More Praise for Intelligent Credit Scoring

Once again, Naeem gives us a detailed and insightful book for risk managers and non-risk managers alike on the importance of credit risk scorecards as a core competency for powerful business decisions.
—Ricardo Plaisant, Consumer Chief Risk Officer,
Citi-Banamex

The most comprehensive, simple, and practical reference for risk professionals dealing with credit risk scorecards. It encompasses in detail the entire credit risk scorecard lifecycle right from scorecard development and validation to implementation and monitoring. In addition to quantitative techniques, *Intelligent Credit Scoring* also covers the practical aspects of credit scoring critical for business users.
—Faizan Iqbal Saleh, Director and Head,
Risk Strategy–Risk Analytics, Al Rajhi Bank

Naeem's book has been a highly valuable resource for BNI in developing in-house scoring capabilities since 2012 by providing us with solid reference and insight about the scorecard development and implementation process. His approach is simple and easy to understand. This new book will surely be another comprehensive reference for scorecard developers.
—Harri Suhendra, Head of Scoring and Modeling,
Bank Negara Indonesia

Once again, Mr. Naeem Siddiqi, the guru of credit scoring, has come out with a book that is easy to understand and gives in-depth information on credit scoring model development methodologies, that will be helpful for all levels of participants who want to develop a predictable and usable credit scoring model.
—Khairul Perera, Chief Credit Officer,
Bank Islam Malaysia Berhad

Intelligent Credit Scoring

Wiley & SAS Business Series

The Wiley & SAS Business Series presents books that help senior-level managers with their critical management decisions.

Titles in the Wiley & SAS Business Series include:

Analytics in a Big Data World: The Essential Guide to Data Science and Its Applications by Bart Baesens

Bank Fraud: Using Technology to Combat Losses by Revathi Subramanian

Big Data Analytics: Turning Big Data into Big Money by Frank Ohlhorst

Big Data, Big Innovation: Enabling Competitive Differentiation through Business Analytics by Evan Stubbs

Business Analytics for Customer Intelligence by Gert Laursen

Business Intelligence Applied: Implementing an Effective Information and Communications Technology Infrastructure by Michael Gendron

Business Intelligence and the Cloud: Strategic Implementation Guide by Michael S. Gendron

Business Transformation: A Roadmap for Maximizing Organizational Insights by Aiman Zeid

Connecting Organizational Silos: Taking Knowledge Flow Management to the Next Level with Social Media by Frank Leistner

Data-Driven Healthcare: How Analytics and BI Are Transforming the Industry by Laura Madsen

Delivering Business Analytics: Practical Guidelines for Best Practice by Evan Stubbs

Demand-Driven Forecasting: A Structured Approach to Forecasting, Second Edition by Charles Chase

Demand-Driven Inventory Optimization and Replenishment: Creating a More Efficient Supply Chain by Robert A. Davis

Developing Human Capital: Using Analytics to Plan and Optimize Your Learning and Development Investments by Gene Pease, Barbara Beresford, and Lew Walker

The Executive's Guide to Enterprise Social Media Strategy: How Social Networks Are Radically Transforming Your Business by David Thomas and Mike Barlow

Economic and Business Forecasting: Analyzing and Interpreting Econometric Results by John Silvia, Azhar Iqbal, Kaylyn Swankoski, Sarah Watt, and Sam Bullard

Foreign Currency Financial Reporting from Euros to Yen to Yuan: A Guide to Fundamental Concepts and Practical Applications by Robert Rowan

Harness Oil and Gas Big Data with Analytics: Optimize Exploration and Production with Data Driven Models by Keith Holdaway

Health Analytics: Gaining the Insights to Transform Health Care by Jason Burke

Heuristics in Analytics: A Practical Perspective of What Influences Our Analytical World by Carlos Andre Reis Pinheiro and Fiona McNeill

Human Capital Analytics: How to Harness the Potential of Your Organization's Greatest Asset by Gene Pease, Boyce Byerly, and Jac Fitz-enz

Implement, Improve and Expand Your Statewide Longitudinal Data System: Creating a Culture of Data in Education by Jamie McQuiggan and Armistead Sapp

Intelligent Credit Scoring: Building and Implementing Better Credit Risk Scorecards, Second Edition by Naeem Siddiqi

Killer Analytics: Top 20 Metrics Missing from Your Balance Sheet by Mark Brown

Predictive Analytics for Human Resources by Jac Fitz-enz and John Mattox II

Predictive Business Analytics: Forward-Looking Capabilities to Improve Business Performance by Lawrence Maisel and Gary Cokins

Retail Analytics: The Secret Weapon by Emmett Cox

Social Network Analysis in Telecommunications by Carlos Andre Reis Pinheiro

For more information on any of the above titles, please visit www.wiley.com.

Intelligent Credit Scoring

Building and Implementing Better Credit Risk Scorecards

Second Edition

Naeem Siddiqi

WILEY

Cover image: background © Candice Cusack/iStockphoto; spreadsheet © Pali Rao/ Getty Images, Inc.

Cover design: Wiley

Published by John Wiley & Sons, Inc., Hoboken, New Jersey.
Published simultaneously in Canada.

For general information on our other products and services or for technical support, please contact our Customer Care Department within the United States at (800) 762-2974, outside the United States at (317) 572-3993 or fax (317) 572-4002.

Wiley publishes in a variety of print and electronic formats and by print-on-demand. Some material included with standard print versions of this book may not be included in e-books or in print-on-demand. If this book refers to media such as a CD or DVD that is not included in the version you purchased, you may download this material at http://booksupport.wiley.com. For more information about Wiley products, visit www.wiley.com.

Library of Congress Cataloging-in-Publication Data:

ISBN 9781119279150 (Hardcover)
ISBN 9781119282334 (ePub)
ISBN 9781119282297 (ePDF)

Printed in the United States of America

10 9 8 7 6 5 4 3 2 1

For Saleha

Contents

Acknowledgments

As with the first edition, I am indebted to many people who have provided ideas, advice, and inspiration for the content of this book.

- I would like to thank Dr. Billie Anderson, Dr. Hendrik Wagner, Clark Abrahams, Bradley Bender, and Charles Maner for graciously agreeing to contribute very informative guest chapters to this book.
- The Roman poet Ovid once said, "A horse never runs so fast as when he has other horses to catch up and outpace." I am grateful to the incredibly talented group of people I work with at SAS who continue to enhance my knowledge of risk management and analytics.
- I want to thank Nikolay Filipenkov and Clark Abrahams for reviewing this book and providing excellent ideas for improvements.
- I continue to learn about the contemporary issues in the industry, the challenges, and innovative ways to deal with them from my customers and colleagues in the credit scoring business. What we know today is due in large part to the generous sharing of knowledge and research work done by credit scoring practitioners. We are indebted to them.

My family—Saleha, Zainab, and Noor—who have been incredibly supportive and tolerant of my frequent work-related absences from home, and have done much of the heavy lifting at home during those times (especially during snowstorms in Markham while I am at warmer locales).

Finally, as always, I want to acknowledge my parents for encouraging me to continuously seek knowledge, and for their constant prayers and blessings, without which there would be no success.

Intelligent
Credit Scoring

CHAPTER **1**

Introduction

"The only virtue of being an aging risk manager is that you have a large collection of your own mistakes that you know not to repeat."

—Donald Van Deventer

Much has changed since the publication of the first edition of this book in 2006. The use of credit scoring has become truly international, with thousands of lenders now developing their own scorecards in-house. As a benchmark, The SAS Credit Scoring[1] solution, which started out around that time, now has hundreds of customers—but more importantly, they are spread out across 60-plus countries. Many more banks, of course, use products from other vendors to build and use credit risk scorecards in-house, but in general, the trend has moved away from outsourcing the development of scorecards to internal builds. The following factors, listed in the order discussed, have led to more widespread usage of scorecards and the decision by banks to build them in-house.

Factors driving the increased use of scorecards include:

- Increased regulation.
- Ease of access to sizable and reliable data.
- Better software for building scorecards.
- Availability of greater educational material and training for would-be developers.
- Corporate knowledge management fostering retention and sharing of subject-matter expertise.
- Signaling capabilities to external and internal stakeholders.
- Efficiency and process improvement.
- Creating value and boosting profitability.
- Improved customer experience.

In the past decade, the single biggest factor driving banks to bring credit scorecard development in-house has been the Basel II Accord.[2]

Specifically, banks that have opted to (or were told to) comply with the Foundation or Advanced Internal Ratings Based approaches of Basel II were required to internally generate Probability of Default (PD) estimates (as well as estimates for Loss Given Default [LGD] and Exposure at Default [EAD]). Larger banks expanded their production and usage of credit scoring, and were compelled to demonstrate their competence in credit scoring. In many countries, particularly in Europe, even small banks decided to go for these approaches, and thus had to start building models for the first time. This led to some challenges—when you have never built scorecards in-house (and in some cases, not really used them either), where do you start? Many institutions went through significant changes to their data warehousing/management, organizational structure, technology infrastructure, and decision making as well as risk management cultures. The lessons from some of these exercises will be shared in chapters on creating infrastructures for credit scoring, as well as the people who should be involved in a project.

While there is a lot of variance in the way Basel II has been implemented in Europe, it is largely a finished process there.[3] Some of the lessons, from Basel II, specifically on how the default definition should be composed will be detailed in a guest chapter written by Dr. Hendrik Wagner. The implementation of Basel II is still ongoing in many countries, where the same exercise is being repeated many times (and in most cases, the same questions are being asked as were 10 years ago in Europe). Many institutions, such as retail credit card and automotive loan companies, that were not required to comply with Basel II, voluntarily opted to comply anyway. Some saw this as a way to prove their capabilities and sophistication to the market, and as a seal of approval on the robustness of their internal processes. But the ones who gained most were those who saw Basel II compliance not just as a mandatory regulatory exercise, but rather as a set of best practices leading to an opportunity to make their internal processes better. This theme of continuous improvement will be addressed in various parts of the book, and guidance given on best practices for the scorecard development implementation process.

In some countries where Basel II was not a factor, local banks decided to take on analytics to improve and be more competitive. In many developing countries, the banking industry became deregulated or more open, which allowed international banks to start operating there. Such banks generally tended to have a long history of using advanced analytics and credit scoring. This put competitive pressures on some of the local banks, which in many cases were operating using manual and judgmental methods. The local banks thus started investing in initiatives such as data warehousing, analytics, and in-house credit scoring in order to bring costs down, reduce losses, and create efficiencies. Another factor that points to a wider acceptance of credit scoring is the tight market for scorecard developers globally. In almost all the countries, whether those with Basel II or not, the demand for experienced credit scoring resources has continued to be high.

In more recent times, the introduction of International Financial Reporting Standards (IFRS) 9 to calculate expected losses has expanded the usage of predictive models within all companies. Those institutions that have already invested in fixing their data problems and establishing sustainable and robust analytics functions will find it easier to comply.

In mature markets, banks that had been developing models and scorecards before have now been looking at how to make the process efficient, sustainable and more transparent. Investments in data warehousing, tools to enable analysts to access the data quickly and easily, integrated infrastructure to reduce model risk, governance processes, and other such areas have increased. Many banks that had invested a lot of money into data warehousing were also looking to increase return on investment (ROI). Credit scoring offered a quick and proven way to use the data, not just for reducing losses but also lead to greater profitability.[4]

Scarcity of modeling/credit scorecard (these two words are used interchangeably throughout this book) development resources has led institutions to try to reduce human resources risk by using modeling tools that encourage sharing and retention of corporate knowledge, reduce training cycles and costs, and are easier to use. Some of the challenges and risks of developing scorecards in-house will be discussed in the chapter on managing the risks of in-house scoring.

In other banks not specifically impacted by the preceding, increasing competition and growing pressures for revenue generation have led credit-granting institutions to search for more effective ways to attract new creditworthy customers and, at the same time, control losses. Aggressive marketing efforts have resulted in a continuously deeper penetration of the risk pool of potential customers, and the need to process them rapidly and effectively has led to growing automation of the credit and insurance application and adjudication processes. The risk manager is challenged to produce risk adjudication solutions that can not only satisfactorily assess creditworthiness but also keep the per-unit processing cost low, while reducing turnaround times for customers. In some jurisdictions without a credit bureau, the risk manager faces an additional challenge of doing so using data that may not be robust or reliable. In addition, customer service excellence demands that this automated process be able to minimize denial of credit to creditworthy customers, while keeping out as many potentially delinquent ones as possible.

At the customer management level, companies are striving ever harder to keep their existing clients by offering them additional products and enhanced services. Risk managers are called on to help in selecting the "right" (i.e., low-risk) customers for these favored treatments. Conversely, for customers who exhibit negative behavior (nonpayment, fraud), risk managers need to devise strategies to not only identify them but also to deal with them effectively to minimize further loss and recoup any monies owed as quickly as possible.

It is in this environment that credit risk scorecards have continued to offer a powerful, empirically derived solution to business needs. Credit risk scorecards have been widely used by a variety of industries for predicting various types of payment delinquencies, fraud, claims (for insurance), and recovery of amounts owed for accounts in collections, among other things. More recently, as mentioned previously, credit scoring has been used widely for regulatory compliance. Credit scoring offers an objective way to assess risk, and also a consistent approach, provided that system overrides are maintained below acceptable policy-specified thresholds.

In the past, most financial institutions acquired credit risk scorecards from a handful of credit risk vendors. This involved the financial institution providing their data to the vendors, and the vendors then developing a predictive scorecard for delivery. For smaller companies, buying a generic or pooled data scorecard was the only option. While some advanced companies have had internal modeling and scorecard development functions for a long time, the trend toward developing scorecards in-house has become far more widespread in the past few years. Some of the regulatory and operational reasons for this phenomenon were covered at the beginning of this chapter. Others will be discussed later.

First, there are more powerful and easy-to-use data mining software today than ever before. This has allowed users to develop scorecards without investing heavily in advanced programmers and infrastructure. Growing competition and the entry of several new data mining vendors made such tools available at ever cheaper prices. Complex data mining functions became available at the click of a mouse, allowing the user to spend more time applying business and data mining expertise to the problem, rather than debugging complicated and lengthy programs. The availability of powerful "point-and-click"–based Extract-Transform-Load (ETL) software enabled efficient extraction and preparation of data for scorecard development and other data mining. Second, advances in intelligent and easy-to-access data storage have removed much of the burden of gathering the required data and putting it into a form that is amenable to analysis. As mentioned earlier, banks and other lenders have made significant investments in data warehousing and data management, and are now looking to use that data to increase profitability.

Once these tools became available, in-house development became a viable option for many smaller and medium-sized institutions. The industry could now realize the significant ROI that in-house scorecard development could deliver for the right players. Experience has shown that in-house credit scorecard development can be done faster, cheaper, and with far more flexibility than any outsourcing strategy. Development was cheaper since the cost of maintaining an in-house credit scoring capability was less than the cost of purchased scorecards. Internal development capability also allowed companies to develop far more scorecards (with enhanced segmentation) for the same expenditure. Scorecards could also be developed more rapidly by internal resources using the right software—which meant that better custom scorecards could be implemented more rapidly, leading to lower losses.

In addition, companies have increasingly realized that their superior knowledge of internal data and business insights led them to develop better-performing scorecards. Seasoned modelers understand that the single biggest contributor to model quality is the data itself, followed by the knowledge level of the analyst of that data. This book will cover in detail how internal knowledge can be applied to build better scorecards. In every phase of the project, we will discuss how appropriate judgment can be applied to augment statistical analyses.

Better-performing scorecards also came about from having the flexibility to experiment with segmentation and then following through by developing more finely segmented scorecards. Deeper segmentation allows for more fine-tuned predictions and strategies. Combined with software that can implement champion/challenger scorecards, this becomes a great way to experiment with different configurations of models. Performing such detailed segmentation analysis through external vendors can become expensive.

Banks have also realized that credit risk scorecards are not a commodity to be purchased from the lowest bidder—they are a core competence and knowledge product of the institution. Internal scorecard development increases the knowledge base within organizations. The analyses done reveal hidden treasures of information that allow for better understanding of customers' risk behavior and lead to better strategy development. We will cover some of this knowledge discovery in the section on model development, specifically the grouping process.

In summary, leaving key modeling and strategy decisions to "external experts" can prove to be a suboptimal route at best, and can also be quite costly.

This book presents a business-focused process for the development and usage of credit risk prediction scorecards, one that builds on a solid foundation of statistics and data mining principles. Statistical and data mining techniques and methodologies have been discussed in detail in various publications and will not be covered in depth here. I have assumed that the reader is either familiar with these algorithms, or can read up on them beforehand, and is now looking for business knowledge pertaining to scorecard development.

The key concepts that will be covered in the book are:

■ The application of business intelligence to the scorecard development process, so that the development and implementation of scorecards is seen as an intelligent business solution to a business problem. Good scorecards are not built by passing data solely through a series of programs or algorithms—they are built when the data is passed through the analytical and business-trained mind of the user. This concept will be applied in all the sections of this book—taking statistical analyses and overlaying business knowledge on it to create better results.

■ Building scorecards is a business process—as much as we use statistical algorithms, simple or complex, to build models, at the end of the day it is a business exercise. The purpose of the exercise is to enable a better business decision and not merely the creation of a great formula. As such, each process—whether selecting a "bad" definition, deciding appropriate segmentations, best bins for attributes, or the best scorecard—will be viewed through the lens of a business decision.

■ Collaborative scorecard development, in which end users, subject matter experts, implementers, modelers, validators, decision makers and other stakeholders work in a cohesive and coherent manner to get better results and avoid costly setbacks and potential disasters during the process.

■ The concept of building a risk profile—this means building scorecards that contain predictive variables representing major information categories, usually between 8 and 15 variables. This mimics the thought processes of good risk adjudicators, who analyze information from credit applications or customer behavior and create a profile based on the different types of information available. They would not make a decision using four or five pieces of information only—so why should anyone build a scorecard that is narrow based? In statistics, parsimonious models are usually preferred. However, in this case, where the modeler is attempting to more fully capture the business reality, more variables are preferred in order to construct a proper and representative risk profile. The point of the exercise is to make the best decision-making tool possible, not just a statistical one.

■ Anticipating impacts of decisions and preparing for them. Each decision made—whether on the definition of the target variable, segmentation, choice of variables, transformations, choice of cutoffs, or other strategies—starts a chain of events that impacts other areas of the company as well as future performance. By tapping into corporate intelligence and working in collaboration with others, the user will learn to anticipate the impact of each decision and prepare accordingly to minimize disruption and unpleasant surprises.

■ View of scorecards as decision support tools. Scorecards should be viewed as a tool to be used for better decision making and should be created with this view. This means they must be understood and controlled; scorecard development should not result in a complex model that cannot be understood enough to make decisions or perform diagnostics.

Individual scorecard development projects may need to be dealt with differently, depending on each company's unique situation—for example, amount and type of data available, knowledge level, staff, and regulatory limitations. This methodology should therefore be viewed as a set of "best-practice" guidelines rather than as a set of definitive rules that must be followed. Many processes and calculations described in this book can be changed and customized by individual users once they understand what is going on. Finally, it is worth noting that regulatory compliance plays an important part in ensuring that scorecards used for granting consumer credit are statistically sound, empirically derived, and capable of separating creditworthy from noncreditworthy applicants at a statistically significant rate.[5] Users should be aware of the regulations that govern models in their jurisdictions, and change the process accordingly.

SCORECARDS: GENERAL OVERVIEW

Credit risk scoring, as with other predictive models, is a tool used to evaluate the level of credit risk associated with applicants or customers. While it does not identify "good" (no negative behavior expected) or "bad" (negative behavior expected) applications on an individual basis, it provides statistical odds, or probability, that an applicant with any given score will be "good" or "bad." These probabilities or scores, along with other business considerations such as expected approval rates, profit, churn, and losses, are then used as a basis for decision making.

In its simplest form, a scorecard consists of a group of characteristics, statistically determined to be predictive in separating good and bad accounts. For reference, Exhibit 1.1 shows a part of a scorecard.

Exhibit 1.1 Sample Scorecard (Partial)

LTV	LTV< 89	41
	89<= LTV< 98	27
	98<= LTV< 111	18
	111<= LTV< 119	11
	119<= LTV, _MISSING_	7
Mth_oldest_trade	Mth_oldest_trade< 42, _MISSING_	16
	42<= Mth_oldest_trade< 58	17
	58<= Mth_oldest_trade< 86	19
	86<= Mth_oldest_trade< 125	20
	125<= Mth_oldest_trade< 178	22
	178<= Mth_oldest_trade< 216	26
	216<= Mth_oldest_trade	29
Total_lim_cc	Total_lim_cc< 1100, _MISSING_	15
	1100<= Total_lim_cc< 1902	16
	1902<= Total_lim_cc< 3970	18
	3970<= Total_lim_cc< 12500	20
	12500<= Total_lim_cc< 21218	25
	21218<= Total_lim_cc	31
Utilisation	Utilisation< 2, _MISSING_	20
	2<= Utilisation< 12	29
	12<= Utilisation< 27	25
	27<= Utilisation< 39	24

Scorecard characteristics may be selected from any of the sources of data available to the lender at the time of the application. Examples of such characteristics are demographics (e.g., age, time at residence, time at job, postal code), existing relationship (e.g., time at bank, number and types of products, payment performance, previous claims), credit bureau (e.g., inquiries, trades, delinquency, public records), real estate data, and so forth. The selection of such variables and creation of scorecards will be covered in later chapters in much more detail.

Each attribute ("age" is a *characteristic* and "23–25" is an *attribute*) is assigned points based on statistical analyses, taking into consideration various factors such as the predictive strength of the characteristics, correlation between characteristics, and operational factors. The total score of an applicant is the sum of the scores for each attribute present in the scorecard for that applicant.

Exhibit 1.2 is an example of the gains chart, one of the management reports produced during scorecard development.

The gains chart, which will be covered in more detail in later chapters, tells us the expected performance of the scorecard. Several things can be observed from this exhibit:

- The score bands have been arranged so that there are approximately 10 percent of accounts in each bucket. Some analysts prefer to arrange them in equal score bands.

- The marginal bad rate, shown in the column "marginal event rate," rank orders from a minimum of 0.2 percent to a maximum of about 15.7 percent. There is some variability between the bad rate based on counts and the predicted bad rate from the model (average predicted probability) due to low counts.

- For the score range 163 to 172, for example, the expected marginal bad rate is 5.31 percent. This means 5.31 percent of the accounts that score in that range are expected to be bad.

- For all accounts above 163, the cumulative bad rate, shown in the column "cumulative event rate," is 2.45 percent. This would be the total expected bad rate of all applicants above 163.

- If we use 163 as a cutoff for an application scorecard, the acceptance will be about 70 percent, meaning 70 percent of all applicants score above 163.

Exhibit 1.2 Gains Chart

Gains Table

Bucket	Score Bucket	Data Role	Count	Cumulative Count	Event Count	Non-Event Count	Cumulative Event Count	Cumulative Non-Event Count	Marginal Event Rate	Marginal Non-Event Rate	Cumulative Event Rate	Cumulative Non-Event Rate	Average Predicted Probability	Low Predicted Probability Threshold	High Predicted Probability Threshold	Cumulative Approval Rate
10	Score >= 232	TRAIN	2465.5	2465.5	5	2460.5	5	2460.5	0.202799	99.7972	0.202799	99.7972	0.004772	0.00312	0.006819	10.60852
9	220 <= Score < 232	TRAIN	2315	4780.5	16	2299	21	4759.5	0.691145	99.30886	0.439285	99.56072	0.008167	0.006419	0.010231	20.56947
8	207 <= Score < 220	TRAIN	2263.75	7044.25	36	2227.75	57	6987.25	1.590282	98.40972	0.809171	99.19083	0.012515	0.009648	0.01603	30.30991
7	193 <= Score < 207	TRAIN	2425.25	9469.5	55	2370.25	112	9357.5	2.267807	97.73219	1.182745	98.81726	0.019892	0.014836	0.02602	40.74524
6	182 <= Score < 193	TRAIN	2349.75	11819.25	84	2265.75	196	11623.25	3.574848	96.42515	1.658312	98.34169	0.03	0.023839	0.037466	50.85572
5	172 <= Score < 182	TRAIN	2331.75	14151	85	2246.75	281	13870	3.645331	96.35467	1.985725	98.01427	0.042729	0.034268	0.051626	60.88874
4	163 <= Score < 172	TRAIN	2297.5	16448.5	122	2175.5	403	16045.5	5.31012	94.68988	2.450071	97.54993	0.056533	0.047773	0.068489	70.77439
3	154 <= Score < 163	TRAIN	2328.5	18777	191	2137.5	594	18183	8.202706	91.79729	3.163445	96.83556	0.07829	0.065195	0.092712	80.79343
2	143 <= Score < 154	TRAIN	2214.5	20991.5	248	1966.5	842	20149.5	11.19892	88.80108	4.011147	95.98885	0.104679	0.086111	0.131602	90.32196
1	Score < 143	TRAIN	2249.25	23240.75	354	1895.25	1196	22044.75	15.73858	84.26142	5.146133	94.85387	0.168506	0.12092	0.277842	100

Based on factors outlined above, as well as other decision metrics to be discussed in the chapter on scorecard implementation, a company can then decide, for example, to decline all applicants who score below 163, or to charge them higher pricing in view of the greater risk they present. "Bad" is generally defined using negative performance indicators such as bankruptcy, fraud, delinquency, write-off/charge-off, and negative net present value (NPV).

Risk score information, combined with other factors such as expected approval rate and revenue/profit potential at each risk level, can be used to develop new application strategies that will maximize revenue and minimize bad debt. Some of the strategies for high-risk applicants are:

- Declining credit/services if the risk level is too high.
- Assigning a lower starting credit limit on a credit card or line of credit.
- Asking the applicant to provide a higher down payment or deposit for mortgages or car loans.
- Charging a higher interest rate on a loan.
- Charging a higher premium on insurance policies.
- Adjusting payment terms for business customers.
- Asking the applicant to provide a deposit for water/electricity utilities services, or for landline phones.
- Offering prepaid cellular services instead of postpaid, or offering a lower monthly plan.
- Denying international calling access from telecommunications companies.
- Asking high-risk applicants for further documentation on employment, assets, or income.
- Selecting applicants for further scrutiny for potential fraudulent activity.

Conversely, high-scoring applicants may be given preferential rates and higher credit limits, and be offered upgrades to better products, such as premium credit cards, or additional products offered by the company.

Application scores can also help in setting "due diligence" policies. For example, an applicant scoring very low can be declined outright, but those in middling score ranges can be approved but with additional documentation requirements for information on real estate, income verification, or valuation of underlying security.

The previous examples specifically dealt with credit risk scoring at the application stage. Risk scoring is similarly used with existing clients on an ongoing basis. In this context, the client's behavioral data with the company, as well as bureau data, is used to predict the probability of ongoing negative behavior. Based on similar business considerations as previously mentioned (e.g., expected risk and profitability levels), different treatments can be tailored to existing accounts, such as:

- Offering product upgrades and additional products to better customers.
- Increasing or decreasing credit limits on credit cards and lines of credit.
- Allowing some revolving credit customers to go beyond their credit limits for purchases.
- Allowing better customers to use credit cards even in delinquency, while blocking the high-risk ones immediately.
- Flagging potentially fraudulent transactions.
- Offering better pricing on loan/insurance policy renewals.
- Setting premiums for mortgage insurance.
- Deciding whether or not to reissue an expired credit card.
- Prequalifying direct marketing lists for cross-selling.
- Directing delinquent accounts to more stringent collection methods or outsourcing to a collection agency.
- Suspending or revoking phone services or credit facilities.
- Putting an account on a "watch list" for potential fraudulent activity.

In addition to being developed for use with new applicants (application scoring) or existing accounts (behavior scoring), scorecards can also be defined based on the type of data used to develop them. "Custom" scorecards are those developed using data for customers of one organization exclusively, for example, if a bank uses the performance data of its own customers to build a scorecard to predict bankruptcy. It may use internal data or data obtained from a credit bureau for this purpose, but the data is only for its own customers.

"Generic" or "pooled data" scorecards are those built using data from multiple lenders. For example, four small banks, none of which has enough data to build its own custom scorecards, decide to pool their data for auto loans. They then build a scorecard with this data and share it, or customize the scorecards based on unique character-istics of their portfolios. Scorecards built using industry bureau data, and marketed by credit bureaus, are a type of generic scorecards. The use of such generic models (and other external vendor built models) creates some unique challenges as some of the know-how and pro-cesses can remain as black boxes. We will discuss how to validate and use such models in a guest chapter authored by experienced industry figures Clark Abrahams, Bradley Bender, and Charles Maner.

Risk scoring, in addition to being a tool to evaluate levels of risk, has also been effectively applied in other operational areas, such as:

- Streamlining the decision-making process, that is, higher-risk and borderline applications being given to more experienced staff for more scrutiny, while low-risk applications are assigned to junior staff. This can be done in branches, credit adjudication centers, and collections departments.
- Reducing turnaround time for processing applications through automated decision making, thereby reducing per-unit process-ing cost and increasing customer satisfaction.
- Evaluating quality of portfolios intended for acquisition through bureau-based generic scores.
- Setting economic and regulatory capital allocation.
- Forecasting.
- Setting pricing for securitization of receivables portfolios.
- Comparing the quality of business from different channels/ regions/ suppliers.
- Help in complying with lending regulations that call for empiri-cally proven methods for lending, without potentially discrimi-natory judgment.

Credit risk scoring, therefore, provides lenders with an opportu-nity for consistent and objective decision making, based on empirically derived information. Combined with business knowledge, predictive modeling technologies provide risk managers with added efficiency and control over the risk management process.

Credit scoring is now also being used increasingly in the insurance sector for determining auto[6] and home insurance[7] premiums. A unique study conducted by the Federal Reserve Board even suggests that couples with higher credit scores tend to stay together longer.[8]

The future of credit scoring, and those who practice it, is bright. There are several issues, discussed later, that will determine the shape of the industry in the coming 5- to 10-year span.

The rise of alternate data sources, including social media data, will affect the industry. In reality, the change has already begun, with many lenders now starting to use such data instead of the more traditional scores.[9] This issue will be discussed in more detail in several chapters. In many countries, the creation of credit bureaus is having a positive impact on the credit industry. Having a centralized repository of credit information reduces losses as lenders can now be aware of bad credit behavior elsewhere. Conversely, it makes it easier for good customers to access credit as they now have strong, reliable evidence of their satisfactory payment behavior. In addition, the access to very large data sets and increasingly powerful machines has also enabled banks to use more data, and process analytics faster. We will cover this topic in more detail in its own chapter authored by Dr. Billie Anderson.

Regulatory challenges will continue, but banks are better prepared. Basel II has overall improved the level of analytics and credit scoring in banks. It has introduced and formalized repeatable, transparent, and auditable processes in banks for developing models. It has helped create truly independent arm's-length risk functions, and model validation team that can mount effective challenges. Basel II, as well as Basel Committee on Banking Supervision (BCBS) regulation 239,[10] has also made data creation, storage, and aggregation at banks far better than before. IFRS 9 and other current regulatory initiatives such as Comprehensive Capital Analysis and Review (CCAR), Current Expected Credit Loss (CECL), and stress testing, as well as their global equivalents, will continue to expand and challenge analytics and credit scoring.

One factor that users of credit scoring will need to be cautious about is the increasing knowledge of credit scoring in the general population. In particular, in the United States, knowledge of bureau scores such as the FICO score, is getting very common. This is evidenced by the number of articles, discussions, and questions on how to improve the score (I personally get such questions via e-mail and on social media at least every week or two weeks—questions such as "How do I maximize my score in the shortest time?"; "If I cancel my card, will it decrease my score"; etc.). This factor can work in two ways. On the positive side, it may drive people to improve their payment and other credit habits to get better scores. On the negative side, this may also lead to manipulation. The usage of robust bureau data will mitigate some of the risk, while the usage of unreliable social media or demographics data may not.

The ever-present discussion on newer, better algorithms will continue. Our quest to explain data better, and differentiate useful information from noise, has been going on for decades and will likely go on for decades more. The current hot topic is machine learning. Whether it or the other more complex algorithms replaces the simpler algorithms in use in credit scoring will depend on many factors (this topic will also be dealt with in the later chapter on vendor model validation). Banks overwhelmingly select logistic regression, scorecards, and other such methods for credit scoring based on their openness, simplicity, and ease of compliance. Complex algorithms will become more popular for nonlending and nonregulatory modeling, but there will need to be a change in regulatory and model validation mind-sets before they become widely acceptable for the regulatory models.

The credit crisis of 2008 has been widely discussed and dissected by many others. Let us firstly recognize that it was a complex event and its causes many. Access to cheap money, a housing bubble in many places, teaser rates to subprime borrowers, lack of transparency around models, distorted incentives for frontline staff, unrealistic ratings for mortgage-backed securities, greed, fraud, and the use of self-declared (i.e., unconfirmed) incomes have all been cited.[11] Generally, I consider it a failure of both bankers in exercising the basic rules of banking, and risk management in failing to manage risks. Some have even suggested that models and scorecards are to blame. This is not quite accurate and reflects a failure to understand the nature of models. As we will cover in this book, models are built on many underlying assumptions, and their use involves just as many caveats. Models are not perfect, nor are they 100 percent accurate for all times. All models describe historical data—hence the critical need to adjust expectations based on future economic cycles. The amount of confidence in any model or scorecard must be based on both the quality and quantity of the underlying data, and decision-making strategies adjusted accordingly. Models are very useful when used judiciously, along with policy rules and judgment, recognizing both their strengths and weaknesses. The most accurate model in the world will not help if a bank chooses not to confirm any information from credit applicants or to verify identities. As such, one needs to be very realistic when it comes to using scorecards/models, and not have an unjustified level of trust in them.

> *"... too many financial institutions and investors simply outsourced their risk management. Rather than undertake their own analysis, they relied on the rating agencies to do the essential work of risk analysis for them."*
>
> —Lloyd Blankfein, CEO Goldman Sachs
> (*Financial Times*, February 8, 2009)

NOTES

1. www.sas.com/en_us/industry/banking/credit-scoring.html
2. Basel Committee for Banking Supervision, Basel II: International Convergence of Capital Measurement and Capital Standards: A Revised Framework, Bank for International Settlements, November 2005.
3. European Banking Federation, Study on Internal Rating Based (IRB) models in Europe, 2014.
4. L. Einav, M. Jenkins, J. Levin, "The Impact of Credit Scoring on Consumer Lending," *RAND Journal of Economics*, 44, no. 2, (Summer 2013): 249–274.
5. Reg. B, 12 C.F.R. §202.2(p)(2)(iii)(1978)
6. http://time.com/money/3978575/credit-scores-auto-insurance-rates/
7. www.cbc.ca/news/credit-scores-can-hike-home-insurance-rates-1.890442
8. Jane Dokko, Geng Li, and Jessica Hayes, "Credit Scores and Committed Relationships," Finance and Economics Discussion Series 2015-081. Washington, DC: Board of Governors of the Federal Reserve System, 2015; http://dx.doi.org/10.17016/FEDS.2015.081
9. www.wsj.com/articles/silicon-valley-gives-fico-low-score-1452556468
10. Basel Committee on Banking Supervision document, BCBS 239, Principles for Effective Risk Data Aggregation and Reporting, Bank for International Settlements, January 2013.
11. www.forbes.com/sites/stevedenning/2011/11/22/5086/#c333bf95b560

CHAPTER **2**

Scorecard Development: The People and the Process

"Talent wins games, but teamwork and intelligence wins championships."

—Michael Jordan

M any years ago, I developed a set of scorecards for a risk management department of a bank. The data sent to us by the risk folks was great, and we built a good scorecard with about 14 reasonable variables. About two weeks after delivering the scorecard, we got a call from the customer. Apparently, two of the variables that they had sent to us in the data set were not usable, and we needed to take them out. I have had bankers tell me stories of changing scorecard variables because information technology (IT) gave them estimates of three to four months to code up a new derived variable. IT folks, however, tell me they hate to be surprised by last-minute requests to implement new scorecards or new derived variables that cannot be handled by their systems. Almost every bank I've advised has had occasions where the variables desired/expected by the risk manager could not be in models, where models built could not be used because other stakeholders would not agree to them, or where other surprises lay waiting months after the actual work was done.

These are some of the things that cause problems during scorecard development and implementation projects. In order to prevent such problems, the process of scorecard development needs to be a collaborative one between IT, risk management (strategy and policy), modeling, validation, and operational staff. This collaboration not only creates better scorecards, it also ensures that the solutions are consistent with business direction, prevent surprises, and enable education and knowledge transfer during the development process. Scorecard development is not a "black box" process and should not be treated as such. Experience has shown that developing scorecards in isolation can lead to problems such as inclusion of characteristics that are no longer collected, legally suspect, or difficult to collect operationally, exclusion of operationally critical variables, and devising of strategies that result in "surprises" or are unimplementable. In fact, since the credit crisis of 2007–2008, the tolerance at most banks for complex/black box models and processes is gone. The business user expects a model that can be understood, justified, and where necessary, be tweaked based on business considerations, as well as an open and transparent process that can be controlled.

In this chapter, we will look at the various personas that should be involved in a scorecard development and implementation project. The level of involvement of staff members varies, and different staff members are required at various key stages of the process. By understanding the types of resources required for a successful scorecard development and implementation project, one will also start to appreciate the business and operational considerations that go into such projects.

SCORECARD DEVELOPMENT ROLES

At a minimum, the following main participants are required.

Scorecard Developer

The scorecard developer is the person who performs the statistical analyses needed to develop scorecards. This person usually has:

- Some business knowledge of the products/tasks for which models are being developed. For example, if someone is responsible for building models for an auto loan product or a mobile phone account, they should be familiar with the car-selling business or the cell phone/telco business. Similarly, a person building scorecards for collections needs to understand the collections process. This is to make sure that they understand the data and can interpret it properly in the context of each subject. This would include knowing which types of variables are generally considered important for each product, how decisions and data collection at source impacts quality, and how the model will be used for decision making.
- An in-depth knowledge of the various databases in the company and the data sets being used. The single most important factor in determining the quality of the model is the quality of the data. When the users understand the quirks in the data, where and

how the data was generated, deficiencies, biases, and interpretation of the data, they will be able to conduct intelligent analysis of that data. Otherwise, their analysis will be devoid of context. This task may also be covered by someone other than the scorecard developer—for example, a data scientist playing an advisory role.

- An in-depth understanding of statistical principles, in particular those related to predictive modeling. For example, knowledge of logistic regression, fit statistics, multicollinearity, decision trees, and so on.

- A good understanding of the legal and regulatory requirements of models and of the model development process. This includes documentation requirements, transparency, and any laws that control the usage of certain information. For example, in many countries the use of gender, marital status, race, ethnicity, nationality, and the like are prohibited. They would also need to know requirements expected by internal model validation teams so that minimum standards of model governance are met. Detailed knowledge of this subject is usually with model validation groups.

- Business experience in the implementation and usage of risk models. This is related to the business knowledge of the product. If analysts understand the end use of the model, it enables them to develop the one best suited for that task. The analyst will not develop a model that merely meets statistical acceptance tests.

This person ensures that data is collected according to specifications, that all data quirks are taken into account, and that the scorecard development process is statistically valid.

Data Scientist

The data scientist is the person who helps source and extract the required records and fields of information in order to populate the scorecard development database. This person usually has:

- An in-depth knowledge of the various databases in the company, and the data sets being used.

- Proficiency in the tools and systems to determine and document data lineage, to perform field-specific code mappings to common values and definitions from a variety of internal legacy transaction systems and external data reporters.
- Ability to merge/combine information from disparate sources and perform necessary preprocessing to deal with data issues, such as undefined codes, missing information, or extreme/suspect values.
- Familiarity with file formats and fields of information available from the different credit bureaus, rating agencies, and other third-party data providers.

A good example of the required knowledge for data sourcing and extraction is in mortgage lending, where there can be up to four co-applicants, and records for each must be found and joined into a single complete applicant record with individual and combined characteristics derived. These include characteristics such as combined loan-to-value ratio, combined income, payment to combined income, combined debt-to-income ratio, and payment shock to combined current housing payments. Even in a data warehouse, the co-applicant records may reside in a different table that the primary applicant record and matching logic must be used to associate related records. Typical scorecard developers do not possess this type of in-depth knowledge, especially in the larger, more complex financial institutions.

Product or Portfolio Risk Manager/Credit Scoring Manager

Risk managers are responsible for the management of the company's portfolio and usage of scorecards. They are usually responsible for creating policies and strategies for approvals, credit limit setting, collections treatment, and pricing. In most companies, this person would be the business owner of the scorecard. This person usually has:

- Subject matter expertise in the development and implementation of risk strategies using scores.
- An in-depth understanding of corporate risk policies and procedures.

- An in-depth understanding of the risk profile of the company's customers and applicants for products/services.
- A good understanding of the various implementation platforms for risk scoring and strategy implementation in the company.
- Knowledge of legal issues surrounding usage of particular characteristics/processes to adjudicate credit applications.
- Knowledge of credit application processing and customer management processes in the company.
- Knowledge of roll rate models; delinquency trends by product, region, and channel; and reports and the average time to charge-off.

When a modeler is asked to build a model (typically a process initiated by the business area), the first question they should ask the businessperson is "why?" That businessperson is typically the risk manager. The answer to that question determines everything else that is done from that point forward, including deciding the target, variable mix in the model, picking the best model, conditions, appropriate model fit measures, and, of course, the final cutoff for any decisions. This person ensures that business considerations are given sufficient thought in the design and implementation of scorecards. Early on in the process, the risk manager can tap their knowledge of the portfolio risk dynamics and performance experience to help with determining the definition of what constitutes "bad" performance for the population of interest. A good practice is to involve risk managers (or a representative) in each phase of the scorecard development process, and get their approval at the end of each one. Risk managers should be able to use some of their experience to point scorecard developers in a particular direction, or to give special consideration to certain data elements. For example, in cases where data is weak or biased, risk managers may use their experience to adjust weight of evidence (WOE) curves or to force certain variables (weak but logical) into the model. Experienced risk managers are also aware of historical changes in the market, and will be able to adjust expected performance numbers if required. They would also contribute heavily to the development of strategies and to gauging possible impacts of those strategies on customers and the various areas of the organization. Scorecards are developed to help in decision making—and anticipating change is key.

Product Manager(s)

The product manager is responsible for the management of the company's product(s) from a marketing or customer retention perspective. Their main objectives are usually revenue related, and they would have:

- Subject matter expertise in the development and implementation of product-marketing strategies.
- An in-depth knowledge of the company's typical client base and target markets, including its best/most valued customers.
- Knowledge of future product development and marketing direction.

Product managers can offer key insights into the client base and assist during segmentation selection, selection of characteristics, and gauging impact of strategies. They also coordinate design of new application forms where new information is to be collected. Segmentation offers the opportunity to assess risk for increasingly specific populations—the involvement of marketing in this effort can ensure that scorecard segmentation is in line with the organization's intended target markets. This approach produces the best results for the most valued segments and harmonizes marketing and risk directions. In other words, the scorecard is segmented based on the profile that a product is designed for, or the intended target market for that product, rather than based on risk considerations alone.

We will cover the gauging of impact on key customer segments post-cutoff selection in later chapters. This involves, for example, measuring metrics like expected approval rates for high-net-worth and similar premium customers. Marketing staff should be able to provide advice on these segments. The product managers typically do not have a say in the selection of final models or variables.

Operational Manager(s)

The operational manager is responsible for the management of departments such as Collections, Application Processing, Adjudication (when separate from Risk Management), and Claims. Any strategy developed using scorecards, such as changes to cutoff levels, will impact these departments. Operational managers have direct contact with customers, and usually have:

- Subject matter expertise in the implementation and execution of corporate strategies and procedures.
- An in-depth knowledge of customer-related issues.
- Experience in lending money.

Operational managers can alert the scorecard developers on issues such as difficulties in data collection and interpretation by frontline staff, impact on the portfolio of various strategies, and other issues relating to the implementation of scorecards and strategies.

A best practice that is highly recommended is to interview operational staff before starting the modeling project. For example, if analysts are looking to develop a mortgage application scorecard, they should go talk to adjudicators/credit analysts who approve mortgages, or other senior staff who have lending experience. Similarly, talking to collections staff is useful for those developing collections models. I normally ask them some simple questions. For applications models, I typically get about 8 to 10 approved and another 8 to 10 declined applications, and ask the adjudicator to explain to me why they were approved or declined. I often ask collectors if they can identify which debtors are likely to pay before talking to them, and which specific variables they use to decide. Staff from Adjudication, Collections, and Fraud departments can offer experience-based insight into factors that are predictive of negative behavior (i.e., variables that they think are predictive), which helps greatly when selecting characteristics for analysis, and constructing the "business optimal" scorecard. This is particularly useful for analysts who don't have a lot of banking/lending experience, and for cases where you may be developing scorecards for a new product or a new market. In some cases, I have obtained ideas for some interesting derived variables from talking to adjudicators. In one example, when dealing with "thin" files, an adjudicator used the difference in days between the date of the first trade opened and the first inquiry as a measure of creditworthiness. The idea was that a creditworthy applicant would be able to get a credit product soon after applying, while a bad credit would take a while and several inquiries before getting money. Internationally, I have found a lot of nuances in lending, as well as uniquely local variables, from country to country simply by talking to bankers. In Western countries for example, the variable "Time at Address" is useful for younger people as they tend to live on their own soon after turning 18 or graduating. However, in other cultures where young people tend to live with their parents, often into middle age, a high number for that variable may not be fully indicative of financial stability for young people. Interviews with local bankers have helped me understand the data better and construct scorecards that would be most valuable to the business user.

Another good exercise to better understand the data is to spend some time where the data is created. For example, spending time in bank branches, as well as auto and mobile phone dealers, will help understand if and why certain fields are left blank, whether there is any data manipulation going on, and what the tolerance level is for filling out long application forms (relevant when determining the mix of self-declared versus bureau variables to have in the scorecard). This will help gauge the reliability of the data being studied.

In organizations where manual adjudication is done, or where historically applications have been manually adjudicated, interviewing the adjudicators also helps understand data biases. Manual lending and over-riding biases data—understanding the policies and lending guidelines, as well as the personal habits of individual adjudicators—will help understand which variables are biased and how. This is similar to studying an organization's policy rules to understand how its data is biased; for example, if above 85 percent loan to value (LTV), all decisions are exceptions only, then performance for all accounts with LTV greater than 85 percent will be biased and will appear to be much better than reality.

The objective here is to tap experience and discover insights that may not be obvious from analyzing data alone. This also helps interpret relationships later on and identify biases to be fixed. As mentioned earlier, superior knowledge of data leads to better scorecards—this exercise enables the analyst to apply business/experience to the data. Application scorecards are usually developed on data that may be more than two years old, and collections staff may be able to identify any trends or changes that need to be incorporated into analyses. This exercise also provides an opportunity to test and validate experience within the organization. For example, I have gone back to adjudicators and shown them data to either validate or challenge some of their experience-based lending ideas.

Model Validation/Vetting Staff

Model oversight function has always been an important part of the model development process. Their role has become even more critical with the introduction of banking regulations and model risk management guidelines in most countries. The role of model validation and key responsibilities are detailed in documents such as the Supervisory Letter 11-7 from the Federal Reserve Board (SR11-7)[1] and Basel II Working Paper 14.[2] Ideally, model validation should have:

- A good understanding of the mathematical and statistical principles employed in scorecard development.
- In-depth knowledge of corporate model validation policies, all relevant regulations, and the expectations of banking regulation agencies.
- Real-life experience in developing risk models and scorecards in financial institutions.
- A good understanding of the banking business.
- A good understanding of the data within the bank.

Model validation staff should have regular checkpoints with the model developers and define clearly what is expected in terms of documentation standards. Any divergence from the expected and other red flags should be identified as early as possible.

The better banks have created an environment where the model development, risk management, and model validation teams work in a collaborative way, each with clearly defined roles and accountabilities. This reduces the chances of delays and "surprises," as well as deadlocks where no one is willing to make a decision. Banks that have long, dysfunctional scorecard development processes usually have:

- Model developers who work in isolation, employ black box processes, and don't share their knowledge with others.

- Risk management business staff who refuse to participate or are not invited to participate in the scorecard development process, nor share knowledge of how they use the scorecards and downstream decisions.
- Risk management staff who don't have even the most basic idea of how scorecards are developed.
- People afraid to make decisions because of vague accountabilities.
- Model validation staff who have never built scorecards themselves. This is a major problem with many banks worldwide. Model validation staff who ask the wrong questions and treat the development process as an academic exercise enable the production of statistically perfect but ultimately useless models.
- Model validation staff with no banking experience.
- Vague model validation processes and policies.

Project Manager

The project manager is responsible for the overall management of the project, including creation of the project plan and timelines, integration of the development and implementation processes, and management of other project resources. The project manager usually has:

- Subject matter expertise in the management of projects.
- An in-depth understanding of the relevant corporate areas involved in the project.

IT/IS Managers

IT managers are responsible for the management of the various software and hardware products used in the company. They sometimes have added responsibilities for corporate data warehouses. They usually have:

- Subject matter expertise in the software and hardware products involved in risk management and risk scoring implementation.
- In-depth knowledge of corporate data, data governance policies, and internal procedures to introduce changes to data processing.
- Knowledge of processing data from external data providers.

IT managers can alert scorecard developers to issues related to data collection and coding—particularly when new data is introduced—and to implementation issues related to the software platforms being used to implement scorecards and manipulate data. They must be notified of changes to maintain timelines for implementation. In particular, where scorecards are being developed using complex transformations or calculations, and they need to be implemented on real-time software, the IT department may be able to advise if these calculations are beyond the capabilities of the software. The same is true for derived bureau variables where the derivations have to be done on credit bureau interfaces or using other software. If scorecards are to be implemented within tight timelines, a good idea is to talk to IT to find out how many can be implemented within timelines. This can then drive segmentation strategy, where the number of scorecards to be developed would be consistent with what can be implemented, rather than a larger number.

Enterprise Risk/Corporate Risk Management Staff (Where Applicable)

Enterprise risk departments are responsible for the management of both financial and operational risks at a corporate level (as opposed to the product level). They are usually also involved in capital allocation and oversight of the risk function. They usually have:

- Subject matter expertise on corporate policies on risk management and risk tolerance levels.
- In-depth knowledge of impacts on capital allocation/hedging, and so forth, of introductions to changes in risk adjudication.
- In-depth knowledge of actuarial practices.

Enterprise risk staff is usually advised when new strategies change the risk profile of the company's portfolio. Increasing or decreasing risk levels affect the amount of capital a company needs to allocate. Taking significant additional risks may also be in contravention of the company's stated risk profile target, and may potentially affect its own credit rating. Enterprise risk staff will ensure that all strategies comply with corporate risk guidelines, and that the company is sufficiently capitalized for its risk profile.

Legal Staff/Compliance Manager

Credit granting in most jurisdictions is subject to laws and regulations that determine methods that can be used to assess creditworthiness, credit limits, and characteristics that cannot be used in this effort. A good practice is to submit a list of proposed segmentation and scorecard characteristics to the legal department, to ensure that none of them is in contravention of existing laws and regulations. In the United States, for example, issuing arising from the Equal Credit Opportunity Act,[3] Fair Housing Act,[4] Dodd-Frank,[5] Regulation B,[6] as well as "adverse" and "disparate" impact are all areas that need to be considered during scorecard development and usage.

INTELLIGENT SCORECARD DEVELOPMENT

Involving these resources in the scorecard development and implementation project helps to incorporate collective organizational knowledge and experience, prevents delays, and produces scorecards that are more likely to fulfill business requirements. Most of this corporate intelligence is not documented; therefore, the only effective way to introduce it into credit scoring is to involve the relevant resources in the development and implementation process itself. This is the basis for intelligent scorecard development.

 NOTE

Bearing in mind that different companies may have differing titles for similar functions, the preceding material is meant to reflect the typical parties needed to ensure that a developed scorecard is well balanced, with considerations from different stakeholders in a company. Actual participants may vary.

SCORECARD DEVELOPMENT AND IMPLEMENTATION PROCESS: OVERVIEW

When the appropriate participants have been selected to develop a scorecard, it is helpful to review the main stages of the scorecard development and implementation process, and to be sure that you understand the tasks associated with each stage. The following list describes the main stages and tasks. Detailed descriptions of each stage are in the chapters that follow. The following table also summarizes the output of each stage, whether signoff is recommended, and which team members should sign off. Note that while the chapter recommends getting advice from those in the marketing or product management areas, they are not involved in any signoff. The abbreviations used in the Participants columns are:

MD: Model development, usually represented by the head of the model development team.

RM: Risk management, usually the portfolio risk/policy manager or end user on the business side.

MV: Model validation or vetting, usually those responsible for overseeing the process.

IT: Information technology or equivalent function responsible for implementing the models.

Stage	Output	Sign Off	Participants
STAGE 1. PRELIMINARIES AND PLANNING			
Create business plan Identify organizational objectives and scorecard role Determine internal versus external development and scorecard type Create project plan Identify project risks Identify project team and responsibilities	Business plan Project plan	Y	RM, MD, MV, IT
STAGE 2. DATA REVIEW AND PROJECT PARAMETERS			
Data availability and quality	Agreement to proceed	Y	MV, MD, RM
Data gathering for definition of project parameters	Data set		MD
Definition of project parameters Performance window and sample window Performance categories definition (target) Exclusions	Parameters analysis report	Y	RM, MD, MV

Stage	Output	Sign Off	Participants
Segmentation	Report	Y	RM, MV, MD
STAGE 3. DEVELOPMENT DATABASE CREATION			
Development sample specifications Sampling Development data collection and construction	Development data set with derived and original variables	Y	RM, MV, MD, IT
STAGE 4. SCORECARD DEVELOPMENT			
Exploring data Identifying missing values and outliers Correlation, collinearity Distributions etc.			MD
Initial characteristic analysis (Binning)	Report with agreed bins and reasons	Y	MD, RM, MV
Preliminary scorecard (Regression)	Model/scorecard	Y	MD, RM, MV, IT (if additional variables are derived)
Reject inference	Combined data set	Y	MD, RM, MV
Final scorecard production (exploration, binning, and regression)	Final model(s)/ scorecard(s)	Y	MD, RM, MV
Choosing the final scorecard/model to implement	Report detailing stats and business reasons for selection	Y	MD, RM, MV
Validation	Qualitative and quantitative model validation report	Y	MD, MV
STAGE 5. SCORECARD MANAGEMENT REPORTS			
Gains tables Characteristic reports Business reports			MD
Pre-implementation validation	Stability report and analysis	Y	RM, MV

The following stages are for post-development work for strategy development, and are usually handled by the business risk management function.

STAGE 6. SCORECARD IMPLEMENTATION

- Scoring strategy
- Setting cutoffs
- Policy rules
- Override policy

STAGE 7. POST-IMPLEMENTATION

- Scorecard and portfolio monitoring reports
- Scorecard management reports
- Portfolio performance reports

The preceding stages are not exhaustive—they represent the major stages where key output is produced, discussed, and signed off. The signoff process, which encourages teamwork and identifying problems early, will be discussed in the next chapter. Involvement by the Model Vetting/Validation unit is dependent on the model audit policies of each individual bank as well as expectations from regulators.

NOTES

1. Supervisory Guidance on Model Risk Management, Federal Reserve Bank, www .federalreserve.gov/bankinforeg/srletters/sr1107a1.pdf
2. Bank of International Settlements, Working Paper No. 14, 2005.
3. https://www.justice.gov/crt/equal-credit-opportunity-act-3
4. https://www.justice.gov/crt/fair-housing-act-2
5. https://www.congress.gov/bill/111th-congress/house-bill/4173
6. https://www.federalreserve.gov/boarddocs/supmanual/cch/fair_lend_reg_b.pdf

## CHAPTER 3

Designing the Infrastructure for Scorecard Development

As more banks around the world realize the value of analytics and credit scoring, we see a corresponding high level of interest in setting up analytics and modeling disciplines in-house. This is where some planning and long-term vision is needed. A lot of banks hired well-qualified modelers and bought high-powered data mining software, thinking that their staff would soon be churning out models at a regular clip. For many of them, this did not materialize. Producing models and analytics took just as long to produce as before, or took significantly longer than expected. The problem was not that their staff didn't know how to build models, or that the model fitting was taking too long. It was the fact that the actual modeling is the easiest and sometimes fastest part of the entire data mining process. The major problems, which were not addressed, were in all the other activities before and after the modeling. Problems with accessing data, data cleansing, getting business buy-in, model validation, documentation, producing audit reports, implementation, and other operational issues made the entire process slow and difficult.

In this chapter, we look at the most common problems organizations face when setting up infrastructure for analytics and suggest ways to reduce problems through better design.

The discussion in this chapter will be limited to the tasks involved in building, using, and monitoring scorecards. Exhibit 3.1 is a simplified example of the end-to-end tasks that would take place during scorecard development projects. These are not as exhaustive as the tasks that will be covered in the rest of the book, but serve only to illustrate points associated with creating an infrastructure to facilitate the entire process.

Based on the most common problems lending institutions face when building scorecards, we would suggest consideration of the following main issues when looking to design an architecture to enable analytics:

- *One version of the truth.* Two people asking the same question, or repeating the same exercise should get the same answer. One way to achieve this is by sharing and reusing, for example, data sources, data extraction logic, conditions such as filters and segmentation logic, models, parameters and variables, including logic for derived ones.

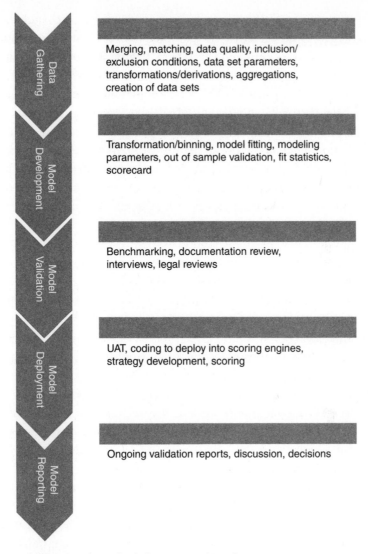

Exhibit 3.1 Major Tasks during Scorecard Development

■ *Transparency and audit.* Given the low level of regulatory tolerance for black box models and processes, everything from the creation of data to the analytics, deployment, and reporting should be transparent. Anyone who needs to see details on each phase of the development process should be able to do so easily.

For example, how data is transformed to create aggregated and derived variables, the parameters chosen for model fitting, how variables entered the model, validation details, and other parameters should preferably be stored in graphical user interface (GUI) format for review. Although all of the above can be done through coding, auditing of code is somewhat more complex. In addition, one should also be able to produce an unbroken audit chain across all the tasks shown in Exhibit 3.1—from the point where data is created in source systems, through all the data transformations and analytics, to scoring and production of validation reports as well as regulatory capital and other calculations. Model documentation should include details on the methods used and also provide effective challenge around the choice of those methods as well as the final scorecard. That means discussion and coverage is necessary for scorecards that were tested and rejected, not just the final scorecard, and competing methods to the one used to produce the scorecard.

■ *Retention of corporate intellectual property (IP)/knowledge.* Practices such as writing unique code for each project and keeping it on individual PCs makes it harder to retain IP when key staff leave. Using programming-based modeling tools makes it more difficult to retain this IP as staff leaving take their coding skills with them. Most modelers/coders also choose to rewrite code rather than sort through partial code work previously written by someone else. This results in delays, and often ends with different answers obtained for the same question. To counter this, many banks have shifted to GUI software to reduce this loss and to introduce standardization.

■ *Integration across the model development tasks.* Integration across the continuum of activities shown in Exhibit 3.1, from data set creation to validation, means that the output of each phase seamlessly gets used in the next. Practices such as rewriting Extract-Transform-Load (ETL) and scoring code, as well as that for deriving and creating variables into different languages is not efficient, as it lengthens the production cycle. It also presents model risk, as recoding into a different language may alter the interpretation of the original variable or condition coded.

These would include parameters and conditions for both data sets and models. An integrated infrastructure for analytics also means a lowered implementation risk, as all the components across the continuum will likely work together. This is in addition to the integration and involvement of various stakeholders/personas discussed in the previous chapter.

■ *Faster time to results.* It sometimes takes months to build a model and implement it in many institutions, resulting in the use of inefficient or unstable models for longer than necessary. Efficient infrastructure design can make this process much faster based on integrated components, faster learning cycles for users, and reduction of repetition (such as recoding).

In discussing the points to consider when designing architecture/infrastructure to enable in-house scorecard development and analytics, we will consider the major tasks associated with performing analytics in any organization.

DATA GATHERING AND ORGANIZATION

This critical phase involves collecting and collating data from disparate (original) data sources and organizing them. This includes merging and matching of records for different products, channels, and systems.

The result of this effort is a clean, reliable data source that ideally has one complete record for each customer and includes all application and performance data for all products owned. This would mean customer's data from their mortgage, credit card, auto loan, savings and checking accounts, and ATM usage would all be in the same place. Later in the book, we will refer to using such variables in scorecard development. In some banks this is known as the enterprise data warehouse (EDW).

In any analytics infrastructure project, this is typically the most difficult and lengthiest phase. Organizations have dirty data, disparate data on dozens and sometimes hundreds of databases with no matching keys, incomplete and missing data, and in some cases coded data that cannot be interpreted. But this is the most important phase of the project, and fixing it has the biggest long-term positive impact on the whole process. Without clean, trusted data, everything else happening downstream is less valuable. We recognize, however, that waiting for perfectly matched clean data for all products before starting scorecard development, especially in large banks with many legacy systems, is not realistic. There is a reason EDW is known as "endless data warehouse" in far too many places. In order to get "quick hits," organizations often take silo approaches and fill the data warehouse with information on one product, and then build and deploy scorecards for that product. They then move on to the next set of products in a sequential manner. This helps in showing some benefit from the data warehouse in the short term and is a better approach than waiting for all data for all products to be loaded in.

Ideally, all data cleansing and matching should be done using automated ETL before the data is put into the EDW (or in any other data repository). Once this is done, users can extract data from here and use it for their own analytics. It also helps to standardize logic of how fields such as "days past due" and others are calculated so that there is no discrepancy across the organization.

Some organizations have departmental data marts that have a subset of the information found in corporate EDWs. For example, the retail credit scorecard modeling department may extract information on retail products only and store it in a star schema to enable scorecard development. A good approach is to make sure all variable transformations, derivations, and aggregations are done via standardized ETL, that is, the code that reads from the EDW and populates the departmental mart. This is beneficial for several reasons. First, it standardizes things like derived variables and definitions of targets, thus reducing errors. Second, auditing is easier, as one only needs to audit the source code once, not each individual project code. Once the code for the creation of variables has been checked, it can be trusted from there on, and any derived variables created from these trusted base variables will also be good. Third, it maintains corporate knowledge. In many banks, code used to generate data is kept on local hard drives or on servers and known only to its creators. By standardizing the code and keeping it in a central location, we create reusable content. This can be done through the usage of GUI software to create data sets or through a centralized repository of code for various tasks.

CREATION OF MODELING DATA SETS

This phase consists of the business user (and sometimes IT) writing code to read data and create smaller data sets with which to develop models. The tasks involved are those such as applying inclusion and exclusion conditions/filters, specifying variables, deriving new variables, deriving and specifying a target(s), and specifying performance windows and sample windows, as well as segmentation and sampling.

Although seemingly a trivial exercise, the creation of data sets for analytics or modeling is still a lengthy and cumbersome one at too many places. Ideally, this task should be done by scorecard developers, as they are most familiar with data items and the objectives of the exercise. This also ensures efficiency, and getting the data set exactly as expected with no interpretation problems. In many banks in particular, this task is done by IT or some other department. The result is a repetitive exercise that takes longer and often produces data sets that have errors. To ensure fewer errors, preservation of corporate IP, efficiency, and full audit, the better banks have incorporated the following practices:

- The use of GUI interfaces for the preceding tasks, to reduce programming error and reduce training time for new hires. There is commercial software available, such as SAS Credit Scoring,[1] that can help create data sets through point-and-click interfaces.
- Create a centralized repository of codes/macros for defining inclusion/exclusion filters, segments, derived variables, common target variables, and nonstandard sampling. This code is used by all modelers to enable standardization and retention of corporate IP. Audit is also easier, as those in model validation only have to audit each code once. For example, code defining specific filter conditions (e.g., exclusions), is created for each segment and each product, so that it can be reused in future redevelopment.

DATA MINING/SCORECARD DEVELOPMENT

This is where the data sets created earlier are then used to perform analytics, including model development. In general, this is the most well understood and, in most institutions, the shortest part of the end-to-end process. Scorecard development will be covered in detail in the rest of the book. Similar to the data gathering phases, banks and other institutions have incorporated several practices to make the data mining process better. These include:

- *The use of GUI software.* While everyone recognizes the ultimate flexibility of using code-based language such as SAS, there are some benefits of using point-and-click software. In particular, when dealing with heavily regulated and audited industries such as banking, GUI software provides standardization, reduces errors, and retains corporate IP better than programming alternatives. What this means is more transparency, shorter training cycles and time to model, easier compliance, and repeatability. In places where scorecard development resources are scarce, this has also helped to manage human resource risk (more on that in a later chapter), and allowed validation staff to perform their duties without having to learn complex programming.

- *Integration with deployment tool.* Once models are developed, they should be able to be implemented easily. Ideally, the scoring code outputted by the data mining software should be read directly into the scoring engine. This not only saves time but also reduces model risk through consistency.

- *Centralization of key macros and code.* Similar to data set creation, the concept of shared standardized code is useful here as well. Where organizations elect to use code, some store key macros for tasks like variable binning, variable selection, model fitting, validation, and so on in a centralized location. Everyone uses the same code base for the same task, therefore ensuring some degree of standardization and repeatability. In addition, if modeling resources leave while working on a project, others can continue with some ease.

- *Control over derived variables.* In cases where new variables are derived in the data mining software and are expected to be used in the future, the ongoing creation of such variables is then transferred to a centralized ETL process. This means such variables are automatically created in the ETL that loads EDWs or departmental data marts. This again ensures efficiency and fewer errors.

VALIDATION/BACKTESTING

Once several models are built, out-of-time and out-of-sample validation takes place (in addition to the qualitative validation). This topic
will also be covered in more detail later on. In some banks in particular, this task is done by teams at arm's length from the original modelers. The validation may involve independently re-creating models and
benchmarking. Many banks have found problems where the validation team has used software programs different from the modelers.
This makes it difficult to re-create exact variables and compare models. In addition to creating regulatory risk by recoding models (and
hence introducing "lost in translation" issues), this process also causes
delays. An integrated modeling plus validation environment reduces
the chances of these errors. If both teams use the same software, auditing also becomes simpler. For example, I have many customers where,
once scorecard developers have built the models, the validation teams
use the same project in the same software to build additional models
for benchmarking. In addition, where resources are scarce, standardizing software enables banks to share and transfer resources with less
disruption and utilize their training budgets more efficiently.

MODEL IMPLEMENTATION

Once validated, the final candidate model(s) are then implemented in
batch or real time. Some banks have faced regulatory scrutiny because
their model implementation environment used software different
from the modeling one. As during model validation, the issues of concern here were continuity, repeatability, and lost-in-translation when
derived variables, filters, conditions, and models are recoded into a
different language. Many banks have found platform integration from
data to analytics to implementation using a single common software
language to be helpful in avoiding these issues. Difficulties and delays
in model implementation can have greater impact than just translation. Many banks will not redevelop scorecards or use new variables
because it just takes too long to implement them. They continue to
reweight scorecards using the same variables just to get new scorecards
into production quickly. This, needless to say, is suboptimal behavior

driven by reality in many places. Seamless deployment options therefore mean the opportunity to use better scorecards and, in the long run, lower losses and higher profits. In addition, for operational purposes, lenders have also found it useful to have the same environment for strategy management as well.

REPORTING AND ANALYTICS

Models and scorecards are monitored for stability, performance and calibration, and various portfolio metrics produced once they are in production. Again, this topic will be covered in later chapters. From an architecture perspective, these reports are best produced in an automated environment, on a monthly, quarterly, or annual basis. The majority of banks worldwide have business intelligence (BI) or reporting software that takes care of their reporting. Much like the previous tasks, a reporting environment integrated with the analytics and implementation tools helps. It reduces project implementation timelines, reduces project risks, and makes compliance and maintenance easier, as there are no breaks in logic for critical scoring code.

NOTE

1. www.sas.com/en_th/industry/banking/credit-scoring.html

## CHAPTER 4

Scorecard Development Process, Stage 1: Preliminaries and Planning

"Give me six hours to chop down a tree and I will spend the first four sharpening the axe."

—Abraham Lincoln

"If you don't know where you are going, you'll end up someplace else."

—Yogi Berra

As discussed briefly in a previous chapter, scorecard development projects do not start with the acquisition of data. Intelligent scorecard development requires proper planning before any analytical work can start. This includes identifying the reason or objective for the project, identifying the key participants in the development and implementation of the scorecards, and assigning tasks to these individuals so that everyone is aware of what is required of them. The point is to make sure that the project will be viable and run smoothly.

CREATE BUSINESS PLAN

Identify Organizational Objectives and Scorecard Role

The first step in any scorecard development project is the identification and prioritization of organizational objectives for that project. This provides a focus point and helps in prioritizing competing issues (e.g., increasing revenue vs. decreasing losses or selection of variables) that come up during development and implementation. It also ensures no "surprises"—for example, deciding whether to set the application approval score cutoff lower to get more accounts or to set it higher to reduce losses.

Examples of organizational objectives, which may be targets for the model, include:

- Reduction in bad debt/bankruptcy/claims/fraud.
- Increase in approval rates or market share in areas such as secured loans, where low delinquency presents expansion

46

opportunities, or in the Telco sector where moving low-risk customers from prepaid to postpaid accounts may be a customer acquisition priority.

- Increased profitability. Note that while profitability is an excellent target to have, in reality, it is exceedingly difficult to measure accurately in complex environments such as multiproduct banks. In many places, proxy numbers are used where known revenue and some cost/loss figures are used in calculations. This forms the basis for a minimum benchmark where at least unprofitability levels are known with some confidence.

- Increased operational efficiency or cost savings. For example, many banks where credit adjudication is still done manually, wish to process applications faster via automation. They may not necessarily have a delinquency problem, and therefore wish to build scorecards to maintain current portfolio metrics but improve turnaround times for applications. This is quite common in the emerging markets, where banks are transitioning from manual to automated adjudication. In such cases, there is an increased emphasis on the scorecard being accepted by the end users, and hence more judgmental alterations to scores are used. In some cases, collections scores are used to assign specific cases to groups of collectors based on matching the collector's ability to the difficulty in recovery. For example, accounts with high recovery may be sent to junior collectors, while the more difficult cases are referred to senior, more experienced ones.

- Better predictive power or improvement over current (compared to existing custom or bureau scorecard).

- Regulatory compliance. Models built for compliance with regulatory initiatives such as Basel II, Comprehensive Capital Analysis and Review (CCAR), the Dodd-Frank Act Stress Test (DFAST), or International Financial Reporting Standard (IFRS) 9 which may require adherence to specific standards.

- Change of corporate decision making from judgmental/manual lending to using credit scorecards. This can come from policy change or acquisition of other banks.

- Routine. Many banks routinely redevelop scorecards at regular intervals, typically every two to three years. The objective is to use the latest information possible and rebuild pro-actively, rather than wait for the scorecard to become unstable.

Organizational objectives, as well as the target to be modeled, will impact many stages of the project. The selection of appropriate performance and sample windows, targets, segmentation options, mix of variables (e.g., bankruptcy or charge-off models, which require isolation of the worst few, will have more negative isolating variables like "Ever Bankrupt" or "Number of Times 90 DPD," whereas behavior scorecards, which require risk ranking across all score ranges, will have more positive data), and modeling technique will all be influenced. The objective will also determine how post-development validation is done as well as the selection of "best" scorecard where more than one has been developed. Typically, most organizations will have a mixture of objectives, including those from the preceding list.

An additional issue that should be clarified at this stage is the extent of the scorecard's role in the adjudication process—is it a sole arbiter, or will it be used as a decision support tool? This is particularly important for organizations that have not previously used risk scoring, since the introduction of scorecards will likely have an impact on organizational culture and operations. Scorecards can be used in the decision-making process to differing extents, depending on product applied for, organizational risk culture and structure, confidence in models, and legal and compliance issues. For example, a credit card company may use risk scorecards as the primary adjudication tool, a sole arbiter, with a small portion—for example, 1 percent—of selected applicants (typically based on scores and policy rules) referred to a credit analyst for additional checks. In this case, the majority of decisions will be made automatically and solely by the scorecard, with no human intervention beyond keying data. This is quite typical with low-exposure, high-volume businesses such as credit cards and telecommunications, as well as in countries where human subjectivity in credit decisioning invites extra regulatory scrutiny or where staffing costs are high.

On the other end of the spectrum, a commercial banker, mortgage company, or insurance underwriter may use risk scoring as one of several measures to gauge the creditworthiness (or claims risk) of applicants, with substantial human involvement and judgmental considerations. This approach is quite common with large value products such as corporate loans and mortgages, or in nations/banks where manual lending is the cultural norm.

Understanding these issues will help in designing effective scorecards and strategies that are appropriate for the organization, as well as the intended purpose. The goal here is to position scorecards as part of a coherent and consistent decision-making process within an organization. The contents of the scorecard should preferably not be duplicated elsewhere, such as in policy rules or adjudicator guidelines. Ideally, in a sole arbiter setting, the scorecard should be based on as many independent data items as possible (as opposed to a scorecard with few characteristics representing limited information types). Conceptually, the scorecard here should mimic what a good, experienced adjudicator would look for in a credit application (i.e., an overall evaluation of the person's creditworthiness). The scorecard should therefore be as complete a risk profile of an applicant as possible. For ideas on what a good risk profile for the particular product or region should look like, a good practice is to speak to experienced adjudicators and risk managers, as suggested in Chapter 2.

In decision support settings, the scorecard characteristics should complement the other considerations being used to evaluate credit. For example, if policy rules are being used, then the factors contained in those policy rules should preferably be kept out of the scorecard. If the decision is manual, then adjudicator guidelines and individual lending criteria need to be understood. This is to further understand the biases in the data, as well as variables to avoid in the model. In addition, if overriding is taking place, understanding its extent and some of the factors that are used to override will further help in identifying any biased data.

Internal versus External Development and Scorecard Type

Where relevant, the business plan should address whether the scorecards are better developed in-house or by external vendors, and provide reasoning.

Where sufficient and clean in-house data exists to build custom scorecards, this decision can depend on factors such as resource availability, expertise in scorecard development for a particular product, time frame for internal versus external development, and cost of acquiring scorecards compared to internal development. Custom scorecards, built in-house on the organization's own data, are generally the best options and most relevant. In the past 10 years or so, the majority of banks in most countries have recognized this and shifted scorecard development in-house. However, paying an external vendor to develop scorecards can be a viable and better option in some cases.

In order to help decide whether scorecards should be developed internally or outsourced, we review the main benefits and drawbacks of each.

The main benefits and drawbacks of *outsourced* scorecard development involve the following main points:

- *Cheaper for very small portfolios, expensive for others.* If a bank has a very small customer base and needs only two or three models a year, it is cheaper to pay someone to build a model or to buy generic ones. Note that this is based only on scorecard development—banks may want to do other types of analytics in-house regardless. Such banks are also more likely to opt for the standardized approach under Basel II and are not required to show in-house competency in model development. For larger banks, however, outsourcing strategies are almost always more expensive, as the charges are per scorecard built. Many large institutions build dozens of scorecards and models annually (in many cases 100+), and this can get very expensive if outsourced.

- *Credibility/track record of developer.* As has been discussed continuously in this book, the knowledge level of the modeler in terms of statistics, data quirks/weaknesses/strengths, products concerned, economic conditions of the country and regions, local lending laws, geography, and other local nuances impacts the quality of the scorecard. Selecting the right company and modeler becomes important, as the person developing the model is no longer under your control. Merely having a company with a long track record of building models is not enough, as work done by junior employees can sometimes be suspect. Banks should ensure that staff identified by vendors to build their models have the requisite knowledge mentioned earlier.

- *Lower risk, lower reward.* Outsourcing strategies are lower risk for the lender, as most of the risks we will discuss in this chapter are transferred over to the vendor. There is no need to manage resources, technology, or stagnation for scorecard development. However, the lower risk also comes with lower rewards, both in terms of lower return on investment (ROI) and less learning.

- *Little knowledge gain or insights.* An external vendor analyzing bank data solely for scorecard development will generally not come up with better ideas for lending strategies or policy rules. Without deep knowledge of the bank data, they are also unlikely to spot some biases or question relationships that look normal but are not. External scorecard development does not increase the knowledge level of the bank as much as internal development does.

- *Less regulatory oversight.* Many banks opt for external sourcing of scorecards as it lowers the regulatory scrutiny they face. This is true in countries such as the United States, where such scrutiny can involve significant bank resources. This strategy transfers some of the burden over to the vendor for the model development—the lender is still responsible for implementation and proper usage.

- *Three- to six-month cycle.* Typically, external vendors would take between three and six months to build models. This is dependent on how quickly the bank can generate and send data to the vendor.

- *Lower flexibility.* External development can be inflexible in two ways. First, due to cost constraints, exploring detailed segmentation strategies can be a limited exercise. Only major, known industry standards or vendor/bank-suggested segments are likely to be investigated. In many cases, these will suffice. However, for more mature lenders, better segmentation through more detailed analysis can generate significant benefits. Second, when a scorecard is deemed to be unstable or not performing well based on other measures, and a decision is made to redevelop, outsourcing strategies will not be as responsive as internal development. The redevelopment (or reweighting, for example) effort will depend on the vendor's schedule and availability (although there are cases where internal staff cannot deal with higher volumes, and in that case it makes sense to get help from external vendors on a temporary basis). Any delays will result in additional losses, as suboptimal scorecards will still be in use.

- *Black box.* As noted in the guest chapter on vendor models, in some cases the methodology used by the vendor, as well as their assumptions, may not be available. This can make compliance and ongoing validation trickier.

In-house scorecard development, however, provides the following main benefits and challenges:

- *Cheaper for larger companies.* In general, if a company is acquiring more than three to five scorecards per annum, it is cheaper to build scorecards in-house, based solely on costs. This is due to the wide availability of economical but powerful data mining software, as well as knowledge and training. In addition, once the tools and staff are established, there is little to limit the number of models and scorecards that can be built. Often, companies who bring credit scoring in-house end up building far more models than when they were outsourcing. Some smaller organizations opt to do this anyway—not for the direct ROI, but for indirect benefits such as creating knowledge and establishing a culture of analytics-based decision making in the company.
- *Higher risk, higher reward.* Developing scorecards in-house is a higher-risk activity compared to outsourcing. The lender takes on human resource and other risks that the vendor would have taken under outsourcing scenarios. Some of those risks are discussed here, and the mitigation of these risks is discussed in a later chapter. However, with that risk comes higher reward in terms of greater ROI, speed, learning, and flexibility.
- *Need to develop and retain talent.* Bringing this discipline in-house means that the lender has to hire, develop, and retain talent for

a strategic activity. Scorecard development goals for any period of time, long or short term, depends on the stability of analytical staff. In some high-growth markets, these resources can be scarce, and can quickly escalate hiring costs and salaries. Mitigation strategies for this risk are discussed in more detail in a separate chapter.

- *Maintain infrastructure.* Lenders must build and maintain internal infrastructure for scorecard development. This, which includes data marts as well as data mining software, has been covered in some detail in a different chapter. However, the impact of this issue is relatively minor as most of the infrastructure involved would have been created anyways for general analytics work, as well as for validating and using scorecards.

- *Regulatory/Vetting scrutiny.* Internal development does mean that there will be increased internal validation/vetting as well as external regulatory scrutiny on the model development itself. This, however, is not a matter of choice for the larger institutions who opt for, or are expected to build their own models for regulatory purposes. Proper governance of data and processes can make dealing with this scrutiny easier. Internal development also means there will be long-term consistency in things such as methodology, validation, scaling, and documentation, which makes compliance easier.

- *Knowledge gain, insights for better strategies/products.* The kind of analysis we discuss in this book, including grouping variables, creates a lot of knowledge within the company, and leads to better strategies, policy rules, and segmentation. Analytics enhances the knowledge base of any institution, which is why doing it in-house makes sense.

- *Two-week to two-month cycle.* This is the average time frame for organizations that have built some maturity and processes around scorecard development. It means automating data gathering, using convenient GUI software for binning, modeling, validation, and other tasks. Usually, for lenders starting from scratch, it could take 9 to 12 months, and the building of three to four scorecards to get to this point (to fine-tune all the processes). The ability to develop models faster has direct ROI benefits. Being able to use a better model sooner can result in lower losses, especially if the older model is unstable or otherwise defective.

■ *Maximum flexibility.* When the development is done in-house, lenders do not have to wait for vendor availability. They can build new models faster and when required. Internal development also makes exhaustive segmentation analysis possible. Superior internal and local knowledge can be used to experiment with better segmentation strategies, and subsequently build better models. The better segmentation can result in lower overall losses, and the discovery of pockets of high/low risk customers, which can then lead to better business strategies and policy rules.

■ *Must get over confidence gap.* External vendors have a long history of building scorecards, and have therefore built corporate memory and expertise. However, once internal staff learn how to build scorecards, and are given the right tools, they too can become knowledgeable and start building that expertise in-house. Many lenders need to get over the confidence gap that they, or their staff, can in fact do this in-house. While the ROI numbers are compelling, they will only come when lenders gain the confidence to take the leap from outsourcing to in-house development.

■ *Localized.* Ideally scorecards should be developed by local staff in any country. Internal development assures that local laws, regulations, lending culture, geography, economy, and other nuances are taken into account during all phases of scorecard development.

■ *Full disclosure.* Internal model development assures full disclosure to validation staff as well as regulators, as long as the software being used for development is also open and transparent. This has the added advantage of understanding better the strengths and weaknesses of the model, since the developer now knows the data, assumptions, parameters, and methodology used.

The mitigation of some of the risks of in-house model development will be discussed in some detail in a later chapter.

In cases where sufficient data does not exist (e.g., low default portfolios) or where accessibility and quality of data are questionable, generic scorecards from an external vendor or credit bureau may be needed. Further cases for generic scorecards occur when a company is marketing to a new segment, channel, or product for which it has no previous data, but where industry data is available; when the business volume of a product does not justify the cost of developing a custom scorecard; or when a product launch schedule does not allow for enough time to develop a custom scorecard.

Generic scorecards are best when their development sample/purpose matches closely with that of the bank's customers. For example, if a bank wants to target first-time homebuyers with loan to value ratio (LTV) greater than 80 percent in Canada, its best to get a generic scorecard for exactly that type of mortgage customers with data from Canada. It may not be possible to have such deeply segmented generic scorecards available in every country. In such cases, the closest alternatives are used. However, lenders should realize that generic scorecards built on regional or global data, with data from countries with very different lending environments, or on population segments that are very different from the intended target market, will not perform very well. For example, using a generic score from the bureau to target unbanked or prepaid Telco customers may not be ideal. Most bureau data is based on people who have credit cards, auto loans, or mortgages, whereas the average Telco customer, and specifically the prepaid customer in most countries, is quite different.

In some cases, it may not be possible to use statistically developed scorecards, custom or generic. This is usually due to very low volumes, perceived benefits that do not justify the costs associated with any externally paid scorecard development, or to a product for which no generic model is available or appropriate. In these circumstances, it may be necessary to develop a judgment-based adjudication model. Such models are also known as judgmental, expert systems, or experience-based models.

The development of such a model involves selecting a group of characteristics judged to be good predictors of risk, and assigning points to each attribute, as with statistically developed models. The exercise, however, is done based on collective experience and intuition, and the resulting model is typically implemented in conjunction with a lot of policy rules. Although not statistically developed, the judgmental model can provide a more consistent and objective decision-making tool than adjudication by individual credit analysts. Judgmental scorecards have also been shown to be effective in microfinance lending.[1]

The development of judgmental models should be done with participation from Credit Adjudication, Credit Policy, and other risk management–related functions. In most cases, the assembled risk experts follow a process like this:

- Pick a group of risk factors/variables normally used to assess creditworthiness, and relevant for the product in question.
- Rank-order the variables in terms of importance. The ranking does not have to be individual—groups of variables can also be created in decreasing order of "strength." This is equivalent to rank-ordering by chi square when doing statistical analysis.
- These variables are then judgmentally "grouped" or broken up into distinct classes; for example, "debt service ratio" is grouped into several bands such as "0–10 percent," "10–15 percent," and so on, that represent different risk levels. Decile distribution by accounts can also be used here. As with statistically based binning, these are also adjusted/created based on knowledge of policy rules and other business factors.
- The different attributes of each variable are then assigned points based on relative riskiness, as well as relative strength of the variable. For example, if LTV is believed to be very strong, there may be an 80-point difference from the minimum to maximum score for its attributes. So someone with 0–10 percent LTV will get 80 points, while a 90–95 percent LTV will get 0 points. If "age of used car" is deemed weaker, the maximum difference between a very old and very new car may only be 30 points, for example.
- Once the judgmental scorecard is created, some prerated applications are scored to make sure there is risk ranking and consistency.

CREATE PROJECT PLAN

The project plan should include a clearly defined project scope and timelines, and address issues such as deliverables and implementation strategy. When dealing with organizations that have not worked with scorecards before, it's a good idea to give the decision makers a sample copy of the scorecard results documentation to set expectations. In general, the risk manager and risk strategy managers are given gains charts and other such analytics that will help them make decisions. I normally generate expected losses, approval rates, revolve rates, recovery rates, and the like by distinct subpopulations. At this point, it is useful to show the decision makers examples of such reports and ask them which subpopulations they would like to study. The point is to generate analytics that will be useful to the decision makers. It is also useful to walk the model vetting or validation team thru a sample project plan and show them the output of each. They then have the opportunity to add or adjust based on the specific requirements of their internal policies or regulator guidelines. This reduces the chances of misunderstandings and other problems later on.

The project plan should include all foreseeable contingencies and risks, and ensure that continuity between development and post-development processes is present. This is to allow seamless transition from the development team to those responsible for testing, strategy development, and implementation. Proper planning at this stage will prevent scenarios such as scorecards being developed by a group but not being implemented, because the IT department was not told early enough, or because reporting for new scorecards cannot be produced in time for implementation. All the stakeholders involved should be aware of what needs to be done, by whom, and when.

Identify Project Risks

The success of scorecard development projects is dependent on various connected processes, with each ensuing process only able to start once the previous one is satisfactorily completed. As an empirically derived solution, the process is also completely reliant on development data. As a result, there are several risks associated with scorecard development projects, including:

- Nonavailability of data or insufficient data. Low-default portfolios have caused issues for many banks who have chosen to comply with the Foundation or Advanced Internal Ratings Based requirements of Basel II. We will look at data sufficiency later on in more detail; at this point, we want to be aware that not having enough data is a risk for model development.
- Poor quality of data (dirty or unreliable).
- Delays/difficulties in accessing data. In many banks it can take several months for modeling staff to get data needed for analytics. This can greatly affect project timelines and cause losses from using outdated models.
- Nonpredictive or weak data. This is something that can only be discovered once the development process has started, and is particularly acute in banks where lending is heavily manual or similarly biased. Variables appear to be unpredictive of risk as the risky accounts are mostly cherry picked, thereby equalizing their risk with the low–risk ones.
- Scorecard characteristics or derivations that cannot be handled by operational systems. This can be easily avoided via communications with the IT teams.
- Changes in organizational direction/priorities.
- Possible implementation delays due to issues such as recoding of models, especially if outsourced.
- Other legal or operational issues.

Project risks, "showstoppers," and other factors that can potentially affect the quality of the scorecard should be identified at this stage and, where necessary, backup plans should be formulated. The point is that merely having data, or having a lot of it, does not guarantee an institution a scorecard or model of any type. In particular, this needs to be explained to senior management of banks that do not have a history of using models and scorecards, so as to make sure that their expectations are realistic.

Identify Project Team

The project plan also identifies all the stakeholders for the project and assembles a multidepartmental project team. A list of suggested team members has been provided in Chapter 2.

The list of project team members should identify roles and responsibilities, executive sponsors, and members whose signoffs are required for successful completion of various development stages. The signoff requirement is a best practice that introduces the idea of continuous consultation and vetting to the process. A list of the major phases in the scorecard development process, outputs of each stage and the suggested signoff parties has been provided toward the end of the previous chapter.

A further list should also be created for those who need to be kept informed of interim results, timelines, and proposed strategies. These are typically departments that do not have a direct role in the development itself, but that will be impacted by changes in strategy.

Following the approval of a business plan outlining the case for using scorecards, the complete project plan, scope, and deliverables are signed off by the executive sponsors and managers from departments performing the actual scorecard development and implementation.

This chapter, as well as the previous one, are designed to encourage planning and cooperation. The purpose of such business planning is not to create additional bureaucratic layers for scorecard developers. The concept is simple—in large organizations where disparate departments share the work involved in the development, implementation, validation and management of scorecards, some coordination is necessary for efficiency and for managing expectations. The scorecard delivery meeting is not a good time to find out that the scorecard you just spent two months developing cannot be implemented.

The majority of problems with scorecard development projects that I have seen do not involve mathematics or statistics issues; they inevitably have to do with data issues, IT issues, communications problems, decision deadlocks, vague policies, vague guidelines from national regulators, as well as internal and external validators/regulators who are not familiar with scorecard development.

Such business planning need not be formal—as long as all the issues have been given sufficient thought.

WHY "SCORECARD" FORMAT?

This book deals with the development of a traditional points-based scorecard, as shown in Exhibit 1.1. While it is recognized that predictive models are also developed in other formats, such as SAS code, using a variety of modeling methods, the scorecard format is the most commonly used one in the industry. Some of the reasons why this format is preferred are:

- This format is the easiest to interpret, understand, implement and use. The increasing or decreasing scores for attributes are intuitive, in line with business experience and therefore appeal to a broad range of risk managers and decision makers who do not have advanced knowledge of statistics or data mining. Scorecards in some cases can be implemented on paper, although this is not recommended.

- Reasons for declines, low scores, or high scores can be explained to customers, auditors, regulators, senior management, model validators and other staff, in simple business terms. This enables simpler decision making when scores change, or applications get declined.

- The development process for these scorecards is not a black box, and is widely understood. As such, it can easily meet any regulatory or internal model validation requirement on method transparency.

- The scorecard is very easy to diagnose and monitor, using standard reports. The structure of the scorecard also means that analysts can perform these functions without having in-depth knowledge of statistics or programming. This makes the scorecard an effective tool to manage risk.

"Creating things that you don't understand—that the buyer doesn't understand, that the rating agency doesn't understand, that the regulator doesn't understand—is

really not a good idea no matter who owns it. The fact that the firms that created them were stupid enough to own them doesn't make me feel any better."

—John Thain, former CEO of Merrill Lynch, speaking at
Wharton College on September 30, 2009[2]

NOTES

1. L. Simbaqueba, G. Salamanca, and V. Bumacov, "The Role of Credit Scoring in Micro Lending," LiSim, 2011.

2. www.finextra.com/news/fullstory.aspx?newsitemid= 20584

CHAPTER **5**

Managing the Risks of In-House Scorecard Development

"Every noble acquisition is attended with its risks; he who fears to encounter the one must not expect to obtain the other."

—Pietro Metastasio

"Risk comes from not knowing what you're doing."

—Warren Buffett

In previous chapters, we have discussed at length the various benefits of in-house credit scoring, including the ability to develop scorecards faster, cheaper, and with far greater flexibility than outsourcing. While these and other advantages of in-house credit scorecard development are well understood, the risks are not. We have previously recognized that internal scorecard development has some risks associated with it. In this chapter, we will discuss ways in which successful lenders have mitigated some of the risks. Note that we are discussing the issue within the narrow realm of in-house scorecard development only, not the entire area of model risk governance. Whether an organization builds the scorecards internally or has someone else build it for them, there are some risks that will always be there—data risks, model validation issues, policies governing usage, internal controls on approvals, and so on. The following are some of the major risks that a lender takes on when it decides to build credit risk scorecards in-house:

- Human resource (HR) risk
- Stagnation
- Technology
- Quality

HUMAN RESOURCE RISK

When banks or lenders decide to start building their own scorecards, they usually set up a department or team to do so. These teams need to be staffed and managed appropriately. The bank now takes on the responsibility to recruit, train, and retain scarce modeling resources. With the outsourcing option, the vendor traditionally carried this risk.

Critical staff can leave—this can put projects at risk for several reasons. First, new resources will need to be hired as replacement. These new hires will then need to be trained to use software and informed about the bank and its data. In the meantime, existing modelers may have to pick up the work left by their departed colleague. The speed at which each of these tasks can be completed will determine the final impact of staff departure. Departing staff can also take a lot of corporate knowledge with them.

Given the strategic nature of model development—recall the widespread usage of credit risk scorecards for operational and regulatory usage, managing this risk is critical to the success of any internal development.

Other than being a great place to work and ensuring that compensation and benefits are competitive, this sort of HR risk can be mitigated through several strategies.

The choice of technology can help manage risk. While programming-based tools for data mining provide ultimate flexibility, they are also less transparent, harder to learn, and involve skills that are scarce in many places. Risk reduction can happen through the use of products that allow faster learning, more transparency, and sharing of work. This issue is more acute in countries where model development and coding resources are scarce. In general, it takes between 9 and 12 months of training to get someone with a good statistics or banking background to a point where they can produce production quality models using a coding-based approach. This is assuming the resources are not familiar with the programming tool being used at the organization. However, graphical user interface (GUI)/point-and-click-based data mining tools normally require about a one- or two-month training cycle, therefore enabling new resources to more quickly become productive.

Traditional programming-based approaches as well as work practices also made it harder to share work. Each person developing models wrote their own code to do so, with their own derivations and logic. Normally, when coders leave their employer, a big chunk of their knowledge leaves with them, as others are reluctant to sift through thousands of lines of someone else's code. Restarting partially finished work often means starting from scratch. Some companies have set up centralized libraries of macros and other code to encourage sharing. An easier way to do this is to use/create GUI software where projects, data conditions/filters, exclusions, derived variables, and other project artifacts are available to everyone and can be shared (this was emphasized previously in Chapter 3). The net result of such arrangements is to lower risk when key staff leave. Unfinished work can be picked up and continued, and training new resources is much faster, allowing them to be productive more quickly. In recent years, there has been a shift to the usage of more point-and-click software, especially for the development of regulatory models, as a way to reduce model risk and meet aggressive timelines for compliance.

When deciding to build scorecards in-house, the right technology/platform partner can make a difference. Lenders have a choice of software/infrastructure provider, and given that they are now bringing a critical function in-house, the selection of such providers should be made in a way that reduces the risk. In particular, attention should be paid to the following:

- *Availability of regular training for statistics, software usage, and best practices.* When new staff are brought on board, one of the factors that influences how quickly they can become productive is the availability of training. Waiting for the next class in seven months halfway across the world is not a great option. Ideally, the new hires should already have some coding skills; however, in reality this is not always the case. In tight markets, it is also common for lenders to hire people with some numerical background but who are experienced in lending policy and strategy for model development roles. These people often need refresher courses on some statistics before they can produce models. Outside of software usage and statistics, scorecard developers often need to be coached in business thinking and taught tips/tricks of the trade. Very often, the more senior staff members fulfill this function, but vendors who can do such knowledge transfer would make things easier.

- *Partner whose "go-to-market" strategy is aligned with your goals.* There are boutique consulting companies and others available who will help transfer knowledge to enable in-house model development, rather than try to convince you to keep outsourcing. Once a lender has decided to develop in-house, it needs to seek partners whose goals are aligned with the lender's own goals. This does not preclude temporary help in scorecard development services.

- *Vendors that can step in and provide short-term scorecard development, consulting, and mentoring.* Many development teams face temporary crunches either due to too much demand for models or temporary staff shortage. In such situations, it is useful to have a partner who can step in and provide scorecard development services, preferably using the same tools as used by the lender. In addition, and related to the previous point, consulting and mentoring services should also be available but with aligned goals. The point is that when these services are provided, the ultimate objective is to empower and train the lender's staff to be self-sufficient in the future, and not to create a cycle of dependency on an external provider.

- *Vendors that have local presence for quick turnaround and knowledge.* Local presence is beneficial in two ways: it allows for faster responses to questions and problems, and if using them for scorecard development services, local knowledge allows for the development of better, more relevant models.

- *Products that are widely used.* The process of hiring and training staff to develop scorecards is easier if the chosen development tool is being widely used in the local market. This is even more critical if a lender chooses to use programming heavy products. The availability of a good pool of resources that can be hired when needed reduces risk. Using products that are less common means that this same process will take longer.

■ *Creating a risk culture where documentation and sharing of knowledge is mandatory.* This means the scorecard developers as well as validators must document the process, decisions, and reasoning for the entire process. Proper documentation not only reduces model risk but also ensures continuity and retention of corporate knowledge.

TECHNOLOGY AND KNOWLEDGE STAGNATION RISK

One of the reasons cited by lenders that decide to outsource model development is that the external vendor has the advantage of greater knowledge, better technology, and continuous learning. In theory, the vendor brings industry experience and new knowledge gained from doing similar work for many others. They also have access to the latest proprietary data mining software and methodologies, which may not be available to the outside world. The risk of in-house development is that knowledge can become stale and isolated, and the bank can fall behind others in the use of the latest methodologies.

Lending institutions that decide on a particular vendor/technology for scorecard development may also face the loss of previous skills and investment in specific software training. This would be the scenario where a switch is being made in the underlying coding language or technology. The risks of this issue include delays in getting value from internal modeling, and increased expenditure.

Almost all lending institutions have existing analytics, data management, and reporting infrastructure in place. When they decide to start scorecard development, the choice of technology may be disruptive. Specifically, integration problems are quite widespread, and can delay/disrupt the benefits of internal model development or, worse, cause regulatory problems. Challenges frequently seen include new technologies and platforms not communicating with existing infrastructure; models that need to be recoded (regulatory and governance risk); validation and development teams that use different products, making benchmarking more difficult; model implementation into scoring and decisioning software becoming very onerous and expensive; proprietary implementation software where internally built scorecards cannot be installed easily; and problems implementing scorecard monitoring and other reports into reporting environments. Some of these have been discussed in some detail in Chapter 3.

Many lenders are hesitant to develop scorecards themselves, as they don't believe their own staff can do as good a job as the external vendor. They believe there is a quality risk should they start developing scorecards in-house.

Those who have been successful in creating an in-house modeling function have mitigated this risk through the following main actions:

- Some banks and lenders engage outside scorecard vendors every three to four years and have them build a custom scorecard. The intention here is to "buy" current knowledge, to see if the vendor has any unique ideas around segmentation, methodologies, and interesting new variables.

- Most lenders have set budgets for continuous education of their resources. This includes attending classroom and online training programs and seminars, as well as conferences. In addition, a lot of academic/peer reviewed and other industry research is also available for public download from the Internet. Resources are encouraged to spend a set amount of time on research—which can include reading journals and papers, and following conversations in online discussion forums. While some of this is immediately useful, a lot of "cutting-edge" methodology is not. As has been discussed in this book, regulatory model development operates under many constraints, and not every new algorithm is usable in practice. However, it is always useful to expand one's knowledge and to keep abreast of the most recent innovations.

- Understand that building a knowledge base takes time. Larger organizations do sometimes hire entire teams with significant industry and modeling experience, and hence get a running start in their journey to internal development. Many others, however, build the knowledge base slowly through the passage of time. As their modelers build more and more scorecards and get comfortable with methodologies, data, and internal processes, they become better and more efficient (and more valuable).

This can sometimes take three to four years, depending on the volume of models built, and so expectations must be managed.

■ Where possible, maintain continuity of coding platforms and software. If you have existing packages that staff are familiar with and have been trained on, the lower-risk proposition is to stick with the status quo. The only exception is when that software package does not have scorecard development capabilities at all, or is well below the industry standards. Many institutions will forgo advanced features and functionalities in order to preserve continuity. Again, this depends on the level of commitment and investment already sunk into the existing product.

■ Integration must not be underestimated. As mentioned in Chapter 3, integration between data, analytics, implementation, and reporting reduces risk and increases governance. Before making any investment decisions, perform an analysis of existing infrastructure and future state with internal scorecards. Identify the various integration points, end products of each component and handoffs to others, validation and governance requirements, and all known gaps/red flags. Prioritize and plan the least disruptive options. This way, implementation, governance, and other risk is reduced. Internal data will be read by the scorecard development tool; scorecards can be benchmarked, validated, and implemented without recoding or expensive outside help; and reports can be produced in a reasonable time frame.

■ Explore engaging the local credit bureaus to get industry trends and changes. In some countries, credit bureaus are able to provide information on how major indicators are changing, for example, the trends in the average number of inquiries, utilization, or trades. Such information can allow a lender to benchmark its own information against the market.

■ Get return on investment (ROI) from your vendor. All vendors perform research and development (R&D) work and create new products. There are two aspects of vendor selection that can reduce the technology risk/gap for the lending institution. First, select vendors that dedicate significant resources to R&D and offer you the benefit of that work regularly. For example, data mining vendors should offer the latest algorithms in their products, preferably without "black boxes." Keeping the work secret may work for some business models, but not one where the customer (i.e., the bank/lender) wants to be self-sufficient and be able to explain what it is doing to various stakeholders. Second, if a vendor is offering short-term consulting or score-card development help (in addition to helping you become self-sufficient), it is a good idea to make sure they use the same software product that they have sold you. If a vendor uses a different product internally, there will be a technology gap.

■ You can do better. Quality risk/gap is an understandable confidence gap for companies without a history of doing data mining or modeling. Mitigating this risk involves pretty much all of the points that have been made in this chapter. Again, this is more acute in developing countries where credit scoring itself is an immature discipline, but very rarely a problem in the more mature geographies. What that tells us is the following: hundreds/thousands of financial institutions have, and are, building their own models and scorecards. Adaptation of analytics is nearly universal, with very clear benefits. Even those who are not required to do so internally for reasons such as Basel II compliance, are doing so, clearly recognizing the advantages. Banks have discovered that the superior internal knowledge of data does produce better scorecards and segmentation, enables creation of knowledge and better strategies, and with time the quality gap can very easily be overcome.

■ Is there really a knowledge gap? While in theory outside vendors are expected to bring new knowledge and variables, this needs to be verified in practice as well. Some of the questions lenders must ask to confirm this are:

  ■ *Have predictive variables changed much?* In most countries there is a set group of variables that have always been used to lend money and build models. These are almost inevitably related to the basic rules of lending, such as the "five C's of lending." Unless there is a brand new data source, such as new credit bureau, these will not change much. The variables themselves, in reality, have not changed significantly, although the attribute bins for some have (e.g., number of inquiries and trades).

■ *How much of the latest information is usable?* While talking about the newest trends and algorithms is interesting, how much of it is useful in real life. Again, considering the various regulatory, validation, technological, and others constraints, an honest assessment needs to be made on the value of the knowledge gap between the vendor and the bank.

The preceding are just some of the ways banks have mitigated the risks of bringing the credit scorecard development process in-house. As mentioned earlier, this is in addition to setting up internal oversight and validation functions. This book aims to equip lenders with knowledge that can be used to develop their own scorecards; however, it must be reemphasized that setting up the right infrastructure and planning well to reduce the chances of operational risks are just as important as the methodology.

## CHAPTER 6

Scorecard Development Process, Stage 2: Data Review and Project Parameters

"Facts are stubborn things, but statistics are more pliable."

—Mark Twain

T his stage is sometimes the longest and most labor-intensive phase of scorecard development. It is designed to determine, first, whether scorecard development is feasible, and if it is, second, to set high-level parameters for the project. The parameters include exclusions, target definition, sample window, performance window, and subsegments for the scorecard.

DATA AVAILABILITY AND QUALITY REVIEW

This phase first addresses the issue of data availability, in the contexts of quality and quantity. Here, we answer the question, "Do we have enough data to start the project?" Reliable and clean data is needed for scorecard development, with a minimum acceptable number of "goods" and "bads." This process is made easier and more efficient where the data is housed within data marts or data warehouses.

The quantity of data needed varies, but in general, it should fulfill the requirements of business confidence, statistical significance, representativeness, and randomness. At this phase, exact numbers are not critical, since that is dependent on the "bad" definition to be set in the next phase. What we are interested in is whether we are broadly "in the ballpark." The subject of sampling is itself a very detailed one and will be covered in the next chapter. There is a large body of work dedicated to finding the "optimal" sample, but none with a definitive answer. The modeling methodology, number of customers in the total population, type of data, and the measure used to determine what the "best" model is all play a role in determining the best sample size. For credit scoring, a good reference is one by Crone and Finlay,[1] who look at the effects of both sample size and the ratio between goods and bads. Their research seems to suggest that for logistic regression models, a sample of about 5,000 bads for applications scorecards and 12,000 for behavior scorecards results in maximum Gini Coefficient (after which no significant improvement in Gini occurs).

Having worked with many data sets for different products and from banks with varying approval processes, my experience has shown several things: First, data quality can compensate for a lack of data. I have seen reasonable scorecards produced with small data sets (1,000 bads) with mostly (clean) bureau data for credit card portfolios, whose application adjudication tends to be largely unbiased. Second is the general industry opinion that while we may not agree with what the "optimal" data set is, we agree that more data is better. Third, the greater issue is not in defining the optimal sample, but rather having a minimum number of goods and bads. In the age of Big Data, where banks can and do develop models with millions and sometimes billions of observations, the upper optimal number has not been one which banks limit themselves to, especially when they have large data sets. The problem is in institutions that have very few bads. Finally, in addition to the model fit and other statistical factors that have been discussed in many papers on sampling, specifically for scorecards that have binned variables, the minimum required data is needed to enable a reasonable number of bins to be constructed. When you have a low number of bads, you may only be able to create two to four bins for a variable such as loan-to-value (LTV), for example, because you need a minimum number of bads in each bin. The two to four bins for a variable like LTV will not offer sufficient differentiation between the different levels of risk, and the accounts in each very large bin will be far from homogeneous. Again, the discussion here is in the context of a minimum number of data points needed to build a scorecard. The ratio between goods and bads is a separate issue that will be dealt with later. Based on this experience, I have generally had success where for application scorecard development there were approximately a *minimum* of 2,000 "bad" accounts and 2,000 "good" accounts that can be randomly selected for each proposed scorecard, from a group of approved accounts opened within a defined time frame. For behavior scorecards, these would be from a group of accounts that were current at a given point in time or at a certain delinquency status for collections scoring. A further *minimum* 2,000 declined applications may also be required for application scorecards where reject inference is to be performed.

The organization's loss, delinquency, claims, or other performance reports and volume of applications should provide an initial idea of whether this target can be met. Typically, it is more difficult to find enough "bad" accounts than "good" ones.

The project team will also need to determine whether internal data intended for scorecard development has been tampered with, or is unreliable for other reasons. Demographic data and other application data items that are not verified, such as income, are more susceptible to being misrepresented, but items such as credit bureau data, real estate data, financial ratios, and so forth are more robust and can be used. If it is determined, for example, that data from application forms or branches is not reliable, scorecards can still be developed solely from bureau data. This is also a common case with models in the Telco industry, where data collected by vendors at point of sale is of low quality.

Once it is determined that there is sufficient good-quality internal data to proceed, external data must be evaluated, quantified, and defined. The organization may decide to develop scorecards based on internal data alone, or may choose to supplement this data from external sources such as credit bureaus, central claims repositories, geo-demographic data providers, and so forth. Some organizations obtain and retain such data for each applicant in electronic databases. In cases where data is not available electronically or is retained in paper-based format, the organization may have to either key it into databases or purchase data on a "retroactive" basis from the external provider. The time frame for "retro" data extracts is specified in line with the performance and sample window definitions to be specified.

At the end of this phase, when it is determined jointly by the key signoff personas discussed in the preceding chapter that both quality and quantity of internal and external data can be obtained, the initial data gathering for project parameters definition can begin.

DATA GATHERING FOR DEFINITION OF PROJECT PARAMETERS

In order to define the project parameters for the scorecard development project, data must first be gathered in a database format. As mentioned earlier, project parameters primarily include determining the definitions of *good, bad,* and *indeterminate;* establishing the performance and sample windows; defining subsegments; and defining data exclusions for use in producing the development sample and in the development process itself.

Data items are then collected for applications from the previous two to five years (the exact number is dependent on the bad definition, prediction horizon needed, and time normally taken for the portfolio to mature) in the case of application scorecards, or from a large enough sample. Note that certain regulations, such as International Financial Reporting Standard (IFRS) 9 may require longer analysis horizons. Typical data items collected include:

- Account/identification number.
- Date opened or applied (to measure time since customer/ applied).
- Accept/reject indicator.
- Arrears/payment/claims history over the timeline being analyzed (to measure bad rate and assign good/bad flag).
- Nonperforming, forced default, or charge-off flag.
- Product/channel and other categorical segment identifiers.
- Current account status (e.g., inactive, closed, lost, stolen, fraud, etc.) used for exclusions and other definitions.
- Loan underwriting/lending policies, to identify sources of bias.
- Major marketing/cross-sell campaigns to identify seasonality and other biases that may cause the sample window to be inappropriate.
- Other data to understand the business.

For behavior scorecard development, accounts are chosen at one point in time, and their behavior analyzed over, typically, a 6- or

12-month period. Again, this can vary based on regulations and other factors. Similarly, those building proportional hazard or transition state models would need to build appropriate data sets for those situations.

Since one of the secondary objectives of the next phase is to understand the business, further relevant data items can be added as required. I have typically analyzed data such as distributions of customers by demographics such as age, housing status, existing banking relationships, number and types of products, pre- versus postpaid Telco, time-of-day usage, geography, brands of car purchased, timing of special customer acquisition initiatives; average values of different bureau-based indicators; and any other criteria that will help in constructing a comprehensive profile of your organization's client base. The point is to understand the data and the business that you are in. In business terms, I try to answer questions like "who is/are my typical customer(s)?"; "who is my best/worst customer"; and "what are my most important segments?" so that when I am analyzing the data I am able to identify any abnormal trends.

Loan underwriting policies help understand the biases in the data, as has been covered in previous chapters. Similarly, knowledge of past marketing or cross-sell campaigns will help understand seasonality or any other abnormal trend in the development sample. The sample we use for scorecard development must be from a normal time period and indicative of future applicants. Once the sample window is identified, understanding major marketing campaigns can help identify if that sample is not representative of the normal through-the-door population.

DEFINITION OF PROJECT PARAMETERS

The following analyses are done not only to define project parameters but also as a way to understand the business through data.

Exclusions

Certain types of accounts and applications need to be excluded from the development sample. In general, accounts used for development are those that you would score during normal day-to-day credit-granting operations, and those that would constitute your intended customer. The question you need to ask is: Who am I going to score using this scorecard on a daily basis? Accounts that have abnormal performance—for example, frauds—and those that will be adjudicated using some non-score-dependent criteria should not be part of any development sample. These can include designated accounts such as staff, VIPs, out of country, preapproved/selective invites, lost/ stolen cards, deceased, underage, and voluntary cancellations within the performance window. Note that some developers include canceled accounts as "indeterminate," since these accounts were scored and approved and therefore fall into the "score during normal day-to-day operations" category. This is a better approach from a logical perspective. Preapproved applications and those that were sent invitations to apply (via cross-sell campaigns) are also excluded because they are a highly biased subpopulation. Typically, these applicants are put through risk as well as marketing filters before the best among them are selected for *occasional* marketing campaigns. Adding them into a scorecard project that includes those in the general population who voluntarily apply for credit products will bias the data—unless the campaigns are going to be run constantly in the future, thereby making them the norm.

Most analysts also exclude applicants that have been declined using policy rules, where the decline rate is almost 100 percent, and the lender has no plans to change that rule in the future. For example, if you decline all applicants that have had a bankruptcy in the past two years, and you will continue to have this policy in the future, it does not make sense to include these applicants in the development sample and analyze them.

If there are geographic areas or markets where the company no longer operates, data from these markets should also be excluded so that the development data represents future expected status. For example, an auto loan company used to provide financing for the purchase of recreational vehicles such as snowmobiles, watercrafts, and all-terrain vehicles (ATV). However, a year ago it decided to focus on its core personal auto financing business, and stopped financing all other assets. For scorecard development purposes, the development data for this company should include only loan applications for personal autos. All others should be excluded because they will no longer be part of the applicant population for this company in the future when the scorecard is implemented.

In other words, we are looking at exclusions as a sample bias issue. For example, if you wanted to develop a scorecard to be applied to the residents of large cities, you would not include those who live in rural areas in the development sample. Similarly, any account or applicant type that is not going to be scored or that is not a normal customer should not be included.

Performance and Sample Windows and *Bad* Definition

Scorecards are developed using the assumption that "future performance is reflected by past performance." Based on this assumption, the performance of previously opened accounts is analyzed in order to predict the performance of future accounts. In order to perform this analysis, we need to gather data for accounts opened during a specific time frame, and then monitor their performance for another specific length of time to determine if they were good or bad. The data collected (the variables) along with good/bad classification (the target) constitutes the development sample from which the scorecard is developed. For behavior scorecards, the same is done for existing accounts, where we take accounts at a point in time and monitor their payment behavior for a designated length of time to determine the target. For example, all accounts not delinquent as of January are monitored for the next 12 months to determine which ones subsequently went into default.

In Exhibit 6.1, assume a new account is approved and granted credit at a particular time, or an existing account at a particular time. At some point in time in the future, you need to determine if this account had been good or bad (to assign performance). "Performance window" is the time

Exhibit 6.1 Performance Definition

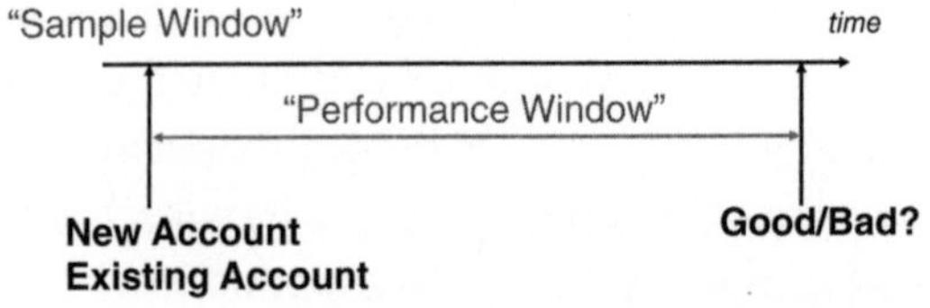

window where the performance of those accounts is monitored to assign class (target). "Sample window" refers to the time frame from which known good and bad cases will be selected for the development sample. For example, if we take all cases that applied for a product from January of 2014, and looked at their performance from opening until December 2015, the sample window would be January 2014, and the performance window 24 months. Later, we will cover some analysis that can be used to determine these parameters. In some cases, such as fraud and bankruptcy, the performance class is already known or predetermined. It is still useful, however, to perform the analysis described next, in order to determine the ideal performance window.

There are several approaches to determining the sample and performance windows.

In some cases, regulatory requirements will determine the performance window, that is, the model prediction horizon. For example, Basel II required a 12-month prediction window, and therefore probability of default (PD) models built for Basel II usage had performance windows of 12 months.[2] More recent initiatives such as IFRS 9,[3] suggest a longer prediction horizon for losses, up to lifetime of the loan.

The second approach, which I call the "decision horizon" approach, matches the performance window with that of the term of the loan or agreement. For example, if the term of a car loan is four years, application scoring for that loan should be based on a four-year performance window. Logically, the relationship that the lender is entering into is for four years; therefore, the risk must be assessed over a four-year horizon. This is similar to the loan lifetime approach, and works well for term loans. If the term of the loan is very long (say more than 8 to 10 years), the time to maturity approach can also be applied to get a shorter performance window, so that more recent data can be used.

For revolving-type loans such as credit cards, services such as postpaid mobile phones, and other credit products with long terms, looking at portfolio maturity may be a better option. Here, we establish the performance window by analyzing payment or delinquency performance of the portfolio (represented by one or several cohorts), and plot the development of defined "bad" cases over time. A good source of this data is the monthly or quarterly cohort or vintage analysis report produced in most credit risk departments.

Exhibit 6.2 Sample Vintage/Cohort Analysis

Bad = 90 days past due						Time on Books							
		1 Qtr	2 Qtr	3 Qtr	4 Qtr	5 Qtr	6 Qtr	7 Qtr	8 Qtr	9 Qtr	10 Qtr	11 Qtr	12 Qtr
	Q1 13	0.00%	0.05%	1.10%	2.40%	2.80%	3.20%	3.50%	3.70%	3.80%	3.85%	3.85%	**3.86%**
	Q2 13	0.00%	0.06%	1.20%	2.30%	2.70%	3.00%	3.30%	3.50%	3.60%	3.60%	**3.60%**	
	Q3 13	0.00%	0.03%	0.90%	2.80%	3.20%	3.60%	4.10%	4.30%	4.40%	**4.45%**		
Open Date	Q4 13	0.00%	0.03%	1.00%	2.85%	3.20%	3.50%	3.80%	4.00%	**4.10%**			
	Q1 14	0.00%	0.04%	1.00%	2.20%	2.40%	2.70%	2.90%	**4.10%**				
	Q2 14	0.00%	0.05%	1.20%	2.50%	2.90%	3.30%	**3.50%**					
	Q3 14	0.00%	0.04%	1.30%	2.60%	3.00%	**3.35%**						
	Q4 14	0.00%	0.08%	1.40%	2.60%	**3.00%**							
	Q1 15	0.00%	0.02%	0.09%	**2.20%**								
	Q2 15	0.00%	0.08%	**1.50%**									
	Q3 15	0.00%	**0.05%**										
	Q4 15	**0.00%**											

An example of a vintage analysis, for a "bad" definition of 90 days past due (DPD) and a 12-quarter (three-year) performance window, is shown in Exhibit 6.2. The report shows the cumulative rate of 90 DPD delinquency by time on book (or time as customer) for accounts opened from Q1 2013 until Q4 of 2015. For example, in the first line, 2.8 percent of accounts opened in the first quarter of 2013 were 90 DPD after five quarters as customers. While the delinquency rates are similar, we can see that some cohorts have higher delinquency rates for the same maturity. This phenomenon is quite normal as marketing campaigns, economic cycles, and other factors can determine the mix of accepted accounts as well as their performance.

In order to generate the delinquency maturity curve from the data in Exhibit 6.3, we have several options.

Exhibit 6.3 Options for Selecting Maturity Curves

Bad = 90 days past due						Time on Books							
		1 Qtr	2 Qtr	3 Qtr	4 Qtr	5 Qtr	6 Qtr	7 Qtr	8 Qtr	9 Qtr	10 Qtr	11 Qtr	12 Qtr
	Q1 13	0.00%	0.05%	1.10%	2.40%	2.80%	3.20%	3.50%	3.70%	3.80%	3.85%	3.85%	**3.86%**
	Q2 13	0.00%	0.06%	1.20%	2.30%	2.70%	3.00%	3.30%	3.50%	3.60%	3.60%	**3.60%**	
	Q3 13	0.00%	0.03%	0.90%	2.80%	3.20%	3.60%	4.10%	4.30%	4.40%	**4.45%**		
Open Date	Q4 13	0.00%	0.03%	1.00%	2.85%	3.20%	3.50%	3.80%	4.00%	**4.10%**			
	Q1 14	0.00%	0.04%	1.00%	2.20%	2.40%	2.70%	2.90%	**4.10%**				
	Q2 14	0.00%	0.05%	1.20%	2.50%	2.90%	3.30%	**3.50%**					
	Q3 14	0.00%	0.04%	1.30%	2.60%	3.00%	**3.35%**						
	Q4 14	0.00%	0.08%	1.40%	2.60%	**3.00%**							
	Q1 15	0.00%	0.02%	0.09%	**2.20%**								
	Q2 15	0.00%	0.08%	**1.50%**									
	Q3 15	0.00%	**0.05%**										
	Q4 15	**0.00%**											

The first option is to use the diagonal represented by bolded numbers in Exhibit 6.3. This shows the most recent delinquency rates by time on book for accounts opened at different dates. In portfolios whose vintages can vary in quality, this may produce curves that are not very useful (the vintage curve will not be increasing in a smooth fashion as there may be "dips"), and therefore this is a better option for products where the applicant and account quality are fairly stable over time, such as mortgages. In the case of fluctuating numbers, there are two additional options that can help smooth the numbers out and give us a more realistic long-term delinquency growth chart. We can use averages of the most recent six cohorts for example, as highlighted by the ovals in Exhibit 6.3, or we can select one single cohort, such as accounts opened in Q1 of 2013, as highlighted by the rectangular box in Exhibit 6.3.

Exhibit 6.4 is a plot of cumulative bad rate by quarters opened (tenure or time on book) for two cohorts: accounts opened in Q1 of 2013 and those opened in Q1 of 2014.

This exhibit shows an example from a typical credit card portfolio where the cumulative bad rate grows over time, and starts right at the beginning. For accounts opened in Q1 of 2013, it shows the bad rate developing rapidly in the first few months and then stabilizing as the account age nears 10 quarters.

The development sample is chosen from a time period where the bad rate is deemed to be stable or where the cohort is deemed to have

Exhibit 6.4 Bad Rate Development

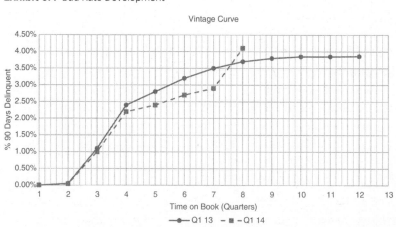

matured (i.e., where the cumulative bad rate starts to level off). In other words, we wait until all the accounts that should have gone bad have gone bad. In the preceding example, a good Sample Window would be with accounts that opened anywhere between 10 and 12 quarters in the past, which would have an 11-quarter average Performance Window.

Selecting development samples from a mature cohort is done to minimize the chances of misclassifying performance (i.e., all accounts have been given enough time to go bad), and to ensure that the "bad" definition resulting from an immature sample will not understate the final expected bad rates. For example, if the development sample were chosen from accounts opened in the first quarter of 2014, about 4.1 percent of the sample would be classified as bad. However, as we can see in Exhibit 6.4, the bad rate is still growing. A mature sample for this cohort will have a bad rate much higher than that at eight quarters. Therefore, some accounts that are actually bad would be erroneously labeled as good if the development sample were to be taken from this time period.

The time taken for accounts to mature varies by product and by "bad" definition selected. Credit card accounts typically mature after 18 to 24 months, and car loans usually between two and four years, while four-to five-year-old accounts are the minimum for mortgage scorecard development. In some cases, low-risk mortgage portfolios may not mature for over 10 years, as the nature of mortgage delinquencies is different from that of credit cards. This is a somewhat self-fulfilling prophecy, since credit card portfolios are by nature of a higher risk than mortgage ones, and therefore would yield the same level of delinquency much faster. Customers in distress are also more likely to stop paying their credit card accounts first than to default on their mortgage payments (there is, however, evidence of "strategic defaulting" in some countries where debtors default on mortgages first because they expect to not be evicted from the home for years). Similarly, and for obvious reasons, analysis done for a "bad" definition of 30 days delinquent will show faster maturity than for a "bad" definition of 60 or 90 days. Scorecards for insurance claims, fraud, bankruptcy, and other definitions will likely have unique stabilization profiles that can be determined by performing similar analyses.

In the example shown in Exhibit 6.4, we can see that the bad rate stabilizes at around 10 quarters, and we suggest that the development sample be taken from accounts open for around that long. The fact is, any cohort open beyond 10 quarters should also have a stable bad rate, but we recommend choosing the latest/newest one. The reason has to do with relevance and stability of the development sample. The accounts opened around 10 quarters ago are the newest mature sample and are most likely to be similar to future applicants. Accounts opened 15 or 20 quarters ago will also be mature, but the information is more likely to be outdated due to changes in product, policies, economic conditions, and demographic change.

Behavior scorecards for operational use are typically built for performance windows of 6 or 12 months. Collections models are typically built for performance windows of one month, but increasingly, companies are building such scorecards for shorter windows of up to one or two weeks, to facilitate the development of more timely collection path treatments. It does not make sense to build collections models that predict recovery over 90 days, and use this probability to develop strategies on a monthly basis. It is far more logical and relevant to build a scorecard, for example, for accounts that are one day delinquent and predict recovery over one month, and use this to develop a collections path for the first month. Then take accounts that are still delinquent at 31 days, and use these to predict recovery for the next 30 days, and create strategy for days 31 through 60. When developing predictive models for specific regulatory requirements— for example, the Basel II Accord—the performance window will be dictated by the regulation. There are other approaches to determining the performance window and default definition, including the usage of Markov chain analysis.[4]

When delinquency scorecards are being built, this analysis may be repeated for several relevant delinquency definitions. This is done because the different definitions will produce differing sample counts. Various factors such as the sample window and the good/bad definition need to be juggled in some cases to obtain a large enough sample (see next section). In cases of bankruptcy or charge-off scorecards, only one analysis is sufficient since there is only one possible definition of *bad*.

Exhibit 6.5 24-Month Delinquency History for an Account

Month	1	2	3	4	5	6	7	8	9	10	11	12
Delq	0	0	1	1	0	0	0	1	2	3	0	0
Month	13	14	15	16	17	18	19	20	21	22	23	24
Delq	0	0	1	2	0	0	0	1	0	1	0	0

Where possible, this analysis should be done using the *ever bad* definition (i.e., the account is deemed to be bad if it reaches the defined delinquency status at any time during the performance window). If this is not possible, normally due to data difficulties, then a "current" definition of bad will suffice, where the delinquency status of accounts is taken from the most recent end-of-month performance. An example is illustrated in Exhibit 6.5, showing a 24-month delinquency history for a particular account. Month "24" is the current month and the number in each "Delq" cell refers to number of months past due.

Using an *ever bad* definition where *bad* is defined as three months past due, the delinquency status of this account can be classified as bad, as it reached the three months delinquent milestone at one point. However, using a *current bad* definition, this account would be classified as good/not delinquent (i.e., zero months delinquent).

Effects of Seasonality

The variation of application and approval rates across time, and the effect of any seasonality, should also be established at this point. This is to ensure that the development sample (from the sample window) does not include any data from "abnormal" periods, so that the sample used for development is in line with normal business periods, representing the typical "through-the-door" population. The objective here is to conform to the assumption that "the future is like the past," so that the development sample is representative of future expected applicants (i.e., the "normal" customer). In practical terms, this also helps to generate accurate approval rate/bad rate predictions and, more importantly, produces scorecards that will be robust and stand the test of time (rather than scorecards that model every quirk or temporary effects in the data and not long-term behavior). In reality, such exercises are done largely to catch extreme behavior, since establishing a standard for "normal" is difficult.

There are several ways to counter the effects of abnormal periods when the applicant population does not represent the normal through-the-door population. In all cases, the reasons for the abnormality must first be established.

A good practice is to perform what I call Pro-Forma Variable Distribution Analysis. This involves comparing the distributions of a recent sample (say, from past two to three months) with that of the intended sample window, for selected characteristics.

I normally pick 40 to 50 of the typical characteristics that are known to be strong and almost always end up in scorecards, and compare their distributions. Previous scorecards, experience, and speaking to seasoned lenders can provide good ideas on the sorts of variables that normally go into scorecards. From the example in Exhibit 6.4, I would compare variables for applicants opened in Q1 of 2013 with applicants from the most recent quarter.

Exhibit 6.6 shows an example of such an analysis, where the most recent quarter is assumed to be the last quarter of 2015. For simplicity, variables can be arbitrarily grouped into deciles for the comparison, since the scorecard has not been built and we don't know the actual final binning. Otherwise, one can group variables based on that of the

Exhibit 6.6 Pro-Forma Variable Distribution Analysis

Loan to Value	Q1 2013	Q4 2015
1–22	10.40%	12.30%
23–37	9.80%	8.20%
37–47	10.80%	9.00%
48–56	10.00%	11.40%
57–61	9.00%	9.30%
62–70	9.80%	8.70%
71–77	10.60%	12.00%
78–82	11.00%	8.90%
83–88	9.80%	9.30%
89–95	8.80%	10.90%
	100%	100%

current or last scorecard where such a variable was used. Based on the distributions shown in Exhibit 6.6, we can visually see any shifts. We can also calculate many measures based on the differences in the two distributions, such as Gini, Kolmogorov-Smirnov (KS), chi-square, Hosmer-Lemeshow, Population Stability Index, and so on, and use the relevant thresholds to decide if the distributions are close enough and therefore stable. If some variables show significant shifts, we can avoid their usage in the model. Using only stable variables ensures that the final model built will be stable when implemented (pre-implementation stability analysis will be covered in later chapters). We can also try to find out reasons for the shift by looking at the specific unstable variables.

Further reasons for profile shifts can also be gleaned from information on marketing campaigns active during the sample window, or any other factor that can affect the profile of credit applicants. For example, an organization expects credit card applicants to be mostly mature men and women but discovers that the applicants from its desired one-month sample window are mostly young men. An analysis of marketing campaigns shows that the company was actively pursuing applications at a booth in an auto show during that month (auto shows typically attract young men as customers). Equipped with this information, the company can then expand the sample window to three or more months long, to smooth out the effects of that particular month, or use some other time frame as the sample window.

Another technique to "normalize" data is to filter out the source of abnormality. In the preceding example, if the company is certain that it will not consistently target young males in the future, and that the performance of these young males will distort their overall expected portfolio, then the company may choose to exclude young males from its development sample. The resulting development sample (and portfolio statistics) will then be in line with the normal day-to-day operations of this company. This would be similar to fixing sample bias by removing the cause of the bias. The same can be done in cases where policy rules and regulations have been changed more recently. For example, if a few months ago regulators changed the rule to cap mortgage LTV at 80 percent from a previous 90 percent level, then the development sample from the past can be altered by removing all applications between 80 and 90 percent to make it relevant for future conditions.

The effects of seasonality can also be countered by taking multiple sample windows, but with each having an equal performance window. This is also referred to as "stacked sampling." For example, three samples can be taken from each of Q1, Q2, and Q3 of 2013, with performance windows of 24 months each. Therefore, the "bad" for each sample will be determined for performances up to Q1, Q2, and Q3 of 2015, respectively. This is in contrast to keeping the observation date the same for all samples (e.g., determining performance as of June 2015 for all three cohorts in the example—which will result in cohorts with differing performance windows within the same sample).

In cases where taking staggered samples or expanding the sample window is not possible, and the reasons for abnormality are known and understood to be confined to one particular month, for example, it is also possible to create a sample by excluding outlying records. This, however, requires detailed information on existing distributions of characteristics during normal business periods, and it is recommended that a sample of the excluded records be analyzed for trends before being discarded.

Definition of *Bad*

This phase categorizes account performance into three primary groups: bad, good, and indeterminate. For bankruptcy, charge-off, or fraud, the definition of *bad* is fairly straightforward. For contractual delinquency–based definitions, however, there are many choices based on levels of delinquency. It has been mentioned that each analysis (as shown in Exhibit 6.4) for different definitions of *bad* will produce a different sample count for "bad" accounts. Using some of the factors listed next, an appropriate definition is chosen for these cases.

The definition of what constitutes a bad account relies on several considerations:

■ The definition must be in line with project objectives, and decision to be made. If the objective is to increase profitability, then the definition must be set at a delinquency point where the account becomes unprofitable. This can get complicated where accounts that are, for example, chronically paying late by a month but do not roll forward to two or three months may be profitable. For insurance applications, a dollar value on claims may be appropriate. If delinquency detection is the objective, the definition will be simpler (e.g., "ever" 60 or 90 DPD). In business terms, the bad is a customer whom you would have declined had you known their performance. This helps in deciding, for example, between picking a 60 DPD vs. a 90 DPD definition.

- The definition must be in line with the product or purpose for which the scorecard is being built—for example, bankruptcy, fraud, claims (claim over $1,000), and collections (less than 50 percent recovered within one month).

- A tighter, more stringent definition—for example, write-off or 120 days delinquent—provides a more extreme (and precise) differentiation, but in some cases may yield low sample sizes.

- A looser definition (e.g., 30 days delinquent) will yield a higher number of accounts for the sample but may not be a good enough differentiator between good and bad accounts, and will thus produce a weaker scorecard.

- The definition must be easily interpretable and trackable (e.g., ever 90 DPD, bankrupt, confirmed fraud, claim over $1,000). Definitions such as "three times 30 days delinquent or twice 60 days delinquent, or once 90 DPD or worse," which may be more accurate reflections, are much harder to track and may not be appropriate for all companies. Choosing a simpler definition also makes for easier management, and decision making—any bad rate numbers reported will be easily understood (e.g., 4 percent bad means 4 percent of accounts have hit 90 days' delinquency during their tenure). I have in the past used roll rates to charge-off to gauge whether using more complicated *bad* definitions are yielding any value. If the roll rate to charge-off for a more complicated *bad* definition is significantly higher than a simpler one, it might be worth using it.

- Companies may also select definitions based on accounting policies on write-offs.

- In some cases, it may be beneficial to have consistent definitions of *bad* across various segments, products, and previous scorecards in use within the company. This makes for easier management and decision making, especially in environments where many scorecards are used. Coupled with consistent scaling of scores, this also reduces training and programming costs when redeveloping scorecards. The new scores will mean the same as the previous ones.

- There may be regulatory or other external requirements that govern how delinquency is defined (distinct from the organization's own operational definition). Basel II and IFRS 9 are examples of this at present. *Bad* definitions in the future may be required to be linked to economic loss, a specific default level, or a particular level of expected loss. Based on the Basel II Capital Accord, the definition of *default* is generally 90 days delinquent.

In some cases, *bad* definitions are chosen by default, due to a lack of data or history (e.g., an organization only kept records for a 12-month history), so that the only *bad* definition that showed maturity during analysis (see Exhibit 6.4) was "ever 30 day." Some organizations do not keep monthly payment data, and the only option for defining *bad* is current delinquency status (compared to "ever").

Dealing with Low-Default Portfolios

Data mining and predictive modeling are best suited for larger portfolios. The widely known Law of Large Numbers tells us that predicted probabilities will work only when applied to a large number of cases. It follows that predictive models will work better when developed on a large number of cases. Conversely, our confidence levels in models should be realistically lower then dealing with smaller numbers.

Before we explore options for scorecard development with low defaults, it is important to realize two points:

- A low-default portfolio (LDP) is not necessarily a business problem. Putting aside opportunity cost of being too tight with credit granting, a portfolio with very low losses is not a bad thing. It is also not a ratings problem, as judgmental ratings are widely used and are obviously effective if you have low defaults.

- Based on the Law of Large Numbers and the fact that most predictive modeling algorithms are designed for large data sets, none of the options for LDPs will be anywhere near optimal. The developers and users of models developed on small samples need to be realistically skeptical, and use them with caution. In most cases this means tweaking based on judgment and qualitative criteria, and the use of more policy rules.

There are several ways to deal with LDPs. The method that may be most appropriate will depend on the actual number of bads. Some methods may enable a portfolio with 600 bads to yield a few hundred more and enable the development of a fairly reasonable scorecard. However, a portfolio with, say, 40 bads will obviously have limited choices. The idea is to consider all the options and pick the one that will be possible (rather than chasing an impossible "optimal" outcome).

Change Performance/Sample Window

When the organization has several hundred cases of "bad," trying various sample windows can often yield good results. These techniques include:

- *Taking stacked samples.* Instead of using accounts opened during one quarter, use two or three, but each with the same performance window. Samples taken over a one-year period have been justified on the basis of seasonality as well. Note that the longer the sample window, the less the homogeneity of the sample.
- *Taking a longer performance window.* In some cases where the regulatory model is needed for a 12-month prediction window, this short time period may generate very few bads. Organizations have developed models on longer performance windows, say two or three years, and then annualized the results to get the 12-month prediction. This way, the actual model, with a large sample, is more robust and will yield the same 12-month predicted probabilities.

Change Bad Definition

If a bank is required to predict, for example, 90-day delinquency, and it finds that the number of 90 DPD bads are low, it can choose to build scorecards to predict 60 DPD, and then use roll rates to calculate the 90-day one. For example, if the 60 day PD for a rating grade is 5 percent and the roll rate to 90 DPD is 50 percent, then the approximate 90 day PD for that grade will be 2.5 percent. The advantage of using this method is that with a higher number of cases, the 60 DPD model will likely be more robust. The number of bads can also be expanded by using more complex *bad* definitions, such as those who are 30 DPD multiple times.

Take Recent Bads

Ideally, the entire development sample should come from the same sample window, for example, accounts opened in January 2013. This is to ensure homogeneity. However, if you have an LDP issue, you may choose to take additional bads from more recent cohorts. Based on the chart in Exhibit 6.4, we would normally take our development sample (goods, bads, rejects) from applications and accounts opened in Q1 of 2013. But we also know that there are immature accounts, that is, those that opened between Q2 of 2013 and the most recent quarter, that have gone 90 DPD and are therefore classified as bad. Based on the *ever bad* definition, these accounts will not be reassigned as good regardless of behavior. Therefore, in order to boost the number of bads in the sample, we will add them to the original development sample from Q1 of 2013. Note that only the immature bads are being added to the development sample, not the goods, since an immature good has the potential to become bad later on. Again, this is not ideal as the more recent bads may have been approved under different conditions. Also note that in this case, calculations of actual default rates should be based on the accounts opened in Q1 of 2013 only, and any probabilities of default will need to be adjusted post-model fitting (this is similar to the case of using oversampled data).

Non-Scorecard Model

As discussed earlier, the scorecard is just one among many types of models. For predictive modeling, the user has the option of using many other formats and types, some of which are better for smaller data sets compared to scorecards. Specifically in the context of Basel II (which was a major reason for smaller banks facing LDP issues), while there are a few suggested methods, including those from Cathcart and Benjamin,[5] Tasche and Pluto,[6] Hanson and Schuermann,[7] and Wilde and Jackson,[8] in practice, many banks globally with very low default portfolios have used Pluto-Tasche.

External Ratings and Scores

In countries where external credit rating agencies such as credit bureaus exist, the bank can use those external ratings to both rank-order accounts and calculate their expected probabilities of default. For retail accounts, bureau-based generic scores can be used for the same purpose. Again, as mentioned earlier, the end users need to be satisfied that those generic scores and probabilities have been calculated using large and relevant data sets. This approach has been allowed by regulators for Basel II internal ratings-based approach for small portfolios, based on the test of materiality. For example, a large bank in Asia that had a very small portfolio in the United States was allowed to use a generic bureau score from an American credit bureau to calculate PD for that portfolio, but had to use internally built models for its significantly larger home portfolio. Another possible route is for many smaller institutions to pool their data via a third party, and develop a consortium model from this data. All the members would then have access to the same, usually anonymized, data set or the resulting pooled data model.

Shadow Ratings Approach

In the case of portfolios where some of the accounts or exposures are rated externally, while others are not, the shadow ratings approach may be helpful. This method consists of:

1. Building a good/bad model on the known rated accounts. This can be a hybrid model incorporating both statistical analysis as well as judgment, given the small data sets.
2. Based on the distribution of scores for each rating, establishing cutoffs to determine score ranges to assign an individual rating.

For example, scores of 600 to 680 are AAA, 550 to 600 are AA, and so on.

3. Score the un-rated exposures/accounts and assign ratings/PD based on the ranges determined in step 2.

Other Methods

Banks globally have tried other methods for assigning ratings and predicted PDs to LDPs. Given the prominence of regulations like Basel II, specifically the internal ratings-based approach, in this exercise, the final method chosen also depends on what the bank's internal validation team as well as the country regulator will allow. In addition, regulators have tended to allow banks greater latitude for smaller portfolios, based on the test of significance/materiality. Some of the methods that have been used globally include:

- *Using proxies from similar countries/products.* For example, one bank used a Hong Kong–based scorecard to score a small Singapore portfolio, assuming the two small nations to be fairly similar. Likewise, one bank used a larger mortgage ratings model to rate its very small auto loans portfolio, under the assumption that those are both secured products and similar metrics are used to adjudicate them.

- *Judgmental ratings.* Banks have developed internal judgmental scorecards and used those to rate their exposures. The risk ranking of these scorecards was then validated externally by independent third parties, whose ratings were compared to that of the internal judgmental model. The PDs were generated by assuming a minimum number of defaults per rated class. Other approaches cited in the Non-Scorecard Model section can also be used for this.

Confirming the *Bad* Definition

For most banks and other lenders that have been developing scorecards for a while, the selection of a definition for *bad* or default is a routine matter. For others that are still trying to find the right one, once an initial *bad* definition is identified using the analysis described in previous sections, further analysis can be done to confirm it and to make sure that those identified are indeed truly bad. This is more relevant where the "bad" class assignment is not definitive (i.e., based on some level of days delinquent or amount recovered). The confirmation can be done using expert judgment, analysis, or a combination of both, depending on the resources and data available. It is important to note that the methods described here can only provide a comfort level for the analysis performed previously—they are not definitive measures that prove any definition of *bad* as optimal.

Consensus Method

The judgmental or consensus method involves various stakeholders from Risk Management, Model Validation, Marketing (sometimes), and Operational areas getting together and reaching a consensus on the best definition of a "bad" account, based on experience and operational considerations, as well as the analysis covered in the previous sections.

Analytical Methods

Two analytical methods to confirm *bad* definitions will be described:

1. Roll rate analysis
2. Current versus worst delinquency comparison

In addition to these two, profitability analysis can also be performed to confirm that those defined as bad are unprofitable, or produce negative net present value (NPV). While this can be done easily at organizations that have only one product (e.g., retail card providers), it is not an easy task in multiproduct environments such as banks.

Roll Rate Analysis

Roll rate analysis involves comparing worst delinquency in a specified "previous *x*" months with that in the "next *x*" months, and then calculating the percentage of accounts that maintain their worst delinquency, get better, or "roll forward" into the next delinquency buckets.

Exhibit 6.7 Delinquency History for an Account

"Previous" 12 Months												
Month	1	2	3	4	5	6	7	8	9	10	11	12
Delq	0	0	1	1	0	0	0	1	2	3	0	0
"Next" 12 Months												
Month	13	14	15	16	17	18	19	20	21	22	23	24
Delq	0	0	1	2	0	0	0	1	0	1	0	0

The point of this exercise is to find some delinquency status beyond which the chances of recovery are very low.

For example, Exhibit 6.7 shows the delinquency status of a revolving account over a 24-month period, broken into two equivalent 12-month "previous" and "next" periods.

Based on these numbers, the worst delinquency of this account in the "previous" 12-month period is 3 months past due (in month 10), and 2 months past due (in month 16) in the "next" 12 months. This information is gathered for all accounts, and is then graphed as shown in Exhibit 6.8.

The purpose here is to identify a "point of no return" (i.e., the level of delinquency at which most accounts become incurable).

Exhibit 6.8 Roll Rate Chart

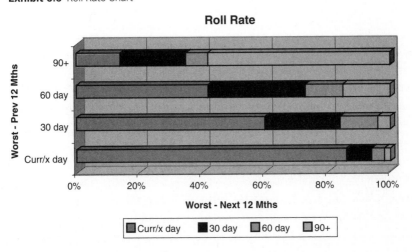

Typically, a vast majority of accounts that reach 90-day delinquency do not cure—they become worse (roll forward), thus confirming that this definition of *bad* is appropriate. In the preceding example, only about 18 percent of accounts that were ever 30 days delinquent in the previous 12 months rolled forward to being 60 and 90+ days delinquent, but almost 70 percent of accounts that reach 90-day delinquency roll forward to worse delinquency. In this case, the "ever 90 days delinquent" definition of *bad* makes more sense, as it truly isolates those that remain delinquent. Conversely, the 30-day *bad* definition will be inappropriate, since most of those accounts roll back (cure) to being current. Inconclusive evidence in this analysis may point to potential "indeterminate" status. The same information can also be gleaned by analyzing cure rates at each delinquency milestone and using some number (e.g., less than 50 percent) to determine "bad."

It is worth noting that the Basel II Capital Accord defines *default* as any point at which the bank considers the obligor unlikely to repay the debt in full, and specifies 90 days past due as a definition (individual regulators can change this to 180 for certain products). In my experience, 90 DPD is also the most widely used *bad* definition globally. In North America, however, I have noted a trend toward the use of 60 DPD as a *bad* definition for secured loans such as mortgages and car loans. This is partly due to the low number of defaults when using the 90 DPD definition.

Current versus Worst Delinquency Comparison

This method is similar in concept to the roll rate analysis, but is simpler to execute. It compares the worst (ever) delinquency status of accounts with their most current delinquency status. As with roll rate analysis, the objective here is also to look for a "point of no return." An example is shown in Exhibit 6.9.

The example shows again that out of all accounts that ever go to 30-day delinquency, a vast majority—84 percent—have no delinquency at present. In contrast, 60 percent of all accounts that go to 90-day delinquency stay at 90 days or become worse. This again confirms that a 90- or 120-day definition of *bad* is an adequate one, as long as enough cases of bads can be obtained.

Exhibit 6.9 Comparing Ever to Current Delinquency

		Worst Delinquency					
		Current	30 Days	60 Days	90 Days	120 Days	Write-Off
Current	Current	100%	84%	53%	16%	7%	
Delinquency	30 days		12%	28%	10%	8%	
	60 days		4%	11%	14%	10%	
	90 days			8%	44%	13%	
	120 days				16%	62%	
	Write-off						100%

It should be noted that the preceding analyses to determine and confirm *bad* definitions could be performed for both application and behavior scorecards. Even though behavior scorecards are usually developed to predict over a six-month window, it is still useful to perform this analysis to determine *bad* definitions.

Good and *Indeterminate*

Once the bad accounts are defined, the same analysis performed earlier can be used to define a good account. Again, this must be in line with organizational objectives and other issues discussed earlier. Defining good accounts is less analytical, and usually obvious. Some characteristics of a good account are:

- Never delinquent, maximum ever delinquency of up to *x* days delinquent (usually less than a week), or delinquent to a point where forward roll rate is less than, for example, 10 percent.
- Profitable or positive NPV.
- Paid up/voluntarily closed with no delinquency <u>beyond</u> performance window.
- No claims.
- Never bankrupt.
- Not fraud.
- Recovery rate of, for example, greater than 50 percent of outstanding in collections, or recovery amount greater than the average cost of collections.

A point to note is that, while good accounts need to retain their status over the entire performance window, a bad account can be defined by reaching the specified delinquency stage at any time during the performance window (as per the *ever* definition).

We have seen how a "good" is an account that has never been delinquent, while a "bad" is one that reaches 90 DPD. What about those whose worst arrears were between 1 and 89 DPD? What do we do with them? This is where the concept of indeterminate cases comes in.

Indeterminate accounts are those that do not conclusively fall into either the good or bad categories. These are generally accounts that do not have sufficient performance history for classification, or that have some mild delinquency with roll rates neither low enough to be classified as good nor high enough to be bad. Indeterminates can include:

- Accounts that hit 30- or 60-day delinquency but do not roll forward (i.e., are not conclusively bad). These can include accounts that are habitual late payers, who are delinquent many times but have a high cure rate.

- Inactive accounts and those with insufficient usage/activity—for example, credit card accounts with a high balance of less than $20, accounts with no purchase activity for over 12 months (some banks have used 6 months for this), or accounts with unused/undrawn lines of credit.

- Voluntarily canceled/closed accounts without delinquency, within the performance window. Note that closed non-delinquent accounts beyond the performance window are usually classified as good.

- "Offer declined" accounts (those who were approved by the bank but walked away) and similar applications that were approved but not booked. This is most common with secured products.

- Insurance accounts with claims under a specified dollar value.

- Accounts with NPV = 0.

Note that some scorecard developers assign all canceled/closed and "offer declined" accounts as rejects or exclude them, assuming that these were likely not their intended customers. However, accounts that cancel voluntarily are your intended customers and may have canceled due to customer service issues. If they reapplied, they would be rescored and likely approved again. Therefore, these should be included in the scorecard development process as indeterminate.

Note that while we are looking at indeterminates as a modeling problem, it is very often a business one as well. In cases where the proportion of indeterminates is very high (e.g., where a large portion of inactive accounts is present), analyses should be done to address the root causes of inactivity—for example, presence of other cards with higher limits or lower interest rates, channel effects such as credit cards that are obtained at point of sale (where the incentive for the customer was to get an immediate discount) or cards obtained through storefront booths (where the incentive was to obtain some free gift), presence of other cards with better loyalty programs, or inactivity with all other cards as well. Some of these factors can be determined by looking at the credit bureau reports of inactive customers and identifying activity of other credit cards, or confirming that there are no other active credit cards elsewhere either. Once the reasons for the credit card customers not using the product are found, appropriate actions can be taken to remedy the situation, such as increasing limits or lowering interest rates for better customers, offering bonus loyalty points to spur activity, offering product discounts for retail store cards, or canceling credit cards for those who appear inactive on all their other credit cards as well. Following this logic, companies may choose to treat some inactives differently as exclusions, a separate target altogether, or as indeterminate.

Indeterminates are issues only where there is a gap between the *bad* and *good* definitions, and are usually not required where the definition is clear-cut (e.g., bankrupt). As a rule of thumb, indeterminates should not exceed more than 10 to 15 percent of the portfolio.

The treatment of indeterminates can vary, depending on things such as the standards set by corporate model validation departments, as well as the preferences of the risk manager and model development staff. In general, indeterminates can be dealt with in three different ways:

1. Only accounts defined as good and bad (and rejects for application scorecard) are used in the actual development of the

scorecard. Indeterminates are then added when forecasting to adequately reflect the true "through-the-door" population, since these are applicants who will be scored and adjudicated, and therefore all approval and bad rate expectations must reflect their presence. For example, assume a portfolio with 50,000 goods, 5,000 bads, and 5,000 indeterminates. The model developed on goods and bads will show a bad rate of 5,000 / 55,000 = 9.1 percent. For better forecasting, we add the indeterminates to the denominator so that the expected bad rate shows 5,000 / 60,000 = 8.33 percent.

2. If the number of indeterminates is very low, they can be excluded or all assigned as good.

3. Where the number of indeterminates is significant (and therefore presenting a sample bias issue if only goods and bads are used for modeling), several methods can be used to assign/infer performance. This would be similar to the reject inference exercise discussed in later chapters. For example, the performance of "offer declined" and inactive customers can be inferred through credit bureau data. If the inactive credit card holder uses someone else's credit card, we can check their payment performance at the credit bureau and use the 90 DPD counter to assign class. For those who declined the lender's offer, we assume that the person has a better offer elsewhere. In this case, we can also check their credit bureau report to see how they behaved with the bank whose offer they accepted. Note that this is dependent on being allowed to access the credit bureau for this purpose. In cases where bureau data is not available, some lenders assume all "offer declined" customers in the highest ratings classes as good. In other cases, lenders have proportionally classified indeterminates based on their in-house behavior or bureau scores. For example, if there are 1,000 indeterminates with a 700 bureau score, and the expected PD is 4 percent, then we can randomly assign 40 of them as bad and the rest as good.

Once the *bad, good,* and, if required, *indeterminate* definitions are established, the actual portfolio bad rate is recorded for use in model development for cases where oversampling is done.

The discussion to this point has been limited to accounts where the performance is known (i.e., approved customers). In cases such as application scorecards, where reject inference is to be used, an additional performance category needs to be included in the development sample for "declined" applications (i.e., those who were declined credit or services). This enables a development sample to be created that reflects the performance of the entire applicant population, and not just that of the approved. Reject inference is covered later in Chapter 10.

SEGMENTATION

In most cases, using several scorecards for a portfolio provides better risk differentiation than using one scorecard on everyone. This is usually the case in large portfolios where there are many distinct subpopulations, and where one scorecard will not work efficiently for all of them. For example, a separate scorecard for high-net-worth individuals will work better for them. The process of identifying these subpopulations is called segmentation. There are two main ways in which segmentation can be done:

1. Generating segmentation ideas based on operational, experience, and industry knowledge, and then validating these ideas using analytics. For credit scorecard development globally, this is how the vast majority of banks determine segments.
2. Generating unique segments using statistical techniques such as clustering or decision trees.

In either case, any segments selected should be large enough to enable meaningful sampling for separate scorecard development (see discussion on data availability and quantity at the beginning of this chapter). Segments that exhibit distinct risk performance, but have insufficient volume for separate scorecard development, can still be treated differently using different cutoffs or other strategy considerations.

It should also be noted that in risk scorecard development, a "distinct" population is not recognized as such based only on its defining characteristics (such as demographics), but rather on its performance.

The objective is to define segments based on risk-based performance, not just risk profile.

Detecting different behavior on its own is, however, not a sufficient reason for segmentation. The difference needs to translate into measurable effects on business (e.g., lower losses, higher approval rates for that segment). An example of how to measure this is given in the Comparing Improvement section of this chapter. The difference must also be explainable in simple business terms—this is a requirement increasingly asked for by model validation teams. Segmentations must be justified, similar to explaining causality for model variables.

Segmentation, whether using experience or statistical methods, should also be done with future plans in mind. Most analysis and experience is based on the past, but scorecards need to be implemented in the future, on future applicant segments. One way to achieve this is by adjusting segmentation based on, for example, the intended market for a particular credit card. What this means is that, instead of assuming that segmentation maximizes predictiveness for unique segments in the population, and then asking the question "what is the optimal segment?," we ask "what segments would I like to maximize predictiveness for?"

Traditionally, segmentation has been done to identify an optimal set of segments that will maximize statistical performance—the alternative approach suggested here is to find a set of segments for which the organization requires better business performance, such as target markets, high-delinquency segments, high-net-worth customers, and superprime and subprime markets. This approach underscores the importance of trying to maximize performance where it is most needed from a business perspective, and ensures that the scorecard development process maximizes business value. This is an area where marketing staff can add value and relevance to scorecard development projects.

The Basel II Capital Accord takes a pragmatic view of segmentation by defining segments as "homogenous risk pools." This leaves individual banks across the world with the option of defining their own unique segments, without a prescriptive recipe for everyone.

Experience-Based (Heuristic) Segmentation

Experience-based segmentation includes ideas generated from business knowledge and experience, operational considerations, and common industry practices. Examples of these sources include:

- Marketing/Risk management departments detecting different applicant profiles in a specific segment.
- A portfolio scored on the same scorecard with the same cutoff, but with segments displaying significantly different behavior (e.g., higher or lower bad rates).
- New subproduct development.
- Need to treat a predefined group differently (e.g., "golden group" of customers or a high-risk segment such as subprime).
- Future marketing direction.

Typical segmentation areas used in the industry include those based on:

- *Demographics.* Regional segments such as those based on sales regions, urban/rural (based on rank-ordered populations of major and minor cities), postal-code based (this approach is better than state/province, which is too high level for effectiveness), and neighborhood; age, lifestyle code, time at bureau, tenure at bank, and high net worth.
- *Product type.* Based on gold/platinum cards, loan terms for mortgages and auto loans, insurance type, secured/unsecured, new versus used cars, lease versus finance for auto loans, size of loan, loyalty program type (travel, retail, cash back, premium, etc.), brand of car or phone, low-interest-rate cards, fixed-versus floating-rate mortgages, secured versus unsecured lines of credit, Internet/Cable TV/land line.
- *Sources of business (channel).* Storefront or at point of sale, "take one" (where the person picks up an application and submits it), branch, Internet, dealers, brokers.
- *Data available.* Thin/thick file (thin file denotes inquiry only with no trades present or less than, say, two trades) at the bureau,

clean/dirty file at bureau or internally (*dirty* denotes some historical negative performance such as missed payments. This allows the use of model variables such as worst delinquency, number and types of delinquencies, balances, time to repayments, time since last missed payments, etc., which would be irrelevant for "clean" accounts), revolver/transactor for revolving products, SMS/voice user, heavy user versus light user.

- *Applicant type.* Existing/new customer (this should be the first obvious one for multiproduct banks. It allows the usage of internal behavior data for new application scorecards), first-time home buyer/mortgage renewal, professional trade groups (e.g., engineers, doctors, etc.), insured versus uninsured mortgage, owner-occupied home versus rental property, automated versus manual decision.
- *Product owned.* Mortgage holders applying for credit cards at the same bank (the segmentation of such premium groups allows the majority of them to be approved and treated better), internet or cable TV customers applying for additional products.

Once ideas on segmentation are generated, further analysis needs to be done for two reasons. First, these ideas need to be confirmed with at least some empirical evidence to provide a comfort level. Second, analysis can help in better defining segments such as thin/thick file, postal code groups, high-/low-risk LTV, and young/old age, by suggesting appropriate breakpoints. For example, they can help answer the question "What is a thin file?" or "What is a 'young' applicant?"

One simple method to confirm segmentation ideas and to establish the need for segmentation is to analyze the risk behavior of the same characteristic across different predefined segments. If the same characteristic (e.g., "renter") predicts differently across unique segments, this may present a case for segmented scorecards. However, if the characteristic predicts risk in the same way across different segments, then additional scorecards may not be required, since there is no differentiation.

Exhibit 6.10 shows observed bad rates for Residential Status and Number of Bureau Trades, segmented by age above and below 30. Observed bad rate by unsegmented attributes is also shown in the column on the far right.

Exhibit 6.10 Bad Rates by Attributes for Age-Based Segmentation

Bad Rate			
	Age > 30	**Age < 30**	**Unseg**
Res Status			
Rent	2.1%	4.8%	2.9%
Own	1.3%	1.8%	1.4%
Parents	3.8%	2.0%	3.2%
Trades			
0	5.0%	2.0%	4.0%
1–3	2.0%	3.4%	2.5%
4+	1.4%	5.8%	2.3%

In the example, there are differences in the bad rates of both renters and those living with parents, above and below 30. The same information (i.e., the attributes "Rent" and "Parents") is predicting differently for older and younger applicants. This shows that segmenting by age is a good idea, and 30 is likely a good point for the segmentation split. Note that if only one scorecard was used, all renters, for example, would get the same points. With segmenting, renters above and below 30 will get different points, leading to better risk rankings.

Let's remember that the point of predictive modeling in businesses is to establish causality, not just correlation. In the same spirit, we should be able to explain the differences in performance across segments. For example, while homeowners have lower bad rates than renters, younger homeowners tend to have higher delinquencies, as they may have lower salaries.

The same is true for applicants with "0" and "4+" trades—the same information predicts differently above and below age 30. Both of these examples are based on North American data and are explainable. Those who are over 30 and have no trades at the credit bureau (i.e., they hold no reported credit product) are considered higher risk. In North America, one is expected to have obtained and showed satisfactory payment behavior for several credit products by age 30, especially credit cards, and therefore the absence of trades at this age is considered high risk. It may denote unbanked, low income segments or recent immigrants.

Those who are familiar with predictive modeling will note the similarity of the above with interaction terms. Interaction terms are a great way to detect and identify segmentations. If a particular characteristic interacts with many others, it may be a good candidate as a basis for segmentation.

Another way to confirm initial segmentation ideas, and to identify unique segments, is to look at observed bad rates for different selected subpopulations. This method involves analyzing the bad rates for different attributes in selected characteristics, and then identifying appropriate segments based on *significantly different* performance. In general, categorical variables are used for segmentation purposes. Continuous variables may be used if there is a significant cutoff point such as requirement for mortgage insurance above a certain LTV. Otherwise, it is usually better to have continuous variables inside the models as they provide good risk ranking throughout the score range.

An example of such an analysis is given in Exhibit 6.11. This exhibit shows typical examples of three segmentations based on age, source of business, and applicant type. In the "Age" example, it can

Exhibit 6.11 Bad Rates by Predefined Segments

Attributes	Bad Rates
Age	
Over 40 yrs	1.80%
32–40 yrs	2.50%
28–32	6.50%
23–28	8.60%
18–22	10.80%
Source of business	
Internet	20%
Branch	3%
Broker	8%
Phone	14%
Applicant type	
First-time buyer	5%
Renewal mortgage	1%

be clearly seen that the bad rate has a significant change between the "32–40" and "28–32" segments. In this case, segmentations for "Over 32"/"Under 32" may make sense. More finely defined groupings for age can also be used instead of the broadly defined groups shown in the example, if there is a need to produce more than two segments.

In the "Source of Business" example, all four attributes have different bad rates, and may qualify as unique segments. While this analysis is being used to illustrate segmentation, it can also be done on a quarterly basis to identify potential areas of concern for delinquency.

Both the methods described above are fairly simple to implement, and can provide some measure of comfort that the segments chosen through experience and intuition are appropriate. They can also help in selecting the right breaks—for example, for age, as shown in Exhibit 6.12—for characteristics used as a basis for segmenting.

Statistically Based Segmentation

Clustering

Clustering is a widely used technique to identify groups that are similar to each other with respect to the input variables. Clustering, which can be used to segment databases, places objects into groups, or "clusters," suggested by the data. The objects in each cluster tend to be similar to each other in some sense, and objects in different clusters tend to be dissimilar. Two of the methods used to form clusters are K-means clustering and self-organizing maps (SOMs).

Clustering can be performed on the basis of Euclidean distances, computed from one or more quantitative variables. The observations are divided into clusters such that every observation belongs to at most one cluster.

The SOM is inspired by the way various human sensory impressions are mapped in the brain, such that spatial relations among input stimuli correspond to spatial relations among the neurons (i.e., clusters).

Exhibit 6.12 illustrates clustering based on two variables. It shows the data points forming three distinct clusters, or groups. An outlier is also visible at the bottom right-hand corner.

Exhibit 6.12 Clustering

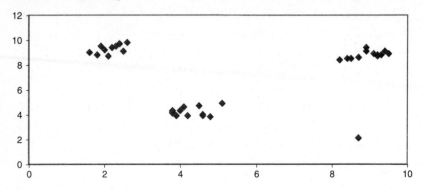

An example of an output for one cluster using this technique is shown in Exhibit 6.13, where the *y*-axis is the normalized mean.

This cluster shows the following characteristics:

- Lower-than-average age.
- Higher-than-average inquiries in the last six months.
- Tendency to live in Region A.
- No residents in Region B.
- Less likely to own their residence.
- More likely to have delinquencies in the past six months.

Exhibit 6.13 Details for a Cluster

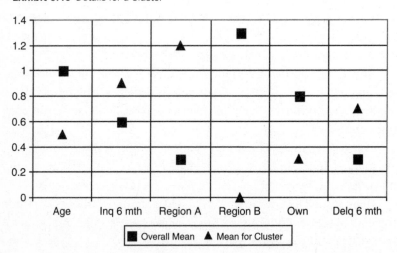

Other clusters can be analyzed for their defining characteristics using similar charts. Further analysis, including the distribution of characteristics within each cluster, may also be performed to obtain a set of rules to define each unique group. For the example in Exhibit 6.13, clusters may be defined as:

- Young homeowners in Region A.
- Young renters in Region A.
- Older homeowners in Region A.
- Older renters in Region A.

Alternatively, the clustering can be based on any of the other characteristics that provide the best differentiation between the clusters.

It should be noted that clustering identifies groups that are similar based on their characteristics—not performance. Thus, clusters may seem to be different, but may have similar risk performance. The clusters therefore should be analyzed further, using, for example, bad rate analysis, to ensure that the segmentation produced is for groups with different risk performance profiles.

Decision Trees

A further technique to perform statistical segmentation is the use of decision trees. Decision trees isolate segments based on performance criteria (i.e., differentiate between good and bad). They are also simple to understand and interpret, and therefore can be explained easily to management and others. In most data mining software, decision trees can also be adjusted based on business requirements. For example, if a jurisdiction requires mandatory mortgage insurance at 75 percent LTV, then the user can force a split at that point to be in line with policies. In addition to identifying characteristics for segmentation, decision trees also identify "optimum" splitting points for each characteristic—thus representing a very powerful and convenient method for segmenting. The example in Exhibit 6.14 shows segmentation based on two levels.

In the preceding example, the first split, by new and existing customer was forced by the analyst for business reasons. The outcome after that is based on the default decision tree algorithm. The results show that there are four possible segments for this portfolio, based on

Exhibit 6.14 Segmentation Using Decision Trees

existing/new customer, length of tenure, and age. This means that the user will now develop four separate scorecards. The bad rates for each segment is different and the splits can be explained to business users. Note that based on the minimum number of cases required, each of the four segments identified through this analysis needs to have at least 2,000 to 5,000 bads. In some cases decision trees will identify segments with very few bads or goods. Most analysts will then adjust the splits manually in order to get viable segments.

Comparing Improvement

Both experience-based and statistical analyses will yield ideas for potential segmentation, and may confirm that there are sufficient reasons for segmenting—but they do not quantify the benefits of building multiple segmented models. There are fairly simple ways available to estimate whether the improvement through segmentation is worth pursuing.

The following exercise involves building "quick and dirty" models for a base case/unsegmented data set, as well as for the proposed segments, and then comparing their performances. The numbers generated are therefore ballpark estimates that can be used for comparison purposes without spending months building more fine-tuned scorecards.

The first step is to measure the improvement in predictive power through segmentation, as one of our reasons for building segmented models was the belief that segmentation maximizes predictiveness for unique segments. This can be done using a number of statistics such as the KS, c-statistic[9] (which is equal to the area under the receiver

Exhibit 6.15 Comparing Improvements through Segmentation

Segment	Total c-stat	Seg c-stat	Improvement
Age < 30	0.65	0.69	6.15%
Age > 30	0.68	0.71	4.41%
Tenure < 2	0.67	0.72	7.46%
Tenure > 2	0.66	0.75	13.64%
Gold Card	0.68	0.69	1.47%
Platinum Card	0.67	0.68	1.49%
Unsegmented	0.66	—	—

operating characteristic [ROC] curve), and so on. Exhibit 6.15 shows an example of this analysis using the c-statistic (details on the c-statistic are covered later, in Chapter 10).

This exhibit shows c-statistic calculations for an unsegmented scorecard and for six scorecards segmented in various ways. "Total c-stat" refers to the c-stat for *that segment* based on an unsegmented scorecard. "Seg c-stat" refers to the c-stat for that segment, using a scorecard built specifically for that segment. For example, a scorecard built specifically for those under 30 years old has a c-statistic of 0.69, while the c-statistic for those under 30 using one unsegmented scorecard is 0.65. In most cases, using segmented scorecards yields better predictive power than using an overall scorecard. Segmentation by platinum/gold cards did not yield significant improvement—probably because the credit grantor did not differentiate enough between its gold and platinum card customers from a risk perspective. This is quite true as platinum and gold have now become fairly meaningless from both a features and risk perspective. The best segments seem to be tenure based, likely due to the more powerful behavior data available for use with existing clients. The break at two years is also interesting, as credit card portfolios tend to mature around that time, which means the population with tenure more than two years is likely much lower risk than the newer one (the bad rates shown in Exhibit 6.14 confirm this). This analysis is based on a single-level segmentation; similar analysis can be done for more complex segmentation as well. The user then needs to decide what level of improvement is significant enough to warrant the extra development and implementation effort.

Exhibit 6.16 Gauging Business Benefit of Segmentation

Segment	Size	After Segmentation		Before Segmentation	
		Approve	Bad	Approve	Bad
Total	100%	70%	3.5%	70%	4.1%
Age < 30	65%	70%	4.1%	70%	6.3%
Age > 30	35%	70%	2.7%	70%	3.6%
Tenure < 2	12%	70%	4.2%	70%	5.7%
Tenure > 2	88%	70%	2.1%	70%	2.9%
Gold Card	23%	70%	3.9%	70%	4.3%
Platinum Card	77%	70%	3.1%	70%	3.8%

That question is best answered using business, not statistical, measures. Businesses are not run to maximize c-statistics or KS—they are run based on performance indicators such as approval rates, profits, loss rates, and so forth. It would therefore be useful to convert improved predictive power into expected portfolio performance, as shown in the example in Exhibit 6.16.

The exhibit compares two common performance measures, namely the approval rate and expected bad rate, for each segmented scorecard. The data comes from the gains chart for the "quick and dirty" scorecards built. It also lists the approximate size of each segment so that we can decide how big of an impact the change will have. Using a template such as this, one can decide if the combination of the size of the segment and the improvement in performance is enough to justify additional scorecard development and implementation. Approval and bad rates used for comparison should be based on some desired portfolio objective, preferably the one agreed to in the business plan discussed in Chapter 4. For example, if the future desired approval rate is 70 percent, then the bad rate metrics should be generated for this number so that an apples-to-apples comparison can be done. In the preceding example, segmentation by tenure provides improvements in bad rates from 5.7 percent to 4.2 percent, and from 2.9 percent to 2.1 percent for those with less than two years and more than two years tenures with the bank, respectively. Using these improvements, some idea of the reduction in losses in terms of dollars can be estimated from write-off numbers. If the number is significant enough, then building extra segmented scorecard is a worthwhile activity.

Choosing Segments

But why would someone not implement all the scorecards built, as long as there is an improvement in predictive power or performance, regardless of size?

There are many factors to consider in selecting the number of segments, including:

- *Cost of development.* This includes the effort involved internally and externally to produce scorecards with full documentation. In recent years, the validation and vetting efforts for scorecards have become a significant undertaking in most countries, most notably the United States. This regulatory/audit burden can add significant cost to developing new scorecards, and in some cases, even to adding new variables.

- *Cost of implementation.* Additional scorecards cost system resources to implement, especially if nonstandard characteristics are used, if complex code needs to be written, or if an external third party needs to be paid to implement scorecards into loan origination systems or core banking systems.

- *Processing.* There are additional processing costs associated with more scorecards, however, once in production, this cost can be small.

- *Strategy development and monitoring.* Each scorecard requires a set of associated strategies, policy rules, and monitoring reports. Creating, managing, and maintaining them require resources that may need to be hired if many scorecards are developed and used. This can be a significant cost especially for any models or scorecards used for regulatory purposes, and for those that require active portfolio management such as in credit cards. Annual reviews of such models are in most cases, fairly lengthy and labor-intensive processes.

- *Segment size.* In some cases, the size of certain portfolios will necessitate the building of several scorecards as the payback can be significant (see previous section).

In cases of larger portfolios, the available resources and savings may mean that these costs and efforts are insignificant compared to the benefits. However, in smaller portfolios and organizations, such analysis may be required to determine if the improvement in performance is significant enough to warrant the additional effort, complexity, and cost required.

METHODOLOGY

There are various mathematical techniques available to build risk prediction scorecards—for example, logistic regression, neural networks, decision trees, and so on. The most appropriate technique to be used can depend on issues such as:

- The quality of data available. A decision tree may be more appropriate for cases where there is significant missing data, or where the relationship between characteristics and targets is nonlinear.
- Type of target outcome, that is, binary (good/bad) or continuous ($ profit/loss given default).
- Type of outcome desired (i.e., predictions or just risk ranking).
- Sample sizes available.
- Implementation platforms (i.e., whether the application-processing system is able to implement a particular type of scorecard). For example, a neural network model may be ideal, but unusable, if the application-processing system is unable to implement it.
- Interpretability of results, such as the ease with which regression-developed points-based scorecards can be maintained.
- Skill levels of both the model development as well as validation staff.
- Legal compliance on methodology, usually required by local regulators to be transparent and explainable.
- Ability to track and diagnose scorecard performance.

At this point, the scaling and structure of the scorecard can also be discussed (i.e., the potential score ranges, points to double the odds, if the score itself represents the expected bad rate, etc.). The technique and intended format of the scorecard should be communicated to the risk and IT managers to ensure that data and theoretical issues on the identified techniques are understood—so that the results of the scorecard development exercise will be interpreted correctly, and the scorecard will be implementable when developed.

REVIEW OF IMPLEMENTATION PLAN

The additional information obtained in this phase may require changes to the original implementation plan and project timelines. In particular, if the number of scorecards needed after segmentation analysis is more than previously expected, the methodology suggested is more time consuming or requires changes to implementation platforms, or the data requirements are expanded, the project will need more time. To ensure realistic expectations, the testing and implementation plans should be reviewed at this point. This is crucial at companies where different areas have responsibility for data gathering, development, testing, implementation, and tracking of scorecards. The project manager ensures that changes are understood and their impacts on the original project plan quantified, so that each phase of the project leads seamlessly into the next.

At the end of this phase, we have determined the following:

- Enough good and bad cases exist to build scorecards.
- The data is clean and accessible.
- List of exclusions.
- The performance and sample windows.
- The definitions of the good, bad, and indeterminate target variables.
- The development sample is from a normal time frame and is not affected significantly by seasonality and other factors.
- The segments required.

All of the above are agreed to and signed off by the major stakeholders, as described in Chapter 2. At this point, all data requirements and project plan documentation are complete, and the works related to database construction can begin.

NOTES

1. Sven F. Crone and Steven Finlay, "Instance Sampling in Credit Scoring: An Empirical Study of Sample Size and Balancing." *International Journal of Forecasting* 28, no. 1 (January 2012): 224–238.

2. Basel Committee on Banking Supervision, "Basel II: International Convergence of Capital Measurement and Capital Standards: A Revised Framework," 2006.

3. http://www.ifrs.org/current-projects/iasb-projects/financial-instruments-a-replacement-of-ias-39-financial-instruments-recognitio/Pages/Financial-Instruments-Replacement-of-IAS-39.aspx

4. M. Choy and Ma Nang Laik, "A Markov Chain Approach to Determine the Optimal Performance Period and Bad Definition for Credit Scorecard." *Research Journal of Social Science and Management* 1, no. 6 (October 2011): 227–234.

5. A. Cathcart and N. Benjamin, "Low Default Portfolios: A Proposal for Conservative PD Estimation." Discussion paper, UK Financial Services Authority, 2005.

6. D. Tasche and K. Pluto, "Estimating Probabilities of Default for Low Default Portfolios," December 2004. Available at SSRN: http://ssrn.com/abstract=635301

7. S. G. Hanson and T. Schuermann, "Estimating Probabilities of Default." FRB of New York Staff Report No. 190, July 2004. Available at SSRN: http://ssrn.com/abstract=569841 or http://dx.doi.org/10.2139/ssrn.569841

8. T. Wilde and L. Jackson, "Low-Default Portfolios without Simulation." *Risk*, August 2006: 60–63.

9. T. Hastie, R. Tibshirani, and J. H. Friedman, "The Elements of Statistical Learning: Data Mining, Inference, and Prediction," 2nd ed. (New York: Springer Science, 2009).

## CHAPTER 7

Default Definition under Basel

By Hendrik Wagner

INTRODUCTION

When building a credit risk scorecard, the definition of the good/bad target flag is one of the key prerequisites for model development and was discussed in an earlier chapter. In this chapter, we expand this discussion to cover further aspects of the default definition from the perspective of the Basel II Accord[1] for regulatory capital calculation.

For the past 10 years and longer, the Basel II accord has shaped the way default is defined in all areas of credit risk analysis and management, even outside of models developed for regulatory capital calculation. A standardized default definition is important for regulatory purposes because it helps make analytics and calculations across institutions comparable. At the same time, however, it presents problems of interpretation and implementation even for regulatory capital calculation, and may not always be the most adequate definition for all other purposes. For example, a default definition used for a 10-year mortgage loan–granting decision may need to be different. We will touch on some of these problems and possible solutions in this chapter.

As we have seen, any definition of the default yes/no flag that serves as a target for developing Probability of Default models (including scorecards) will consist of two components: a definition of the default *event* and a definition of the prediction *horizon*. In addition, a default *rate* is associated with groups of cases, such as characteristic attributes, pools, rating grades, or segments.

In the next section, we will discuss the default event. We will present two fundamentally different ways of interpreting the "90 days past due" criterion for establishing a default event. Other topics include the various "unlikely to pay" criteria, materiality, and the aggregation level.

In the third section, we will discuss various ways of calculating the default rate of a group of cases. Topics include accounting for multiple defaults over the prediction horizon, quarantine periods, and the effects of cases that are in default at observation.

This leads us to the fourth section, on model validation and recalibration under Basel II. Here, we will extend the validation discussion in earlier chapters by focusing on dynamics over time and, in particular, over an economic cycle. We will discuss calibration to a long-run average and differentiate between Through the Cycle and Point in Time models.

Finally, we will come back to the concept of the prediction horizon in the context of building application scoring models. We have seen in earlier chapters how the dynamics of default rate maturation vary between products and segments, and how to choose useful prediction horizons (performance windows) as a function of these dynamics. We will discuss if and how this approach may need to be reconciled with a prescribed prediction horizon of 12 months under Basel II specifications.

DEFAULT EVENT

In previous chapters, the default event has been more generically referred to as the "bad" event. It has been pointed out, among other things, that the *bad* definition may depend on profitability consider-ations, may be "looser" (earlier) or "tighter" (later), and that typically for delinquency-based *bad* definitions, one would try to determine a "point of no return" delinquency level, after which a vast majority of cases would not cure.

The "point of no return" idea is important, as it attempts to cre-ate a tight or late definition that allows for a rather straightforward analysis of expected losses: Under such a definition the portion of cases defined as bad that actually do not cause a loss, but instead repay the amount owing and revert to current/paid-up status is made negligible. Otherwise, an additional analysis of perhaps segment- or case-dependent cure rates (a cure model) would be required to correct for this negligence.

The Basel II definition of the default event, however, includes a delinquency-based component in which the delinquency level is set to 90 days past due. This level generally tends to constitute a rather early definition, and often a large number of cases may cure. Therefore, cure models are abundantly used in conjunction with Basel II Probability of Default models (as part of the Loss Given Default model).

The Basel II definition of the default event is best characterized as consisting of a specific delinquency-based criterion, as noted earlier, and a second somewhat general criterion that requires the lender to assess if a borrower is deemed unlikely to pay. The latter relies on information from processes or policies other than delinquency tracking and is sometimes referred to as *process default.*

The delinquency level that constitutes a Basel II delinquency default is 90 days past due. National supervisors may opt to set it to 180 days past due for specific portfolios (retail loans secured by real estate, public-sector entities), but this option has been rarely exercised. A frequent cause for concern is how the 90-day criterion is interpreted and implemented, specifically regarding the way in which the delinquency level is established. This is handled differently across countries, and even between different institutions in the same country.

In one popular method, delinquency refers to the (possibly fractional) number of missed payments as calculated from the outstanding amount. Any partial payment reduces that number. According to this method, a person may continuously have a delinquency status of two monthly payments, or 60 days past due. As long as their outstanding amount doesn't reach the amount corresponding to three monthly payments, that person will not be considered to be in default.

In another common method, it is not the relative amount outstanding that establishes the delinquency level, but rather the length of time passed since there was no outstanding amount (material outstanding, that is; see below). According to this method, the chronic late payer described earlier would be considered in default after 90 consecutive days in material arrears. The partial payments made would not matter, only that the person was in some form of delinquency for 90 days.

As of the writing of this text, national supervisors were not necessarily enforcing one view or the other. However, they would try to ensure that within the same banking group a single consistent approach is chosen. The approach advocating consistent behavior has also been used in other situations, including the treatment of low-default portfolios.

We have previously mentioned that the materiality of the outstanding amount matters. The 90 days counter resets whenever the outstanding amount becomes immaterial. An outstanding is classified as material according to criteria set by national supervisors. Typically, an outstanding is considered immaterial if it is either lower than a certain fixed amount (e.g., 200€) or is below a certain portion of the remaining exposure (e.g., 2 percent). The European Banking

Authority is currently in the process of creating a Europe-wide rule on materiality.[2]

The second criterion that establishes a Basel II default event is an assessment of how unlikely the borrower is to pay. The materiality issue described earlier is not considered in the context of such process defaults. According to the regulation, indications of "unlikeliness to pay" include, but are not limited to, nonaccrued status, specific credit risk adjustment, sale at a loss, distressed restructuring, and bankruptcy. In order to implement this part of the default event definition, a large number of disparate systems may need to be monitored so that any sign of default is quickly picked up, including information from bookkeeping, collection, and workout, or even external sources such as credit bureaus and court records. In some cases, ongoing reviews of small and medium-sized enterprise (SME) or corporate loans by credit officers may be used to make such decisions.

Finally, an important aspect of the interpretation and implementation of the default event definition is the level to which it is applied, namely, account level or customer level. This includes how default events are "inherited" from customer level down to account level or "aggregated up" from account level to customer level.

In retail portfolios, it is permissible to consider cases on account level. However, there are two aspects of the default event definition that imply the need to also consider the customer level: first, some types of process defaults, such as bankruptcy, are inherently defined at a customer level. Therefore, even if a bankruptcy event is first officially logged for one specific type of account, once it occurs, all other accounts of that bankrupt customer need to be flagged as defaulted immediately.

Second, if a default event is strictly related to a specific account, such as a delinquency default, one then needs to consider whether the underlying reason for the delinquency of this account also implies an unlikeliness to pay for the remaining accounts. One would typically affirm this if a significant portion of the overall exposure is in default, and a 20 percent threshold has been suggested as a general rule.

In nonretail portfolios, cases must be considered at a customer (company) level and all account-level defaults immediately imply a customer default. This means that the default of a relatively minor account can and will lead to the default of the whole, potentially very large company. Still, it is not permissible to alleviate the strictness of this rule by calling extreme default situations "merely technical" or having the default overruled by some expert opinion. However, in the case of a delinquency default (but not a process default), the effect is alleviated by the materiality thresholds. Since these are now also calculated at a customer level, a minor account-level exposure, even if 90 days past due, will not be in default if the outstanding is sufficiently small relative to the overall exposure.

PREDICTION HORIZON AND DEFAULT RATE

For regulatory capital calculations, one is concerned only with the default risk within the existing portfolio and not with the risk of applications that have not yet been approved. Therefore, the prediction horizon is not dependent on the dynamics of default risk maturation, unlike in application scoring. We'll come back to that in a later section.

As is generally practiced in behavioral scoring, in order to create a target flag for model development, one would pick an observation date (Sample window, as discussed earlier in the book) sufficiently long into the past (more than 12 months), and then observe the payment performance of accounts opened for 12 months from the observation date to see if a default event has occurred or not.

This process can be replicated with multiple observation dates, to make sure that the default information is not biased toward one particular 12-month time period. This is practiced quite often in the industry via the creation of stacked samples, in particular, for low default portfolios as well as those that have seasonality. One can either reuse the same cases over again or, if there is a sufficient number of cases, use different random samples for different observation dates in order to assure independence of the observations.

The above procedure ensures that every single case is associated with a default flag based on a 12-month performance period. This is necessary in order to develop models such as regression models, including scorecards. However, for Basel II purposes, such a case by case flag is not strictly required. Instead, what is generally required is that the default rate be measured for a group of cases, such as rating grades or the overall portfolio, expressing default risk over a 12-month horizon. This may be achieved in ways other than averaging individual flags.

One example is a situation where multiple defaults of the same case within a 12-month horizon must be accounted for. In such a case, we would count the number of all default events occurring within a 12-month horizon, for a group of accounts that were not in default at observation date, and we would include redefault events after cures. Such a way of defining default rate has been enforced in some countries. However, this was done under the condition that the cure rate model associated with that same portfolio had been correspondingly created in a way that accounted for redefaults of the same case. Hence, relatively higher cure rates would be countered by relatively higher default risk.

As this discussion shows, a full definition of a default event must also include a description of the circumstances under which a state of default no longer applies. This is to ensure that the effects of "false" cures and multiple defaults can be properly measured. In this context, a situation where an account cures and then very quickly redefaults may be interpreted as a sign that the cure event should not have been declared in the first place. In some cases, a high amount of quick and even oscillatory redefaults may be caused by technical difficulties and time delays in the implementation of the default event detection across various databases. As a remedy for such phenomena, a "probation" or "quarantine" period is commonly used. A period of three months has been suggested as a general rule.[3]

Finally, one should be aware of the fact that the measured default rate for a particular portfolio depends not only on what happens after the observation date but also on which cases are at default at the observation date itself. These cases are not considered for default rate measurement because, obviously here no default prediction is necessary, and as such probabilities of default of 100 percent are used in the regulatory capital calculation. So sometimes, when a default event definition is changed, where we expect a higher default rate as a result, this may not actually happen, or at least not to the extent we expected. This is because more high-risk cases may now be considered being in default already at observation.

VALIDATION OF DEFAULT RATE AND RECALIBRATION

Two of the core criteria underlying model quality are discriminatory power and calibration. A powerful model is one where the default predictions differentiate the population in such a way that there is maximum separation between actual defaulters and nondefaulters: Actual defaulters will be concentrated in the group of cases with high probability of default and vice versa. A well-calibrated model is a model where the average prediction matches the actual default rate, either overall or in subsegments such as rating grades. A powerful model may be poorly calibrated, for example, if the probability of default is, say, 10 percent too high for every single case, but the rank ordering is still maintained. A well-calibrated model may have poor power, for example, if every case is given the same probability of default equal to the overall default rate.

Depending on the use of the model predictions, power and calibration may not be equally important. For example, when using application scores to make approval decisions, a good separation of good and bad cases is essential, especially around the cutoff score. As will be covered later in this book, such separation is usually calculated using measures such as the Kolmogorov-Smirnov (KS). Calibration problems may be taken care of in the process of selecting an optimal cutoff. However, stronger calibration may be considered the more important quality for regulatory capital calculation because here the objective of the exercise is to determine capital levels through calculations of expected and unexpected losses. Hence, in this case, a correct prediction of the overall level of risk is typically more important than a strong differentiation of cases.

A poorly calibrated model is also more easily rectified than one with poor separation power. It is possible to transform predictions in such a way that the average transformed prediction equals a desired value, while not changing model power. A popular method for doing this is the so-called "Bayes Rule," which is the one such transformation that leaves Weight of Evidence values constant. This method can also be described as a shift of the intercept in a logistic regression model. The precise formula for this transformation will be discussed in Chapter 8.

The Bayes Rule needs to be applied to individual cases. If it is applied to predictions that have been averaged by rating grade, and the size of the rating grades is restricted to not change, then the average transformed prediction (weighted by rating grade size) will be slightly off the desired target value. However, a new virtual target value can then be found using optimization techniques so that eventually the original target will be matched when using the virtual target in the Bayes Rule.

As we said before, under Basel II the default rate (and hence the probability of default) is calculated over a 12-month prediction horizon. The Basel II accord additionally prescribes that the calculated default rate shall be one corresponding to a "long-run average." The reason for this requirement lies in the use of the probability of default values as input to a risk function that outputs a stressed probability of default corresponding to a worst-case economic scenario, and accounting for default correlation between individual cases. In this framework, since it is the risk function that simulates an economic downturn, the inputs themselves should not correspond to a stressed economic scenario or any other specific phase in the economic cycle, but rather to an average value across a cycle.

This long-run average requirement in real life is interpreted in two different ways: In one approach (Through the Cycle models), it is understood as a requirement that the probability of default of a specific case does not change as long as a set of noncyclical basic characteristics do not change. So in this approach, the model will contain a set of the most important risk drivers (variables), but it would not contain those that are strongly correlated with the economic (or business) cycle. The former set would include demographic risk drivers such as Age and Time at Address, collateralization (for secured loans), product type, or application score, while the latter set of cyclical characteristics that are not to be used would, for example, include variables derived from delinquency levels (e.g., Number of Times 30 Days Past Due in Last 12 Months). These cyclical variables are not included, as they would likely be affected by the economic climate in the sense that high delinquency levels would be more frequently found in bad economic times. So in a Through the Cycle model, the same cases would be found in the same rating grade throughout the cycle. It is interesting to note that, from a Point in Time validation standpoint, these models would almost always be miscalibrated, as the actual default rate over a cycle would oscillate around the constant probability of default.

Even though this type of model may be theoretically ideal from the standpoint of regulatory capital calculation (via stable predictions), it has serious drawbacks for almost all other operational purposes. First and foremost, this is because of the obvious sacrifice of discriminatory power that stems from ignoring the highly significant risk drivers that are the cyclical variables. For most practical purposes it is far more important to know which cases have a high probability of going to default than to have a case remain in the same rating grade throughout an economic cycle. Therefore, instead of building Through the Cycle models in the strict sense, typically Point in Time models are built that make use of all the relevant important information, whether cyclical or not. In order to somewhat fulfill the long-run average requirement, these models are then calibrated in such a way that, over a cycle, at least their average prediction would match the average default rate.

Finally, it is important to note that an important practical problem in calibrating Through the Cycle or Point in Time models to a cycle average default rate lies in the fact that case-specific data histories are often not available for a whole economic cycle. As a compromise, it is common practice to calibrate instead to a five-year moving average default rate. Alternatively, one can try to obtain the time period for which data is available in an economic cycle using external reference data and then extrapolate.

APPLICATION SCORING AND BASEL II

Finally, we now want to come back to the discussion of prediction horizon in the context of application scoring. There is a common misconception that under Basel II one is obliged to use a 12-month prediction horizon when building application scoring models. This is, however, not the case, as regulatory capital calculation is concerned only with models for existing clients. As we know, application scores are used for making approval decisions that cannot be revoked over the lifetime of the contract. As such, they must be built using performance windows that allow the default rate to substantially mature, or at least stabilize, as has been shown using vintage curves in previous chapters. In order to differentiate well between cases, one must wait long enough so that all types of defaulters have shown up. In some portfolios such as credit cards or other consumer credit, the necessary performance window can be shorter; in others, such as home loans, it may need to be longer in order to build meaningful scorecards.

It is true that for regulatory capital calculation one is usually interested in building specific models for new clients for whom so far only application information is available. It may even be efficient to use the existing application scores as the only input to such a model. However, the resulting model would be fundamentally different from the application scoring model, as for Basel II purposes, a 12-month prediction horizon would need to be used.

SUMMARY

In this chapter, we have seen how regulatory requirements influence the way Probability of Default models are built. In particular, the regulatory definition of the default event, the prediction horizon, the default rate calculation, and Through the Cycle calibration requirements set the framework for most Probability of Default modeling for institutions looking to qualify for the foundation or advanced Internal Ratings Based requirements under the Basel II regime.

One may ask the question as to why the specifics of an important but limited purpose, like regulatory capital calculation, has such a strong influence on the way Probability of Default models are built in general. The answer lies in a regulatory concept that is known as the "use test." In order to prevent a possible gaming of the system, which could arise from allowing models to be specifically built for regulatory capital calculation purposes, models are approved for use in these calculations only if they are also used in other relevant credit risk management operations, such as credit risk reporting or credit approval. What's more, supervisors require that the regulatory definition of default be the only operational definition of default to be used across all operations of the bank from front end to back end.

This use-test requirement, when interpreted very literally, causes conflict in a variety of ways. In particular, two areas find it difficult to reconcile the specific requirements for regulatory capital calculation with their own intrinsic operational requirements for model development. First, after the discussion in this chapter, it should be clear that models for existing clients such as those used for regulatory capital calculation cannot be directly used for credit approval. Second, for many day-to-day credit risk management tasks, in particular in the management of existing clients, it is important that a very up-to-date, short-term risk assessment is available. This means that Through the Cycle models cannot be used for these purposes, even if they may be the preferred model type for regulatory capital calculation.

Today, supervisors acknowledge this and focus more on a state-of-the-art model development process in which provably all important information is used, instead of demanding a strict one-to-one adoption of the regulatory capital calculation models in all other areas.

NOTES

1. Bank for International Settlements, "Basel II: International Convergence of Capital Measurement and Capital Standards: A Revised Framework—Comprehensive Version," June 2006.
2. European Banking Authority, "Draft Regulatory Technical Standards on Materiality Threshold of Credit Obligation Past Due." Consultation Paper, October 2014.
3. European Banking Authority, "Guidelines on the Application of the Definition of Default." Consultation Paper, September 2015.

CHAPTER **8**

Scorecard Development Process, Stage 3: Development Database Creation

"Today's scientists have substituted mathematics for experiments, and they wander off through equation after equation, and eventually build a structure which has no relation to reality."

—Nikola Tesla, 1934

Following the parameters defined in Stage 2, creation of a database for scorecard development can now begin. This database will contain a set of characteristics (or predictor variables) plus a target variable for each case. This data set will then be used for the scorecard development/modeling itself.

DEVELOPMENT SAMPLE SPECIFICATION

Once the sample parameters, segmentation, and methodology for the project are established, specifications need to be produced for the creation of development sample databases to be used in the modeling stage. Based on the results of the preceding phases, the following are specified and documented:

- Number of scorecards required and specification of each segment, including coding instructions on how to identify the various segments.
- Definitions of *bad, good,* and *indeterminate*.
- Portfolio bad rate and approval rates for each segment.
- Performance and sample windows.
- Definitions of exclusions.

In addition, the following are specified and added in this stage:

- Sample size required for each segment and performance category (including "declined" for application scorecards).
- Detailed list of characteristics, from internal and external sources, required in the development sample for each segment.

132

- Derived characteristics, with details on exact calculations and logic.
- Target variable, with details on exact coding.

Selection of Characteristics

The selection of characteristics to be included in the development sample is a critical part of the development process. This step, where characteristics are carefully and deliberately selected by the analyst, reinforces the need for some business thought to be put into every phase of the scorecard development project. The alternative is to import the contents of entire data marts or other data repositories into the scorecard development database—which is inefficient, and unlike characteristic selection, does not enhance or use the analysts' knowledge of internal data. In particular, where there are thousands of variables available, this exercise can quickly get out of control.

The exercise I normally do with customers involves getting a list of all variables that they have access to, and then having a discussion around their inclusion into the scorecard development database. Usually, the model developer, the risk/strategy or policy manager, model validation staff, and, in some cases, subject matter experts such as adjudicators or collectors are involved in the process. A limited number of characteristics are picked to make the process efficient and controlled, and these should be selected based on a variety of factors, including:

- *Expected predictive power.* This information is derived from collective experience (collectors, adjudicators, and risk analysts), previous analysis/experience including old scorecards, and literature on modeling. This is where interviewing adjudicators and collectors can help greatly, especially for analysts who are new to credit risk. Most predictive variables are fairly well known, and there is a limited set of about 30 to 50 variables that almost always gets into application scorecards globally.
- *Reliability and robustness.* Some unconfirmed data may be manipulated or prone to manipulation (e.g., income, time

at employment), especially in cases where data input is being done by staff motivated to sell products, such as bank branches, auto dealers, cell phone vendors, or loan brokers. In some cases, it may be cost prohibitive to confirm such data (e.g., in a low-value lending product or where cost of staffing is high), and in such cases the potential payback should be evaluated against costs. Some high-level analytics can be performed to detect manipulated data. For example, comparing the changes in confirmed data such as age, with related unconfirmed data such as "time at employment" or "time at address" can help. Large deviations in related variables such as the preceding may suggest manipulation. Older data such as stated income may also be prone to inflationary effects and therefore cannot be used in their absolute form. Variables affected by market growth such as Number of Inquiries, as well as those related to trades, purchases, and balances also tend to increase over time for the population, and may need to be adjusted based on current norms. For data that is inputted by the applicant or sales agents online, certain drop-down lists should also be analyzed, for example, occupation. I have seen cases where a significant chunk of applicants and sales staff automatically select the first option on the list in order to save time. Social media data presents a growth area but can also be very unreliable. This will be dealt with in more detail later in this section.

■ *Missing data.* Some missing data can be useful in analyzing the causes of why they are missing. We will cover how to deal with such situations in the Chapter 10. In selecting variables, normally those that are largely missing should not be included, especially when there is enough choice of complete variables. In particular, this is the case with self-declared data on application forms that have historically been left blank by applicants, and the lender has made no effort to get that missing information. While there is no definitive threshold for how much missing is acceptable, industry practitioners usually discard anything more than 40 to 50 percent missing.

- *Ease in collection.* Data elements in application forms that are optional (and are therefore left blank by applicants) should also be avoided or considered only for scorecards if they are made mandatory.
- *Interpretability.* Some characteristics, such as occupation and industry type, are prone to subjective interpretation. Different people can put the same person into different occupation or industry types, and as nontraditional occupations grow, it is becoming harder to slot people into traditionally defined occupation types. In addition, most banks have overly broad categories for occupation such as sales, technical, managerial, government, and so on. This is the reason that, in most institutions, the "Other" category often has as much as 75 percent of all cases for occupation. Even in cases where such characteristics have been shown to be predictive, concerns about future interpretation can bring their robustness into question. An exception can be made when the subjective interpretation of a variable is backed by credit risk experience. An example of this is a field such as "management quality," which can be used in scorecards for commercial/small businesses (also known as "small and medium-sized enterprises," or SMEs). While this is a subjective field, the judgment is made (or should be) by experienced adjudicators which allows this field to be used with a higher confidence level than those mentioned previously.
- *Human intervention.* This refers to characteristics that have been *significantly* influenced by human intervention such as those used for broad policy rules (e.g., bankruptcy indicators should be avoided where almost all bankrupts have been declined as a policy). While reject inference can remedy this situation to some extent, policy rule and scorecard characteristics should preferably be independent for coherence. For example, a very predictive binary variable with a lop-sided distribution (such as 99 percent "yes") is not very useful for models but is an excellent policy rule variable. On the other hand, continuous ones are best suited for models.
- *Legal issues surrounding the usage of certain types of information.* If there are characteristics that have been collected historically

(e.g., marital status, number of children, gender, nationality), but are legally or politically suspect, it is better to leave them out of scorecard development. This is where knowledge of the regulatory and legal requirements for lending comes in handy.

■ *Creation of ratios based on business reasoning.* Users need to avoid the "carpet bombing" (if you throw enough explosives near a target, you might hit it, but you'll also do a lot of collateral damage and waste resources) approach to creating ratios. This involves taking pretty much all somewhat related numeric variables in the data set, dividing them by everything else, and then letting statistical algorithms tell you if they are useful. This generates hundreds, and sometimes thousands, of derived ratios that may (by chance) be statistically predictive but are unexplainable and hence not very useful. Recall that the objective of the exercise is to understand causation, not just correlation. Any ratio created needs to be justified and explained. For example, ratio of credit bureau inquiries in the past month divided by inquiries in the past 12 months provides an indication of short-term credit hungriness compared to long-term. Similarly, short-term to long-term comparisons of other indicators such as purchases, payments, utilization, balances, payment ratios, and others, have proven to be good indicators of risk—all due to good business reasons. The point of creating these recent versus long-term comparison variables is to identify abnormal behavior such as changes in payments, purchasing, deposits, withdrawals, and utilization. In countries where credit card usage is not widespread, I have used ratios of changes in ATM withdrawals, cash withdrawals, and activities in savings and checking accounts to predict financial distress. In the retail business, companies have used changes to shopping behavior in terms of the types of stores customers shop at to what you actually purchase to predict credit risk.[1]

■ *Future availability.* Ensure that any data item being considered for scorecard development will be collected in the future. In addition, ensure that the definitions of these data items will also be consistent—for both internal and bureau-based variables. When definitions change after implementation, scorecard stability as well as its predictive performance may be impacted.

- *Changes in competitive environment.* Characteristics that may not be considered strong today may be strong predictors in the future due to industry trends such as higher credit lines or new products.

It is now known that the scorecard will be developed based on data up to two to three years old and is expected to be in use for approximately the next two years. Past and expected future trends should therefore also be considered at this time. One way to do this is to consult with credit bureaus on how information has changed over the past two to three years—for example, whether indicators like balance, number of trades, utilization, credit lines, and time at bureau changed significantly over the past few years and if they are trending upward or downward. While this will not change development data, it can be used to manage expectations and design appropriate strategies. For example, an increase in competition will increase the average number of inquiries an applicant has at the bureau. Scorecards developed with historical data will treat those with, for example, over four inquiries in 12 months as high risk, based on historical performance. However, new data may suggest that having four inquiries is now associated with normal, medium-risk performance. Consequently, one has the option of either changing the score allocation for inquiries artificially, or adjusting the cutoff in recognition of these changes in trend. At the least, this creates an awareness of this issue that can then be addressed rather than ignored.

One area that is currently generating significant buzz is the use of alternate data sources for credit scoring. These generally include two main sources: payment data from products not traditionally reported to credit bureaus such as utility and cell phone bills, and social media data from sources such as LinkedIn, Facebook, and Twitter.[2] There are several reasons why institutions are looking at these, including:

- The continuous effort to create better scorecards through usage of new and innovative data sources.
- Searching for ways to market credit products to the unbanked population,[3] those who are not in the traditional credit cycle,

and those who do not have credit bureau records ("no hits") such as new immigrants.

- The absence of a centralized credit bureau in many countries.

In most countries where there are credit bureaus present, banks tend to use that data since it is considered very reliable and directly related to credit behavior. The incentive in such countries to use social media data is somewhat less. Between the different types of alternate data sources mentioned earlier, payment data from utility bills, for example, is the better option. While recognizing that the amount values are low, proof of regular ongoing fixed payments is a good indication of character and responsible behavior in making sure monthly obligations are met. These customers may well be suited for low-exposure products such as credit cards. Additionally, banks may choose to exercise conservatism by establishing lower-than-normal starting credit limits for them. This can be a good way to bring additional customers into the traditional credit cycle and establish future loyal clients.

Social media data, however, needs to be approached with some caution. There are several factors that should be causes for concern when dealing with such data. Recognizing that there is a shortage of regulations around usage of such data for credit, the conditions specified in the points below may change in the future.

- *Privacy laws/public opinion.* In many jurisdictions, usage of such data may run afoul of privacy laws. In addition, usage of personal domain areas such as Facebook posts may also create negative public opinion for the bank using such data to lend money. Again, these can change in the future, both in the development of regulations and greater public acceptance of such actions. Much will depend on convincing the public that such data is indeed relevant and necessary for credit lending decisions, and not merely coincidental.

- *Reputational risk.* While credit bureau data, based on credit repayment behavior, is widely accepted as a legitimate source of information for a bank to use for credit decisions, social media is not (as yet). A bank that chooses to use such data may be exposing itself to reputational risk. How this plays out in the future is largely dependent on the first point, dealing with public opinion.

- *Dubious causality.* The Internet is littered with examples of dubious correlations. A strong chi-square, for example, does not necessarily imply causation. While information such as "using 'wasted' in your Facebook post may imply higher credit risk"[4] makes for interesting Internet memes, the causality behind such things is somewhat dubious. The decision to lend money to someone needs to be based on far more robust and explainable measures of creditworthiness than your tweets or Facebook posts.

- *Reliability.* Perhaps the most important factor when considering social media data is its reliability. What makes credit bureau data so valuable is that it is reliable. Social media profiles, however, are self-created and not often reflective of reality. In addition, knowledge of credit scoring among the general population is growing, and with it the chances of borrowers adjusting their online profiles to game the system. For example, evidence of continuous employment on LinkedIn[5] and "likes"/"follows" for universities and financial press may indicate a better credit risk, and some commercial lenders use online ratings for businesses as an indicator of how well the business is run. There is nothing stopping someone from arbitrarily following or liking such things, or creating artificial reviews, merely to try to boost their chances of getting a loan (although using information such as how long the profile has been up can mitigate some of this). Such information should be treated as any other self-reported data that is not confirmed by the bank. In most cases, educational background, social circle, and reading interests are generally correlated to employment and income — both of which can be confirmed by a lender.

The preceding exercise is not meant to deter experimentation. On the contrary, it encourages thoughtful creativity with the data, with results that can be explained. For example, the idea of using variables such as "Average Fast Food Purchase Last Month/Average Last 12 Months" and similar measures for purchases of organic food, gym memberships, and at designer stores was inspired by the concept behind fraud models, that is, abnormal short-term behavior. Now that the concept is established, we can then design variables where changes from long-run averages may indicate financial distress, such as greater purchases in cheaper stores, purchasing more store-brand goods, or lower weekly withdrawals from the ATM. Depending on the regulations and privacy laws in different countries, you may also want to include psychometric data.[6] Such behavior data is limited to credit and debit card usage, and checking and savings account activities, and is an excellent leading indicator of financial distress. Behavior data for term loans such as mortgages is somewhat limited, which is why many analysts use data from other products to build behavior scorecards for term loan products.

The breadth of issues covered in this task of choosing characteristics again underscores the need for scorecard developers to cooperate and consult with other members of the project team. At the end of this phase, analysts will have a list of variables with which they will start the scorecard development process.

SAMPLING

There are two tasks that require sampling in scorecard development, namely, splitting the total sample into development and validation data sets, and deciding the proportion of goods, bads, and rejects to include in the total samples. There are numerous studies on the topic of sampling, with very few providing conclusive answers. As such, sampling in financial institutions in particular is mostly dictated by the model validation units as a policy, or driven by the preferences of the model development manager.

Development/Validation

There are various ways to split the development (sample on which the scorecard is developed) and validation ("hold") data sets. Normally, 70 to 80 percent of the sample is used to develop each scorecard; the remaining 20 to 30 percent is set aside and then used to independently test or validate the scorecard. Where sample sizes are small, the scorecard can be developed using 100 percent of the sample and validated using several randomly selected samples of 50 to 80 percent each. While this is not ideal, it's a reasonable compromise when dealing with small data sets.

Good/Bad/Reject

As mentioned earlier, typically about a minimum of 2,000 each of goods, bads, and rejects are sufficient for scorecard development (and there is no upper limit — using more data usually gets you better results). That ratio indicates a 50 percent bad rate (considering only the goods and bads), which usually does not represent reality. This method is called oversampling and is used in the industry, especially when modeling rare events such as fraud and bankruptcy. Adjustments for oversampling (to be covered later in this chapter) are later applied to get realistic forecasts.

A more recent trend, especially with larger banks, is to use either proportional sampling or full data sets (i.e., all their data). This has been helped by the availability of powerful machines that can perform modeling on millions and, in some cases, billions of records. Proportional sampling can still be used, as long as there are enough individual cases of goods and bads for statistical validity (minimum 2,000 to 5,000 of each). Using proportional sampling, for example, in a portfolio with a 4 percent bad rate, one would need a development sample that has a 4 percent distribution of bads, for example, 4,000 bads and 96,000 goods; and if the approval rate is 50 percent, then you would add another 100,000 rejects to this sample. There is no need to adjust this data set to prior probabilities, since the sample already reflects actual proportions. An added benefit of using a larger samples is that it reduces the impact of multicollinearity and makes the result of logistic regression statistically significant.[7]

There are also various other statistical techniques available to determine optimal sample sizes based on the number of characteristics under consideration and the variability of these characteristics.

It must, however, be kept in mind that the numbers stated above are minimum sample sizes. As there are many competing theories on sampling, users should follow the sampling method they feel most comfortable with, as long as the sample sizes are sufficient to ensure satisfactory statistical and business results. Where grouped characteristic scorecards are being developed (as is detailed in this book), the end objective of any sampling method used should be that each group has a sufficient number of goods and bads to make the analysis meaningful. This includes the calculation of weight of evidence (WOE) for individual groups as well as establishing the WOE trend across attributes. It should also be noted that sample sizes, in addition to being related to statistical significance, also affect business confidence. For example, building a scorecard for a portfolio segment with 1 million customers with 5,000 goods and 5,000 bads will likely not give management a sense of comfort around representativeness. It is for this reason that, in many banks that I know of, scorecards are built on anything from 50 to 75 percent of the total population (if not using the entire sample). These numbers typically come from the model validation or vetting groups.

DEVELOPMENT DATA COLLECTION AND CONSTRUCTION

Based on the development sample specification, all required application (or account data for behavioral scorecards) and performance data is collated from the different sources (e.g., internal databases, credit bureaus, claims repositories, real estate databases). If some of the required data is kept in nonelectronic format, it may need to be keyed in. The end result of this exercise is a data set that contains selected independent variables (characteristics) and a target variable (good/bad indicator). As with preparing for other modeling exercises, the following points are worth noting.

Random and Representative

The selection of applications and accounts must be random and representative of the segment for which the scorecard is to be developed (i.e., representative of the population that will be scored in the future) and must exclude the specified account types. A data set skewed to a certain campaign, channel, region, or age group may not be effective for the overall applicant population, as it may penalize others or make them seem a lesser relative risk.

Nonsegmented Data Set

For projects where more than one scorecard is being developed, a separate data set should to be constructed for every segment, as well as one that is nonsegmented, that is, one that represents the total population. The nonsegmented data set is used for analysis to measure any additional "lift," or advantage, provided by segmented scorecards, such as that shown in Exhibit 6.16.

Data Quirks

When gathering this data, the user needs to be aware of historical changes to the databases, especially in the time period during and after the sample window. Most analysts who have dealt with data in financial institutions are painfully aware of situations where formats or data collection has changed—for example, the code for write-off changed from "W" to "C"; housing status was collected at field 32 until December, and is now at field 22; "other cards" is no longer collected, since last March; occupation codes grouping was changed four months ago, and so forth. Awareness of such changes ensures that the code or queries written to build the sample actually get the data as specified and ensures "no surprises."

In most organizations, such data quirks are not documented. Unless these quirks are taken care of via automated ETL programs, this leaves data miners at the mercy of their own memory or the collective memories of those who have worked at the organization for a length of time. Clearly, such situations are neither sustainable nor efficient. Ideally, every database in the organizations should have an associated *Data Change Log*, which documents all changes to the database since inception. Changes such as those listed in the previous paragraph can then no longer be surprises, since everyone working with databases has access to known data quirks. This knowledge of internal data, both its quirks and biases caused by judgment and policy rules, is the main reason why scorecards developed internally at banks are better than those developed by external parties. The data itself, and intelligent interpretation of it, is what makes a great scorecard. In recent times, however, most banks have undertaken data warehousing and risk data mart projects where data cleansing is taken care of in an automated fashion. Such data issues have been reduced somewhat, but are still the biggest challenge most banks face in analytics.

ADJUSTING FOR PRIOR PROBABILITIES

Oversampling has been a prevalent practice for many years for predictive modeling exercises (and especially when modeling rare events), and refers to cases where the proportion of good and bad cases in the development sample is different from that in the actual population. Oversampling is also known as separate, biased, choice-based, stratified, or outcome-dependent sampling.

In such cases, the development sample will need to be adjusted for prior probabilities. This method, also known as *factoring*, is used to statistically adjust the development sample case counts such that the sample bad rate (and approval rate) reflects the actual population bad rate. This is useful both in the development process and when generating management reports for scorecards, such as the gains chart. Adjusting for oversampling produces realistic forecasts and gives insights into account performance during attribute groupings—thus providing a valuable business advantage, as well as statistical benefits. Adjustments for oversampling are also necessary for generating true model validation and strength statistics such as the Kolmogorov-Smirnov, c-statistic, Gini, and so forth.

The adjustment is therefore useful when forecasts need to be produced. It is not necessary if the objective of the modeling exercise is to investigate relationships between variables and a target, or where only the rank-ordering of scores is required (i.e., where a higher score is needed to denote lower risk, but not necessarily a specific bad rate). It is safe to assume that for most credit scorecard development, this adjustment will be required. Credit scoring is used to reach realistic decisions, to make very specific calculations, and to set cutoffs, and it therefore requires relationships between score and bad rates to be known. Note again that if proportional samples are used, these adjustments are not necessary.

Exhibit 8.1 Adjusting an Equal Sample to Simulate a 10,000 Through-the-Door Population

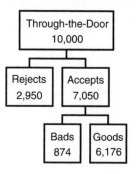

For example, if the development sample consists of 2,000 each of goods, bads, and rejects, the sample bad rate and approval rate would be 50 percent and 67 percent. Assuming the actual approval rate is 70.5 percent and actual population bad rate is 12.4 percent, the sample factored to a 10,000 "through-the-door" population is shown in Exhibit 8.1.

While adjusting for oversampling can be done before or after the model is fitted, when developing grouped variable scorecards, it is beneficial to do so before the grouping exercise. This is so that the relationships between variables and the target can be assessed better—a realistic distribution of bad rate and approval rate by attribute can provide information on whether policy rules or other manual intervention have artificially affected performance (e.g., if a known negative attribute has a low approval rate, and a low bad rate, or if a known positive attribute has a high bad rate). It also provides a sanity check for any groupings done, to ensure that each group has a distinct enough performance.

There are two main methods for adjusting for oversampling: using an offset and using sampling weights.

Offset Method

The standard logit function used in regression for joint sampling is:

$$\text{Logit } (p_i) = \beta_0 + \beta_1 x_1 + \ldots + \beta_k x_k$$

Where p_i, β_k, and x_k are the posterior probability, regression coefficients, and variables, respectively.

When oversampling, the logits are shifted by an *offset*, $ln\ (\rho_1\pi_0\ /\ \rho_0\pi_1)$, and the new logit function (the pseudomodel) becomes:

$$\text{Logit } (p*_i) = ln\ (\rho_1\pi_0\ /\ \rho_0\pi_1) + \beta_0 + \beta_1 x_1 + \ldots + \beta_k x_k$$

Where ρ_1 and ρ_0 are proportion of target classes in the development sample, and π_1 and π_0 are proportion of target classes in the actual population.[8]

The above is for adjustment before the model is fitted. The adjusted posterior probability can similarly be calculated after fitting the model, by using:

$$p^\wedge_1 = \frac{(p^\wedge *_i\ \rho_0\pi_1)}{\left[(1 - p^\wedge *_i)\rho_1\pi_0 + p^\wedge *_i\ \rho_0\pi_1\right]}$$

Where $p^\wedge *_i$ is the unadjusted estimate of posterior probability.

Both of these adjustments can be done in SAS Enterprise Miner using the prior probabilities vector, or alternatively in the SAS PROC LOGISTIC step using an offset option,[9] as shown in Exhibit 8.2. Note that in both cases, the "offset calc" is $ln\ (\rho_1\pi_0\ /\ \rho_0\pi_1)$.

Exhibit 8.2 SAS Code to Adjust for Oversampling Using the Offset Method

Premodel Adjustment	Postmodel Adjustment
Data develop;	Proc logistic data=develop …;
Set develop;	Run;
Off=(offset calc);	Proc score … out=scored…;
Run;	Run;
Proc logistic data=develop …;	Data scored; set scored;
Model ins=……/ **offset=off;**	**Off = (offset calc);**
Run;	**p=1 / (1+exp(-(ins-off)));**
Proc score ….;	Run;
p=1 / (1+exp(-ins));	Proc print data=scored …;
Proc print;	Var p ……;
Var p ….;	Run;
Run;	

Sampling Weights

In adjusting for oversampling using sampling weights, each case is multiplied by a set weight to make the sample reflect true population. The weights in this case are $\rho_1\pi_1$ and $\rho_0\pi_0$ for target classes 1 and 0, respectively.

Alternatively, the weight of each bad can be set at 1, and the weight of each good then set at $p(\text{good})/p(\text{bad})$, where $p(\text{good})$ and $p(\text{bad})$ are the probabilities of goods and bads in the actual population. For example, if the bad rate—that is, $p(\text{bad})$—of a portfolio is 4 percent, and the development sample contains 2,000 goods and 2,000 bads, the adjusted sample will show 2,000 bads and 48,000 (i.e., 0.96/0.04 * 2000) goods.

This method can be applied by using the "sampwt" option in SAS programming or a frequency variable in SAS Enterprise Miner. An example using SAS programming is shown in Exhibit 8.3.[10]

It should be noted that the resulting regression parameter estimates will be different when using the above two adjustment methods.

In general, when the linear-logistic model is correctly specified, the offset method is considered superior. When the logistic model is an approximation of some nonlinear model, then weights are better.[11] Statisticians prefer to use the offset method when developing ungrouped variable predictive models. In the case of grouped variable, points-based scorecards, however, the weight method is better, as it corrects the parameter estimates used to derive scores, instead of merely correcting the predicted probabilities. The normalization that occurs when sampling weights are used also causes less distortion in p-values and standard errors.

Exhibit 8.3 SAS Code to Adjust for Oversampling Using the Weights Method

```
Data develop;
Set develop;
sampwt=(π₀/ρ₀)* (ins=0) + (π₁/ρ₁)* (ins=1);
Run;

Proc logistic data=develop ...;
Weight=sampwt;
Model ins=.......;

Run;
```

NOTES

1. www.creditcards.com/credit-card-news/how-shopping-can-affect-credit-1282.php

2. www.forbes.com/sites/moneybuilder/2015/10/23/your-social-media-posts-may-soon-affect-your-credit-score-2/#1ade9f3a3207

3. "Using Data Mining Technology to Identify and Prioritize Emerging Opportunities for Mortgage Lending to Homeownership-Deficient Communities." SAS White Paper, SAS Institute, 2001.

4. https://next.ft.com/content/d6daedee-706a-11e5-9b9e-690fdae72044

5. www.huffingtonpost.com/aryea-aranoff/could-your-linkedin-profile-be-your-new-credit-score_b_7313454.html

6. R. Anderson, "Psychometrics: A New Tool for Small Business Lending," Paper presented at Credit Scoring and Control XII conference, Edinburgh, Scotland, August 24–26, 2011.

7. C. H. Achen, *Interpreting and Using Regression* (Beverly Hills, CA: Sage, 1982).

8. A. J. Scott and C. J. Wild, "Fitting Regression Models to Case-Control Data by Maximum Likelihood," *Biometrika* 84 (1997): 57–71.

9. W. J. E. Potts and M. J. Patetta, *Predictive Modeling Using Logistic Regression: Course Notes* (Cary, NC: SAS Institute, 2001).

10. Ibid.

11. A. J. Scott and C. J. Wild, "Fitting Logistic Regression Models under Case-Control or Choice Based Sampling," *Journal of the Royal Statistical Society. Series B* (Methodological), 48, no. 2 (1986): 170–182.

## CHAPTER 9

Big Data: Emerging Technology for Today's Credit Analyst

By Billie Anderson

THE FOUR V'S OF BIG DATA FOR CREDIT SCORING

It has been estimated that 2.5 quintillion bytes of data are generated each day.[1] An interesting way to visualize this much data is to imagine this: this amount of data would fill 10 million Blu-ray discs, which, stacked, would equal the height of four Eiffel Towers arranged on top of each other.[2] These astonishing amounts of data are often referred to as *big data*. For this chapter, big data will mean data sets that are too large for traditional data-processing hardware and software to handle, and that require new technology. Generally, when describing big data, the definition includes data that is structured, semistructured, and unstructured.

The earliest use of large data sets does not differ substantially from how big data is being used today. What has changed is that computers have become more powerful, computing resources have drastically dropped in price, many different sources of data are now available, and several big data technologies exist that allow for efficiently managing and extracting information from large data sets.

The financial and credit scoring industries are no strangers to big data. These sectors have been accustomed to big data ever since credit bureaus first started gathering consumer credit information a few decades ago. The ability of a financial institution to use all of the data, whether structured or semistructured, is crucial in the age of big data analytics. Using data to make decisions that span across the entire financial institution can make that institution more efficient, and drive an increase in revenue by, for example, better selecting which applicants to accept or reject for a credit loan.

There are four V's that characterize big data. These four V's are discussed below in the context of credit scoring.

Volume

Massive amounts of data can strain a traditional data storage system. Unless action is taken to deal with this issue, it will cause performance bottlenecks as financial institutions that perform credit scoring collect increasingly massive amounts of data. There are now multiple ways of analyzing consumer behavior and preferences through data sources such as electronic payment systems, online banking, and the usage of credit and debit cards. What is a bank to do with all of this data? According to Peter Graves, CIO of the Independent Bank in Ionia, Michigan, the volume of financial data generated can enable a bank to understand customers better, which will lead to an increase in profits. He states:

> This would be to understand [customer] buying habits. In banking, it might be what products they have, how often they change banks, how often they refinance their mortgage. It's taking every aspect digitally of that relationship. It may not just be what they have with you; it may be their entire financial picture. Then you can try to make sense of that and match products and services in an efficient way that meets their needs.[3]

Velocity

The velocity aspect of big data refers to the rate at which data is being collected, and the speed at which that data can be collected, stored and analyzed. The data generated by increasingly powerful computers, such as online processing engines, is produced at a faster speed than the more traditional data-collection techniques. For example, in the past, it would take several weeks for a bank's direct marketing team to extract the appropriate information from a large data warehouse and determine who should be targeted for a credit card offer. With the rise of dynamic databases that are updated on a daily, sometimes minute-by-minute basis, a marketer can now select which credit applicants they want to send personalized offers to in a matter of milliseconds.[4]

For example, US Bank is using the velocity of big data sources to help detect customer leads. If US Bank detects that a customer has been searching on their web site, the bank can determine how deep the level of engagement was and how long the visitor stayed on their web site. Using a cloud-based solution, US Bank can ascertain how many pages deep into the web site the visitor viewed, if any tools were used, and where the drop-off point occurred.

Once potential customer leads are captured, using a unique customer ID, they are first flagged as an already existing customer (or not). The data is cleansed per the bank's privacy policy, and then prioritized using a predictive model. The models are built using predictors such as the level of visitor engagement, the quality and temperature of the lead, and the product and customer value to the bank.

The bank then uses this information to prioritize customer contact. For example, if a Web visitor shops for a checking account at 8 P.M. and the call center opens the next morning, that customer lead has cooled off. However, if the Web session took place at 8 A.M., it is ranked much higher and is given priority for follow-up and further customer engagement.[5]

Another aspect of the velocity of big data sources is the ability to build predictive models at a much more rapid speed, and use much more data than before big data sources were available. Banks have long used models to predict the probability of default of potential loan applicants. Predictive modeling traditionally uses statistical techniques on sampled historical data to predict what is going to happen next (default/nondefault). With the big data storage and powerful analytical software that is now available, traditional methodologies to build predictive models may not be as relevant as compared to previous years, where powerful computers were not available to analyze billions of records very quickly. As compared to previous years, where sampling was the norm, with big data sources, the bank can now access and model the entire population of applicants or accounts. Building models with all available data provides better insights into predicted default rates and reduces the cycle time of obtaining the results of the predictive models (reducing the cycle time is discussed in more detail later in the chapter).

Variety

Traditional databases are well formatted and tend to change their content slowly. The more modern data repositories need to deal with both today's rapid speed of data collection, as well as its greater variety. In the past few years, banking data sources have undergone a tremendous change.[6] Banking data is currently being captured in both structured and unstructured formats. Banking data in the form of unstructured data can include information from sources such as mobile banking applications, telecommunications sources, social media data such as a credit applicant's connections on LinkedIn, clickstream data (data that allows banks to view the path a potential applicant follows on a web site), application programming interfaces (APIs) via the cloud, and voice response logs. The big data phenomenon has made a larger pool of data sources available for credit analysts to search in order to retrieve information regarding a potential credit applicant. This increase in the variety of data sources allows banks to get a more detailed view of the person, compared to the more traditional data sources such as credit bureau.

Unstructured data sources such as social media data can, for example, verify not only that the applicant really exists, but what types of social connections the applicant has, aspects of the applicant's personality, and whether the applicant is deserving of a loan.[7]

One financial lending institution that is capitalizing on the different varieties of data sources that are now available is Atlanta-based Kabbage. Small businesses seeking loans grant Kabbage access to either an Amazon, e-Bay, PayPal, Square, or QuickBooks account in order to obtain real-time access to a business's customer transaction data. Specifically, they grant Kabbage access to one of these APIs for the credit-making decision.

In addition, Kabbage also examines Facebook and Twitter data from the small business applicants. For example, Kabbage looks at what the small business applicant's customers are saying about them on social media. In making the credit-granting decision, Kabbage would consider information such as whether the business gets a lot of likes on Facebook, the sentiment of online customer reviews that are posted on sites like Facebook and Twitter, and how the business responds to and treats customers on social media sites. Kabbage does admit that just because a business has a lot of likes does not guarantee that it is a good credit risk for a loan, but a glimpse into the social media activity of a business does provide business credibility and a more complete picture of the small business loan applicant.[8] As noted elsewhere in this book, the issue of data reliability is not unique to business applicants when it comes to social media data.

Value

For businesses that loan money, *value* means making money. Lending institutions can generate value from big data sources in several ways. First, the financial institution needs to ensure that it can develop metrics to assess the value being generated from using big data sources.[9] Another way in which value has been derived from using big data sources is from reducing operational costs. For example, the speed at which data can be processed can reduce such costs. Bean cites one example of a bank's investment in big data software and hardware that allowed the bank to process seven years of customer transactional data in the same amount of time that it previously took to process a year's worth of data.[10] Processing and analyzing data faster can lead to quicker, more frequent decisions, which can lead to substantial return on investment (ROI).

Additionally, value can be derived from the use of more diverse data sources. In 2014, the Bank of England hosted an event named "Big Data and the Central Banks." Bholat[11] reports on this event and provides an example of a mortgage loan company deriving value from using a variety of different big data sources. The loan company used proprietary, open source as well as purchased data sources. The combined data set contained up-to-date information on property prices and applicant's credit scores from credit rating agencies. The report noted that the value of this combined data set was greater than the sum of its individual parts. At the same time, because each part had been collected by an organization with a comparative advantage in its provision, the speaker claimed that a cost–benefit ratio had been optimized.

Banks and other lending institutions can derive value from big data and use big data sources to remain competitive. Some of the initiatives that can help are:

- *Eliminate data silos.* Data must be pooled from across all departments in order to benefit the entire organization. Personal deposit accounts are often in different silos than borrowing accounts, which are both separated from mortgage and credit card data. Transactional information needs to be linked with conversations at call centers and e-mail requests to assist in increasing customer engagement, cross-selling of products, or retention initiatives. In addition, as has been noted in this book, the use of information from other existing products can help in generating better credit risk models as well.

- *Start simple.* Create a clearly defined small pilot project that is governed by a business manager. The manager needs to obtain "buy-in" from a cross-functional team of members such as information technology (IT), credit analysts (may be a data scientist), and any other stakeholders. Following are some suggestions on how to implement a big data pilot project.

  - Define the big data sources that will be used and make sure the data is accessible.

  - Incorporate the organization's data privacy and security policies.

  - Determine the objectives of the exercise, and measurable results.

  - Limit the length of the pilot to a very short window of time.

  - The pilot project should not require a substantial investment in time or money.

  - Determine if the big data analysis is repeatable and whether the analysis could be used within other parts of the organization.

  - Quantitatively measure the success of the pilot. For example, it is common practice for many banks to model loan default via regression models using predictor variables that are found in structured data sources. Many times, these models are assessed using a metric such as the area under the Receiver Operating Characteristic curve (AUC).[12] Credit scoring start-ups such as ZestFinance, rely solely on unstructured data sources to grant loans—the bank could try and replicate this for its portfolios, and measure the improvements. One interesting fact is that ZestFinance found that applicants who fill out their loan application using all capital letters are more risky than applicants that do not.[13] Note that this in itself is not conclusive evidence that people who use capital letters are riskier—further evidence is needed to establish causality. A binary indicator variable could be created to indicate whether an applicant filled out the credit application using all capital letters or not and feed the binary variable into the predictive model. Determine if the incorporation of the binary variable increases the AUC of the model.

- If the pilot project does fail, fail fast and discard any big data sources that were not important in adding value to the project.

  A big data pilot project needs to be backed up by a well-defined data strategy and a data governance model. The pilot needs to go beyond traditional uses of an IT department and demonstrate that using big data sources can impact the bottom line of the entire organization.

- *Realize that it takes time to properly analyze big data sources.* Big data sources are not the simple Excel and Access-type spreadsheets of yesteryear. Big data sources are extremely messy and dirty and will require many hours to clean, merge, and organize before the analyzing can even take place. Analyzing big data sources is not as simple as computing descriptive statistics or building simpler predictive models such as regression models or decision trees. Analyzing big data sources involves "data discovery" far more than traditional methods and volumes of data. The idea of using data as a discovery tool is a nontraditional data analytics approach, especially for traditional businesses like banking.[14] Analyzing big data requires time to discover patterns, events, and customer opportunities.

- *Recruit highly trained data scientists.* A data scientist has a different persona than a traditionally trained mathematician, statistician, or programmer. A data scientist is someone who does possess the requisite academic knowledge, but they can also effectively communicate the results of big data to the end users, who are usually the decision makers. Big data sources are difficult to collect, store, and interpret. It takes individuals with a very specialized set of skills in order to analyze and interpret big data sources. There is currently a shortage of data scientists, so attractive salaries and benefits have to be offered in order to obtain top talent.

■ *Invest in software and hardware that is needed to properly collect, store, and analyze big data sources.* Surging volumes of data require major upgrades and improvements to traditional databases and analytical software. Hadoop is one emerging big data technology that allows for the storage and query of big data sources. Hadoop has reached some level of acceptance within the financial industry, and many mainstream analytical software products such as SAS can interface with it. The topic of setting up infrastructure for analytics has been covered in some detail in Chapter 3.

Spark, a much newer entrant into the market, is an open source big data processing framework. It has several advantages over Hadoop in that applications can be written in Java or Python (not the complicated MapReduce code that Hadoop requires) so data queries can be completed in a less complicated manner.

One financial firm has used Spark as a layer on top of Hadoop. The firm used the text mining capabilities of Spark to analyze the text of regulatory filings, to look for patterns of changing regulatory requirements, to get a better understanding of what was happening around them.[15]

Davenport[16] has reported that banks use a variety of hardware and software to manage and analyze big data sources. The author cites an example of one bank using four applications: a Hadoop cluster, a Teradata Aster big data appliance, a traditional data warehouse and a heavy duty Teradata enterprise data warehouse. The challenges come in when a bank tries to incorporate the big data hardware and software to work within their existing data management systems. It is not uncommon for data to be stored across multiple data warehouses, which results in the duplication of data. Data integration issues will occur when an organization attempts to incorporate big data hardware sources like Hadoop or Spark into the traditional and existing mainframes and databases. As such, integration of the various hardware and software platforms needs to be thought of fully before embarking on any big data initiatives.

One question for senior management is what to do with existing traditional data storage systems. If the bank has bought into the idea of utilizing big data sources, the data stored in the traditional databases will need to be accessed and streamlined into the new big data sources hardware. This data integration challenge is going to be timely and costly.

In summary, big data initiatives are time and resource intensive. In order to generate value from big data sources, banks need to gravitate toward a model where analytics derived from big data sources is an organization-wide priority; everyone from branch manager to the CEO needs to use data in their daily decision making.

CREDIT SCORING AND THE DATA COLLECTION PROCESS

Traditionally, the data used by financial institutions to determine a credit score included items such as the applicant's income, length of current employment, time at residence, home ownership status, payment history on other types of credit lines, and the type of credit lines held by the applicant (e.g., retail accounts, installment loans, mortgage loans, and finance company accounts). These types of data items can be stored in columns in a database, and are called *structured data.* Other traditional sources of data frequently used are bureau scores (e.g., FICO score in the United States) and credit bureau information. Information obtained from the credit bureau can provide the financial institution with a broader view of the applicant's background than other data sources, such as the bank's own customer data. For example, credit bureau data can provide information on whether an applicant has ever been arrested or filed for divorce.

In jurisdictions with legal restrictions on the types of information that can be used to grant credit, structured data makes it convenient to filter out legally suspect variables such as gender, race, and nationality of a credit applicant. However, in the era of big data and access to unstructured data sources, it is relatively easy for the algorithms that comb through these big data sources to detect such items as race, gender, or geographic location, even if such results are not intended. For example, it would not be difficult for a machine learning algorithm to use the ratio of vowels to consonants in an applicant's name to predict race. Telecommunications data may not directly have access to an applicant's address, but every time an applicant drives by a cell tower the location is tracked, so it would not take much effort to determine where an applicant lives and works. Note that in the United States, geographical variables such as postal code of the applicant are legally suspect for credit scoring as they may cause the bank to be in contravention of fair banking laws.

CREDIT SCORING IN THE ERA OF BIG DATA

A major shift that may significantly change traditional credit scoring is the ability of many financial institutions to access unstructured big data sources. In addition, given the increased interest of banks globally in such data sources, the question is not of when, but of how banks will use the unstructured data to assist existing credit scoring processes. At the present time, however, we recognize that the use of such data sources globally is far from widespread.

There are a few start-up companies that are trying to capitalize on unstructured data and using it to determine a credit applicant's score. Of the many new companies that now exist in this space, Lenddo, established in 2011, is one of the more established ones. The co-founders of Lenddo realized that more than one billion people in developing countries were starting to move into the middle class and would need access to credit.[17] Lenddo's plan was to offer small, targeted loans to individuals in developing countries who lack credit histories, simply because no financial infrastructure, such as credit bureaus, exist for them to establish credit history. The purpose of the loans was to give that rising middle class access to credit to enrich their life through education, health care, or home improvement. These loans could work well, for example, for an individual who wants to take a career-development class, but lacks cash and cannot qualify for a traditional loan due to a lack of credit history. The applicant can leverage what he or she does have—a connected network of online friends and colleagues.

Lenddo uses only social media data to compute credit scores and determine the creditworthiness of applicants. To apply for a loan, the individual connects to social networks and invites friends and family to be part of what Lenddo calls the "trusted network." Lenddo then uses a social network algorithm to evaluate the "trusted network" and develop a Lenddo score, which is similar to a traditional ranked-order credit score. If the applicant is granted a loan, her entire social network is kept informed of her payment history.[18] Such public disclosure of what has traditionally been private information does bring up privacy and ethical issues, which have been dealt with in other chapters in this book.

Such access to social media big data has not only helped individuals in developing countries, it may also to help a large segment of U.S. individuals who can now access credit and become potential credit applicants. Currently, 30 to 50 million U.S. consumers are not able to access credit due to their thin or nonexistent credit history; 10 million of these consumers turn out to have credit scores over 600 (for reference, a FICO score of below 600 is considered unacceptable, 600 to 649 a poor score, while anything above 680 is considered good) when nontraditional forms of credit data are used to determine their scores.[19] Established companies like FICO, Experian, TransUnion, and Mastercard have started to partner with companies such as Yodlee and VisualDNA to obtain alternative data such as utility bills and rental payments, and to investigate incorporating them into traditional credit scores.

At present, while the traditional banking world has started to use big data technologies, it remains wary of social media data for credit scoring. However, the interest level in such data remains high, and there is evidence that the traditional credit scoring players are slowly adapting such data, in particular, in countries without credit bureaus and with relatively weak privacy laws.

For example, in a recent profile of First Tennessee Bank, a regional midsized U.S. bank, the CFO discusses the need for more big data incorporation in their credit scoring process. Keenan[20] also reports a survey of 165 retail banks in 2014, in which the banks were asked how important each of the following technologies are in delivering the top retail banking priorities. Exhibit 9.1 summarizes the results.

Exhibit 9.1 Top Retail Banking Priorities and Their Importance

Priority	Percentage
Digital banking channel development	84%
Omni-channel delivery	78%
Customer analytics	72%
Branch channel transformation	56%
Predictive analytics	52%
Business process management	21%
Social media integration	27%
Core system replacement	15%

Thus, the survey results show that almost 30 percent of retail banks are now reporting that integration of big data through social media sources is a priority. The results of this survey demonstrate the growing impact of big data in current banking practices.

Software and hardware companies are working to bring to market solutions that will allow financial institutions to make better decisions and increase profits in a big data world.[21] In a recent survey, 36 percent of bankers said they were looking to sign new contracts with providers of analytical services.[22] Given the many resources including analytical software and hardware now available to house and retrieve the plethora of data that banks can access, the promise and potential of big data for banking will be significant.

The Promise of Big Data for Banks

In an era where there is no shortage of information, the bank with the most actionable insights is the winner. The age of big data has begun to slowly filter through into the banking environment.

There are several ways in which banks can derive value from big data. Having access to multiple sources of data, beyond the traditional structured data sources, allows a financial institution to obtain a personal view and an understanding of a credit applicant at a level of granularity never available previously. While traditional data sources have been helpful, big data provides the ability to more deeply understand the credit applicant, thereby allowing credit strategies at a far more personalized level. Being able to understand the credit applicant translates to higher acceptance rates, streamlined infrastructure costs, increased customer satisfaction, and more bank profitability.

Many banks have yet to focus on using big data sources and customer analytics together to enhance the customer experience. Customer analytics has been a traditional area of analytics in banks for a long time, and has the potential to be super-charged in a world of big data sources. As banks get fully immersed into the digital age with millennials and other tech-savvy new customers, it is now more important than ever to have a one-to-one relationship with such customers. The era of mass communication with banking customers is over. Banking customers want immediate responses to their specific problems (e.g., responses to tweets and social media posts), apps that let them check their balances and apply for credit card increases in a matter of seconds, identify them though selfies, and deposit checks using photos on their smartphones. Banks need to understand what customers are doing on the Internet and on their mobile devices at all times. Big data sources and the associated analytics allow a bank to get to "know" their customers at a very deep level.

Keeping customers happy generates revenue for banks. Groenfeldt[23] reports one European bank, before using big data sources, was only analyzing 5 percent of the total customer complaints via call center logs, e-mails, and texts. By utilizing big data sources, the bank was able to analyze all the complaints, not just a small sampling. By having access to all customer complaints, the bank could determine where on the banking web site customers were having trouble, and then redesign the web site to make it easier for customers to use. The bank was able to reduce complaints by 25 percent. The bank, using big data sources, could also identify customers who had less-than-optimal products, and design cross-sell programs to suggest another product that had more relevant features, and was cheaper. Reacting to customers' needs and wants allowed the bank to not lose customers, which in the long run generates revenue for the bank.

> Merely having access to large data sets, however, is not enough. Banks need a more holistic approach to analytics to take advantage of such data. As covered previously in this book, this data in banks cannot sit in departmental silos. It needs to be integrated across the entire financial institution, from the credit manager to the data scientist. Each of these individuals must understand both the business opportunities and the power of what can be gleaned from the data — and have access to it. Banks will need to extend beyond traditional structured data to include unstructured sources, such as social media sentiment, real-time location services, keyword, semantic analysis of contact center communications and incorporating the "Internet of Things"—the millions of Internet-connected devices that are in the market.[24] Such concepts may well be in their infancy, but they have the potential to change how we grant credit. Again, it should be noted that credit scoring is a highly regulated

business, and the success of such concepts will depend on the regulatory environment as much as the available technology.

The promise of big data to the banking world will come from utilizing all the various big data sources that the bank has available, and can use from a legal and regulatory standpoint. Access and use of the different types of big data sources have completely changed the way a bank uses data to build predictive models. In the past, credit analysts or data scientists would spend time exploring and preparing the data, creating the model and then hand the model off to an outside department, such as IT to deploy them. This process took time and made the business managers wait for results from the analysis.

In the world of big data sources, and the rise of many visual analytics tools and user-friendly big data software interfaces, an individual, with very little data analytics background, can take some data and produce basic reports that are consumable and allows the individual to make a decision using the data almost immediately. One example is Fauquier Bankshares, a midsize bank in Virginia, which uses big data software products to pull data from disparate sources and enables individuals in accounting, finance, and retail support to create their own data reports easily. This helps the bank make better and quicker decisions on simpler tasks, for example, such as whether there are enough branch tellers available on certain days.[25] This empowering of nonanalytical staff then allows the data scientists and credit analysts to work on more complicated analytical tasks.

Population versus Sample in the World of Big Data

One advantage of big data is the ability to use all the available information for any task. Using sampling to detect patterns often loses valuable information in outliers at either end of the curve. One of the main reasons many analysts who work with big data sources do not sample is that they are specifically looking for something odd or extreme. For example, only a few credit card transactions out of millions may be fraudulent. Analysts who are trying to detect fraudulent credit card transactions therefore have a really good reason, and in fact a requirement, to search the entire population of customer transactions. This, of course, leads to the question: is sampling still relevant in the era of big data?

The answer is, it depends on the situation. Just because you can do something does not always mean it is the appropriate thing to do. The question that needs to be asked is whether it makes sense to sample based on the business problem the credit analyst is trying to solve.

If the big data population is the right population to be analyzed for the problem at hand, then you will only employ sampling in few cases, for example, the need to run separate experimental groups for different credit card offers or if the sheer volume of data is too large to capture and process (which should not be an issue with appropriate big data hardware investments).

Statistically speaking, if your sample is sufficiently large and is random, the results of the sample will give you the same answer as if you used the entire population. There is no difference between the results of the sample and the population for most model building and metric calculations. If a credit analyst is not looking for outliers, then from a practical perspective it may make more sense to sample.

One practical reason to support sampling would be that the sample would be easier to work with than the entire population. Any type of data analysis with the amount of data you would have using big data sources is going to be tedious. Instead of using one million (or more) observations, would you rather go through all the data analysis steps using 50,000 observations instead?

ETHICAL CONSIDERATIONS OF CREDIT SCORING IN THE ERA OF BIG DATA

Big data is sexy—it is hip and popular. Banks and financial institutions have only started to explore and understand the benefits and uses of big data for credit scoring purposes. Big data is here to stay, and it is changing the way that the financial industry operates.

As discussed earlier in the chapter, social media data is increasingly used as an alternative to standard credit bureau data, with new scoring methods being created to construct credit ratings for those with thin or poor credit history. Proxies for credit history can be anything from how frequently a person recharges (adds more money in order to continue use) their mobile phone credit, to the number of minutes spent looking at a loan product online. To determine creditworthiness, credit analysts are starting to look at larger trends in the data, comparing the individual to the average and looking for factors that correlate with creditworthiness. For example, on average, people who spend a longer time reading and understanding the terms of a loan online might be more likely to pay the loan on time.

While recognizing that big data is a credit scoring industry game changer, some critical questions need to be addressed. Big data has a great deal of power to transform financial inclusion efforts, but what are its downstream effects? What are the consumer protection and legal implications? Does big data allow for new forms of implicit discrimination? Ultimately, as big data is being used now, is it making life better for consumers?

One "downstream" effect is understanding that big data does a good job of finding correlations, but unstructured big data sources do not perform well at detecting which correlations are meaningful—that is, the causation. The Google flu algorithm is a good example of this scenario. Google developed an algorithm to identify, based on search terms entered into Google search, the parts of the country where the flu was most prevalent. At first, the algorithm showed high accuracy regarding where the flu was occurring, but over time the algorithm failed to detect flu outbreaks. A main reason for the algorithm's failure was that it did not take into account extraneous variables other than the search terms used. For example, if a local news story profiled a county or city with a flu outbreak, that event would prompt individuals to search for flu symptoms, even if the individuals did not have the flu.[26] The Google flu example is a perfect illustration to highlight that unstructured data sources need to be balanced with traditional data sources to ensure the accuracy of the algorithms and predictive models that are developed.

So how does a financial institution balance these new sources of unstructured data that are readily available in a big data world? How does a lender that incorporates social media usage, past bill payments, mobile phone information, and shopping habits and preferences to build better credit scorecards protect the consumer and legal rights of a credit applicant? In order to help financial institutions grapple with this issue, the Federal Trade Commission recently published a report to assist financial institutions with guidance on the ethical concerns of using big data in credit scoring algorithms and predictive models.[27] Following is a summary of some of the report's findings:

- Ensure the data being used to predict an applicant's creditworthiness is representative; that is, take steps to ensure that the data is not missing information on certain populations.

- Take precautions to not include bias in the data. Consider how the data and the algorithms are generated. The methodology used to create data could create bias in the data. For example, if there is a certain type of social media ad that one racial group responds to more than others, this could sway the algorithm to learn to prioritize credit card offers to more individuals of a certain race group over others.

- Incorporate traditional statistical analyses along with big data algorithms. For instance, if a big data algorithm detects that a credit applicant is "risky" based on their social media profile, use traditional predictive modeling with structured data sources and traditional credit scoring data (if available) to double-check the results found from using social media sources.

- Ethical and fairness concerns are major challenges for credit scoring models that incorporate big data. Financial institutions need to think broadly about how they are using big data sources in order to not promote unfairness. Financial institutions need to understand consumer protection laws and how the laws apply to big data.

Potential discriminatory factors that can be introduced into the credit-granting decision need to be considered and avoided when incorporating big data into credit scoring algorithms. U.S. federal regulations do not allow financial institutions to discriminate based on race, gender, or other personal characteristics when determining the creditworthiness of an applicant.[28] However, in this world of abundant unstructured data, the advanced credit scoring algorithms that use big data sources have made it relatively easy for financial institutions to market to and solicit those credit applicants who are perceived as good credit risks. For example, by using social media data, it is fairly simple for algorithms to detect whether an applicant graduated from university or whether they have a high-paying job such as a lawyer or a doctor. Further, a financial lending company could perceive an applicant with a finance or engineering degree who is currently employed at a reputable, well-known company as a better credit risk than someone who studied a less marketable subject and has had many short-term jobs. The financial lending institution could be discriminating against one group of individuals based solely on the results of the social media analysis.

In addition, as noted at the beginning of the chapter, not only can an applicant's social media profile be examined for creditworthiness, the types of social connections an applicant has can play a role in whether an applicant is granted a loan or not. Big data algorithms can assess the degree and strength of a potential applicant's social media connections. This data provides useful information about a consumer's lifestyle, habits, and behaviors, all which can be predictive of repayment of a financial loan.

In order to avoid the potential discriminatory pitfalls when using unstructured data sources, such as social media, to detect creditworthiness, it is important that companies be transparent about how they are using big data sources and communicate the information to potential credit applicants.

So is big data making life better for consumer credit applicants? Two groups of consumers seem likely to benefit the most when a lender incorporates big data sources into their decision: those applicants who have a traditional credit scoring history but have been denied credit for some past mistakes, and those consumers who do not have a credit history. Utilizing nontraditional data sources such as the types of connections on social media, the types of comments a consumer posts to social media that could indicate lifestyle choices, or the records of bill payments, has potential to unlock credit access to millions of applicants who, in the past, would have been denied credit.

As financial institutions move toward incorporating big data sources into their credit scoring process, it is vital that the data is not used to violate any regulations or laws that protect consumers against discrimination. Financial lending institutions need to proceed with caution when using big data sources and take all means necessary to ensure that they are harnessing big data for the public good of the consumer, and not to isolate some groups from accessing credit. For example, if a credit card company detects that consumers who shop at a particular store have a history of late payments, then the company should not lower the credit limit for all customers who shop at the store.

The Rise of "Big Brother" Issues When Using Big Data

For years, credit bureaus and financial institutions have collected and stored a lot of personal information on millions of potential credit applicants as well as borrowers. In parallel with an increase in online social interactions, as well as tasks, there has been a cultural shift in the way that individuals share personal data. As a society, people (credit applicants included) are freer with their personal data than they have ever been. The Internet has made tracking potential credit applicants far easier than ever before. Amazon knows what individuals have historically bought, Google knows search habits, Facebook and Twitter know what is on people's minds with social connections and posts, and smartphone providers know who people talk to and can track every physical movement.

With big data promising valuable insights to banks and other lenders, all signs seem to point to the fact that they will continue to collect, store, and analyze big data sources. The size and scale of data collections will increase by leaps and bounds as storage costs continue to fall and analytic tools become ever more powerful. In the credit scoring world, has big data become Big Brother?

The issue of Big Brother and big data is related to privacy. And for banks, privacy is a larger part of data governance issues. Bank executives need to understand and have policies in place for data ownership, rights, and responsibilities. It is important that executives and those who regularly work with data understand where the data is stored, specifically what it is used for, who can access it, who is responsible for it, and who can use it. They should also have some idea of the privacy and regulatory issues around the use of personal data.

Not knowing where data is located can lead to duplication, which leads to inefficiency and can be costly. If an analyst cannot find data files, a data query has to be performed again. The duplication time is time that the analyst could have spent doing something else. When data cannot be found, storage and manpower costs increase. People have to spend time looking for data and replicating data sources if they cannot find the data they are looking for. Duplicate data also leads to data files becoming out of sync; that is, when data is stored in multiple locations and different people are accessing and modifying the data sources, the data can easily become out of sync. This scenario will lead to data files that will completely diverge.

Big data sources, particularly in the form of unstructured data sources, are more difficult to track than traditional data sources just due to the sheer volume and variety of the data. Many banks have outdated data management tools that cannot track, manage, and provide the appropriate user authorization suitable for big data sources.

Questions about data access and permission are difficult to answer and monitor with traditional IT approaches, especially given the amount of unstructured data that is being created. For example, consider the following scenario:

> One terabyte of data contains 50,000 folders. About 5% (2500) of those folders have unique permissions known as Access Control Lists (ACL). On average, each ACL has an average of four groups.[29]

This scenario becomes more difficult to manage with different data platforms, different user permission structures, and multiple domains. Without automation, an IT specialist would spend hours trying to determine who has access to which specific data sources.

A bank's data governance responsibilities increase when collecting, storing, and analyzing big data sources. The bank must make sure that the information given to them is not misused in any way. The misuse of personal information makes it very difficult for the bank to keep business and remain reputable. It also exposes them to breaches of privacy laws. As with traditional data sources, responsibility must be taken, and appropriate policies and procedures put in place, to protect the information provided by big data sources.

Banks need to strike a balance between becoming Big Brother and having appropriate privacy and security issues put in place to properly use big data sources. Following are some suggestions on how a financial institution can strike this balance.

■ Add data quality checks no matter how big the data is. The old saying "garbage in garbage out" still holds true even when using big data sources. Create a data quality process to ensure that the big data sources you are using reflect the reality of your business decision.

■ Know the appropriate and inappropriate big data sources to use in the credit granting decision. Check the quality of the big data source. Spend time determining whether the big data source being used is reputable and reliable. For example, if there is a regulatory rule that does not permit using a certain type of big data source, be aware of this issue. It's better to spend more time during this phase than to regret any type of misinformation and resulting incorrect credit approval/denial decision.

CONCLUSION

The viability of using big data sources to assess an applicant's creditworthiness will need to be assessed over the long term. The financial lending industry is just on the precipice of the data that is available to be analyzed. There is no question that using big data sources and algorithms can help credit managers make difficult decisions more efficiently and accurately. Big data in the credit scoring arena has the power to improve lives by providing more consumer applicants access to credit. But absent a human touch, its single-minded efficiency can further isolate groups that are already at society's margins. There will always be a need for a credit analyst to examine the results and decisions of the big data credit scoring algorithms and ask the questions:

■ "Does that credit decision make sense?"
■ "Is that credit decision fair and ethical and in accordance with government regulations?"

In a new economic era characterized by networks and databases, the convergence of credit scoring and big data seems logical and natural. With big data, the financial lending industry can quickly acquire useful information from vast resources to support business decisions, and provide more effective precision marketing and risk management to improve business performance and operational efficiency. Yet while big data brings great opportunities, it also presents new challenges and competition, from companies like Lenddo that are making access to credit available to many consumers who previously would not have been able to access credit. Financial players that prepare for the disruptive forces of big data will not only have a better chance for survival but also will be on the leading edge of this new financial market.

NOTES

1. B. Baesens, *Analytics in a Big Data World: The Essential Guide to Data Science and Its Applications* (Hoboken, NJ: Wiley, 2014).
2. B. Walker, "Every Day Big Data Statistics—2.5 Quintillion Bytes of Data Created Daily," April 5, 2015. http://www.vcloudnews.com/every-day-big-data-statistics-2-5-quintillion-bytes-of-data-created-daily/
3. J. Ginovsky, "Big Data at the Bank," *ABA Banking Journal* 104 (2012): 28–32.
4. T. Davenport, P. Barth, and R. Bean, "How 'Big Data' Is Different." *MIT Sloan Management Review* 54 (2012): 22–24.
5. Adobe Systems Incorporated, "Know It All," 2014.
6. S. Lohr, "Banking Start-Ups Adopt New Tools for Lending," *New York Times*, January 18, 2015, p. 1. http://www.nytimes.com/2015/01/19/technology/banking-start-ups-adopt-new-tools-for-lending.html?_r=0
7. Y. Wei, P. Yildirim, C. Van den Bulte, and C. Dellarocas, "Credit Scoring with Social Network Data," *Marketing Science* 35, no. 2 (2015): 234–258.
8. D. Dahl, "The Six-Minute Loan: How Kabbage Is Upending Small Business Lending—and Building a Very Big Business," *Forbes*, May 25, 2015: 56–60.
9. R. Bean, "Just Using Big Data Sources Isn't Enough Anymore," *Harvard Business Review*, February 9, 2016. https://hbr.org/2016/02/just-using-big-data-isnt-enough-anymore
10. Ibid.
11. D. Bholat, "Big Data and Banks," *Big Data & Society*, January–June, 2015: 1–6.
12. N. Siddiqi, *Credit Risk Scorecards: Developing and Implementing Intelligent Credit Scoring* (Hoboken, NJ: Wiley, 2006).
13. J. Lippert, "ZestFinance Issues Small, High-Rate Loans, Uses Big Data to Weed Out Deadbeats. *Washington Post*, October 11, 2014: 1. https://www.washingtonpost.com/business/zestfinance-issues-small-high-rate-loans-uses-big-data-to-weed-out-deadbeats/2014/10/10/e34986b6-4d71-11e4-aa5e-7153e466a02d_story.html
14. T. Davenport, *Big Data at Work: Dispelling the Myths, Uncovering the Opportunities* (Boston, MA: Harvard Business School Publishing, 2014).

15. T. Groenfeldt, "Lenddo Creates Credit Scores Using Social Media," *Forbes,* January 29, 2015. http://www.forbes.com/sites/tomgroenfeldt/2015/01/29/lenddo-creates-credit-scores-using-social-media/2/#196fe40260a1

16. T. Davenport, *Big Data at Work: Dispelling the Myths, Uncovering the Opportunities* (Boston, MA: Harvard Business School Publishing, 2014).

17. J. Groenfeldt, "Banks Turn to 'Spark' Technology to Crunch Big Data, *American Banker,* 2015. http://www.americanbanker.com/news/bank-technology/banks-turn-to-spark-technology-to-crunch-big-data-1076953-1.html?zkPrintable=1&nopagination=1

18. B. Anderson and M. Hardin, "Credit Scoring in the Age of Big Data Analytics and Social Media." *Encyclopedia for Business Analytics and Optimization,* edited by J. Wang (Hershey, PA: IGI Global, 549–557).

19. E. Wolkowitz and S. Parker, *Big Data, Big Potential: Harnessing Data Technology for the Underserved Market* (Chicago, IL: Center for Financial Services Innovation, 2015).

20. C. Keenan, "Big Data and Predictive Analytics: A Big Deal, Indeed," *ABA Banking Journal* 107, no. 4 (2015): 32–34.

21. A. Adams, "Credit Scoring Models Becoming More Agile." *American Banker* 177 (2012): 10–13.

22. K. Broughton, "Teaching Bankers to Be Data Scientists," *American Banker* 179 (2014): 21.

23. T. Groenfeldt, "Lenddo Creates Credit Scores Using Social Media," *Forbes,* January 29, 2015. http://www.forbes.com/sites/tomgroenfeldt/2015/01/29/lenddo-creates-credit-scores-using-social-media/2/#196fe40260a1

24. Federal Trade Commission, *Big Data: A Tool for Inclusion or Exclusion* (Washington, DC: U.S. Government Printing Office, 2016).

25. B. Yurcan, "Why Small Banks Should Be Thinking About Big Data," *American Banker,* November 23, 2015. http://www.americanbanker.com/news/bank-technology/why-small-banks-should-be-thinking-about-big-data-1077955-1.html

26. E. Ramirez, J. Brill, M. K. Ohlhausen, T. McSweeny, and Federal Trade Commission, *Big Data: a Tool for Inclusion or Exclusion?* (Washington, DC: U.S. Government Printing Office, 2016).

27. Ibid.

28. N. Kshetri, "Big Data's Impact on Privacy, Security and Consumer Welfare," *Telecommunications Policy* 38, no. 11 (2014): 1134–1145.

29. Varonis, "10 Insights on Enterprise Data," 2013.

## CHAPTER 10

Scorecard Development Process, Stage 4: Scorecard Development

"The fact that the polynomial is an approximation does not necessarily detract from its usefulness because all models are approximations. **Essentially, all models are wrong but some are useful.** *However, the approximate nature of the model must always be borne in mind."*

—George Box

"All models are right, most are useless."

—Thaddeus Tarpey

Once the development database is constructed, the scorecard developer should have a database that includes a set of characteristics and a target variable. There are various methods that can be used to develop scorecards from this data. All of them involve establishing and quantifying the relationship between the characteristics and good/bad performance (target). Scorecards or models can also be produced in different formats such as SAS code.

This chapter will deal exclusively with model development using grouped attributes and logistic regression. We will also perform reject inference, and the scorecard will have scaled points. The result will be a scorecard that looks like that shown in Exhibit 1.1. This method balances the two key requirements for successful scorecard development: need for sound statistical basis, and a realistic business focus.

Exhibit 10.1 shows the process flow that will be followed using this methodology. Note that this is for an application scorecard; behavior scorecards are developed using the same process flow but without reject inference. For behavior scorecards, therefore, one would perform initial characteristic analysis and then move directly to final scorecard stage.

Exhibit 10.1 Scorecard Development Steps

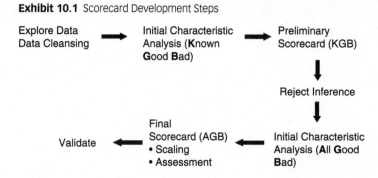

EXPLORE DATA

A good practice before actual modeling work is initiated is to explore the sample data. Simple statistics such as distributions of values, mean/median, proportion missing, and range of values for each characteristic can offer great insight into the business, and reviewing them is a good exercise for checking data integrity. Visual analytics techniques are often excellent for this work. If using samples, sample data distributions should also be compared with overall portfolio distributions to confirm that the sample is representative of the portfolio. Data should also be checked for interpretation (e.g., to ensure that "0" represents zero and not missing values), and to confirm that any special values such as the various special cases of missing bureau data are documented. This step again confirms that the data has been collected as specified, and that all aspects of the data are understood, including data quirks.

MISSING VALUES AND OUTLIERS

Most financial industry data contains missing values, or values that do not make sense for a particular characteristic. These may either be fields that were not captured, were discontinued, were not available, or were not filled out by applicants; miskeyed values; or simply outliers denoting extreme cases.

While some statistical techniques such as decision trees are neutral to missing values, logistic regression requires complete data sets with no missing data (i.e., complete case analysis). There are four main ways to deal with missing values:

1. Exclude all data with missing values—this is complete case analysis, and in most financial industry cases, will likely result in very little data to work with.

2. Exclude characteristics or records that have significant (e.g., more than 50 percent) missing values from the model development, especially if the level of missing is expected to continue in the future.

3. Include characteristics with missing values in the scorecard development process. The "missing" can then be treated as a separate attribute, grouped, and used in regression as an input. The scorecard can then be allowed to assign weights to this attribute. In some cases this assigned weight may be close to the "neutral" or mean value, but in cases where the weight is closer to another attribute, it may shed light on the exact nature of the missing values.

4. Impute missing values using statistical techniques.

While the second option may be more convenient, option 3 offers many benefits, and is the one I normally recommend. Note that we are discussing self-declared missing data, where the reasons for being missing are not known (as opposed to data for which reasons for missing are already known, for example, from the credit bureau). Options 1, 2, and 4 assume that missing data holds no value—that no further information can be gleaned from analyzing the missing data. This is not necessarily true—in the world of credit risk, missing data is generally associated with negative information. They may be part of a trend, linked to other characteristics, or indicative of previous bad performance. Missing values are not usually random. For example, those who are new at their work may be more likely to leave the "Years at Employment" field blank on an application form. If characteristics or records with missing values are excluded, none of these insights can be made. It should be noted that here we are talking about self-declared data that is not overwhelmingly missing. If a field has say 99 percent missing, it would have been dropped in the previous step. For most variables where there is a reasonable number of missing data (up to 25 percent in my experience), analyzing the bad rates or Weight of Evidence (WOE) of the missing, and comparing to other attributes can help point to the types of applicants that are leaving it blank. Therefore, it is recommended that missing data be included in the analysis, and be assigned points in the final scorecard. This method recognizes that missing data holds some information value, and that there is business benefit in including such data in your analysis. In addition, having assigned/calculated points for missing values in the scorecard will facilitate the proper scoring of applicants who leave fields blank in the applications form in the future. In most cases where missing data is excluded, scorecard developers assign a "neutral" score to future missing cases. If the actual performance of missing data is negative, this will reward future applicants for omitting information. At the least, missing data should be analyzed first, and if it is found to be random and performance neutral, it may be excluded or imputed.

In the case where options 1, 2, or 4 are chosen, those observations should be added to the final development database and the scorecard should be recalibrated using all of the data (for completeness). What this means is that while some of the characteristics may be missing, others that are populated can still be used to add value to the scorecard development process.

Some data mining software, such as SAS Enterprise Miner, contain algorithms to impute missing data. Such algorithms include tree-based imputation and replacement with mean or median values. If imputation methods are used, those that consider the values of other characteristics and records for imputing the missing value are recommended for scorecard development. Assigning "most frequent" or "mean" values to missing values will cause spikes in the data, and differentiating between data with assigned mean values and data that actually had that value will not be possible—thus business information may be lost. It may be equally practical to assign special values to the missing (e.g., 99 or 999, or something else beyond the normal range) and include them in the analysis.

Outliers are values that fall outside of the normal range of value for a certain characteristic. For example, a distribution of age may show all the population within the range of 18 to 55, with a few at 99, 112, and 134. While these may be true, they are more likely the result of errant keying. These numbers may negatively affect the regression results, and are usually excluded. In some cases, these can be assigned mean values, since they are usually small in number and will not adversely affect the results. In all cases, however, outliers should be investigated first, since they may point to problems such as fraud. Note that when building grouped attribute scorecards, these outliers are binned with the nearest group which neutralizes their effect.

CORRELATION

The initial characteristic analysis, described in the next section, only looks at individual characteristics—no correlation, multicollinearity, or partial associations are considered at this point. However, correlation does exist and needs to be handled. Again, there are several ways to identify correlation. Such methods include using PROC VARCLUS[1] in SAS, or the Variable Clustering node in SAS Enterprise Miner. These SAS procedures use a type of principal components analysis to identify groups of characteristics that are correlated. One can then select one or more characteristics from each group, and theoretically, represent all the information contained in the other characteristics in each of the groups. Such selection can be done based on outputs from the PROC representing the amount of information of each cluster explained by each variable and the distance of the variable from the next cluster, or a combination of the two measures. In addition, business considerations should also be used in selecting variables from this exercise, so that the final variables chosen are consistent with business preference.

PROC VARCLUS is better than using simple correlation figures, as it considers collinearity as well as correlation, and is therefore a better approach to choosing variables for scorecard development. I also find the graphical output from this exercise to be useful in visualizing the variables that are close to one another.

Multicollinearity (MC) is not a significant concern when developing models for predictive purposes with large data sets. The effects of MC in reducing the statistical power of a model can be overcome by using a large enough sample such that the separate effects of each input can still be reliably estimated. In this case, the parameters estimates obtained through ordinary least squares (OLS) regression will be reliable.[2]

Identifying correlation can be performed before or after initial characteristic analysis, but before the regression step. Both the correlation and grouping steps provide valuable information on the data at hand, and are more than just statistical exercises. While reducing the number of characteristics to be grouped (by checking for correlation first) is a time saver, one is also deprived of an opportunity to look at the nature of the relationship between many characteristics and performance. Therefore, the best approach is likely a combination of eliminating some redundant characteristics and choosing more than one characteristic from each correlated "cluster" based on business and operational intuition. This serves to balance the need for efficiency with the opportunity to gain insights into the data.

INITIAL CHARACTERISTIC ANALYSIS

Initial characteristic analysis involves two main tasks. The first step is to assess the strength of each characteristic individually as a predictor of performance, and the nature of its relationship to the target. This is also known as univariate screening and is done to screen out weak or illogical characteristics.

Once it is established that the characteristic is strong and logical, it is then grouped. This applies to attributes in both continuous and discrete characteristics, and is done for a few reasons, including an obvious one. The grouping is done because it is required to produce the scorecard format shown in Exhibit 1.1.

Models can also be, and are, produced using continuous (ungrouped) characteristics. However, the grouping process offers some advantages:

- It offers an easier way to deal with outliers with interval variables, and rare classes. The impact of the outliers are reduced via grouping.
- The grouping process makes it easy to understand relationships, and therefore gain far more knowledge of the portfolio. A chart displaying the relationship between attributes of a characteristic and performance is a much more powerful tool than a simple variable strength statistic. It allows users to explain the nature

of this relationship, in addition to the strength of the relationship. This helps analysts understand points in the data where behavior changes (useful for strategy) and identify new policy rule variables (e.g., strong binary variables).

■ Nonlinear dependencies can be modeled with linear models.

■ It allows unprecedented control over the development process—by shaping the groups, one shapes the final composition of the scorecard. This allows business judgment to be used, especially when dealing with biased or small data sets.

■ The process of grouping characteristics allows the user to develop insights into the behavior of risk predictors and increases knowledge of the portfolio, which can help in developing better strategies for portfolio management.

Once the strongest characteristics are grouped and ranked, variable selection is done. At the end of initial characteristic analysis, the scorecard developer will have a set of mostly strong, grouped characteristics, preferably representing independent information types, for use in the regression step.

The strength of a characteristic is gauged using four main criteria:

■ Predictive power of each attribute. The Weight of Evidence (WOE) measure is used for this purpose.

■ The range and trend of WOE across grouped attributes within a characteristic.

■ Predictive power of the characteristic. The information value (IV) measure is used for this here. However there are many other ways to gauge this.

■ Operational and business considerations (e.g., using some logic in grouping postal codes, or grouping debt service ratio to coincide with corporate policy limits).

Some analysts run other variable selection algorithms (e.g., those that rank predictive power using chi-square, Gini, or R-squared) prior to grouping characteristics. This gives them an indication of characteristic strength using independent means, and also alerts them in cases where the IV figure is high/low compared to other measures.

The variable selection/ranking step should not be treated as just a step to identify the top predictors. When dealing with biased data or low sample sizes, I also pay attention to the variables that appear statistically weak. What we're looking for are variables that are considered predictive based on judgment and experience, yet display low statistical correlation to the target. This can be due to severe selection biases or just sparse data. In such cases, we may need to adjust these variables, as we will discuss later in the chapter. Such variables that sometimes end up statistically weak are quite often variables that are used for manual adjudication and policy rules and appear weak due to that bias.

The initial characteristic analysis process should be interactive, and involvement from business users and operations staff should be encouraged. In particular, they may provide further insights into any unexpected or illogical behavior patterns and enhance the grouping of all variables. Usually, the model developer performs the binning of the variables and then gets input from the risk management staff for adjustments.

The first step in performing this analysis is to perform initial grouping of the variables, and rank order them by IV or some other strength measure. This can be done using a number of binning techniques. In SAS Credit Scoring, the Interactive Grouping node can be used.

If using other applications or coding, a good way to start is to bin interval and ordinal variables into 20 or so equal groups (5 percent of total accounts in each bin), and to calculate the WOE and IV for the grouped attributes and characteristics. The WOE graph is then generated using any spreadsheet software. The analyst can then fine-tune the groupings for the stronger and logical characteristics based on principles to be outlined in the next section. Similarly for categorical characteristics, the WOE for each unique attribute and the IV of each characteristic can be calculated. One can then spend time fine-tuning the grouping for those characteristics that surpass a minimum acceptable strength. Decision trees are also often used for grouping variables—grouping is similar to splitting as done in decision trees. Most scorecard developers, however, use more user friendly interactive binning software applications to interactively fine-tune the groupings as it can be very repetitive and tedious. Note that there are several

Exhibit 10.2 Finely Binned Loan to Value

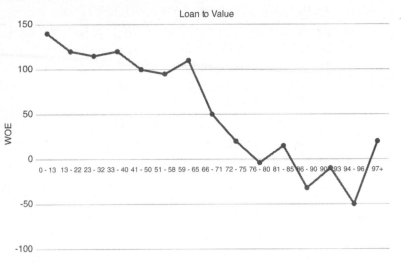

"optimal" binning algorithms available as an alternate starting point.[3] Whether using the optimal binning approach or one based on quantiles, one must then review groupings and adjust them as will be discussed later.

The broad step here is to take a look at an ungrouped or finely grouped WOE curve to decide if it is sensible or not. Once we decide this, we will then spend time working on making the bins better. Exhibit 10.2 shows such a chart for loan to value (LTV).

We note that, in general, the higher the LTV, the lower the WOE (the calculation of WOE is covered in the next section). This seems to be logical from a business perspective. We also note that there are significant differences from the lower to higher WOEs. This tells us that this is a generally logical variable, with sufficient statistical strength. There are some reversals in the chart, but we will deal with those later via fine-tuning of the bins.

Statistical Measures

Exhibit 10.3 shows a typical chart used in the analysis of grouped characteristics. The example shows the characteristic "age" after it has been grouped. In the exhibit, "Tot Distr," "Distr Good," and "Distr Bad" refer

Exhibit 10.3 Analysis of Grouped Variables

Age	Count	Tot Distr	Goods	Distr Good	Bads	Distr Bad	Bad Rate	WOE
Missing	1,000	2.50%	860	2.38%	140	3.65%	14.00%	−42.719
18–22	4,000	10.00%	3,040	8.41%	960	25.00%	24.00%	−108.980
23–26	6,000	15.00%	4,920	13.61%	1,080	28.13%	18.00%	−72.613
27–29	9,000	22.50%	8,100	22.40%	900	23.44%	10.00%	−4.526
30–35	10,000	25.00%	9,500	26.27%	500	13.02%	5.00%	70.196
35–44	7,000	17.50%	6,800	18.81%	200	5.21%	2.86%	128.388
44+	3,000	7.50%	2,940	8.13%	60	1.56%	2.00%	164.934
Total	**40,000**	**100%**	**36,160**	**100%**	**3,840**	**100%**	**9.60%**	

Information Value = 0.668

to the column-wise percentage distribution of the total, good, and bad cases, respectively. For example, 17.5 percent of all cases, 18.81 percent of goods, and 5.21 percent of bads fall in the age group 35–44.

A few things to note in Exhibit 10.3:

- "Missing" is grouped separately. The WOE of this group implies that most of the missing data comes from an age group between 23 and 29.

- A general "minimum 5 percent in each bucket" rule has been applied to enable meaningful analysis. There are also a sufficiently high number of good and bad cases in each bucket. At minimum, industry practitioners look for a minimum of 80 to 100 cases in each bin, but this number may be higher when dealing with larger data sets.

- There are no groups with 0 counts for good or bad. When using auto binning algorithms on low default portfolios, if a bin is formed with 0 goods or bads, analysts normally assume a small number (1 or 0.5) of goods or bads in order to calculate the WOE.

- The bad rate and WOE are sufficiently different from one group to the next (i.e., the grouping has been done in a way to maximize differentiation between goods and bads, and from one group to the next). This is one of the objectives of this exercise—to identify and separate attributes that differentiate well.

While the absolute value of the WOE is important, the difference in WOE between the groups is key to establishing differentiation. The larger the difference between subsequent groups,
the higher the rank ordering ability of this characteristic.

■ The WOE for nonmissing values also follows a logical distribution, going from negative to positive without any reversals. This
confirms business logic.

The WOE, as mentioned previously, measures the strength of each
attribute, or grouped attributes, in separating good and bad accounts.
It is a measure of the difference between the proportion of goods and
bads in each attribute (i.e., the odds of a person with that attribute
being good or bad). The WOE is based on the odds calculation[4]:

$$(\text{Distr Good} / \text{Distr Bad})$$

The formula above measures odds of being good (e.g., for the 23–26
attribute above, this would be 13.61 / 28.13 = 0.48). A person aged
23–26 has 0.48:1 odds of being good:bad.

A more user-friendly way to calculate WOE, and one that is used
in Exhibit 10.3, is:

$$[In \, (\text{Distr Good} / \text{Distr Bad})] * 100.$$

For example, the WOE of attribute 23–26 is:

$$In \, (0.1361/0.2813) * 100 = -72.613.$$

Multiplication by 100 is based on personal preference, and done to
make the numbers easier to work with. Negative numbers imply that
the particular attribute is isolating a higher proportion of bads than
goods.

Information Value, or total strength of the characteristic, comes
from information theory,[5] and is measured using the formula:

$$\sum_{i=1}^{n} (\text{Distr Good}_i - \text{Distr Bad}_i) * In(\text{Distr Good}_i / \text{Distr Bad}_i)$$

Note that "Distr Good" and "Distr Bad" are used in this formula in
decimal format, for example, 0.136 and 0.28.

Based on this methodology, my rule of thumb regarding IV is:

- Less than 0.02: generally unpredictive
- 0.02 to 0.1: weak
- 0.1 to 0.3: medium
- 0.3+: strong

Characteristics with IV greater than 0.5 should be checked for overpredicting—they can either be kept out of the modeling process, or used in a controlled manner, such as will be described later in the "Preliminary Scorecard" section.

IV is a widely used measure in the industry, and different practitioners have different rules of thumb regarding what constitutes weak or strong characteristics. Other measures commonly used in the industry for this include Gini and chi-square. In many cases, where a variable is weak, but has a logical relationship and is considered useful from a business perspective, risk managers will often include it in the model.

Where the scorecard is being developed using nongrouped characteristics, statistics to evaluate predictive strength include R-squared and chi-square. Both these methods use goodness-of-fit criteria to evaluate characteristics. The R-squared technique uses a stepwise selection method that rejects characteristics that do not meet incremental R-square increase cutoffs. There are many opinions on what constitutes an acceptable R-squared value/cutoff, from 0.1 to above 0.67. Chi-square operates in a similar fashion, with a minimum typical cutoff value of 0.5. The cutoffs can be increased if too many characteristics are retained in the model. As with the technique using grouped variables, the objective here is to select characteristics for regression (or another modeling step).

Again, it is important to note that univariate screening, whether using grouping or not, does not account for partial associations and interactions among the input characteristics. Partial association occurs when the effect of one characteristic changes in the presence of another. Multivariate methods that consider joint subsets may be preferable in this case. In any case, the purpose of doing the exercise is the same—choosing a set of strong variables for input into regression (or another technique, as appropriate).

Exhibit 10.4 Model Characteristics

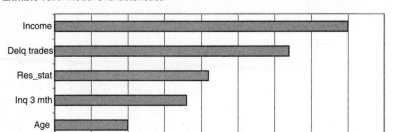

Some modeling software offer options to group characteristics using the R-squared and chi-square methods, and to test interactions for categorical inputs. Examples of two-way interactions that can be tested are "income * residential status," "age * income," and so forth. This methodology goes beyond individual characteristic analysis and can produce more powerful results by considering interactions between characteristics. As discussed in the segmentation section, interaction terms are also a way of generating ideas for segmentation. Note that interaction terms are not normally used in scorecards, as the binning process relies on establishing a logical relationship, which is not always possible with interactions. However, if the logical relationship is not a concern, interaction terms used in credit scoring has shown to add value.[6]

A typical output from an R-squared analysis is shown in Exhibit 10.4, where the incremental increase in R-squared value is shown as characteristics are added to the model starting with age and ending with income.

Logical Trend

The statistical strength, measured in terms of WOE and IV, is, however, not the only factor in choosing a characteristic for further analysis, or designating it as a strong predictor. In grouped scorecards, the attribute strengths must also be in a logical order, and make operational sense. For example, the distribution of attribute weight for age, from Exhibit 10.3, is plotted in Exhibit 10.5.

Exhibit 10.5 Logical WOE Trend for Age

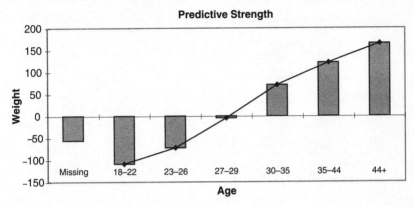

As can be clearly seen, apart from "missing," the other groupings in this characteristic have a linear relationship with WOE; that is, they denote a linear and logical relationship between the attributes in age and proportion of bads. This confirms business experience both in the credit and insurance sectors that younger people tend to be, in general, of a higher risk than the older population. Establishing such logical (not necessarily linear) relationships through grouping is the purpose of the initial characteristic analysis exercise. The process of arriving at a logical trend is one of trial and error, in which one balances the creation of logical trends while maintaining a sufficient IV value.

Another part of creating logical relationships is identifying and fixing biases in the data. These biases can take several forms. Let's take a look at a few.

Exhibit 10.6 shows the WOE relationship for a variable "Age of Used Car in Years," for an auto loans scorecard.

The chart shows a trend where generally, the older the used car the borrower is buying, the worse their performance. This seems to make sense, except the last bucket, where people buying cars older than 15 years old perform better than expected. The fix for this illogical relationship will depend on what is causing the reversal. There are two possible explanations:

- ▪ The data in "15+" is biased due to a very low number of applicants being approved in that category. Perhaps they are overrides only, as generally the quality of applicants purchasing

Exhibit 10.6 WOE for Age of Used Car in Years

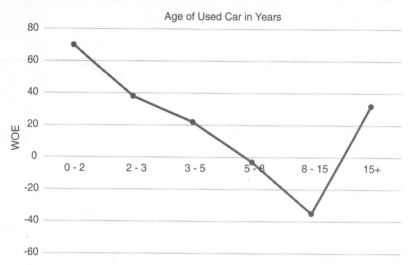

such old cars cannot be very high, and so the bank selectively approved very few of them, who then performed well.

■ The data in "15+" is correct, and represents people who are buying expensive vintage cars. These would tend to be richer people, who presumably are better at paying their loans.

Depending on the reason, we may choose to manually fix the WOE for "15+," rebin with a separate break at a number that represents truly vintage cars (perhaps at 40 years and above), or leave it as it is.

One of the major causes of biases in banking data for application scoring is lending policies and adjudication based overrides. This is why we recommended studying lending policies and talking to adjudicators in previous chapters. If such policies are not known, a good way to detect possible biases is to calculate the approval rate for each bin. The higher the approval rate, the less the bias; that is, a 100 percent approval rate would represent the full "through the door" population, while a 1 percent approval rate would represent a highly biased sample. This may help determine the cause of the WOE reversal in Exhibit 10.6. If the data in "15+" is from overrides, the approval rate should be very low.

Another way variables are biased is through policy rules. Let's look at another example, debt service ratio (Exhibit 10.7).

Exhibit 10.7 WOE for Debt Service Ratio

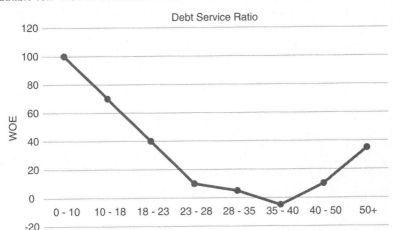

The chart shows the WOE relationship for debt service ratio (DSR), which is generally defined as the percentage of income going towards servicing debt. For example, if a borrower's income is $10,000 per month, and their monthly payments for debt servicing is $2,300 ($1,200 for mortgage, $800 for car loan, $300 for credit cards), then their DSR would be 23 percent. Note that in some countries, banks will add other significant expenses to this ratio, which then becomes a broad measure of percentage of income going towards major fixed expenses. Examples of such expenses include electricity/heating costs, car /home insurance, education, medical insurance, and so on.

Exhibit 10.7 shows three broad sections in the chart. We can see that there is a fairly linear trend from 0 up to 28 percent DSR. Between 28 and 40, the trend is still logical, but the gradient seems to have changed. Beyond 40 percent, there is a reversal in logic, since experience and business sense dictates that the higher the DSR, the worse the performance. The trend seen in the exhibit came about through deliberate binning, based on knowledge of the customers lending policies:

- The bank followed normal lending policies up to 28 percent DSR. This zone has largely unbiased performance.

- From 28 to 40 percent, due to elevated risks, the bank had instituted additional policy rules based on higher bureau scores, stricter previous delinquencies and higher income levels. This zone has performance biased by policy rules.

- Above 40 percent, the lending policy allowed only manual approvals by experienced adjudicators. This is the most biased zone.

This illustrates an example of how knowing lending policies can help in isolating biases during binning. DSR, along with loan to value, previous delinquencies, employment history and income are some of the most frequently used variables for policy rules. If the scorecard developer had not known the policy rules mentioned before, these biases could have been detected via approval rates by DSR as well.

Now that we have identified and isolated the biased sections, how do we fix the trend? We cannot keep the existing trend since that will assign undeservingly higher points to the high risk applicants (remembering that this is an applications scorecard that will score all applicants, but the data being used is for approves only).

There are a couple of ways to fix biases like these. Some of them can be fixed via judicious use of reject inference, which will be covered later. The other option is to manually change the WOE curve to reflect the most probable trend for the "through-the-door" population.

Exhibit 10.8 shows two examples of how the original WOE can be adjusted.

The first line, "Adjusted WOE-1," is based on an extrapolation of the part of the chart with normal lending policies. The second line, "Adjusted WOE-2" assumes a worse performance. I have used the approval rates in the normal lending ranges to adjust WOE's in such cases. "Adjusted WOE-1" is based on the assumption that the vast majority of the applicants in the range below 28 percent DSR are approved, and therefore their performance represents the though-the-door population. If this is not the case, "Adjusted WOE-2" can be used, which assumes that the approval rate for the 10 to 28 percent DSR is in the mid-ranges and therefore biased as well. This is based on judgment, and to obtain the most probable performance of the total population.

Exhibit 10.8 Adjusted WOE for Debt Service Ratio

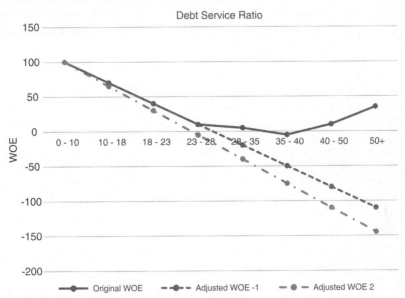

In such cases, looking for the "optimal" or 100 percent correct answer is not possible, unless we lend money to all our applicants and find out the real bad rates for the worst customers with greater accuracy. In the absence of such data, we rely on judgment and extrapolation. The exact right answer in the preceding example may be different from either one of the suggested adjusted WOE lines. The model developer and risk manager need to work together to establish the *best answer realistically possible*. Sometimes, risk managers will have scorecards developed using several adjustment schemes to see what the final scores look like, and then decide on the appropriate adjustment based on the score distributions that satisfy business sense and conservatism.

The shape of the WOE curve will determine the shape of the scorecard. What this means is that if the WOE curve is linear, the resulting final scores will also be linear. If the WOEs are near each other, the scores for the attributes will also not have much difference between them once the final scorecard is created. Reversals in the WOE curve will also be reflected in the final scores. When binning, it is useful to envisage the shape of the scorecard when viewing the WOE curve.

Some companies that are merely looking for risk ranking, rather than a predictive model, often use the WOEs themselves as scores. For example, in Exhibit 10.3, the WOE column, rounded up, would then be used as scores for age.

Experimenting with different groupings (regrouping or merging bins, for example) mostly eliminates reversals (where the trend reverses itself) and other illogical relationships. General trends can be seen by looking at the relationship between WOE and raw (ungrouped) attributes or broad quantile groups such as 20—grouping merely smooths out the curve. In some cases, however, reversals and other nonlinear trends may be reflecting actual behavior or data, and masking them can reduce the overall strength of the characteristic. These should be investigated first, to see if there is a valid business explanation for such behavior. In general, grouping serves to reduce "overfitting," whereby quirks in the data are modeled rather than the overall trend in predictiveness. Where valid nonlinear relationships occur, they should be used if an explanation using experience or industry trends can be made. Again, what needs to be confirmed is that an overall explainable trend or profile is being modeled, and not data quirks. Business experience is the best test for this. For example, in North America, "Utilization" (balance/limit for revolving trades) has a unique-shaped curve with respect to WOE, similar to a second-order parabolic or quadratic Bezier curve. An example is shown in Exhibit 10.9.

Exhibit 10.9 WOE Graph for Utilization

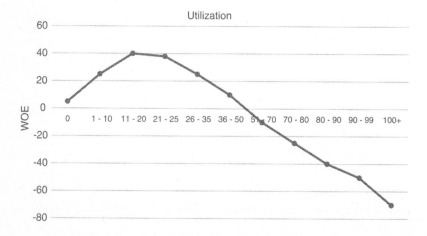

The chart shows that very low utilization accounts are higher risk, then the risk decreases up to a point, and finally risk starts increasing as utilization increases. The rationale behind this is that those with 0 utilization are inactive customers who don't use the credit card. At some point in the performance window, if they start using it, it likely means they need the money and are hence not the best risk. The ideal utilization where the card holder has manageable debt is, according to this data set, around 20 to 25 percent. These numbers may be different in other nations, indeed, the whole curve may be. Other valid relationships may be "U" shaped/normal distributions, and these should be kept as that, as long as the relationship can be explained.

Nominal variables are grouped to put attributes with similar WOE together, and, as with continuous variables, to maximize the difference from one group to the next.

An example of a WOE relationship is shown in Exhibit 10.10, which is a screen print from the Interactive Grouping node in SAS Enterprise Miner.

We would start grouping this variable by first identifying the plateaus, that is, where the WOE is generally flat across several groups. This can be seen in groups 7 to 10, 13 to 20, and 26 to 30, and would suggest that performance/risk level is the same within these bands. As performance is homogeneous within them, these can be merged to

Exhibit 10.10 WOE Example

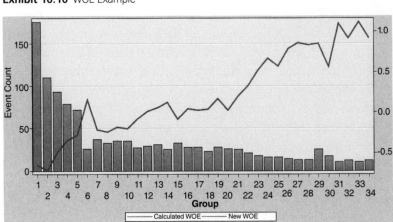

reduce the number of bins. Once the scorecard is built, for example, all applicants in the groups 7 to 10 will then get the same points. We then analyze the major reversals and assign the nonlogical bins into the groups before or after them to create something continuously linear for this variable. Note that this does not preclude adjusting for biases, as has been discussed earlier.

Clearly, this process can be abused when it is done by someone who is not familiar with the business, which again underscores the need for it to be a collaborative process with other project team members. The value of talking to businesspeople to understand the art of lending, and the relevant business should also be clearer now to the reader. For example, someone not familiar with policy rules may simply create linear trends and hence mask actual biased behavior. Usually, this tends to assign much higher points to high risk customers than they deserve.

The number of bins for each characteristic can vary. As a rule, higher number of bins will yield a more granular scorecard, as long as the WOEs are not too close, and the trend is logical. For example, having three bins for LTV is likely not enough to sufficiently differentiate between the various levels of risk in that variable. A low number of (large) bins can also hide changes in the population that should affect risk. In this situation, while the scores will remain stable, the actual riskiness of the population will change. For continuous variables like LTV, I have normally used anywhere from 6 to 10 bins depending on the size of the data set. Analysts who wish to have a distribution closer to an unbinned one will sometimes create individual bins for each value of LTV. However, due to data quirks, there will likely be reversals in the trend, which will need to be smoothed out individually for logical scores. The number of bins are also highly dependent on the size of the data set being used—the more data you have the more bins you can create, and the smaller the size of each bin. Note that in general, binning is done using whole numbers only, without decimal points. Including decimal points results in an unwieldy number of potential values.

Exhibit 10.11 illustrates an example of an illogical trend. In this particular data set, this characteristic is weak and shows no logical relationship between age and good/bad performance.

Exhibit 10.11 Illogical WOE Trend for Age

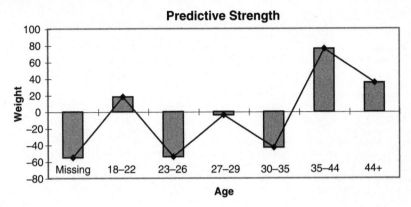

Exhibit 10.12 shows two WOE relationships, both of which are logical. However, the steeper line (square markers) represents a stronger predictive relationship between age and performance. This will be reflected in its IV number.

Initial characteristic analysis involves creating business logical relationships through grouping of attributes that exceed minimum IV criteria. Logic is not a function of correlation or statistical strength, it is a function of causality and depends on the user being able to explain the relationships. The alternate, purely statistical approach involves establishing relationships that only maximize IV or other measures, whether grouped or not.

Exhibit 10.12 Logical Trend and Strength

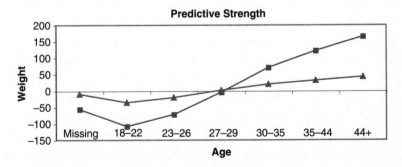

The business-based approach is better for several reasons, including:

- Logical relationships ensure that the final weightings and scores after regression make sense. This also ensures that when attributes are allocated points to generate a scorecard, these points are logical (e.g., an older person gets higher points than a younger person always).

- Logical relationships ensure buy-in from internal end users, such as risk managers, model validators and adjudicators. When the scorecard confirms general experience, it provides a higher level of confidence in both the scorecard, as well as subsequent decisions made with it, in particular, automated decision making. Especially for firms building scorecards for the first time, this can mean less opposition and hence faster acceptance as well.

- Logical relationships confirm business experience, thus going one step further than a purely statistical evaluation. This allows the usage of business experience to enhance predictive modeling and makes it more useful for business purposes.

- Logical binning also filters out the biases and makes the scorecard more relevant and accurate, as we have seen in previous examples.

- Most importantly, generalizing relationships by grouping them in a logical fashion reduces overfitting. You are no longer modeling every quirk in the data by assigning an unlimited number of weights to ungrouped attributes. You are now risk-ranking and modeling trends, so that the scorecard can now be applied to an incoming population with some elasticity (able to withstand some changes in the population), and that will remain stable for a longer period of time. A legitimate concern here would be that of overgeneralization, whereby the model will seem to work even when the changes in the population dictate otherwise. The solution to this issue is to make sure that there are enough separate bins to capture all the different levels of risk within each variable, to build a widely based risk profile model, and not one with a limited number of characteristics. This is also why scorecards built with small data sets tend to be less stable and less robust. The long-term application differentiates credit risk scorecard development from marketing models, which are often built for specific campaigns and then discarded. Therefore, one cannot afford to model quirks.

■ The result of creating logical bins means that you create an overall risk ranking mechanism, where you differentiate not just the highest and lowest levels of risk, but also the intermediate ones.

While the best types of variables are the ones which are both strong and logical, in many cases risk managers will also select variables that are relatively weak, but logical. In such cases, while the points distributions will not be as far apart as the stronger ones, there will still be risk ranking.

Business/Operational Considerations

Statistical considerations and business logic have been discussed as measures used to group attributes. The third consideration is business or operational relevance.

For categorical—that is, nominal—variables, such as postal codes or lifestyle code, the automated groupings are normally done based on similar weights and will always produce a logical trend (i.e., attributes with similar weights are grouped together), based on calculated WOE. These auto groupings must be investigated for logic.

Groupings should be done based on business logic such as regional, urban/rural, similar occupation types, luxury versus cheaper brands, voice/SMS versus data users, similar products purchased, national brand name versus store brand, and other such considerations. For example, if you are building a scorecard to predict default for mortgages, grouping of postal codes should be done by similar real estate markets. I have had success by ranking cities by population size and also by average house price, and then creating bins. The risk associated with borrowers is dependent on the real estate market, which tends to differ in large urban areas and rural areas. For example, in Canada, it may not make sense to group Ontario or British Columbia as province or region, as the housing market in the entire province is not uniform. Grouping Toronto, Montreal, and Vancouver together, and rural areas in both provinces together, makes far more sense.

Establishing logic in categorical variables is somewhat more difficult than the continuous ones we have seen before. In general, biases
and illogical results in categorical results are due to two main issues.

First, policy rules based on regions, products, housing status, and,
in some cases, types of employment will result in certain categories performing better than they should, due to overriding and cherry-picking.
These are similar to the DSR example discussed earlier, and is "negative"
bias—people who are considered higher risk looking better in the data.

Second, the most common reason for positive bias—people considered to be good but look bad in the data—in categorical grouping (the algorithms putting similar WOEs together) is low counts or
sparse data. For example, one particular luxury car brand may have
been grouped with several low-end brands, based on negative WOEs,
or one high income-earning occupation with those of lower incomes.
When faced with situations like this, the first thing one should do
is check the individual category to make sure it has enough counts.
If the data in that category is sufficiently large, then the reasons for
the seemingly illogical result needs to be investigated. Perhaps those
who bought the luxury brand were low income, or had higher than
average LTVs. Similarly, the company's product or pricing may have
attracted high income earners in financial distress. Typically, however, such cases are due to sparse data. This should be confirmed by
looking at the good and bad counts. There may be only five people
who bought a particular luxury car and, by chance, three of them
defaulted on the loan. That does not mean that in the general population, 60 percent of those buying that brand are bad. The fix to this
situation is usually to take that category and move it into a different one with similar luxury brands. Due to the low counts in that
attribute, the WOEs, IV, Gini, and so on of the variable will not be
affected. However, from a logic and business sense perspective, it will
make a significant difference.

It also makes sense to have breaks concurrent with policy rules, as
they are almost always the source of bias. For example, if a company
policy requires loans with LTV of 90 percent and above to be manually
adjudicated, then there should be a break at 90 percent. The benefits of
grouping in such a way is that the distortion caused by the policy rule
on the scorecard is minimized, since those affected by the policy rule

are now isolated somewhat. We have covered such an example in the previous section. Such groupings can also test conventional wisdom and previous policies—for example, to see if the 42 percent rule makes sense at that point, or if it would be better situated at a higher debt service ratio to maximize risk discrimination.

The binning process is interactive and manually intensive, as it requires a lot of user input to get useful results. This is why we short-listed characteristics in the previous chapter, rather than start with thousands of them. The requirement to interpret and create logic out of WOE relationships is also why the model builder needs to understand each variable, what it means, how it is derived, and the nature of why it is useful for risk management; for example, DSR is used to determine the ability to take on more debt or capacity. Again, this reinforces some of the reasons why we picked characteristics for analysis in the previous chapter.

At the end of this phase, we have:

- Identified and grouped all the strong and preferred variables.
- Screened out the very weak and illogical variables (some weak but logical ones are kept).
- Established, via interaction with risk/policy managers, that the WOE relationships are logical. This is best done by going through the variables with the risk manager, as well as model validation staff. In some cases, the risk manager will request changes to the bins, elect to use variables that are weak but logical or choose to drop variables for other reasons. These should all be documented. Note that marketing/business staff may be consulted at this stage to help explain phenomena, but they should not have the final say on any variables, nor be able to veto them.
- Understood the data better—in addition to identifying variables with strong statistical correlations to the target, we now also know how they are related. We recognize the types of customers that are high/low risk, the points where behavior changes, and how the data is biased.
- Obtained the WOE for each attribute, for all the binned variables. These WOEs will be used in the regression model to be built in the next section.

PRELIMINARY SCORECARD

Initial characteristic analysis identifies a set of strong characteristics that should be considered for the final model, and it transforms them into grouped variable format. At the preliminary scorecard stage, various predictive modeling techniques can be used to select a set of characteristics that, together, offer the most predictive power. Some of the techniques used in the industry are logistic regression, discriminant analysis, partial least squares, decision trees, Cox proportional hazard, and neural networks. There are also upcoming methodologies like machine learning that are attracting much attention. For credit risk models and scorecards, however, the majority of banks that I have met use logistic regression and decision trees. For the purposes of this scorecard, we will use logistic regression.

In general, the final scorecards produced in this stage consist of between 8 and 15 characteristics, although in larger banks with a lot of data, I have seen those with 18 to 30 characteristics. This is done to ensure a comprehensive risk profile that includes all the reasonable variables, as well as a more stable scorecard whose predictive powers will be strong even if the profile of one or two characteristics were to change. Scorecards with too few characteristics are generally unable to withstand the test of time, as they are susceptible to minor changes in the applicant profile.

Regardless of the modeling technique used, this process should produce a scorecard consisting of the optimal combination of characteristics, taking into account other issues such as:

- Correlation between characteristics.
- Final statistical strength of the scorecard.
- Business sense.
- Compliance with local regulations and laws.
- Interpretability (causality) of characteristics from a business perspective—being able to explain in plain business language why that variable is strong and should be in the model.
- Implementability from a technical perspective.
- Transparency of methodology for regulatory and internal validation requirements.

Risk Profile Concept

Scorecards can be developed with various "optimizing" objectives in mind—maximizing statistical measures, efficiency (using the fewest variables), and so forth. In business terms, scorecards should be developed to mimic the thought process of a seasoned, effective adjudicator or risk analyst. A good adjudicator will never look at just four or five things from an application form or account history to make a decision. What he or she is more likely to do is look at several key measures, to form a *risk profile* of the subject. So why should decision making scorecards be developed that include only four or five characteristics?

The objective of the scorecard development process described in this section is to build a comprehensive risk profile of the customer. This wide-based approach not only makes the scorecard more predictive and stable but also maximizes acceptance and buy-in from business users. This is particularly important in banks and other companies where scorecards are being used for the first time. The seasoned lenders, as well as management in such places, often have a healthy cynicism and suspicion of models. In order to gain their confidence, it is important to show them that scorecards aren't just some mysterious statistical tools, they are based on exactly the sort of information that bankers have been using to lend in the past. The difference is that we will be using more robust analytics to get to it. The binning process described in the previous section also helps in getting that buy-in. In addition, including more variables also makes scorecards more stable and less susceptible to changes in one particular area. Such a risk profile should include characteristics representing as many independent and explainable types of data as possible.

The risk profile should be relevant to the purpose/objective of the exercise. A scorecard to predict 60 days past due (DPD) for applications, used to rate and price the entire risk spectrum, would have a very different set of variables from one designed for fraud detection, where action is taken only on very few accounts. One is built to isolate the worst 2 to 3 percent of cases, while the other needs to differentiate throughout the score spectrum. The desired Lorenz curves for the two cases would be quite different. As experienced risk modelers know, the behavior of models, viewed via Lorenz or Kolmogorov-Smirnov (KS) charts, can be controlled through selective uses of certain variables. For example, continuous data such as LTV and other ratios do not isolate the bottom few percent; rather, they are helpful in identifying a continuum of all the shades of risk (which is also why they are very useful in general delinquency models). However, a variable like "Ever 90 DPD" or "Ever Bankrupt Last 12 Months" will isolate only the very few cases that have such extreme delinquencies—say the bottom 0.5 percent. They do nothing for the other 99.5 percent. A model with just one variable like that will have a massive separation and yield high KS, but wouldn't be very useful for applications scoring. The right scorecard will have a mixture of several of these types of variables—depending on what we want it to do. This is why looking at statistics alone is insufficient in determining the right scorecard. We need to build the right scorecard, with the appropriate mixture of variables that will enable us to meet our business objective.

A credit card applications scorecard, for example, should include some demographic data such as age, residential status, narrowed-down region, time at address, and time at employment; some credit bureau characteristics representing tenure, for example, age of the oldest trade, inquiries (including ratios of near- and long-term inquiries), trades (types of trades, utilization, highest limits, ratio of unsecured to total trades), payment performance (number of times missed payments for 30, 60, or 90 days; time since missed payment; time to cure; balance at missed payment), financial information, and public records; some measure of capacity to service debt, such as gross or total DSR; and, where relevant, internal performance data for existing customers. A scorecard for secured products such as mortgages or car loans should additionally include LTV, type of housing, whether the property is for investment or is owner occupied, type of car, brand, mileage on and age of the used vehicle, and whether the car is used or new. Behavior scorecards for credit cards usually have information on customer tenure; payment history, including ratios of long time and current averages; purchasing history; types of places where the credit card is used; delinquency history, including time since; utilization history; and, in cases of retail companies, types of product bought. In countries where credit card usage is not common as well as for mortgage and auto loans behavior scorecards, I have used information from the customer's savings and checking accounts. These include variables such as average difference between deposits and withdrawals, average balances and their history, average ATM withdrawal, debit card usage, current and historical average debit transactions, and other products held at the bank. These variables all help in identifying customers in financial distress, such as declining balances, lower debit and credit card transaction amounts and declining average ATM withdrawals. Traditionally, banks that have used only credit usage or credit bureau data often miss out on identifying high net worth customers who may not have taken out loans, but have significant deposits. This segment, which may have paid in cash for cars and homes, but requires credit cards for convenience often gets low scores due to a lack of credit payment information. As such, incorporating savings, checking and investment account information into scorecards allows for better insight into these and other low risk customers. The same concept can be applied to SME and corporate risk models where variables representing all the major information categories should be used. The point is that we want to create a scorecard that has as many of these customer characteristics as possible to enable better decision making. A list of common variables used in scorecards is provided for reference in Appendix A.

The risk profile concept also helps in making subsequent monitoring of the scorecard more relevant. Most risk analysts would run reports such as "system stability" or "population stability" on a monthly basis to confirm the validity of the scorecard on current applicant or account populations. What these reports are effectively measuring is the change in the population as *defined by the characteristics in the scorecard* only. A broadly based risk profile scorecard would more realistically capture actual changes in the population, rather than artificially indicate change or stability, as may be the case with limited-variable scorecards.

Creating a scorecard based on a risk profile is in theory no different from other predictive modeling exercises—the difference is only in the method of arriving at the final set of characteristics. Most of the techniques mentioned in previous chapters can be, and need to be, manipulated to include the issues discussed in the preceding paragraphs, since running modeling algorithms without intervention is unlikely to result in a risk profile. The remainder of this section will deal with methods used in the logistic regression technique to build such risk profile scorecards.

Logistic Regression

Logistic regression is a common technique used to develop scorecards in most financial industry applications, where the predicted variable is binary. In cases where the predicted variable is continuous, such as modeling loss given default, linear regression is used. The rest of this section will deal with using multiple logistic regression to predict a binary outcome (good/bad).

Logistic regression, like most other predictive modeling methods, uses a set of predictor characteristics to predict the likelihood (or probability) of a specific outcome (the target). The equation for the logit transformation of a probability of an event is shown by:

$$\text{Logit}\,(p_i) = \beta_0 + \beta_1 x_1 + \ldots + \beta_k x_k$$

where

p = posterior probability of "event," given inputs
x = input variables
β_0 = intercept of the regression line
β_k = parameters

Logit transformation is log of the odds, that is, log (p[event]/ p[nonevent]), and is used to linearize posterior probability and limit outcome of estimated probabilities in the model to between 0 and 1. Maximum likelihood is used to estimate parameters β_1 to β_k. These parameter estimates measure the rate of change of logit for one unit change in the input variable (adjusted for other inputs); that is, they are in fact the slopes of the regression line between the target and their respective input variables x_1 to x_k. The parameters are dependent on the unit of the input (e.g., a percentage number compared to income) and need to be standardized to ease analysis. This can be done using several methods, including using standardized estimates. Another way is to bypass the unit of input altogether and perform the regression not against the input, but rather against the WOE of each grouping created in the previous step.

Regression needs to have a target and a series of inputs. These inputs can have various forms. The most common way is to use the raw input data for numeric variables and create dummy variables for categorical data. Standardized estimates are then used in the analysis to neutralize the effects of input variable units. This approach is, however, not relevant when grouped variable scorecards need to be developed.

In the case of grouped variable scorecards, inputs can be in the shape of group average values for numeric variables, such as average age of each group, or some weighted average, or dummy variables for category groups. Using dummy variables for categorical variables has a drawback—it assumes that the difference from one categorical variable group to the next is the same. A better way to deal with grouped variables is to use the WOE of each grouping as the input. This not only solves the problems of differing input units but also takes into account the exact trend and scale of the relationship from one group to the next. It also helps in the development of scorecards by keeping each characteristic intact. In addition, if the grouping is done right, this will also ensure that the allocation of points to each group during scorecard scaling is logical.

In other words, WOE variables allow the model to take into account nonlinearities in the predictive relationship. For example, the difference between LTV of 10 percent and 20 percent will not be the same as LTV of 70 percent compared to 80 percent. As has been discussed before, the grouping of variables by WOE and its usage in the regression allows a business user to insert the logical relationships of the variable to the target into scorecard coefficients effectively, whereas a single coefficient for a continuous variable may lose some of the predictive power.

WOE scorecards also tend to have fewer degrees of freedom, as compared to using dummy variables. Dummy variables also sometimes result in score reversals and other illogical relationships, particularly where there is collinearity. The WOE binned scorecards will always produce scores exactly as determined by the shape of the WOE curve. While maintaining the relationships, WOE-based scorecards then apply a scaling parameter to deal with the interaction with other scorecard characteristics.

However, as we regress at the characteristic level, WOE variables are inefficient in dealing with interactions at the attribute level. This may lead to "double counting" and awarding more points to better customers than they should get. This problem can be resolved by using negative dummy variables for the affected attribute. However, care must be taken with this approach, as it may cause issues with regulators and internal audit.

Regression can be run to find out the best possible model using all options available. This is commonly known as "all possible" regression techniques and is computationally intensive, especially if there are a lot of independent input characteristics. Far more commonly used are the three types of stepwise logistic regression techniques:

- *Forward selection.* First selects the best one characteristic model based on the individual predictive power of each characteristic, then adds further characteristics to this model to create the best two, three, four, and so on characteristic models incrementally, until no remaining characteristics have *p*-values of less than some significant level (e.g., 0.5), or univariate chi-square/ minimum discrimination information statistic above a determined level. This method is efficient, but can be weak if there are too many characteristics or high correlation. This method can however be modified for business usage, as we will do in the next section.

- *Backward elimination.* The opposite of forward selection, this method starts with all the characteristics in the model and sequentially eliminates characteristics that are considered the least significant, given the other characteristics in the model, until all the remaining characteristics have a *p*-value below a significant level (e.g., 0.1) or based on some other measure of multivariate significance. This method allows variables of lower significance a higher chance to enter the model, much more than forward or stepwise, whereby one or two powerful variables can dominate.

- *Stepwise.* A combination of the preceding two techniques, this involves adding and removing characteristics dynamically from the scorecard in each step until the best combination is reached. A user can set minimum p-values (or chi-square) required to be added to the model or to be kept in the model.

Designing a Scorecard

While it is possible to build a scorecard by putting all the characteristics into the regression model and generating a statistically optimal outcome, this method may not produce results that are operationally ideal. The scorecard developer would typically rely on some statistical measures such as p-values, Gini, chi-square, R-squared, and others to determine the quality of the outcome. There are, however, some business goals that need to be considered when developing scorecards.

The first goal is to choose the best set of characteristics and build the most comprehensive risk profile. The concept of creating a risk profile was discussed earlier in the chapter. Ideally, this profile should be built using as many independent data items as possible, for example, demographics, time-related data, financial data, credit bureau inquiries, trades, payment patterns, and so on. The development process should address standard modeling issues such as correlation and collinearity, and other such factors that affect the reliability of the model itself.

The scorecard developed must be coherent with the decision support structure of the organization. If the model is a sole arbiter, the need to create a comprehensive risk profile becomes even greater. If it is being used as a decision support tool, then the characteristics to be included in the scorecard must be consistent with other measures used and not oppose them. For example, inclusion of characteristics such as bankruptcy, total DSR, previous delinquency, and so forth, that are typically included in policy rules, should be minimized.

The example in Exhibit 10.13 shows characteristics of an application scorecard that is a comprehensive risk profile. Note that it includes

Exhibit 10.13 Example of Risk Profile Scorecard

- Age
- Residential status
- Postal code
- Time at address
- Time in Industry/Profession
- Inquiries 3/12 months
- Inquiries/trades opened last 12 months
- Revolving trades/total trades
- Trades opened the last 3/12 months
- Utilization
- Time since last missed payment
- Number of times 30 days last 12 months
- Total debt service ratio
- Loan to value

characteristics representing various information types, both from internal and external sources. The inclusion of the ratio of inquiries in the past 12 and 3 months is done to gauge short- and long-term credit hungriness. These two could also have been included independently. "Bankruptcy" and "public records" were not included in the scorecard, as they were used in policy rules to automatically reject applicants. "Time in industry" is used instead of "time at recent employment" since time in the same industry or in continuous employment is a better indicator of risk than time at the most current job, especially in urban areas with a mobile workforce. The ratio of inquiries in the last twelve months to the number of trades opened during the same time period is a measure for the applicant's success rate in getting credit. One risk adjudicator I interviewed calls this the applicant's "batting average." The same concept can be applied to any situation where a scorecard is being built to facilitate a business decision. For example, a scorecard to assess the creditworthiness of a small business would include elements such as:

- Financial strength.
  - Liquidity (account balance, cash/assets, quick ratio, current ratio).
  - Indebtedness (debt to income).
  - Profitability (average margin, industry code, average profit).

- Credit history (previous loan payment history with bank, personal bureau characteristics similar to a retail applicant, business bureau data, debt service).

- Stability (time as owner, years of experience in a similar business, number of similar businesses owned, management quality, ability to grow market share, revenue trends, average tenure of employees, address changes, turnover rate).

- Geographic/market influences (average ratings online [with caveats noted earlier], macroeconomic indicators, bankruptcy rate for industry).

Such a scorecard is not usually a result of an autopilot regression algorithm. So how do we get a scorecard like this?

We design one.

The scorecard developer has several methods by which to influence the final shape of the model. These include forcing characteristics in, whereby characteristics deemed operationally necessary or "must have" are forced into the scorecard at the outset, and manipulating regression to maximize the chances of certain characteristics entering the final model.

One way to achieve this involves considering characteristics for entry into the model in steps, where the characteristics to be considered at each step are individually specified by the analyst. This is no different from stepwise regression, other than the fact that the variables are considered for entry into the model based on user input rather than the algorithm itself. This is done to ensure that more variables have the opportunity to enter the scorecard. The default stepwise regression algorithm, as we know, picks the strongest variable first and then goes down the order in terms of strength. This algorithm is designed for efficiency and to produce parsimonious models, among other things. While that is appropriate in certain environments, for banks with large data sets and powerful computers, it may not be relevant. As discussed earlier, we are looking to develop a business optimal model, and we have the ability to analyze very large data sets.

An example of performing this sort of interactive regression using multiple variables at each level is shown in Exhibit 10.14.

Exhibit 10.14 Defining Characteristics for Each Step of Regression

Step 1 : Age, time at address, time in industry, time at bank, oldest trade at bureau
Step 2 : Region, postal code, housing status, occupation type, industry code
Step 3 : Total balance of all credit products at bank, number of products, average balance of checking accounts last 12 months, average ATM withdrawal last month/average withdrawals last 12 months
Step 4 : Inquiries last 3 months, inquiries last 9 months, inquiries 3 mths/inquiries 12 mths, accounts opened last 3 mths/accts opened last 24 mths
Step 5 : Time since last 30 days delinquent at bureau, trades 3 months delinquent as % of total trades, current trades, revolving trades/total trades, max delinquency at bank last 24 months, time since last missed payment at bank
Step 6 : Utilization, loan to value, debt service ratio, price of car/income, max credit limit, max utilization last 6 mths/avg last 24 mths

Using this technique, the regression program first selects characteristics from the same step, using either stepwise, forward, or backward logistic regression (although the majority of bankers tend to use stepwise regression). Characteristics that pass the minimum criterion (e.g., p-value of parameter estimates based on some significance level) are added to the scorecard first (or removed first, in the case of backward regression). Usually, related variables (based on results of correlation exercise or the use of PROC VARCLUS perhaps) are put into the same step. The idea is to have variables representing each information type at one level, and plan regression so that there are at least one or two variables from each information type in the scorecard at the end. In the example shown, age, time at address, time in industry, time at bank, and oldest trade at bureau (representing time related information) would be regressed in the first iteration, taking into account correlation. Assume that "oldest trade at bureau" comes out as having the strongest predictive power—this will then become the first variable to enter the model.

In the second iteration at the same level, the algorithm will consider the four remaining characteristics, taking into account the predictiveness already modeled by "oldest trade at bureau." If either one or all of the remaining characteristics add sufficient predictive power to the scorecard, they would be added. The regression would stop when no further characteristics could be added or removed from the model.

All characteristics that have entered the model in step 1 will start in the model in step 2. The regression at this step, to consider region, postal code, housing status, occupation and industry codes will start with the characteristics from step 1 already in the model. Again, measures such as p-values and significance levels will be used to determine the model at this step.

Similar analyses will then be performed at each subsequent level until a final scorecard is produced. Characteristics entering the model in previous steps will be forced into the model in subsequent steps. In reality, there will be many more variables being used at this step, the ones shown in the Exhibit 10.14 are meant to be an example only.

An experienced user can control this process to maximize the chances of ending up with a risk profile scorecard. Relatively weaker and "preferred" characteristics can be placed in the earlier steps to maximize their chances of addition into the model, and to maximize the influence of certain variables by putting them in first and then letting the others add their respective predictive strengths.

Stronger characteristics are placed at the bottom, and may not enter the scorecard, as their predictive content may already have been modeled by one or several other criteria. Using several weaker criteria to model the behavior of one strong criterion is done for stability, without losing any predictive strength (e.g., five characteristics adding 200 points each to the scorecard are preferable to two characteristics adding 500 each). The model will be as effective, but with a broader base—corresponding to the idea of creating a risk profile.

Similar criteria are placed in the same step (e.g., age, time at work, time at home, or inquiries in the past 3/6/12 months) so that correlation between the characteristics can be further considered, and the best among correlated characteristics will enter the scorecard. Related ratios should also be put in the same step as the type of information of the numerator and denominator. In addition, considering the different independent information types individually at each step maximizes the chances of at least one variable from each information type entering the final scorecard. Again, the point is to maximize the chances of various characteristics, representing the different information types to get into the final model.

The regression is repeated using various combinations of characteristics at the different steps and with differing significance levels in an iterative process to get highest scorecard strength. Characteristics can be moved to higher or lower steps to produce different combinations for scorecards. This way a number of scorecards can be produced, each with a different combination of variables in it. These scorecards are then evaluated later using business criteria, mix of characteristics, and statistical measures of strength.

One practical way to do this is to use the model-ordering option in stepwise regression. There are two approaches that can be used:

1. Single regression
2. Multiple regression

Single Regression

One regression run is performed, and the characteristics are placed in order, based on information type and strength. Exhibit 10.15 provides an example.

Place the overall weaker information types at the top (based on average IV or Gini for example) and the stronger ones at the bottom. Within each information type, characteristics can be ordered from the weakest to the strongest. This ranking of each characteristic can also be done using IV or other measure if variable strength. The example in Exhibit 10.15 shows characteristics type ranked from weakest to strongest based on overall IV. Within each characteristic type, such as "time based" or "inquiries," there is further ranking done based on the

Exhibit 10.15 Inputs for Single Regression

Characteristic	IV
Time 1	0.02
Time 2	0.04
Time 3	0.06
Demographics 1	0.09
Demographics 2	0.12
Demographics 3	0.2
Inquiries 1	0.15
Inquiries 2	0.18
Inquiries 3	0.19
Inquiries 4	0.26
Financial 1	0.25
Financial 2	0.34

Info Type: Weaker → Stronger

Weaker → Stronger (Time)
Weaker → Stronger (Inquiries)

IV within each information type. This would be the sequence in which regression will consider each characteristic. This is a starting point, and the sequence should be adjusted in subsequent regression runs until the desired results are obtained. For example, if no inquiry variable enters the scorecard, we may want to run the regression again with that variable in a higher position, since a well-balanced credit score-card should have measures of credit hungriness.

Another way to rank-order the characteristics for a single regres-sion is to place them in order of increasing strength, from the lowest to the highest, regardless of information type. Using various orders of variables, and substituting different variables to represent the same information type, for example, building one scorecard with age and another with time at address, will yield different models, that can then be compared. In this manner, we can build several different scorecards for the same purpose, using different combinations of variables.

Multiple Regression

Using this approach, the regression step itself is repeated, considering each different information type exclusively at each step. An example of this approach, using information type as a basis for the different levels, has been illustrated in the example shown with Exhibit 10.14. Other ways to perform multiple regression is to set the levels corre-sponding with the strengths of both variable and information type:

- Overall weaker information types are considered first in initial regression steps.
- Within each regression, characteristics are ordered from the weakest to strongest (as in single regression).
- Characteristics entering the scorecard in previous steps are forced into the scorecard in all following steps, and the process repeated as explained in the previous section.

The preceding are only two ways to start *interactive regression*. At the end of each regression run, the composition of the final scorecard is discussed by the key stakeholders such as the model developer and the risk manager. Depending on the outcome of each run, experienced modelers and risk managers will sometimes change the order of the next run or substitute variables for business purposes. Needless to say, in addition to the business considerations discussed in this section, they should of course also consider all the usual statistical issues in building models. These include looking at the Wald chi-square, sign of the estimate and p-values (if one is inclined to), and so on.

In SAS, ordered regression such as the one shown in Exhibit 10.15 can be performed in PROC LOGISTIC using the "SEQUENTIAL=" option, whereby the order of input into the model will follow whatever is specified in the "MODEL y=" statement. The "INCLUDE=" option can be used to force characteristics to remain in the scorecard, for example, business preferred ones that are logical but may have weak power, while the "START=" option starts the stepwise regression with the first n variables specified (not in any particular order), but those variables can be removed at later steps.[7]

Performing regression with specified sequences such as this can be done in SAS Enterprise Miner using the "Model Ordering" option in the Scorecard or Regression nodes.[8]

Again, as with the grouping process, this approach to scorecard development is excellent for risk managers and model developers who want to inject business sense to make a robust statistical process produce a better outcome. But it is also susceptible to abuse due to its flexibility. An understanding of the statistical components, the purpose of the scorecard, as well as the data being worked with, will reduce the chances of abuse. Once again, these issues have been highlighted in the previous chapter—we are now starting to see the practical impact of talking to people like adjudicators and selecting characteristic manually. This approach should be experimented with using several different combinations to understand data dynamics before final scorecard production.

This process combines statistical modeling (i.e., regression) with business considerations in "designing" a scorecard that is strong and stable, contains characteristics from various sources, and represents different independent information types that together form a risk profile (e.g., demographics, inquiries, previous performance, trades). That is exactly how experienced lenders make decisions. Note that the regression is performed with the strongest set of characteristics chosen from the initial characteristics analysis, and that all the very weak criteria have been eliminated. All tests for significance are followed in selecting the final composition of the scorecard, yet that is not the only criterion for inclusion. The scorecard produced has measurable strength (e.g., fit statistics) and impact.

Most importantly, it is a useful business tool that can be accepted with confidence, and used by risk managers and other decision makers to create risk-adjusted strategies.

Once a list of characteristics for inclusion in the scorecard is obtained, these characteristics can then be regressed again as a group, to obtain final regression parameters. Similar processes are followed for each scorecard that needs to be built, in the case of segmentations. Typically, several scorecards using different combinations of characteristics are built for each segment, and evaluated against strategic objectives to determine the final choice. A scorecard with lower "power" may deliver a stronger performance for the strategic objective (e.g., higher profit) than another with a higher power, and it is therefore a valuable exercise to compare several scorecards in this manner rather than relying solely on statistical measures. Note that scorecard selection criteria and validation will be covered in subsequent sections.

The output from this phase is several different scorecards, comprising a list of characteristics and their respective regression parameters each.

REJECT INFERENCE

All the model development analyses performed to this point were on accounts with known performance. These are commonly referred to as the "Known Good/Bad" or "Accepts Only" samples. Application scorecards are developed to predict the behavior of all applicants, and using a model based on only previously approved accounts can be inaccurate, as the development sample is not representative of the population on which we will use the scorecard ("sample bias"). This is particularly true where previous accept/decline decisions were made systematically (meaning based on some deliberate selection criteria using models or judgment) and were not random; that is, the accepts population is a biased sample and not representative of the rejects. A method is needed to account for cases where the behavior is unknown. Note that

Exhibit 10.16 Reject Inference

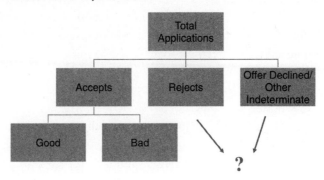

if behavior scorecards were being developed, this phase would not be necessary. It would also be unnecessary if the data being used for modeling were unbiased, or if all the biased were fixed before starting the modeling process itself.

Reject inference is a process whereby the performance of previously rejected applications is analyzed to estimate their behavior (i.e., to assign performance class). Just as there are some bads in the population that is approved, there will be some goods that have been declined. This process gives relevance to the scorecard development process by recreating the population performance for a 100 percent approval rate (i.e., obtaining the "population odds").

Exhibit 10.16 shows what we're doing. The left side shows the data set with known performance. In order to develop a scorecard applicable to the total applicants, we need to answer the question, and therefore generate a sample representing the total applicants, classed as good or bad.

Reasons for Reject Inference

The first reason for performing reject inference is that of relevance—ignoring rejects would produce a scorecard that is not applicable to the total applicant population. The issue of sample bias has already been mentioned.

Reject inference may also incorporate, and fix, the influence of past decision making into the scorecard development process. This is particularly true in manual or policy heavy underwriting environments, where significant bias is introduced by underwriters/adjudicators. We covered some of these biases in the section on binning, and also how to fix them manually. For example, consider a scenario where 1,000 out of 10,000 applicants for credit have some serious delinquency. Adjudicators decline 940 and accept 60 of these applicants. Subsequent performance shows that most of the 60 accepted applicants perform well and are classified as "good," which is hardly surprising given that they were "cherry-picked." If a scorecard is now developed using only the known goods and bads, it will tell us that those who have serious delinquency are very good credit risks. Reject inference can neutralize the distortive effects of such cherry-picking, and even policy rules, by incorporating the likelihood of cherry-picked cases being accepted into their good/bad performance. Note again, that this can be dealt with manually at the binning phase. We will cover other ways to do this in this chapter.

From a decision-making perspective, reject inference enables accurate and realistic expected performance forecasts for all applicants (i.e., the people for whom the scorecard is being developed). For example, consider a bank that has traditionally approved all applicants who scored 200 points and above using their existing scorecard. The bank now feels that it has been overly conservative and wishes now to also approve those who score 170 to 200. If the bank has never approved these applicants in the past, how will it know the incremental level of risk it is taking by moving the cutoff lower? Reject inference, by allowing them to estimate the bad rates by score of those who were previously rejected, will help them make this decision.

It also creates opportunities for better future performance through identifying the "swap set." The swap set is the exchange of known bads with inferred goods, as shown in Exhibit 10.17. Inferred goods are those

Exhibit 10.17 Swap Set

		Old Scorecard	
		Approve	Decline
New	Approve	Known G	Inf G
Scorecard	Decline	Known B	Inf B

who were rejected previously, but have been identified as potential goods using reject inference. During reject inference, we will go through and reassess those that were declined credit and ask the question, "What if they had been approved?" Based on new information or new analysis, we will infer that some of those would have been good. These are the types of applicants that we want to approve in the future. This, coupled with declining the known bads, whose performance we now know, will allow a credit grantor the opportunity to approve the same number of people but obtain better performance through better selection; that is, we will "swap" known bads for inferred goods.

Exhibit 10.18 shows an example of swap set at work. We can see that the existing approval rate is 70 percent, and based on the left side of the chart, the bad rate of the accepted population is 10 percent. Once reject inference is done, we then discover that the inferred bad rate of the rejects is 50 percent, and we split the 3,000 rejects into 1,500 goods and 1,500 bads. Depending on the reject inference method, we will then either perform the binning and regression exercise or repeat it, with the full data set of 10,000 applicants. After building that new model, we will then set the new cutoff for an expected approval rate of 70 percent. However, due to better separation of the goods and bads, and the resulting higher concentration of goods above cutoff and more bads below cutoff, we will bring about 300 of the

Exhibit 10.18 How Swap Set Enables Better Performance

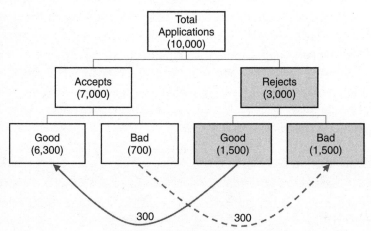

previous declined goods above cutoff. Conversely, 300 of the *previously approved* bads will now be below cutoff. The result is that while we will still approve 7,000 of our applicants, we will approve a better 7,000. The new bad rate for the same 70 percent approval rate will be (400 / 7,000) = 5.6 percent.

The better and more informed decision making underlines the fact that reject inference is more than just an exercise to comply with statistical principles—it has significant business relevance.

Understanding Reject Inference

The previous example mentions the inferred bad rate of the rejects as 50 percent. How do we know that is the accurate right answer? The answer is we don't. We will, in a later section, cover an easy to way get a guesstimate of what the number could be. Let's recognize that other than approving all applicants and finding out their performance, there is no absolutely accurate way to knowing how the rejects would have performed. It is important to accept the fact that reject inference involves predicting an unknown, and will always carry with it a degree of uncertainty. The level of uncertainty can be reduced by using better techniques, and by judicious use. Users must understand that reject inference can lead to better decision making, but it is not, and possibly will never be, 100 percent accurate (other than approving all rejects). It is therefore appropriate to be skeptical about this process and understand what it is and, more importantly, what it is not.

In this chapter, we will discuss a few different ways to perform reject inference. We will discuss how to use it sensibly, knowing all the caveats.

The population with both known and inferred goods and bads, known as the "All Good Bad" data set, is used for the final scorecard production. The sample is factored again after reject inference, as shown in Exhibit 10.19. Based on our previous assumption of a 70.5 percent actual approval rate and a 12.4 percent actual population bad rate, the inference sample shows an overall bad rate of 17.9 percent for a 100 percent approval rate. Note that the bad rate for the inferred population is about 31 percent (914 / 2,950). This is a relevancy check to ensure that reject inference has been done correctly. If the inferred

Exhibit 10.19 Factored Sample after Reject Inference

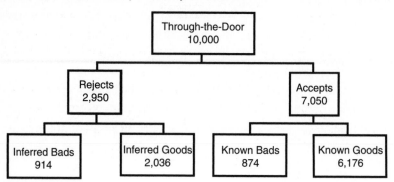

population has a lower bad rate than the known population, it would imply that the rejects are in fact of better quality than those approved by the company.

When Reject Inference Should Be Used

The impact and importance of reject inference in the scorecard development process are dependent on the application acceptance rate and the level of confidence in previous credit-granting criteria. A very high level of confidence, coupled with a high approval rate (allowing the assumption of "all rejects = bad") or a very low level of confidence (assumes near random adjudication) reduce the need for reject inference. In subprime lending, even a medium approval rate may allow the assumption of "all rejects = bad" to be made if the level of confidence in adjudication is high.

Reject inference is also less important in environments with high approval rates and correspondingly high bad rates, since the approved population is fairly close to the total applicant population, and can be safely used as a proxy for the through-the-door population. The same is true for environments where decisions were made either randomly or using an inaccurate adjudication tool. In cases with high approval rates and very low bad rates—that is, denoting a fairly tight adjudication process—it can also be safely assumed that all rejects are bads. Reject inference will not make a significant difference here either.

In environments with either low or medium approval rates and low bad rates, reject inference can help in identifying opportunities to increase market share with risk-adjusted strategies. In this case, if the lender feels that there are enough creditworthy applicants that they are currently rejecting ("leaving money on the table"), reject inference will help them in identifying these applicants. Reject inference will also have a significant impact in cases where there is confidence in the adjudication process, but it is also believed that bad rates could be brought down through better selection. Finally, as discussed previously, reject inference techniques can help in manual adjudication environments in fixing the inherent sample bias.

Reject Inference Techniques

There are various techniques used in the industry to perform reject inference. The appropriate technique that can be used will depend on several factors including the availability of complete rejected data, availability of credit bureau data on the rejects, type of bias, regulatory limitations, directives or preferences of corporate model validation departments, and other such issues. Ideally, the inferring of performance for unknown cases should be done with new data (e.g., from credit bureau)—however, there are situations when this is not possible. We will discuss several methods in the following section.

Assign All Rejects to Bads

The only situation where this would be acceptable is one in which the approval rates are very high, for example, 97 percent, and there is a high degree of confidence in the adjudication process. In this case, the assumption that all rejects are bad can be made with some confidence. This approach may not be satisfactory in other cases because we know that a significant portion of the rejects would have been good, based on competitive information gathered via credit bureau files, and also random override studies conducted by issuers over the years. The benchmark approval rate for making this call depends on how high risk the applicant population is. For example, in a subprime portfolio where a large majority of the applicants have serious delinquencies to start with, this number could be 70 percent.

Assign Rejects in the Same Proportion of Goods to Bads as Reflected in the Acceptees

For this method to be valid, one must assume that there is absolutely no consistency in the current selection system, which implies that the decisions have been made randomly up until now.

Manual Adjustment of WOEs

This involves building the final scorecard on accepted applicants only. However, recognizing that the data is biased, adjustments are made in the WOE curves to reflect what an unbiased performance would look like. This approach was discussed in detail in the Initial Characteristic Analysis section and requires in-depth knowledge of the lending policies and other factors that impact the approved population. This method does not require external data sources and can be used in countries where there is no credit bureau or where rejected data is not available.

Approve All Applications

This is the only method to find out the actual (as opposed to inferred) performance of rejected accounts. It involves approving all applications for a specific period of time. This allows for collection of a sample of the true through-the-door population and their performance. Ideally, the approved applications should be representative of all score ranges, so as not to understate or overstate the bad rate of the rejects. While this method is perhaps the most scientific and simple, the notion of approving applicants that are known to be very high risk can be daunting (the method is also known as "buying data" for this reason). There is, however, no need to approve each and every applicant for a lengthy period of time. Consider the fact that, at minimum, about 2,000 bads are required for scorecard development. If 500 of these are to be from below cutoff, and the bad rate of accounts below cutoff is estimated to be 25 percent, then 2,000 applicants below cutoff will need to be approved. Among options for collecting this data are:

- ■ Approving all applicants for a specific period, say a week or two weeks; enough to generate a sample of 500 estimated bads.

- Approving all applications above cutoff, but only randomly selected ones below. For example, approving 1 out of every 5 applicants below cutoff for a month. Again, just enough to generate a sample of 500 bads. This method, using random approves below cutoff, is the only option is some countries, as selective approvals of applications below cutoff may be against lending regulations.

- Approving all applications up to 10 or 20 points below cutoff, and randomly sampling the rest, in order to get a better sample of applications in the decision-making zone (i.e., where cutoff decisions are likely to be made)

In high-volume environments, it is also advisable that such applications be collected across a few months, to minimize seasonal variations. A further strategy to lower losses during this exercise is to grant lower loans/credit lines to those below cutoff. This does introduce bias into the exercise, but it may be necessary to get buy-in from management.

This method is, and has been, utilized by several banks, most often for the credit card portfolio. A good exercise is to estimate the additional revenues and losses due to giving credit to applicants below the cutoff, and then estimating the lower losses and higher revenues from the swap set (or usage of a better scorecard) in the future. The combination of those factors will enable the calculation of the return on investment (ROI) for this exercise, making the decision easier. For larger portfolios, even small swap sets can make a significant dollar impact.

Similar In-House or Bureau Data–Based Method

Other than approving all applicants, this is the best method for inferring the performance of the rejects. It uses actual performance at other lenders, or performance at the same bank, for similar products. It is superior to the other techniques that involve statistical inference since this is based on additional, external data and therefore adds more value than just inference using the same biased data, or judgment.

Assume a person applies for a car loan in January 2015. They get declined by your bank. The most likely next action by that applicant is that they will try their luck at another bank or other financial institution. This is exactly the behavior we are counting on.

This method involves using in-house performance data for applicants declined for one product but approved for a similar product with the same lender, or using performance at credit bureaus of those declined by one creditor but approved for a similar product elsewhere.

For example, a bank can get a list of applicants that were declined for an unsecured line of credit (overdraft facility) but were approved for a credit card (also an unsecured revolving product) at the same bank. Similarly, a credit card issuer can obtain a list of applicants that it declined but who were approved by other credit card companies. The delinquency performance of these accounts at the other card company or with similar products in-house can then be monitored through their credit bureau reports or monthly performance files. The performance with other products or companies is taken as a proxy for how the declined applicants would have performed had they been originally accepted. So if your declined customer got a car loan somewhere else, and did not get to your bad definition within the performance window, then they would have been a good.

This method approximates actual performance and is a great option but has a few hurdles and caveats. First, regulatory restrictions or privacy laws may prevent a creditor from obtaining credit bureau records of declined applicants (in some jurisdictions there is a time limit for this). In others, this may be possible, but in batches stripped of identifying information. This may, however, be possible if the declined applicant is an existing client of a multiproduct bank, whose credit bureau record is obtained at regular intervals by the bank anyways. Again, in jurisdictions where the use of credit bureau records is strictly regulated, this may not be possible. The rejected applicant may have obtained a loan elsewhere based on different conditions or pricing, or may have submitted higher down payments. This will affect their performance, and the conditions will not be exactly the same as if your bank would have given them the same loan. We must be aware that while this is an excellent approximation tool, it will not be exact.

The applicants chosen must also obtain *similar credit* during a *similar time frame* (i.e., soon after being declined). Generally, risk managers have used windows of between one and two months for this; that is, once declined the applicant has one or two months to get a similar product somewhere else. If they fail in doing so, they are assumed to have been declined everywhere else or they gave up looking; and these applicants are therefore automatically given a "bad" rating. Further, the *bad* definition chosen through analysis of known goods and bads must be used for these accounts using different data sources—which may not be easily done, especially if the credit bureau is not capable of calculating cumulative delinquency counters. In addition, applicants declined at one institution or for one product are also likely to be declined elsewhere, thus reducing the potential sample size of future "goods."

Augmentation in Historically Judgmental Decision-Making Environment (Soft Cutoff)

This method seeks to match up people with like characteristics and count the rejects as assigned by this process. The idea behind augmentation is that people rejected at a given score will behave essentially the same as those accepted at that score. The method consists of first building an Accept/Reject scoring system, which shows the inconsistency in the current credit-granting system. Within each score interval, the number of applicants accepted and rejected is tallied. The augmentation factor is defined as $(A + R) / A$, where A = number of accepts in the interval, and R = number of rejects in the interval. The computer algorithm for augmentation is then:

- Setup
  - Define the number of score intervals.
  - Calculate augmentation factors for all score intervals.
- Loop
  - Select an accepts sample point.
  - Score the sample point in question.
  - Retrieve the augmentation factor for that score interval (from Setup step 2).
  - Identify the performance group for the sample point in question.
  - Tally the sample point as n goods or bads, depending on the performance category (from step 6).
  - Have all accepts been examined? (No—go to step 3; Yes—the process is done).

After the augmentation factors have been applied, the number of augmented goods (*AG*) and augmented bads (*AB*) can be calculated and the population odds (*AG/AB*) are necessarily a convex combination of the accepts population odds (*G/B*) and the reject population odds [(*AG-G*)/(*AB-B*)]. A typical ratio of the accepts population odds to the reject population odds is 1.5 to 4.0. In a hypothetical example, suppose there are 10,000 applicants coming through the door. Suppose further that typically there are 3,500 rejects and 6,500 accepts, composed of 300 bads and 6,200 goods, and that after augmentation there are augmented goods (*AG*) of 9,400 and augmented bads (*AB*) of 600. This implies that among the 3,500 rejects, there are 300 bads and 3,200 goods, and we may calculate the following odds ratios:

Overall population odds: 9,400/600 = 15.7 to 1 Accepts population odds: 6,200/300 = 20.7 to 1
Rejects population odds: 3,200/300 = 10.7 to 1

In this hypothetical case, the accepts population is twice the quality of the reject population. The upshot is that augmentation has allowed the scorecard developer to swap some of the accepted bads for a portion of the accepted goods.

Simple Augmentation

This method, also known as "hard cutoff," involves the following steps:

Step 1: Build a model using known goods and bads (note that this is what has been done in the previous section of this chapter).

Step 2: Score rejects using this model and establish their expected bad rates, or p(bad).

Step 3: Set an expected bad rate level above which an account is deemed "bad"; all applicants below this level are conversely classified as "good." A good and consistent selection point is at the expected marginal bad rate of the worst-quality applicant you are willing to approve today, applied with a safety factor. For example, if the bad rate at your current cutoff is 12 percent, you may want to use 6 to 8 percent for this exercise. This means that any rejects falling into a score bucket where the expected bad rate is more than 6 to 8 percent will be classified as bad.

Step 4: Add the inferred goods and bads to the known goods/bads and remodel.

This method is simple but has some drawbacks. The classification of rejects into goods and bads can be arbitrary, even though one can use iterations with different cutoffs and simple rules of thumb to make sanity checks (e.g., bad rate of rejected population should be two to four times that of the accepts). The known good/bad scorecard here needs to be strong, and unbiased, since it is the only thing being used to assign class. Those who use this method tend to spend some time at the binning stage removing all known biases from the data, so that when the rejects are scored, the results are not biased. This method also does not take into account the probability of a reject being approved, and hence rejects are incorporated into the known on a 1:1 basis. The next method seeks to remedy this particular drawback.

Augmentation 2[9]

This method adjusts the weights of the known good/bad model by an estimate of the probability of acceptance (i.e., the probability of being included in the known population). This is done in two steps:

Step 1: An accept/decline model is built to get the probability of accept or decline for each case.

Step 2: Using only the known goods and bads (i.e., the accepts), a good/bad model is built with the population distribution adjusted using the previously established accept/reject weights. This is done in such a way that the new case weights are inversely proportional to the probability of acceptance, so that cases are weighed to more accurately represent the total population.

This method recognizes the need to adjust bias using the p(approve) and is better than simple augmentation. We briefly discussed this subject in the section on binning—that bias is reflected by the approval rate. A similar technique that uses the rejected population is explained later in the Fuzzy Augmentation section.

Bureau Score Migration

This method may be used where banks have bureau score rules for denying credit, for example, a policy rule that states that all applicants below a bureau score of 400 are declined. The bank then monitors the applicant's bureau score over the performance window (e.g., the next 24 months). It also sets a higher approval benchmark where the probability of being good is very high—in this case, say a bureau score of 550. If in the next two years, the rejected applicant's bureau score climbs to above 550, then they would have been good.

Parceling

This method is similar to simple augmentation, but instead of classifying all rejects at a certain score as good or bad, it assigns them in proportion to the expected bad rate at that score. This is a very widely used method preferred by risk managers in countries where no credit bureau data is available, as well as those with small portfolios where purchasing bureau data for rejects is not considered cost effective.

This method involves the following steps:

Step 1: Build the known good/bad model and score the rejects.

Step 2: Allocate the rejects into goods and bads based on the expected bad rate from the known good/bad model; that is, proportional classification.

Step 3: Combine the data sets and rebuild the model.

Exhibit 10.20 illustrates an example.

The first four columns in the exhibit are distributions by score of the "known good/bad" sample, using the known good/bad scorecard that we built in the previous section. This information can be obtained from the gains chart of the known good/bad model. The data suggests that 200 was the cutoff for the previous scorecard, and this new one is largely similar in separating the goods and bads. Note also the relatively low bad rates for scores below 200. These are likely the overrides from the past, hence showing selection bias.

The "reject" column represents the distribution of rejects as scored by the known good/bad scorecard. The last two columns represent the *random* allocation of the scored rejects into "good" and "bad" classes.

Exhibit 10.20 Reject Inference Using Parceling

Score	# Bad	# Good	% Bad	% Good	Reject	Rej - Bad	Rej - Good
0-169	290	1,028	22.0%	78.0%	3,778	831	2,947
170-179	268	1,221	18.0%	82.0%	2,514	453	2,061
180-189	198	1,452	12.0%	88.0%	5,587	670	4,917
190-199	241	2,437	9.0%	91.0%	6,539	589	5,950
200-209	852	9,798	8.0%	92.0%	3,952	316	3,636
210-219	698	13,262	5.0%	95.0%	2,400	120	2,280
220-229	321	7,704	4.0%	96.0%	1,598	64	1,534
230-239	277	13,573	2.0%	98.0%	2,166	43	2,123
240-249	140	17,360	0.8%	99.2%	1,248	10	1,238
250+	94	18,706	0.5%	99.5%	799	4	795

For example, if there are 3,952 rejects in the score range 200–209, and the expected bad rate is 8 percent, then 316 rejects will be assigned as "bad" and the remaining 3,636 as "good." The assignment of classes within each score band is random.

The major problem here is that while the expected bad rates are from the approved sample, we are applying those same numbers on the rejects. Business sense would suggest that since the proportion of goods and bads in the rejected cases cannot be the same as that of the approved (rejects should be worse), a conservative approach is to assign a higher proportion of rejected ones as bad. We therefore need to calculate a factor to multiply the calculated bad rate with. In my experience, I have seen factors here that range from the bad rate of rejects being 2 to 10 times as high as the approved. But how do we know how bad the rejects are?

One way to obtain a good *guesstimate* is to plot the bad rate of the approved accounts by score, as shown in Exhibit 10.21.

The solid vertical line in the middle denotes the current cut-off, which is 200. We can see the bad rate for the approved population both above and below the cutoff. Note again the bad rate of the accounts below cutoff is lower than it should be. In order to get a guesstimate of the bad rate below cutoff, we can extrapolate the curve above cutoff into the zone below in several ways. "Extrapolate 1"

Exhibit 10.21 Extrapolation of Known Bad Rates

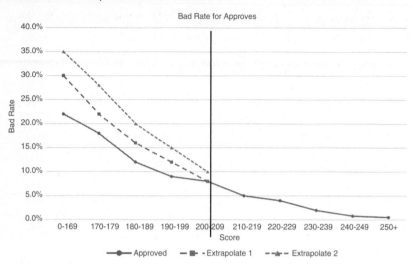

and "Extrapolate 2" represent two ways to do this. "Extrapolate 1" assumes that the bad rates above cutoff are unbiased and therefore tries to create the usual logarithmic relationship between bad rates and scores (dependent on the "points to double the odds" factors). "Extrapolate 2" is a more conservative estimate, and assumes that the curve above cutoff is also biased due to high side overrides. While there is no definitive 100 percent correct extrapolation, we can try either of these approaches to get a broad estimate.

An iterative approach, and rules of thumb can be used here. The factor can depend on the approval rate, confidence level in the previous model, override rates and separation provided by the old scorecard. For example, if the factor was five, then for score range 200–209, instead of 8 percent, we would allocate 40 percent of the rejected cases to "bad." Risk managers apply the factor in different ways:

- Apply it uniformly across all score bands.
- Apply a higher factor in the lower scores (to be more conservative), apply the exact factor in the middle, and a lower factor in the higher score bands. In the above example, we could apply a factor of 10 to the bands lower than 180, a factor of 8 for

200–230, and 4 to those rejects who scored above 230. Risk managers and scorecard developers can adjust these numbers until they get to the overall bad rate desired.

This method is fairly quick and simple to implement, and the ability to adjust the factor to multiply the bad rates, makes it flexible. Risk managers can exercise business judgment and conservatism to get to a number that they feel comfortable with. As with simple augmentation, the known good/bad scorecard here needs to be good, since it is the only thing being used to allocate class. In addition, the allocation needs to be adjusted (e.g., based on the conservative approach) so that the bad rate of the rejects is not understated.

Fuzzy Augmentation[10]

This method combines two steps, namely, proportional classification, and adjustment of the inferred data set based on the probability of approval. The full process involves classification and then augmentation using the following steps:

Step 1: Classification.

- Score rejects with the known good/bad model.
- Determine $p(good)$ and $p(bad)$ for each reject based on expected bad rates.
- Assign each reject as a partial good and a partial bad (i.e., creating two weighted cases from each reject).
- Weigh rejected goods with $p(good)$ and rejected bads with $p(bad)$. As with parceling, each scored reject can be assigned a higher expected $p(bad)$ as a conservative measure, based on the factor discussed in the previous section.

Step 2: Augmentation.

- Combine rejects with accepts, adjusting for approval rate, $p(approve)$.
- For example, frequency of a "good" from rejects = $p(good)$ * weight, where "weight" is the probability of a reject being included in the augmented data set.

The additional weighting at the augmentation step is done since combining accepts and inferred rejects on a one-to-one basis would imply that they both have equal chances of being in the data set.

This method incorporates not just the likelihood of a reject being bad, but also its probability of being accepted in the first place. This is a better approach, as it assigns some measure of importance to a reject in the final sample. In addition, using partial classification makes it better than methods that use arbitrary measures to do so.

Iterative Reclassification[11]

This method involves first building a known good/bad model, assigning classes based on a p(bad) (as in simple augmentation), combining rejects with the accepts, and repeating the process until some convergence is reached.

The steps are as follows:

Step 1: Build a known good/bad scorecard.

Step 2: Score rejects and assign class based on a minimum expected bad rate or chosen p(bad). The cutoff should be set based on some conservatism as has been discussed previously.

Step 3: Combine the inferred rejects and accepts, and rebuild scorecard.

Step 4: Rescore the rejects and reassign class, then combine and rebuild scorecard.

Step 5: Repeat this process until parameter estimates (and p[bad]) converge.

Note that one way to modify this approach is to use partial good/bad classifications instead of classifying on the basis of an arbitrary p(bad).

Convergence can be measured by using parameter estimates or p(bad) for each score group or for each run, or by using a plot of log(odds) against score, as shown in Exhibit 10.22. The dashed lines represent iterations.

Each iteration should be below the known good/bad (KGB) line, confirming that the combined population has a higher bad rate than the accepts alone. If the combined data set line is above the KGB line, it would imply that the rejects are of better quality than the accepts.

Exhibit 10.22 Reject Inference Using Iterative Reclassification

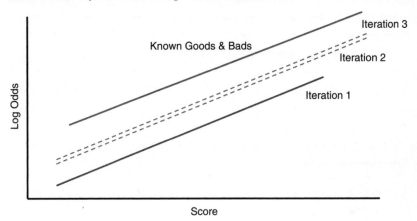

Nearest Neighbor (Clustering)

This technique uses clustering to identify goods and bads in a reject sample, and does not rely on any previously built models. The steps involved are fairly simple:

Step 1: Create two sets of clusters—one each for known goods and bads.

Step 2: Run rejects through both clusters.

Step 3: Compare Euclidean distances to assign most likely performance (i.e., if a reject is closer to a "good" cluster than a "bad" one, then it is likely a good).

Step 4: Combine accepts and rejects to create inferred data set, and remodel.

As further steps to refine this approach, adjustment for p(approve) can be added when creating the inferred data set, and partial classifications can be done. This method is also relatively simple to do with the right tools. Its drawback is that the measures are relative—as compared to the other options discussed in previous sections.

Memory-Based Reasoning[12]

Memory-based, or case-based, reasoning follows a two-step process to assign class. First, it identifies similar cases, for example, good and bad cases in a sample. It then uses the learning from the first step to assign class to a new record. This process mimics the thought pattern that people would go through if they were performing manual reject inference. For example, a person reviews many known good and bad accounts and notes the characteristics of both. He or she then goes through a set of rejected ones and identifies those that have similar characteristics as the known goods or bads. The way adjudicators judgmentally assign risk ratings is based on a similar phenomena.

The steps involved in performing reject inference using memory-based reasoning are:

Step 1: Perform clustering using the known goods and bads, as well as the rejects in the same data set. SAS Enterprise Miner, for example, uses the k-nearest neighbor algorithm to categorize observations in its Memory Based Reasoning node.

Step 2: The distance between each known good/bad observation and the reject case (called a "probe") is then measured. The k known good/bad observations that have the smallest Euclidean distance to a reject case are then the k-nearest neighbor to that reject.

Step 3: The target classes (good/bad mix) of the k-nearest neighbors are then used to assign a probability of good/bad to each reject case. For example, if $k=50$, then the algorithm looks at the nearest 50 cases to determine class.

Step 4: Create a combined sample and remodel.

The classification can be done in absolute terms; that is, the rejected case can be classified as a good or bad. Otherwise, the composition of the nearest neighbors can be used to partially classify each reject. For example, if 40 out of the 50 nearest neighbors to a reject are good, then we can either classify that reject as a good, or assign it as 80 percent good and 20 percent bad.

Inferring Indeterminates

We have discussed inferring the rejects to this point. In addition to those, we can also infer the performance of an "indeterminate" account using the same methods. For example, the performance of inactive and offer declined (not taken up) accounts can be inferred using credit bureau data.

If an applicant was approved by your bank, but they declined the offer and walked away, it would be logical to assume that they had a better offer somewhere else, based on pricing or limit. Using the same logic as the Bureau Data–Based Method discussed earlier, we can check the credit bureau of this account, find similar trades opened within one or two months of them declining your offer, and then use the performance at the other lender to infer their performance had they taken your offer. The same caveats apply. In cases where you are unable to get their full bureau report, some banks use proportional classification or other statistical methods discussed.

For inactive accounts or those with very low balances, we can follow a similar approach, but segment them into:

- *Inactive at your bank, but uses other credit cards.* Check their performance with the other lender and use the delinquency counter to assign class. Some banks will try to use different strategies using credit limits or other offers to try to convert these accounts into active users. Generally, if that doesn't work, and these accounts have no other relationship with the bank, some banks will close down such accounts as they are higher risk.

- *Inactive at your bank, and does not use other credit cards.* In general, banks will evaluate their relationships with such cases. If there is no other banking relationship, some banks choose to close down such accounts, as these are higher risk. If there is a profitable and significant banking relationship (savings/checking accounts, mortgages, etc.) with this account, then most banks do nothing. In this case, the bureau, or some internal score may be used to assign class based on proportional classification.

Verification

Once reject inference is completed, simple analysis can be done to verify the results. This includes:

- Comparing bad rates/odds of inferred and known samples and applying industry rules of thumb as discussed previously. Reject inference can be run with different parameters until these rules of thumb are satisfied. The rules of thumb should be applied based on the approval rate and the level of confidence in previous credit granting. For example, if the previous credit granting was good, and the approval rate was also high, then the inferred rejects should have a bad rate much higher, say 8 to 10 times that of the approves. A medium approval rate may yield an inferred bad rate only 3 to 4 times that of approves.

■ Comparing the weight of evidence or bad rates of grouped attributes for pre- and post-inferred data sets. Attributes with low acceptance rates and high WOE should see lower post-inference WOE—consistent with business experience, as discussed in the section on binning.

There are several global banks and other financial institutions that have conducted in-house research to determine whether specific reject inference techniques are better for certain portfolios. As we have seen in this chapter, the types of biases in secured versus unsecured loans tend to be different. It may be that some inferencing techniques work better on certain types of portfolios. These techniques and parameters can be tested using "fake" rejects. This involves splitting the rank-ordered approved population into accepts and rejects, for example a 70/30 split. A model developed on the 70 percent "approved" sample can then be used for inferring the performance of the remaining 30 percent. Since the actual performance of the 30 percent "rejects" is already known, misclassification can be used to gauge the performance of each reject inference method.[13]

Once reject inference is completed, the combined data set (of approves and inferred rejects) is created and used for the next phase of scorecard development. Now that sample bias is resolved, this final scorecard will be applicable to the entire through-the-door population.

FINAL SCORECARD PRODUCTION

The final models are then produced by running the same initial characteristic analysis (binning) and statistical algorithms (logistic regression) on the post-inferred data set, to generate the final set of characteristics for the scorecard. Note that you are not limited to the characteristics selected in the preliminary scorecard in this phase. Some characteristics may appear weaker and some stronger after reject inference, so the process of selecting characteristics needs to be repeated, considering the entire development data set. In particular, characteristics used in policy rules or those heavily biased very often become more logical and display a higher separation (steeper gradient) after the addition of the rejected data set.

At this point, let's assume that a final model has been produced by performing initial characteristic analysis and logistic regression on the "All Good Bad" data set. What we have now is a set of characteristics, along with the output from logistic regression such as the intercept, parameter estimates, and model performance statistics.

Additional issues that now need to be addressed are scaling of the scores, validity of the points allocation, misclassification, and scorecard strength.

Scaling

Scorecards can be produced in many formats (e.g., SAS code, points system, etc.). In some cases—such as online or real-time scorecard usage that is often dependent on implementation platforms, regulatory instructions requiring the provision of reasons for decline, simplicity and ease of use, and other factors mentioned in the Why "Scorecard" Format? section in Chapter 4—the scorecard needs to be produced in a particular format with grouped variables and points (see Exhibit 1.1). In this case, scaling needs to be applied. Scaling refers to the range and format of scores in a scorecard and the rate of change in odds for increases in score. Scorecard scores can take several forms with decimal or discrete number scores:

- Where the score is the good/bad odd or probability of bad (e.g., score of 6 means a 6:1 odd or 6 percent chance of default).
- With some defined numerical minimum/maximum scale (e.g., −1, 0–1,000, 150–350), or without a defined range but

with a specified odds ratio at a certain point (e.g., odds of 5:1 at 500) and specified rate of change of odds (e.g., odds double every 50 points).

The choice of scaling, or its parameters, does not affect the predictive strength of the scorecard. It is an operational decision based on considerations such as:

- Implementability of the scorecard into application processing software. Certain software can implement scorecards only in the format shown in Exhibit 1.1.

- Ease of understanding by staff (e.g., variables with discrete points are easier to work with and understand, therefore generate confidence among end users).

- Continuity with existing scorecards or other scorecards in the company. This avoids retraining on scorecard usage and interpretation of scores.

Note that at the moment we have a logistic regression equation and binned characteristics. What we want to do is assign points to each attribute in each characteristic, such that the total score (when you add up attributes across characteristics) can then be interpreted to mean odds or probabilities of default, for example.

There are various scales in use in the industry. One of the most common is a scorecard with discrete scores scaled logarithmically, with the odds doubling at every 20 points. To understand this, let's take a look at a typical odds relationship to some rank ordered input. The curve would look something like Exhibit 10.23.

Our objective is to generate a scorecard where the x-axis on that curve is the final score, and each score corresponds to some odds. In order to start the analysis, we will pick two reference points on the curve. The reference points—a score, odds at the score, and points to double the odds—are entirely up to the user and will serve as parameters for calculations to come. However, a good practice is to follow whatever scaling has been in use at the company, or in the previous scorecard so that the new scores will mean the same as the old one.

Let's assume that we would like a scorecard where a total score of 300 means 30:1 odds, and the odds double every 20 points. This gives

Exhibit 10.23 Odds to Rank-Ordered Input Relationship

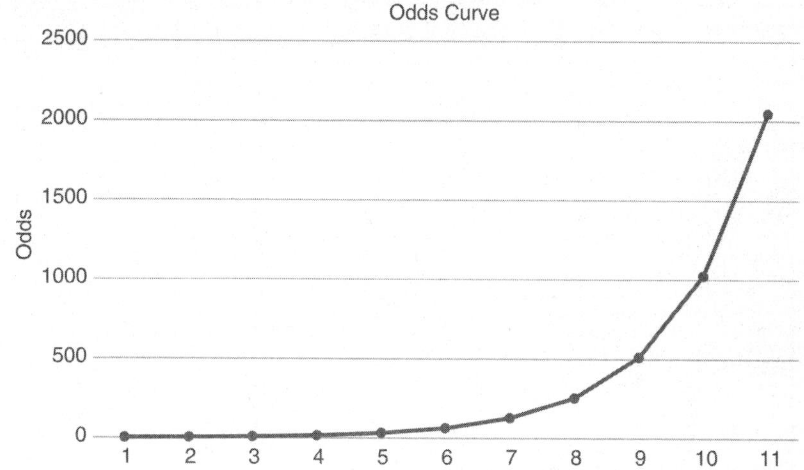

us two reference points on the curve in Exhibit 10.23, namely, where the odds are 30 and 60.

Now let's return to Exhibit 10.23 but add the curve for the ln(odds) to rank ordered input. That curve will look something like that shown in Exhibit 10.24.

Exhibit 10.24 Ln(odds) to Scaled Score Relationship

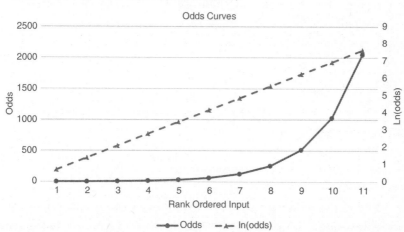

Exhibit 10.25 Example Scorecard Showing Scaling

Age			Delq at Bureau			Score	Odds
18-24	20		0	55		300	30
25-29	32		1-2	40		301	31
30-37	46		3-5	12		302	33
38-45	56		6+	5		303	34
46+	80					.	
			R/O Burden			.	
Time at Res			0	15		320	60
0-6	12		1-9	40		.	
7-18	25		10-25	30		340	120
19-36	38		26-50	25			
37+	50		50-69	20			
			70-85	15			
Region			86-99	10			
Major Urban	20		100+	5			
Minor Urban	25						
Rural	15						
Inq 6 mth							
0	50						
1-3	30						
4-5	15						

We now have the relationship between score and ln(odds) as a convenient linear equation. What we would like to do is to calculate the points for each scorecard attribute, where once we add the attribute points for any applicant, their final scores can be interpreted. Based on the parameters stated, for example, someone who scores 300 points will have good:bad odds of 30:1. An example, using a partial scorecard, is provided in Exhibit 10.25.

We will go through the calculations that describe how to calculate these points in the next section.

Scaling Calculation

In general, the relationship between odds and scores can be presented as a linear one:

$$\text{Score} = \text{Offset} + \text{Factor } ln \text{ (odds)}$$

Where the scorecard is being developed using specified odds at a score and specified "points to double the odds" (*pdo*), the factor and offset can easily be calculated by using the following simultaneous equations:

$$\text{Score} = \text{Offset} + \text{Factor} * ln \text{ (odds)}$$
$$\text{Score} + pdo = \text{Offset} + \text{Factor} * ln \text{ (}\underline{\mathbf{2}} * \text{odds)}$$

From the previous section, we refer back to the two references points, where at a score of 300 the odds are 30:1 and at a score of 320, the odds should be 60:1.

Solving the equations above for *pdo*, we get

$$\text{pdo} = \text{Factor} * ln \text{ (2), therefore}$$
$$\text{Factor} = pdo \text{ / } ln \text{ (2);}$$
$$\text{Offset} = \text{Score} - \{\text{Factor} * ln \text{ (Odds)}\}$$

For example, if a scorecard were being scaled where the user wanted odds of 50:1 at 600 points and wanted the odds to double every 20 points (i.e., *pdo* = 20), the factor and offset would be:

$$\text{Factor} = 20 \text{ / } ln \text{ (2)} = 28.8539$$
$$\text{Offset} = 600 - \{28.8539 \; ln \text{ (50)}\} = 487.123$$

And each score corresponding to each set of odds can be calculated as:

$$\text{Score} = 487.123 + 28.8539 \; ln \text{ (odds)}$$

The same formula can be used to scale scorecards that triple or quadruple the odds every few points. "Points to double the odds," however, is the most widely used scaling in the credit risk industry.

This formula can be used to generate scores for any case, using any model that can generate a probability of bad, or odds. This would include models developed using techniques other than regression, as has been discussed in this book. The formula describes the relationship between total score and odds, and may not be applicable in cases where the score to odds relationship is quadratic or some other higher order one. Once again, what we would like to do is to assign points to each grouped attribute in our scorecard. For this, we go one step further, and break up the *ln(odds)* in the equation above into its components.

Since the scorecard here is being developed using the weight of evidence as input into a logistic regression equation (which, not coincidentally, outputs the odds), the preceding relationship can be modified as:

$$\text{score} = ln(\text{odds}) * \text{factor} + \text{offset} =$$

$$-\left(\sum_{j,i=1}^{k,n}(\text{woe}_j * \beta_i) + a\right) * \text{factor} + \text{offset} =$$

$$-\left(\sum_{j,i=1}^{k,n}(\text{woe}_j * \beta_i + \frac{a}{n})\right) * \text{factor} + \text{offset} =$$

$$\sum_{j,i=1}^{k,n}\left(-\left(\text{woe}_j * \beta_i + \frac{a}{n}\right) * \text{factor} + \frac{\text{offset}}{n}\right)$$

where

WOE = weight of evidence for each grouped attribute (<u>NOT</u> multiplied by 100)

β = regression coefficient for each characteristic

a = intercept term from logistic regression

n = number of characteristics in the model

k = number of groups (of attributes) in each characteristic

This formula is applied to every attribute bin/group in the scorecard. It will calculate the scores to be assigned to each grouped attribute, based on the parameters determined by the end user, for every characteristic in the scorecard developed. Summing up the scores, for each characteristic, for any one account or applicant, would then provide the final score. If the logistic regression was performed on dummy codes instead of WOE, the formula above can be easily modified to calculate the scores for each bin:

$$\sum_{j,i}^{k,n}[-\left(\beta_{ij} + \frac{\alpha}{n}\right) \times \text{factor} + \frac{\text{offset}}{n}]$$

Where β represents the regression coefficient for each dummy variable. At this point, it is worth noting that the trend and difference between weights of evidence in the grouped attributes will affect the points assigned using this approach. This underscores the emphasis placed on both maintaining a logical trend of WOE and trying to maximize the differences in the WOE of successive groups.

Adverse Codes

In some jurisdictions, notably the United States, lenders are required to give borrowers reasons for declining their applications for credit. This is done using adverse codes. Please note that the actual method to generate adverse codes will need to be verified and approved by the compliance function of each bank. The following examples are of two potential ways in which this can be done.

One method uses the methodology for allocating scores as described earlier, and generates adverse codes by calculating a "neutral score." The neutral score would be the score where the WOE is 0 (where the odds of good:bad are equal). Using the equation shown earlier, once the factor and offset are obtained, one can substitute WOE = 0 in the equation to get the neutral score. The equation for neutral score is therefore:

$$-\left(\frac{\alpha}{n} \times \text{factor}\right) + \frac{\text{offset}}{n}$$

Any characteristic for which the applicant scores below the neutral score is then a potential reason for decline, since the odds of being bad based on this characteristic is more than the odds of being good (note, at WOE = 0, the good:bad odds are 1:1). An example of how one applicant scored on a scorecard is shown in Exhibit 10.26. The exhibit also provides the neutral score for this scorecard.

Exhibit 10.26 Reasons for Decline with Neutral Score

Scorecard	
Avg Bal Savings	56
Time at Address	43
Loan to Value	22
Inquiries 3 Mths	20
% Trades Delinquent	43
Oldest Trade	68
Debt Service Ratio	42
Utilization	25
Worst Rating	30
Neutral Score	31

Exhibit 10.27 Neutral Score Using Weighted Average Approach

Time at Res	Distribution	Score	D × S
0–6	18%	12	2.16
7–18	32%	25	8
19–36	26%	28	7.28
37+	24%	40	9.6
Weighted Average			**27.04**

Based on this applicant's scores, his top three reasons for decline would be Inquiries 3 Months, Loan to Value, and Utilization. These are the three lowest-scoring characteristics below the neutral score.

Some institutions also generate the adverse codes based on the weighted average score of each characteristic. This needs to be calculated separately for each characteristic, whereas there is only one neutral score for each scorecard. An example of the weighted average calculation for "time at residence" is shown in Exhibit 10.27.

The weighted average is calculated using the formula:

$$\sum_{I=1}^{n}(\text{Distribution}_i * \text{score}_i)$$

The adverse code is then generated using attributes where the applicant scores below the calculated weighted average score. In the case of our time at residence example above, it the applicant scored 12 or 25 points, based on having time at residence of less than 18 months, then this can be a potential reason for decline. Ranking in this case can be done by calculating the percentage difference between the applicant's score and the weighted average, for all characteristics where the applicant has scored below the weighted average—the three biggest variances would then become the top three reasons for decline. Again, any methodology adopted by any bank in the United States must be approved by its compliance staff. The preceding examples are merely illustrative, and are not to be treated as specific compliance advice.

Points Allocation

Once the final scorecard is produced, the point allocation for each attribute, and the overall strength of the scorecard, should be checked. The allocation of scores needs to be logical, following trends established in the initial characteristic analysis. An example of scores from two separately developed scorecards are shown for "age" in Exhibit 10.28.

The first two columns are for Scorecard 1, which has a logical distribution; as age increases, applicants are given more points. This fits in well with the attribute WOE distribution and with business experience. Scorecard 2, however, contains a reversal at attribute "27–29." This could have been caused by an illogical WOE distribution or correlation (if using dummy variables). This also happens when two groups have weights that are not sufficiently far apart. Note also that "missing" age was allocated 16 points, based on the negative WOE. If we had excluded the missing data, we would likely have given anyone leaving their age missing the neutral score, which would be approximately 26 or 27 points (close to WOE = 0). By including the missing data, and binning the "missing" category, we will now be giving the appropriate points to people leaving their age missing. This is why we followed that option.

Note that if the approach outlined in this book is followed, with logical grouping and regression using WOE, this sort of reversal will not happen. These tend to occur where the raw data is used as an input into regression, and then the scores are assigned using other methods. Since this is the only reversal in this characteristic, and the

Exhibit 10.28 Logical Distribution of Points Allocation

Age	Weight	Scorecard 1	Scorecard 2
Missing	−55.50	16	16
18–22	−108.41	12	12
23–26	−72.04	18	18
27–29	−3.95	26	14
30–35	70.77	35	38
35–44	122.04	43	44
44+	165.51	51	52

rest of the point allocation is logical, a judgmental alteration of the points is normally performed. Depending on the severity of the reversal, and the order of the point allocation for the rest of the attributes, regrouping characteristics and a revision of the stepwise regression may be needed.

Once again, the importance of understanding your data and business, and spending time collaboratively binning the variables must be underscored. This is why we had stated earlier that the shape of the WOE bins you create will determine the shape of the scorecard. The logical WOE distribution, whether linear or some other shape, is critical in making sure that the final scorecard has points that follow that logic. This ensures that the final scorecard meets experience and expectations, and is therefore accepted and used. The binning process is the most critical part of the scorecard development exercise, as it determines exactly what the final scorecard will look like.

This exercise may become an iterative process until a statistically and operationally acceptable scorecard is produced.

At the end of this stage, we have built several candidate models, and scaled all of them into the scorecard format.

CHOOSING A SCORECARD

Most scorecard developers would produce at least two or three different scorecards as part of any project. Developing several different scorecards becomes an easier option given the amount of control and flexibility associated with the development method shown in this book. At this point, choosing a final scorecard from among these involves answering two questions, namely: "Which scorecard is the best?" and "How good is the scorecard?" In most data mining software, the fit statistics and charts for the models are normally produced on both the development and validation samples. As such, in practice, some validation can also be done while we're selecting the best scorecard. Validation and the question of whether the scorecard is compliant with regulations will be covered in more detail in a later section.

The questions above are answered using a combination of statistical and business measures. Model risk management guidance from regulators including the Basel Committee for Banking Supervision, are all fairly consistent in stating that statistical tests alone are insufficient in determining model quality, or in validating any models.[14] Another good resource for model validation statistics is in *Fair Lending Compliance* by Clark Abrahams and Sunny Zhang (see Bibliography). The chapter on model validation describes a number of metrics, including a model performance residual index, model lift decay index, model stability index, model usage index, model aging index, and model profitability index. All of these are relevant aspects both when choosing them and also evaluating scorecards as they are used.

Note that there is no single definitive way to decide which model is the best. The decision depends on the objective of the model, internal practices and personal preferences of the model development, validation, and risk management staff. The method discussed below should be seen as just examples of some of the approaches that can be used to decide.

Misclassification

Scorecards are designed to predict the probability of a case being good or bad. More importantly, as rank ordering mechanisms, they are used for differentiating between good and bad cases. Misclassification statistics are a good way to determine whether a scorecard is providing the right differentiation. For operational purposes, companies normally choose a minimum level of acceptable bad rate (based on a score) as a "cutoff." Applicants scoring below the cutoff are declined for credit or services, or tagged as potential frauds. As a result, there is always a chance that an actual good may be classified as bad and therefore rejected, and vice versa. The same is true for behavior scorecards where a cutoff is used to decide positive or negative actions on certain accounts. To ensure better performance, the final scorecard here should to be chosen such that the level of such misclassification is minimized. The question is, which measure do we need to maximize or minimize?

There are several measures used to gauge the level of such misclassification, and compare different scorecards. These measures compare the number of true goods and bads with the number of predicted goods and bads for a certain cutoff. "Goods" and "Bads" here refer to cases above and below the proposed cutoff.

Exhibit 10.29 Confusion Matrix

		Predicted	
		Good	Bad
Actual	Good	True Negative	False Positive
	Bad	False Negative	True Positive

The measures are based on a confusion (or misclassification) matrix, as illustrated in Exhibit 10.29.

A better scorecard may be one where the "true" cases are maximized, and conversely, "false" cases minimized. However, there are other ways to look at the statistic. There are many statistics that are produced from the above matrix, some of them used to gauge misclassification are:

Accuracy: (true positives and negatives) / (total cases)

Error rate: (false positives and negatives) / (total cases)

Sensitivity, or true positive rate: (true positives) / (total actual positives)

Specificity, or true negative rate: (true negatives) / (total actual negatives)

Precision or positive predicted value: (true positives) / (predicted positives)

Negative predicted value: (true negatives) / (predicted negatives)

False positive rate: (1 – specificity)

False discovery rate: (1 – precision)

If you have four candidate scorecards, all with different statistics from the confusion matrix, which one do you use to pick the best? A good initial step is to convert the statistics into business terms, for example:

- False positive—decline goods
- True positive—decline bads
- False negative—acceptance of bads
- True negative—accept goods

Based on these measures, a company can then decide, for example, to maximize the rejection of bads. In this case, typically where

Exhibit 10.30 Confusion Matrix Numbers for Unadjusted Samples

		Predicted	
		Good	Bad
Actual	Good	$n^*(\text{True } P_s/\text{Actual } P_s)*\pi_1$	$n^*(1-\text{Sens})*\pi_1$
	Bad	$n^*(1-\text{Spec})*\pi_0$	$n^*(\text{Spec})*\pi_0$

the scorecards are being built to reduce losses, it would choose the scorecard that maximizes sensitivity. In the case where the company wishes to get higher market share and does not mind approving some bads, it can minimize the rejection of goods by choosing the scorecard that maximizes specificity. The statistics here are therefore being used in the context of the business goals for which the scorecard is being developed. There is no one right answer—again, the point of this is to illustrate how a commonly produced output of models can be used to make business decisions. This should reinforce the importance of deciding on an objective for scorecard development, as was discussed under the Create Business Plan section of Chapter 4.

Where several models have been developed for comparison, these statistics should be generated for each one, based on similar cutoffs (e.g., based on 70 percent final approval rate or 5 percent bad rate).

Note that where the scorecard has been developed without adjusting for oversampling, the misclassification matrix numbers need to be adjusted to reflect proper counts. This is done by multiplying cell counts by sample weights π_1 and π_2, as shown in Exhibit 10.30.

Another more direct way to pick the best scorecard is to compare them using the measure most relevant to the objective. For example, profitability by score (to compare the one most profitable at the intended cutoff), total recovery rate for the top 25 percent, and so on. The example in Exhibit 10.31 is for the two most common measures used for application scorecards, namely, approval rate and expected total bad rate.

The exhibit shows two scorecards with very different performance profiles. Interestingly enough, they have almost identical Gini, KS, area under the receiver operating characteristic curve (AUC), and so on, so using statistics to compare won't be of much help.

Exhibit 10.31 Trade-off between Approval and Bad Rate for Two Scorecards

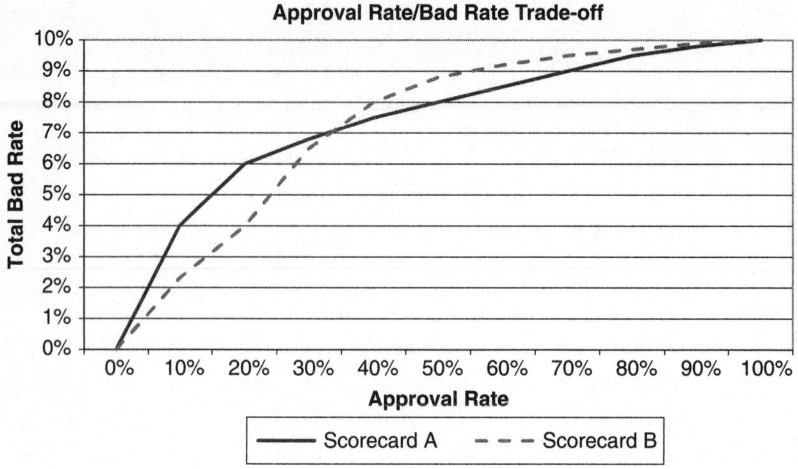

So which one is better? It depends. If your target approval rate is 75 percent, then Scorecard A would be better since it will produce a lower bad rate. However, if your intended target bad rate is 4 percent, then Scorecard B would be a better choice since it will generate that bad rate with a higher approval rate.

This underscores the discussion we had earlier on designing the right scorecard for the business objective at hand or solving the business problem. There is no such thing as an overall best model if you're trying to maximize a fit statistic alone. You must know why you are developing the model and what the preferred trade-off is. Using this information, you will then select the right mix of variables for the model to get the desired performance. For example, if we were building a fraud or bankruptcy model, we would use more negative variables (like ever bankrupt, ever 90 DPD) that would isolate the worst 3-5 percent of the population (a bit like Scorecard A in Exhibit 10.31). We are not so concerned about the other 95 percent because we don't intend to take any action on them. For credit card behavior scorecards, we use mostly continuous positive or financial data because we intend to take different action on the whole spectrum, and we want separation across the scores. This is one of the reasons why we designed a scorecard via judicious interactive regression.

Scorecard Strength

Scorecard strength can be measured many different ways. There is a long list of statistics that measure how well the model describes the data or how well it predicts the cases of goods and bads. Some of these include the usage of KS, chi-square, Hosmer-Lemeshow,[15] AUC, and the confusion matrix we saw earlier. Before we discuss examples of these measures, some issues should be noted.

Most of the measures commonly used in the industry are for comparative purposes, and not absolute. This means that outside of some rules of thumb, there are no absolute acceptable levels of such measures. For example, while application and behavior scorecards at banks typically have KS values of 40 to 60 percent, models built on deep segments such as super- or subprime will have much lower KS values, some below 15 percent. That in itself does not make the model unusable or "not useful." If a user can identify/segment out a group of very low risk customers, then that is operationally very useful, regardless of the model KS. When looking at such fit measures, it is useful to remember that models are built on a "best efforts" basis, and that the fit statistics are not just a function of the methodology used, they are mostly dependent on the data itself. Where modeling is done with good, clean, predictive data, the fit statistics will be good. Severely biased and dirty data is not going to produce a reasonable model, regardless of the method used. Establishing a strict minimum acceptable statistic for using models may not be the best strategy for a bank, especially those with biased or scarce data (notwithstanding measures such as AUC, which do have a 0.5 benchmark). This leads to perfectly usable models not being able to be used simply because of some arbitrary minimum number.

One should also understand exactly what the measure is telling us. There are various ways to measure how well a model will work. Generally, the two most common ones are measures of predictive accuracy and separation. The KS statistic, for example, is a measure of separation. Judgmental scorecards, by definition, have high KS because humans are generally better at identifying the extremes, that is, very good and very bad, than identifying fine shades of gray (although experienced adjudicators may take exception with this statement). But when developed without underlying data, such judgmental models cannot predict the probability of default. However, in cases where judgmental scorecards have been validated with actual data and calibrated, they can, of course, be used to predict probabilities. If predictive accuracy is the main issue, measures such as mean squared error (MSE) or root mean squared error (RMSE) may be better.

In some cases, previously used or current scorecards are compared against new ones being built. One should be very careful of such comparisons, as changes in data, applicant profiles, and marketing strategies may make these comparisons irrelevant or weak at best. For example, if the current scorecard has become unstable and unusable, it would not be relevant to compare, for example, the KS of this new scorecard with the old one when it was developed. As stated earlier, scorecards should always be developed on a "best efforts" basis given the data. Some companies go back into history and use both the new and existing scorecards to score a group of accounts opened in the past, and then track the performance of both scorecards. Again, if the current scorecard is not stable, this exercise is completely irrelevant to the current circumstances. In addition, even if the old scorecard shows better statistics for measures like AUC, Gini, and so on, based on scoring a two- or three-year-old sample, it does not prove that this model will be better for the next two or three years. The newer model may be a better choice if it reflects future market conditions, not what the conditions were three years ago (which the backward looking performance tests measure). Those who do such comparisons are asking the question, "Is the new scorecard better than the old one?"— which is the wrong question to ask.

The better way to answer the correct question at this time, which is "Is this the best that can happen today?" is to benchmark. This involves, preferably, an independent arm's-length team such as the model validation one, developing models using several approaches using the same data.[16] For example, they could build scorecards and models using logistic regression with grouped variables, logistic regression with raw data, neural network, and a decision tree, and then compare the predictive power of each. This way, any significant difference in the fit statistics and behavior can be identified and the reasons for them explored. Otherwise, if those statistics are fairly close to each other, the model can be considered benchmarked. Note again that while this discussion is limited to statistical benchmarking, qualitative and business criteria will also need to be considered before deeming a model acceptable.

The point is to pick the right, relevant measure for the purpose of the model, and make sure that those studying the fit statistics understand what they are measuring. This exercise is as much about generating confidence in the model or scorecard produced as it is about measuring statistically how well the model has described the development data set.

Examples of some methods used to compare scorecard predictive power include statistics such as:

- *AIC (Akaike's Information Criterion).*[17] AIC provides an indication of model quality relative to other models, and is not an absolute measure. It is normally used for model selection, and penalizes for adding parameters to the model (basically trading off goodness of fit with addition of variables). Small values of AIC are preferred.

- *SBC (Schwarz's Bayesian Criterion).*[18] The SBC also penalizes for adding parameters to the model, as with AIC. In order to reduce overfitting, smaller values of SBC are preferred. In the case of "risk profile" scorecards built using the methods described in this book, the SBC and AIC may not be the best methods to gauge strength, since in this book a premium has been placed on having a broad-based scorecard rather than one with the absolute minimum characteristics. While both AIC and SBC have relevance in a particular environment, I tend not to use them for scorecards in financial institutions that are used to make business decisions.

- *Kolmogorov-Smirnov (KS)*[19] *statistic.* This measures the maximum vertical separation (deviation) between the cumulative distributions of goods and bads, and is a very widely used measure of divergence/separation. One issue with KS is that the separation is measured only at the one point (which may not be

Exhibit 10.32 Kolmogorov-Smirnov Statistic

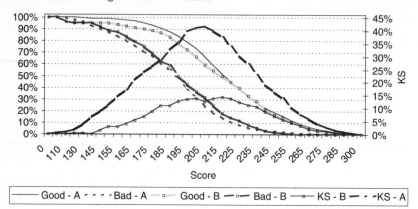

around the expected cutoff point), and not on the entire score range. If the intended scorecard cutoff is at the upper or lower range of scores, this measure may not provide a good method of scorecard comparison, since the statistic would be irrelevant to the decision at hand. In such cases, it might be better to compare the deviation at the intended cutoff, since that is where maximum separation is most required, and indeed, if divergence is a priority. Exhibit 10.32 shows a sample KS calculation for two scorecards where the maximum KS measures occur at scores of 205 and 215, respectively. Scorecard A is stronger than Scorecard B since Scorecard A has a maximum deviation of about 41 percent compared to about 15 percent for Scorecard B.

■ *c-statistic.* This is the most powerful nonparametric two-sample test, and the measure is equivalent to the area under the ROC curve, Gini coefficient, and the Wilcoxon-Mann-Whitney[20] test. It measures classifier performance across all score ranges and is a better measure of overall scorecard strength. The c-statistic measures the area under the Sensitivity versus (1 − Specificity) curve for the entire score range. An example of a scorecard comparison using the c-statistic is given in Exhibit 10.33—where Scorecard A is stronger, as it has a higher area under its ROC curve than Scorecard B.

Exhibit 10.33 ROC Curve

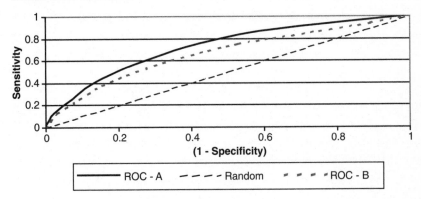

The "random" line denotes c-statistic = 0.5. Therefore for a scorecard to be better than random selection, the c-statistic must be above 0.5. In most cases where good data is being used, a c-statistic of 0.7 and above would be considered adequate, however, this should not be considered an absolute number.

In some scorecard development solutions, such as SAS Credit Scoring, this statistic is automatically generated. The code shown in Exhibit 10.34 shows an example of some SAS code[21] that can be written to calculate the c-statistic.

■ *Lorenz curve.* A measure similar to the ROC curve used in the industry to compare models is to plot the distribution of "bad" cases and total cases by deciles across all score ranges. This is referred to as the Lorenz curve (also known as the Cumulative Accuracy Profile, Gini, and Power curve), and measures how well a scorecard isolates the bads and goods into selected deciles. An example of a Lorenz curve is shown in Exhibit 10.35.

In Exhibit 10.35, for the bottom 60 percent of the total sample, Scorecard A isolates about 90 percent of all bads, whereas Scorecard B only isolates about 80 percent. Therefore, Scorecard A displays stronger performance. Note that the ratio of the area between a scorecard's Lorenz curve and the 45-degree line, to the entire triangular area under the 45-degree line, is also equivalent to the Gini index.

Exhibit 10.34 SAS Code to Calculate c-statistic

```
proc rank data=&_VALID out=rscore d;

   var PREDICTIONVAR IABLE;

run ;


proc sql;

   select sum(TARGET=1) as n1,

          (sum (PREDICTIONVARI ABLE* (TARG ETVARIA BLE=1))-.5*(calculated

n1)*(calculated n1+1))

          /((calculated n1)*(coun t(TARGETVARIA BLE)-(calculated n1)))
as c

          from rscored;

quit;
```

It is important here to compare scorecard performance in operationally logical deciles, meaning that if the expected approval rate is about 60 percent, then performance should be compared at the 60 percent percentile mark. Comparing performance at the lowest 10 percent is irrelevant when what is needed at implementation is best performance,

Exhibit 10.35 Lorenz Curve

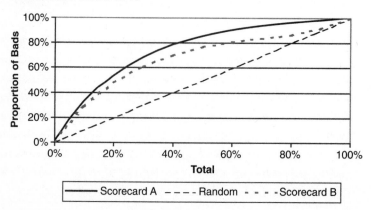

at 60 percent in this case. However, when dealing with scorecards such as bankruptcy or response, making comparisons at the lowest percentiles does make sense and should be done—since in these cases the objective is to isolate the worst/best few performers for action.

As with other decisions that have been made during the scorecard development process, the one to select a final scorecard should also be made with the objectives for scorecard development in mind. This may call for further analysis to determine which scorecard, for example, maximizes profit or minimizes false positives (for fraud scorecards), at a chosen cutoff. The objective is to first choose the scorecard that best helps the company achieve its strategic objectives, and then confirm that it has an acceptable statistical strength.

There are various other commonly used measures available to gauge scorecard strength, including:

- *Gains chart.* Cumulative positive predicted value versus distribution of predicted positives (depth).
- *Lift/Concentration curve.* Sensitivity versus depth.

$$\text{Lift} = \frac{\text{Positive predicted value}}{\% \text{ percent positives in the sample}}$$

- *Misclassification costs.* Where losses are assigned to false positive and false negative cases. The optimal decision rule minimizes the total expected cost.[22]
- *Bayes Rule.* This minimizes expected cost (i.e., total misclassification cost). Bayes Rule and misclassification costs are difficult to implement in practice, due to problems in obtaining accurate loss numbers.
- *Cost ratio.* Cost ratio is the ratio of the cost of misclassifying a bad credit risk as a good risk to the cost of misclassifying a good risk as a bad. When used to calculate the cutoff, the cost ratio tends to max the sum of the two proportions of correct classification. This is done by plotting the cost ratio against sensitivity and specificity. The point where the two curves meet tends to be the point where both sensitivity and specificity are maximized.
- *Somers' D, gamma, tau-a.* Based on the numbers of concordant and discordant pairs. These measures are related to the c-statistic.

VALIDATION

Once the final scorecard has been selected, the results of the modeling need to be validated. This is standard "out-of-sample" validation, where we confirm that the model developed is generally applicable to the subject population, and to ensure that the model has not been over-fitted. The industry norm is to use a random 70 percent or 80 percent of the development sample for building the model, while the remaining 30 percent or 20 percent "holdout sample" is kept for validation. As discussed earlier, in most financial institutions, these numbers are normally specified by the model validation department. If the scorecard is being developed on a small sample, it may be necessary to develop it on 100 percent of the sample, and validate on several randomly selected 50 percent to 80 percent samples.

In recent years there has been increased interest in the validation and oversight of model development and usage, mostly under the "model risk management" umbrella. In the United States, Federal Reserve Bulletin SR 11-7, "Supervisory Guidance on Model Risk Management," is an excellent resource for the qualitative issues and framework for model development, validation, usage, and governance. A similar, but more generic governance document, is the GL-44 Guidelines on Internal Governance issues by the European Banking Authority.[23] An older document is the Basel Committee on Banking Supervision Working Paper 14, which is specific to the development of regulatory models for Basel II, but nevertheless has some good general principles for model governance, qualitative validation, as well as details on the statistical tests that should be performed. Most other documents that deal with the issue also have similar principles that include adequate oversight, the use of qualitative and quantitative measures, independent validation, sound end-to-end systems and processes, and so on. Validation is not an end or a set of statistics, it is a process and framework, designed to provide a level of comfort that the models developed are robust, and can be used with confidence for business decision making. A good resource for ideas on how to perform validation is Appendix 8 of *Fair Lending Compliance*.[24]

Exhibit 10.36 Validation Chart

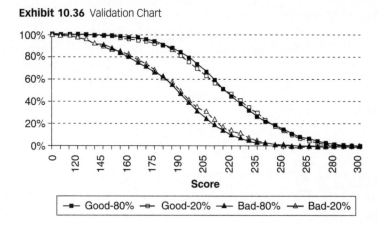

As such, while there are many suggested methods (including in the documents mentioned) to validate models, there is no one set of global standard. The model validation/vetting groups at most banks usually set the documentation and development standards, and they in turn follow broad guidelines set by their national regulators. Therefore, there are many ways to validate models, of which we will cover a few. In addition to statistical out of sample validation, there are also other questions asked at this phase. Those aspects are covered in detail in documents such as SR11-7 as well as Working Paper 14, cited earlier.

The first validation method is to compare the distributions of scored goods and bads across the two samples. Exhibit 10.36 shows an example of validation done on a holdout sample of 20 percent, and compared to the development sample.

The scorecard may be validated if the two sets of data are not significantly different. Usually, a visual examination of the two curves is sufficient for this purpose. However, any goodness of fit measure such as the least squares method or the IV can also be utilized. However, note that there is no global standard or rule of thumb that will conclusively prove that the model is validated.

A second method of validation is to compare development statistics for the development and validation samples. An example is given in Exhibit 10.37.

Exhibit 10.37 Validation by Comparing Performance Statistics

Fit Statistics	Statistics Label	Train	Validation
AIC	Akaike's Information Criterion	5780.93893	NaN
ASE	Average Squared Error	0.045816919	0.04710042
AVERR	Average Error Function	0.177342113	0.18247522
DFE	Degrees of Freedom for Error	16259	NaN
DFM	Model Degrees of Freedom	6	NaN
DFT	Total Degrees of Freedom	16265	NaN
DIV	Divisor for ASE	32530	13951.5
ERR	Error Function	5768.93893	2545.80307
FPE	Final Prediction Error	0.045850734	NaN
MAX	Maximum Absolute Error	0.996439338	0.99473712
MSE	Mean Square Error	0.045833827	0.04710042
NOBS	Sum of Frequencies	16265	6975.75
_NW_	Number of Estimate Weights	6	NaN
RASE	Root Average Sum of Squares	0.21404887	0.21702632
RFPE	Root Final Prediction Error	0.214127846	NaN
RMSE	Root Mean Squared Error	0.214088362	0.21702632
SBC	Schwarz's Bayesian Criterion	5827.119555	NaN
SSE	Sum of Squared Errors	1490.424373	657.121564
SUMW	Sum of Case Weights Times Freq	32530	13951.5
MISC	Misclassification Rate	0.051398709	0.051464
XERR	Sum of Squared Errors	2268.426479	NaN
_KS_	Kolmogorov-Smirnov Statistic	0.418177384	0.40371775
AUR	Area Under ROC	0.774160998	0.75521059
Gini	Gini Coefficient	0.548321996	0.51042117
ARATIO	Accuracy Ratio	0.548321996	0.51042117

The scorecard may be validated where there is no significant difference between statistics for the two samples. I say *may be* since statistics alone cannot conclusively determine that any scorecard is validated.

A further method to perform validation is to compare the divergence statistic for the development and validation holdout samples. Divergence can be calculated using the formula:

$$\text{Divergence} = (mean_G - mean_B)^2 / [0.5\ (var_G + var_B)]$$

where $mean_G$, $mean_B$, var_G, and var_B are the means and variances of the scored good and bad populations respectively.

Validation can also include comparing the good/bad ratio or bad rate by score range for the development and validation samples (and in addition, on out of time samples outside of the sample window). The use of bootstrapping[25] and jack-knifing[26] is also common, particularly with smaller data sets. Some practitioners go further to ensure a robust model fitting by generating the parameter estimates as well as the model fit statistic for the development, validation and out of time samples. In addition, many better banks use arms-length benchmarking as part of the validation process as well.

Significant differences in any of the preceding methods will require further analysis. Typically, characteristics with large score ranges present problems, since a small shift in the population distribution can cause a significant shift in scores. The same is true for scorecards developed with small samples, scorecards with too few characteristics (which tend to be unstable over time), scorecards with too many strong binary variables (again where a small shift in populations can have a large impact ion scores) and those developed on nonrandom samples. These are in addition to the usual causes of bad model development, such where the characteristics selected for the model have overfit the data.

At the end of this phase, we have binned the data, performed reject inference, built several different candidate models and scaled them into the scorecard format, and finally, performed validation of the scorecard.

▶ NOTE

A further pre-implementation validation is also conducted separately to confirm that the recent applicant profile is similar to that of the development sample. This will be discussed later in Chapter 12.

NOTES

1. SAS Institute Inc., *SAS Procedures Guide, Version 6,* 1st ed. (Cary, NC: SAS Institute, 1990).

2. Kent Leahy, "Multicollinearity: When the Solution Is the Problem." In *Data Mining Cookbook,* edited by O. P. Rud (Hoboken, NJ: Wiley, 2001).

3. I. Oliveira, M. Chari, S. Haller, and SAS/OR®, "Rigorous Constrained Optimized Binning for Credit Scoring." SAS Global Forum 2008, SAS Institute.

4. I. J. Good, *Probability and the Weighing of Evidence* (London: Grin, 1950).

5. S. Kulback, *Information Theory and Statistics* (Hoboken, NJ: Wiley, 1959).

6. M. Rezac and J. Kovar, "Influence of Variable Interactions Versus Segmentation in Credit Scoring: A Case Study." Analytics 2012 Conference, 2012.

7. SAS Institute Inc., *SAS 9.1.3 Help and Documentation* (Cary, NC: SAS Institute, 2004).

8. Ibid.

9. G. G. Chandler and J. Y. Coffman, "Using Credit Scoring to Improve the Quality of Consumer Receivables: Legal and Statistical Implications." Paper presented at the Financial Management Association meetings, Seattle, Washington, 1977.

10. B. Anderson, S. Haller, and N. Siddiqi, "Reject Inference Techniques Implemented in Credit Scoring for SAS® Enterprise Miner™." *Proceedings of the SAS Global Forum 2009* (Cary, NC: SAS Institute Inc., 2009).

11. G. J. McLachlan, "Iterative Reclassification Procedure for Constructing an Asymptotically Optimal Rule of Allocation in Discriminant Analysis," *Journal of American Statistical Association* 70 (1975): 365–369.

12. B. Anderson, J. Cox, D. Duling, S. Haller, and N. Siddiqi, "Improving Credit Risk Scorecards with Memory-Based Reasoning to Reject Inference with SAS® Enterprise Miner™." *Proceedings of the SAS Global Forum 2010* (Cary, NC: SAS Institute Inc., 2010).

13. Anderson, Haller, and Siddiqi, 2009.

14. Basel Committee for Banking Supervision, "Basel II: International Convergence of Capital Measurement and Capital Standards: A Revised Framework—Comprehensive Version." Bank for International Settlements, 2006.

15. D. W. Hosmer and S. Lemeshow, "A Goodness-of-Fit Test for the Multiple Logistic Regression Model," *Communications in Statistics.* A10 (1980): 1043–1069.

16. N. Lynas and E. Mays, "Structuring an Efficient Program for Model Governance," *RMA Journal,* March 2010: 44–49.

17. H. Akaike, "A New Look at the Statistical Model Identification," IEEE Transactions on Automatic Control 19, no. 6 (1974): 716–723. doi:10.1109/TAC.1974.1100705, MR 0423716

18. Gideon E. Schwarz, "Estimating the Dimension of a Model," *Annals of Statistics* 6, no. 2 (1978): 461–464. doi:10.1214/aos/1176344136, MR 468014

19. N. Smirnov, "Table for Estimating the Goodness of Fit of Empirical Distributions," *Annals of Mathematical Statistics* 19 (1948): 279–281. doi:10.1214/aoms/1177730256

20. D. J. Hand, *Construction and Assessment of Classification Rules* (Hoboken, NJ: Wiley, 1997).

21. W. J. E. Potts and M. J. Patetta, *Predictive Modeling Using Logistic Regression: Course Notes* (Cary, NC: SAS Institute, 2001).

22. G. J. McLachlan, *Discriminant Analysis and Statistical Pattern Recognition* (New York: Wiley, 1992); B. D. Ripley, *Pattern Recognition and Neural Networks* (Cambridge, UK: Cambridge University Press, 1996); and Hand, 1997.

23. https://www.eba.europa.eu/regulation-and-policy/internal-governance/guidelines-on-internal-governance

24. C. Abrahams and M. Zhang, *Fair Lending Compliance, Intelligence and Implications for Credit Risk Management* (Hoboken, NJ: Wiley, 2008).

25. B. Efron, "Bootstrap Methods: Another Look at the Jackknife." *Annals of Statistics* 7, no. 1 (1979): 1–26. doi:10.1214/aos/1176344552

26. J. W. Tukey, "Bias and Confidence in Not Quite Large Samples." *Annals of Mathematical Statistics* 29 (1958): 614–623. doi:10.1214/aoms/1177706647

## CHAPTER 11

Scorecard Development Process, Stage 5: Scorecard Management Reports

*"There is nothing so useless as doing
efficiently that which should not be done
at all."*

—Peter Drucker

Once the final scorecard is selected, a full suite of management reports is produced. These reports are management tools, and are produced for three major reasons:

1. Making operational decisions such as deciding the scorecard cutoff and designing account acquisition and management strategies.
2. Monitoring future scorecard performance.
3. Helping downstream calculations such as those for expected losses and regulatory and economic capital.

These reports should be designed and produced to help the business user answer questions such as "Where should I set my cutoff to meet my objectives?" and "What impact will that have on my portfolio?" Therefore, a good practice is to get the end users' input on what reports they would find useful for making decisions, and use that as a guide for producing reports.

These typically include development score and scorecard characteristics distributions, expected bad/approval rate charts, and the effects of the scorecard on key subpopulations. These scorecard management reports are run on the scorecard development data set, including indeterminates and inferred rejects where appropriate.

In addition to these management reports, scorecard documentation should be produced detailing the analyses performed at each key phase of the project (i.e., business case development, definitions of good/bad/indeterminate, exclusions, segmentation, sampling and data gathering, initial characteristic analysis, model development, reject inference, scorecard performance statistics, and validation), and the output generated. This serves as reference material

for future scorecard developments, audit and compliance requirements, future employees, and troubleshooting, should scorecard
problems arise. Documentation requirements differ between banks,
and countries, as some of it, particularly in the banking industry, is driven by regulatory and internal model validation/vetting
functions.

The examples addressed in this chapter represent the most common reports produced in the industry. In reality, risk managers and
model developers produce many more custom reports based on their
individual requirement.

GAINS TABLE

A gains table includes a distribution of total, good, and bad cases by
individual scores or score ranges. An example of a section from a gains
table, using individual scores, is shown in Exhibit 11.1.

Gains tables are produced for the overall sample as well as for
selected subpopulations. The key information in this table is:

- The expected bad rates for each score or score range (i.e., interval or marginal bad rate). For example, the expected bad rate
  for people who score 211 is 7.6 percent.
- The expected bad rates for all cases above a certain score
  (i.e., cumulative bad rate). In Exhibit 11.1, the total bad rate for
  all cases above 211 is 5.94 percent.
- Expected approval rates at each score. The approval rate for a
  cutoff at 211 is 66.20 percent.

Exhibit 11.2 shows another example of a gains table, from a screen
shot taken from the Scorecard node in SAS Enterprise Miner.

A few items to note in this report:

- When such reports are run based on equal distribution of
  scores, there is always a possibility of having zero counts for
  goods or bads. This should be avoided where possible and such
  score bands combined to produce nonzero counts. A better
  way to bin the score bands is to have equal distribution of
  accounts.

Exhibit 11.1 Section of a Gains Table

Score	Count	Cumulative Count	Goods	Bads	Cumulative Goods	Cumulative Bads	Interval Bad Rate	Cumulative Bad Rate	Approval Rate
210	345	6,965	311	34	6,538	427	9.86%	6.13%	69.50%
211	500	6,620	462	38	6,227	393	7.60%	5.94%	66.20%
212	450	6,120	418	32	5,765	355	7.11%	5.80%	61.20%
213	345	5,670	323	22	5,347	323	6.38%	5.70%	56.70%

Exhibit 11.2 Detailed Gains Table

Gains Table

Bucket	Score Bucket (Bucket)	Data Role	Count	Cumulative Count	Event Count	Non-Event Count	Cumulative Event Count	Cumulative Non-Event Count	Marginal Event Rate	Marginal Non-Event Rate	Cumulative Event Rate	Cumulative Non-Event Rate	Average Predicted Probability	Population Percentage
	9278 <= Score < 304	TRAIN	489.25	589	0	489.25	0	589	0	100	0	100	0.001678	3.621273
	8252 <= Score < 278	TRAIN	1492.5	2081.5	1	1491.5	1	2080.5	0.067002	99.933	0.048042	99.95196	0.003817	12.79742
	7226 <= Score < 252	TRAIN	2694.75	4776.25	30	2664.75	31	4745.25	1.113276	98.88672	0.649045	99.35096	0.009146	29.3652
	6200 <= Score < 226	TRAIN	3428.5	8204.75	94	3334.5	125	8079.75	2.741724	97.25828	1.523508	98.47649	0.022763	50.44421
	5174 <= Score < 200	TRAIN	4370.5	12575.25	219	4151.5	344	12231.25	5.010868	94.98913	2.735532	97.26447	0.052816	77.31479
	4148 <= Score < 174	TRAIN	2881	15456.25	316	2565	660	14796.25	10.96841	89.03159	4.270117	95.72988	0.114957	95.02767
	3122 <= Score < 148	TRAIN	791.25	16247.5	169	622.25	829	15418.5	21.35861	78.64139	5.102323	94.89768	0.21632	99.89241
	296 <= Score < 122	TRAIN	16.5	16264	7	9.5	836	15428	42.42424	57.57576	5.140187	94.85981	0.370496	99.99385
	1 Score < 96	TRAIN	1	16265	1	0	837	15428	100	0	5.146019	94.85398	0.756296	100
	10 Score >= 304	VALID	23.75	23.75	0	23.75	0	23.75	0	100	0	100	0.000748	0.340465
	9278 <= Score < 304	VALID	194.75	218.5	0	194.75	0	218.5	0	100	0	100	0.001618	3.13228
	8252 <= Score < 278	VALID	589	807.5	0	589	0	807.5	0	100	0	100	0.00384	11.57582
	7226 <= Score < 252	VALID	1128.25	1935.75	12	1116.25	12	1923.75	1.063594	98.93641	0.619915	99.38009	0.00932	27.7497
	6200 <= Score < 226	VALID	1556	3491.75	36	1520	48	3443.75	2.313625	97.68038	1.374669	98.62533	0.022295	50.05555
	5174 <= Score < 200	VALID	1659	5150.75	101	1558	149	5001.75	6.088005	93.912	2.892783	97.10722	0.053223	73.83794
	4148 <= Score < 174	VALID	1413.75	6564.5	155	1258.75	304	6260.5	10.96375	89.03625	4.63097	95.36903	0.114359	94.10458
	3122 <= Score < 148	VALID	410.25	6974.75	54	356.25	358	6616.75	13.16271	86.83729	5.1328	94.8672	0.214813	99.98566
	296 <= Score < 122	VALID	1	6975.75	1	0	359	6616.75	100	0	5.1464	94.8536	0.342699	100
	1 Score < 96	VALID	0	6975.75	0	0	359	6616.75	0	0	5.1464	94.8536		100

- The report has been produced for both the development and validation data sets, a good practice to ensure robustness of results. Charts plotting the bad rate by score can be created for the two populations for comparison and validation.

- The "marginal event rate" is calculated based on the number of bad and total cases in each score band. If there is a low number of bad cases in some buckets, or a low default portfolio, the marginal bad rate will not be uniformly increasing or decreasing due to low counts. This will produce illogical reports, and should be fixed. Options include creating a linear "best fit" line through the values, or using the calculated posterior probabilities.

- Other fields such as expected profitability, net present value (NPV), revenues, inactive rate, revolving rate, recovery, expected average balances and other appropriate fields can also be added as necessary.

This information is used in conjunction with financial and operational considerations to make cutoff decisions for various actions—for example, based on an expected bad rate or approval rate, at what cutoff should new applicants be approved?

In addition to the overall populations, a useful exercise is to produce such reports on selected subpopulations. The objective of producing such tables for subpopulations is to identify any abnormal effects on critical segments of business; for example, typically, scorecards developed on a more mature population will penalize younger clients (a case for segmented scorecards). Typical subpopulations can include geographical, source of business, by existing product owned, existing/new customers, segments to be targeted in future campaigns, and so forth.

Exhibit 11.3 shows an example of expected approvals rates by cutoff for several segments.

Exhibit 11.3 Expected Approval Rate by Segment

Score	Zone 1	Zone 3	Hi Nt Wrth	> 2 Prod	TM2	New Cust	Mort/Auto
210	74%	49%	88%	80%	83%	56%	97%
211	67%	43%	85%	77%	80%	51%	95%
212	61%	39%	80%	70%	76%	46%	92%
213	56%	35%	77%	67%	72%	44%	87%

The segments to be analyzed are entirely decision/context related and should be specified by the risk/portfolio manager or the person responsible for using the scorecard for strategy creation. In this example, we can see segments such as "high net worth" (customers who have more than a certain amount in deposits at the banks), those in certain regions and customers with mortgages and auto loans at the bank. We will cover setting cutoff later on—at this stage assume that we have conducted all our overall portfolio analysis, and determined the cutoff to be 211, for a credit card new application scorecard. Once that cutoff is set, we are now analyzing the impact of it on various segments. In Exhibit 11.3, we can see that the potential approval rate for "high net worth" is 85 percent. This should be a red flag for potential problems, since high-net-worth clientele should have a very high approval rate for products like credit cards. We can also see that customers with existing mortgages and car loans at the bank have an approval rate of 95 percent at the same cutoff, which is more reasonable for that segment. These sorts of unintended/unplanned results do occur due to the nature of models. They have limited information—in the above case, it may be that the scorecard is based heavily on bureau data and performance on existing loans, but does not include deposits. High-net-worth customers tend to have high deposits and may not have any mortgages or car loans; therefore, quite a few of them would have scored low due to missing information, and therefore 15 percent fall under the cutoff. This is information that strategy managers should know before they implement the scorecards. This sort of phenomenon is also why segmentation is helpful, and should be decided based on business considerations. Also as mentioned earlier, knowledge of the various types of customers and nuances in their behavior should be used to select appropriate variables for the scorecard. In this case, information on net deposits or balances could have been added to the scorecard to give higher rankings to high-net-worth customers. Alternatively, if this is a large enough, or important enough, segment, developing a separate scorecard for it may add value.

Similarly, if a secondary objective, for example, were to capture market share in certain zones, improve retention rates by minimizing the decline rate for existing customers, or to maximize the approval of new customers, their approval rates should be estimated before implementation to avoid surprises.

Exhibit 11.4 Expected Bad Rate by Segment

Score	Zone 1	Zone 3	Hi Nt Wrth	> 2 Prod	TM2	New Cust	Mort/Auto
210	2.5%	6.0%	0.6%	4.0%	2.0%	5.5%	1.1%
211	2.2%	5.5%	0.4%	3.3%	1.8%	5.1%	0.9%
212	2.0%	5.2%	0.2%	3.1%	1.5%	4.5%	0.7%
213	1.6%	4.6%	0.1%	2.7%	1.1%	4.0%	0.5%

Financial and other institutions that may be having a delinquency issue may wish to check the bad rates for different segments, based on various cutoffs. Exhibit 11.4 shows an example of such a chart.

We can see, not surprisingly, that the same cutoff yields different bad rates for various segments. The overall cutoff was an average of all the different populations, and the preceding case is common, especially in broad segments. This is why building segmented scorecards makes sense. In the case of Exhibits 11.3 and 11.4, we are assuming that the segments are not big enough to warrant their own models—if they were, based on the difference in the bad rates, we would have certainly explored that first. In this case, the risk manager has several options to try to reduce the bad rate, and treat the low-risk customers better. One common option (dependent on local regulations) is to have different cutoffs for different segments but still use the same scorecard. In Exhibit 11.4, for the high-net-worth or existing mortgage holders, the cutoff could probably be at a 100 percent approval rate, and would still yield very low bad rates for those two segments. This would also mean instead of having one cutoff for everyone, we vary it to treat our low-risk customers better, even if the scorecard does not isolate them into the higher score bands. However, we can also see some higher-risk segments. Again, the strategy for dealing with this is entirely dependent on what risk managers want to do, and the options open to them. They may choose to have a higher cutoff by region or segment, if the problem was delinquency. They may choose to have differential pricing by both segment and score, instead of by score alone. They may choose to change their marketing strategy to target a better class of customers. Once more, if any of these segments had a critical mass of goods and bads to enable the development of its own segmented scorecard, then that would likely be the best option.

Please note that differential cutoff decisions are rarely this simple in real life. In credit cards, for example, higher-risk customers also tend to revolve more and generate higher revenues. In reality, it would be normal to consider other measures in addition to the one shown in the simplified examples here.

The examples discussed above were to illustrate the importance of making well-informed decisions via analytics. The immediate exercise may well be to develop a model to predict default. However, the overall decision using that score has other consequences. It is best to try to predict how that scorecard will affect the key stakeholders, internal and external, before making any final decisions. More discussion on how downstream strategy decisions affect the various operational areas will be done in the next chapter.

The distribution of the sample population by score is also used as a basis for scorecard stability and final score reports used for scorecard monitoring (which will be covered in Chapter 14). The distributions at development, as shown by the gains chart, are what we will expect in the future as well to gauge our "future is like the past" assumption.

CHARACTERISTIC REPORTS

These reports provide distributions for each characteristic included in the scorecard, as well as the approval rate and bad rate for each attribute by score. An example of a characteristic report is shown in Exhibit 11.5.

Exhibit 11.5 Characteristic Report

Age	Distr	Points	Bad Rate
Missing	8%	16	16%
18–22	9%	12	24%
23–26	15%	18	18%
27–29	26%	26	10%
30–35	10%	35	5%
35–44	20%	43	3%
44+	12%	51	2%

The characteristic report is used as a basis for characteristic analysis reports (see Chapter 14) performed as part of regular scorecard monitoring. The report goes deeper into the model inputs to identify variables contributing to instability. As we will cover later in detail, the objective is to measure characteristic stability—we would expect the distribution of age in the future to be similar to that in the development sample.

The production of these reports typically marks the end of the scorecard development project. The next chapters will deal with how these scorecards are implemented and used for decision making.

## CHAPTER 12

Scorecard Development Process, Stage 6: Scorecard Implementation

*"The 50-50-90 rule: anytime you have a
50-50 chance of getting something right,
there's a 90% probability you'll get it wrong."*

—Andy Rooney

This section deals with post-development analyses and will cover three main areas:

1. Understanding the analyses and business considerations in implementing risk scorecards.
2. Understanding how scorecards and management reports are used.
3. Understanding how strategy is developed.

PRE-IMPLEMENTATION VALIDATION

Pre-implementation activities after scorecard development include testing for scoring accuracy and frontend validation (also known as out-of-time stability validation). This validation exercise is similar in concept to the one performed as part of scorecard development, but with different objectives. Whereas the objective previously was to confirm the robustness of the scorecard by comparing distributions of development and validation data sets, the objective here is to confirm that the scorecard developed is valid for the current applicant population. In some cases where the development sample is two or three years old, significant shifts in applicant profile may have occurred, and need to be identified. As mentioned in previous chapters, parts of this exercise can be performed prior to building the model. The stability of the scorecard is dependent on the individual characteristics used. Before starting the model development, the scorecard builder can choose a set of 40 to 50 characteristics that are likely candidates for the model (based on previous experience and scorecards), and then they can compare the distributions of the planned development sample with that of a recent applicant/account population. Avoiding any unstable characteristics will maximize the chances of the scorecard developed being stable. The exercise does not guarantee a stable scorecard as other derived variables may be added to the model during development, but it provides some level of comfort.

The results of this pre-implementation validation are also used as part of the analysis to set cutoffs. In particular, the expected approval rates can be calculated on a more recent applicant population instead of the development sample.

Before the validation can be performed, all new external and internal scorecard characteristics need to be programmed into external data interfaces (e.g., credit bureau) as well as into the application processing and decision-making systems so that these characteristics can be used for scoring.

Once all the characteristics have been programmed, accuracy testing of the scorecard can be done. Validation reports can be produced as part of the accuracy testing to make the process more efficient. Ideally, testing should be done in the same environment where the scorecard is to be implemented (i.e., in test or development regions of the production system). If the test area is not available, programs in, for example, SAS code need to be written to simulate scoring and generate population distributions. This, however, does not give an accurate representation of how the actual production system will interpret the various scoring characteristics, especially calculated ones, and may lead to inaccurate forecasts. It is therefore essential that the accuracy testing be as closely aligned with actual production conditions as possible. In particular, for scorecards to be used for regulatory calculations, having to recode them from the development to validation and implementation environments may create regulatory issues. The recoding of models may result in the original calculations being misinterpreted, and represents a model risk. Ideally, the models should be developed, validated, deployed, and monitored in the same environment to reduce model and regulatory risk.

Once scoring accuracy has been established, frontend validation reports can be generated by scoring recent applications/accounts using the new scorecard, and comparing their distributions with that of the development sample. What constitutes "recent" depends on several factors. In some companies, the monthly application volumes are too low for reliable reports, so they use quarterly, and even annual applications for this purpose. Volume is not usually an issue with behavior scorecards. Model validation teams also sometimes determine this time period via policy. For example, they may choose to perform stability check on a previous 12 months period. In generic terms, the most recent batch of applications with enough numbers is used. However, it is a good practice to do this analysis for several recent time periods where data is available (e.g., past month, past three months, past six months, three months ago, six months ago, and so on) in order to detect any emerging trends, or to confirm that any deviations in one particular month do not represent long-term trends.

Typically, system stability and characteristic analysis reports are produced for this purpose. These reports can be generated both for application and behavior scorecards.

System Stability Report

An example of a system stability report is shown in Exhibit 12.1. Note that the system stability report is also sometimes referred to as the population stability or scorecard stability report.

The "Actual %" and "Expected %" columns denote the distribution of cases for recent and development samples, respectively, for each of the score ranges specified. Note that in Exhibit 12.1, the score ranges have been engineered so that there are 10 percent expected cases in each band. Normally, most people who run this report set

Exhibit 12.1 System Stability Report

Score Range	Actual %	Expected %	(A-E)	A/E	ln(A/E)	Index
0-169	7%	10%	-3%	0.7000	-0.3567	0.0107
170-190	6%	10%	-4%	0.6000	-0.5108	0.0204
191-197	6%	10%	-4%	0.6000	-0.5108	0.0204
198-202	7%	10%	-3%	0.7000	-0.3567	0.0107
203-207	9%	10%	-1%	0.9000	-0.1054	0.0011
208-218	13%	10%	3%	1.3000	0.2624	0.0079
219-225	13%	10%	3%	1.3000	0.2624	0.0079
226-259	11%	10%	1%	1.1000	0.0953	0.0010
260-292	13%	10%	3%	1.3000	0.2624	0.0079
293+	15%	10%	5%	1.5000	0.4055	0.0203
Index						0.108159293

uniform score ranges, for example 10 points apart, and get a more "normal" distribution of expected cases. Both ways are valid—I find that for business purposes, the 10 percent expected in each bucket helps identify shifts easier. In addition, as this index itself, like many calculations, is sensitive to the score bands, I find that making the distribution equal gives me more confidence in it. If using equal score bands, you get some bands with very few customers while others have over 20 percent.

The index as shown measures the magnitude of the population shift between recent applicants and expected (from development sample). This index is calculated as:

$$\Sigma \ (\% \ \text{Actual} - \% \ \text{Expected}) * ln \ (\% \ \text{Actual}/\% \ \text{Expected})$$

for all score ranges.

In general, an index of less than 0.10 shows no significant change, 0.10–0.25 denotes a small change that needs to be investigated, and an index greater than 0.25 points to a significant shift in the applicant population. These are industry rules of thumb, and not definitive. Further investigation is always needed, as will be discussed in the following sections.

Other goodness-of-fit measures, such as chi-square with some level of significance, may also be used to measure the magnitude of the shift. The method shown in Exhibit 12.1 is one used widely in the industry.

The additional suggestion of running this report for historical time periods can also be very helpful. For example, Exhibit 12.2, shows the distribution by score of the expected and actuals for several historical periods.

Exhibit 12.2 shows a simple example, where the most recent applicants ("last month") show a fairly large deviation from the expected. This may produce a stability index of greater than 0.25. However, the data from three and six months ago show fairly stable distributions near the expected. This tells us that the applicant population last month, which shows a shift to higher scores, may be due to a one-time event, and is not usually a cause for concern. The shift to higher scores may be due to, for example, cross selling to existing mortgage holders

Exhibit 12.2 Stability Analysis with Recent History

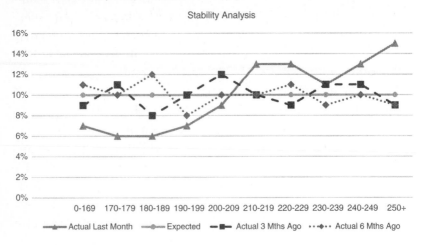

at a bank or to a mailing list from a high end magazine. Presumably, both these segments tend to have higher scores.

Exhibit 12.3 shows a different trend.

In the case of the chart in Exhibit 12.3, we can see that the data from the most recent month shows the same large deviation from expected. However, distributions of the three- and six-month-old data tells us that this trend started more than six months ago, and is not a one-time event. This phenomenon bears further scrutiny into what

Exhibit 12.3 Stability Analysis with Lingering Trend

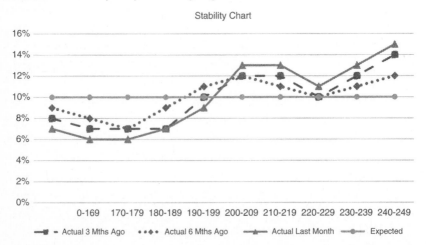

changed, say seven or eight months ago. Did the company start selling premium handsets which gradually attracted a higher income clientele? Perhaps the product or loyalty program changed which did that. Regulatory changes, such as lowering of maximum allowable loan to value for mortgages, will also result in a gradual and permanent change to the applicant population.

Another example is provided in Exhibit 12.4.

We see again that the most recent applicants have a significant deviation from the expected, but as in Exhibit 12.4, the six- and three-month-old data seems to be stable. In this case, we have added a third line, for applications from 12 months ago. That line seems to be much closer to the most recent one, and just as significantly deviated from the expected. Usually, this denotes some sort of seasonal effect. In most countries, new applications for revolving credit trend to spike near major holidays (such as Eid, Chinese New Year, Christmas, Diwali, etc.), and, conversely, the delinquency rates also tend to shift up immediately afterward due to overshopping. In others, mortgage applications tend to rise during the spring and summer months as that is when most people tend to buy homes and move. This is why getting

Exhibit 12.4 Stability Analysis Showing Seasonality

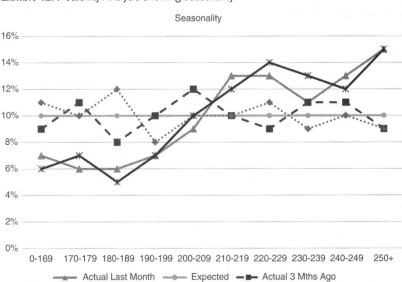

development samples exclusively from such time periods should be avoided, as they represent a departure from the norm. In the case of the above stability analysis, once it is confirmed that the instability of the most recent applicant population is due to seasonality, it is usually not a cause for concern.

Note that while we are doing this exercise just before implementing the scorecard, to confirm that it is valid, the same exercise is done at regular intervals for ongoing validation of the scorecard. We will cover those reports in later chapters.

Some analysts also generate normal distributions of the applicants (via equally spaced score bands). This can provide additional information in addition to whether the shift in scores is downward, upward, or for example, kurtosis.

As with all other data mining exercises, the confidence level in the index is dependent on the volume and reliability of the data. Many banks will only produce these reports on a quarterly or twice yearly basis due to low volumes. Stability analysis is mostly done for application scoring as that is where change happens in short time frames. Changes in the distributions of existing accounts usually takes a much longer time and only happens following sustained change on the application side first.

The preceding examples should underscore the point that the population stability index in itself is not an end-all measure. It is not absolute, and much like model validation, here qualitative factors also matter as much as a single statistic. Factors such as trends (Is the change a temporary occurrence or something more long-term?), magnitude of the shift, and reasons for change must always be taken into account before deciding if a population shift is significant enough, or something that requires further action such as a change in strategy.

Shifts in score distributions can be due to several reasons:

- *Independent change in applicant profile (e.g., demographic change).* This is not normally the case in most developed countries as there is no rapid and significant change of populations applying for credit. However, in some developing economies, there is significant migration, usually of young people from rural to urban areas. Over time, this may change the credit applicant population. In addition, rapidly growing economies tend to add significant numbers to the middle class, which in every country is the primary driver of credit products. In such cases, the demographics does tend to change over shorter periods of time.

- *Marketing campaigns, niche competition, and other business reasons.* For example, if the recent month's applicants were noticeably younger or were concentrated in a particular area, this may be due to focused marketing activity. An example of this has been provided in Exhibit 12.2. Sometimes changes in the underlying product, such as the addition of loyalty programs, changes in fee structure, "no interest for six months"or bonus signup points — type sweeteners, or temporary focus on (or permanent shift to) new channels, can also attract a different type of applicant. Loyalty programs, as discussed in the segmentation section, sometimes attract a very specific segment, and therefore any changes can have a significant impact on stability. External competition, particularly from new entrants into the market who target a narrow demographic—such as monoline credit card companies who target professionals, and online FinTech[1] lenders—may also affect the makeup of your applicants. Pricing changes, both at your institution, as well as at your competition, can impact the quality of your applicants. A lower price elsewhere, and higher risk-based pricing at your institution both tend to decrease the quality of your applicant. In the telco industry, the types of handsets and programs offered often determines applicant profile. In regulated industries such as banking, changes to regulations around credit limits, loan to value and income verification will also introduce changes to the applicant profile. In behavior scoring, more aggressive authorizations or credit line management strategies, introduction of loyalty programs, repricing, cross-selling, strategic closing of inactive accounts and other such activities can change the profile of existing customers. Usually, if the profile of the applicants for credit changes significantly, this has a downstream effect on the booked population as well.

- *Error in coding*. This is typically a systematic error, and can be avoided through UAT.
- *Mistakes in data capture*, whereby the data represents a nonrandom or incorrectly segmented sample, or exclusions from the development sample are included.

A point to note is that for a pure system stability report, the applicant population must be generated using the same exclusion criteria as the development sample. Companies, however, perform a second set of analyses for the scorecard cutoff in which all applicants are included (if the exclusions for the scorecard project are not the same as that during real-life implementations). This is to provide a more realistic analysis of the expected approval rate and of the effects of the cutoff on key segments.

The system stability report only indicates whether a shift has occurred, and gives an indication of the magnitude. For business decision making, finding out the source of the population shift is far more important, since only that allows appropriate actions to be taken where necessary.

Further investigation to pinpoint the cause of the shift can be done through:

- Performing a characteristic analysis to analyze shifts in scorecard characteristics.
- Analyzing shifts in non-scorecard characteristics that are believed to have an impact on the applicant quality and those that can explain underlying reasons for scorecard characteristic shifts (more on this in the next section).
- Gathering information on recent marketing campaigns, economic conditions and other initiatives that can impact applicant or account quality.

Characteristic Analysis Report

If there has been a shift in the distribution of the scores, logically, that shift can only be caused by the variables in the scorecard. The characteristic analysis report provides information on the shifts in the distribution of scorecard (and other) characteristics, and the impact on

Exhibit 12.5 Characteristic Analysis

Age	Expected %	Actual %	Points	Index
18–24	12%	21%	10	0.9
25–29	19%	25%	15	0.9
30–37	32%	28%	25	−1
38–45	12%	6%	28	−1.68
46+	25%	20%	35	−1.75
				−2.63

the scores due to that shift. An example of a characteristic analysis for "age" is shown in Exhibit 12.5.

"Expected %" and "Actual %" again refer to the distributions of the development and recent samples, respectively. The index here is calculated simply by:

$$\Sigma \, (\% \text{ Actual} - \% \text{ Expected}) * (\text{Points})$$

for all score ranges.

Exhibit 12.5 shows a shift toward a younger applicant, resulting in applicants scoring about 2.63 points less than at development for age. Analyses on all the scorecard characteristics are done in the same fashion to more comprehensively pinpoint the possible reasons for score shifts. Some analysts also calculate other goodness-of-fit statistics for characteristics, based on the difference between expected and actual distributions. However, the reliability of all such numbers can be suspect for characteristics with very few bins for example.

Similar analyses to compare development versus current distributions are performed for other characteristics, including:

■ *Characteristics that are not in the scorecard but are believed to have an impact on applicant quality.* These include strong characteristics that did not make it into the scorecard. For example, if shifts in the scorecard characteristics point to a deteriorating quality of applicants, reviewing these strong non-scorecard characteristics will help to confirm that movement. This ensures that judgments on applicant quality are made with a wider variety of information than just the limited variables in the scorecard, and are therefore more robust. For example, an increase in the number of inquiries points to an increased appetite for credit. I would also check the number of trades opened as well as utilization on revolving credit to confirm this. If average loan to value is increasing, meaning a higher risk, then other financial predictive variables should probably tell us the same thing. If not, we should look at other factors such as home prices and incomes to provide further explanations.

■ *Characteristics that are similar to the ones in the scorecard.* A good way to identify these variables is to perform a correlation/collinearity check. In previous chapters we have discussed using the Variable Clustering node in SAS Enterprise Miner (or Proc Varclus) to generate such an analysis. The point of this exercise is to confirm the movements of some variables by comparing them to similar ones. For example, if "age" is in the scorecard, tracking other time-related characteristics—such as time at employment or address and age of oldest trade—may confirm or explain further reasons for the shift in applicant profile. Logically, they should all move in the same direction. For example, if the average age of the applicant is stable, but the average time at address is getting longer, it may point to some manipulation of data. Again, this is not conclusive, but other analysis such as checking frequency of address changes or movements between postal codes can help clarify. If there is evidence of population movement and increased changes in addresses, then the increased time at address is not justifiable, and the case for manipulation is stronger. Another dimension that can help answer such questions is that of time. If for example, "inquiries in the past 6 months" is in the scorecard, tracking inquiries in the past 3 and 12 months will help to further explain the shift in the scorecard inquiries variable. This is similar to the population stability example shown in Exhibit 12.3. At the least, this will help explain whether the shifts are due to recent or historical one-time events, permanent changes such as product, pricing, or regulatory changes; seasonality, or some other factor. Related characteristics should all move in the same direction (e.g., older applicants should have higher tenures at work or older files at the bureau). Examples of other information types for which this can be done include trades, demographics, inquiries, and financial ratios.

■ *Where ratios are used in the scorecard, distributions of the denominator and numerator should also be tracked to explain changes in the ratio itself.* For example, if debt service ratio (monthly debt payments divided by income) has decreased, it may be due to either lower debt balances or interest rates, longer amortizations or terms, or incomes being increased—which all have different impacts on actual risk levels.

Again, these analyses should be performed to compare development data with recent historical data over the past 1 to 12 months, to detect any trends and to validate that the shifts in distributions are not a temporary phenomenon. The preceding is work that is usually done each month or quarter as part of ongoing model validation as well.

In most cases, it is also useful to keep track of major marketing campaigns, pricing changes, regulatory changes, and introduction of or changes to the loyalty program, as well as changes to policy rules. As discussed above, these are the reasons for score shifts in the majority of cases.

The shifts in scored and nonscored characteristics should be consistent and explainable using logic and business considerations. If, for example, analysis shows that applicants are getting younger, yet have higher "time at employment," coding errors may be occurring. Such illogical shifts must be investigated and explained. The point of doing all of the above is to answer the question: Has my applicant population changed significantly, and is it material? This cannot be done via calculated indices alone and therefore further analysis, including qualitative judgment is needed.

What if the Scorecard Does Not Validate?

If analysis shows that the recent population has shifted significantly compared to the development sample, the user is left with a few options.

Before we discuss options on how to deal with such scenarios, we again recognize that the most important task here is to establish the reasons for the shift in the distribution of the scores and characteristics. These reasons for changes will determine which actions are appropriate, or indeed, if any action needs to be taken at all.

Redeveloping the scorecard may not be a viable choice, since the data sample for this redevelopment will likely come from the same time period as the original scorecard (if an exercise similar to the one described in Chapter 6 is done), which did not validate. Ideally, this stability exercise is best done before starting the scorecard development project. The Pro-Forma Variable Distribution Analysis mentioned in Chapter 6 is a great way to increase the chances that the model developed will be stable. In other cases, the user would need to check the sample window again to make sure that effects of seasonality, campaigns, and other one-time events have been incorporated. If they have not, the scorecard can be redeveloped using a different sample window from a more stable time. If the exact reason for the score shift can be identified and isolated, there is also an opportunity here to reengineer the development sample to represent the recent population. For example, if there had been a regulatory change where the maximum allowed loan to value (LTV) for mortgages was changed from say 90 percent to 80 percent, then we can easily reengineer the sample by removing all applications between 80 and 90 percent. Similarly, the effects of more recent policy and other changes can be incorporated into the historical development sample. Note that it is far easier to remove such biases from the data than to add populations that did not exist before. In those cases, extrapolations and adjustments for WOE can be done, and perhaps expectations for predicted bad rates managed rather than expecting stability. Again, this exercise is best done before developing the scorecard, not after.

If the instability is due to one or two related characteristics, another option is to redevelop the scorecard without them. However, it is best to understand why they were unstable to make sure there isn't a larger business problem looming.

If redeveloping the scorecard is not an option, in such cases users sometimes adjust their applicant population expectations based on the new distributions. This means regenerating the scorecard management reports, as outlined in the previous section, with new total distribution numbers, but keeping the odds relationship (or bad rates) at each score the same. Based on qualitative and quantitative analyses, the bad rate expectations can then be changed as well. For example, if it is deemed that the population is of lower quality than expected, conservative measures can be taken to increase bad rate expectations and loan/credit line amounts can be lowered at the margins. A better way to adjust the expected bad rates is to use roll rates or vintages from more recent applicants/accounts. Exhibit 12.6 shows such an example.

In Exhibit 12.6, we can see the long-term vintage curve, for those accounts that opened in Q1 of 2013, as well as the recent vintage for 3 different quarters of 2015 accounts. The scorecard was developed in Q4 of 2015, with accounts opened in Q1 of 2013. In this scenario, the minimum bureau score cutoff policy at a lender was changed in Q1 of 2015, from a minimum of 620 to 580. Consequently, the credit card was now marketed and offered to people with bureau scores of between 580 and 620, in addition to those above 620. This is similar to another case where a bank changed its policy to approve home equity lines of credit (HELOCs) at higher loan to value levels. Whereas in the past a customer could get a HELOC only if their current mortgage was at LTV of 70 percent and lower, they could now get it at up to

Exhibit 12.6 Adjustment of Expected Bad Rates via Recent Vintages

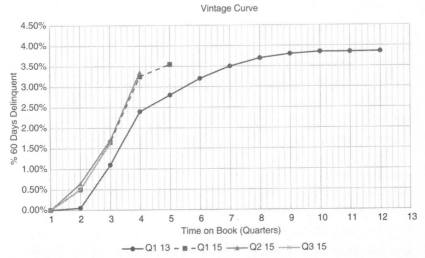

85 percent LTV. As in the preceding case, the bank started marketing this new product to those customers who had current mortgage LTVs of between 70 and 85 percent, and also lowered their cutoff. In the credit card case in Exhibit 12.6, the developed scorecard will point to a bad rate of about 3.8 percent. However, we know that the more recent, and future applicants and accounts will be much higher risk than the development sample. One way to adjust the expected bad rates is to extrapolate the recent vintages to 13 quarters. For Exhibit 12.6, that number would likely fall around 4.6 to 4.8 percent. We would then go back to the gains chart and change expected bad rate from 3.8 percent to say 4.7 percent. Most risk managers would start with this number, and as is normal, adjust it on a quarterly basis.

The qualitative analysis to be done at this point is based on the reasons for shifts in scores. For example, if all analyses point to a younger applicant with higher levels of delinquency and less stability, the expected performance is obvious. In some cases, the shifts may be less so. For example, cases where "credit line utilization" has generally gone down denote lower risk. This could be due to a decline in balances (which truly shows lowered risk), or to an increase in available credit limits due to competitive pressure among banks (which may not be indicative of lowered risk). Understanding such reasons for score shifts will assist in making an educated evaluation of the expected performance, and hence better decision making. Once again, we note that this exercise is not about generating statistics, charts and graphs—it is ultimately about making better decisions.

If the reasons for score shifts are well understood, changes to score points assigned can also be attempted. For example, in growing economies, the number of inquiries for credit products usually increases across time. In particular, when the development data set is old, the average numbers will have gone up by the time the scorecard is implemented. In such cases, it may be necessary to adjust the bins for inquiries to reflect current averages, rather than outdated ones. I have used a method where a profile is built using more stable demographic variables for people with say zero to two inquiries from five years ago. We then plot the number of inquiries for people with similar demographic profiles in the last quarter. This information is then used to adjust the Number of Inquiries bins in the scorecard, while keeping the score points the same. This is not something to be attempted without a thorough understanding of the reasons for score points shift, and is only a "best-fit" business solution to a problem.

Another option is to isolate the reason for shift and develop a separate segmented scorecard. For example, the bank traditionally targeted people with established credit histories but has recently started wooing those who are new debtors. The first step is, of course, to speak to marketing or other departments to find this out. The portfolio can then be split into two segments, one for the established and the other for new debtors, and two separate scorecards developed. Note that if the new debtor market is entirely new for the bank, it will need to get a generic scorecard to start with, but at least the established customer scorecard will work better than the earlier combined alternative.

There are also statistical techniques available whereby the development sample distributions can be "adjusted" to be similar to more recent distributions. However, this only adjusts the characteristics and may not represent the performance behavior of the original sample.

The pre-implementation validation is complete once it is established that the scorecard is valid for the current applicant population. At this point, strategy development work usually begins.

STRATEGY DEVELOPMENT

> *"Be wary, then. Best safety lies in fear."*
>
> —Shakespeare

General Considerations

Scorecards are developed for certain business objectives. Once the scorecard is developed, the user needs to decide how it is to be used to attain those objectives. This involves performing analysis for, and making risk-adjusted decisions on, issues such as the minimum score for approval (cutoff), initial credit lines or automated credit line increases, collections paths, best offers, setting conditions, establishing policy rules, and implementing "challenger" strategies where appropriate. Typically, frontend validation reports in conjunction with expected performance reports are used for this purpose. Strategy development is a very detailed and vast topic. In this section, we will deal with some high level, and simplified activities that are done to create strategies in financial and other institutions. The purpose is to give scorecard developers some idea of how their creation is used to make decisions, rather than provide specific strategy development advice. In reality, I would strongly advise scorecard developers to talk to decision makers and get some details around end usage and use this information to create appropriate models to solve the problem at hand. This topic, of how models must be engineered for specific purposes, has been dealt with in some detail in previous chapters.

Strategy development is decision making, and, as with all decision making, there are several general thoughts one should bear in mind:

- *Effects on key segments.* Any strategy implemented, or decision made, should be analyzed for its effects on key segments (e.g., regional, demographic, and distribution channel). *Key segments* refers especially to those segments deemed valuable to the company or important target markets. This reduces the chances of surprises, and allows the company to take steps such as using the same scorecard, but with different cutoffs for certain segments. The importance of this analysis is even greater where separate scorecards have not been developed for these segments, and where the applicant profile varies significantly between segments (e.g., branch customer vs. Internet, or existing vs. new customer). In some countries it may also be necessary to make sure that cutoff and decision strategies are in compliance with local lending regulations. In the United States in particular, analysis must be done to ensure compliance with fair lending regulations.[2] An example of how to conduct analysis to gauge effects on key segments was discussed in Chapter 11.

- *"What-if" analysis.* Where companies are utilizing a decision-making engine, using scorecards for the first time or using new segments, then "what-if" analysis should to be done for new or "challenger" strategies. The purpose is to get an initial idea of the effects of the intended new strategy on the ongoing business, whether it will perform better than the existing "champion" and the volume of accounts falling into each defined scenario. The purpose is to make the most informed decision possible, and to foresee any negative impacts.

- *Policy rules.* Implementation of new strategies gives the company an opportunity to revisit and enhance policy rules, especially when putting in new scorecards. Special attention needs to be paid to alignment of decisions based on scoring and policy rules, so that they do not negate each other and the effectiveness of each can be tracked and evaluated independently. Some analysts also use the scorecard development analysis to help set policy rule breaks. For example, a very strong binary variable where a small proportion falling into one category has a very high bad rate would be a good idea for a policy rule, for example, Ever Bankrupt. When looking at unbiased data for continuous variables, if the gradient of the WOE curve changes at one particular data point, that may indicate a good place to have a policy rule break.

- *Evaluate options.* More than anything else, real-life decision making is most often a search for "what is the best that can happen today?" rather than some theoretical optimal answer. As has been discussed in the earlier chapters, decisions regarding strategy on low default portfolio, reject inference, and selection of data is largely dependent on what is available and can be done, rather than a perfect solution that is impossible. Decision making should involve identification and ranking of the various options available, and then picking the best one possible.

Scoring Strategy

Most lenders typically start their credit scoring journey with a simple probability of default model. As they then get used to the idea of developing and using that first scorecard, they then start developing and using multiple models to assess different aspects of risk. In environments where a single scorecard is being used for a segment, the scoring strategy is fairly simple. Each applicant, or customer, is scored using that single scorecard and then appropriate decisions made. However, where multiple scorecards are being used, various methods are available. Multiple-scorecard usage occurs when, for example, an applicant is scored to predict different levels of delinquency (30, 60, or 90 days past due), attrition/churn, propensity to revolve, fraud, first payment default, bankruptcy, charge-off and profitability, and when a credit bureau or other externally based scorecard is used to supplement the in-house model.

There are three main approaches to implementing a multiple scoring solution:

1. Sequential
2. Matrix
3. Matrix-sequential hybrid

Sequential

Using this method, the applicant or account is scored on each scorecard sequentially, with separate cutoffs, and the very worst declined outright. Exhibit 12.7 shows an example of this strategy.

Exhibit 12.7 shows a sample sequential scoring flow where three different scorecards are being used, one after the other. Note that depending on the number and types of scorecard used, once an applicant passes the third scorecard, one of two things can happen: Either they are approved, or they can then be scored using other scorecards (see matrix strategy below). For example, a bank can use fraud and bankruptcy scorecard in sequence to filter out the worst few, and then use bureau and in-house scores in a matrix for a more fine-tuned decision. Also in addition to "pass" and "fail," other decisions such as "refer" can also be used here. Given the nature of the actions, this strategy is best implemented where absolute "hurdles" are being used; that is, either you pass or fail, with no gray areas. In practice, such

Exhibit 12.7 Sequential Scoring

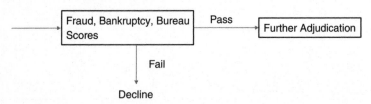

strategies are often used with scorecards such as those for bankruptcy and fraud. The idea is to use a score, or a probability, as a substitute for a policy rule.

A traditional policy rule would be something like "if applicant has been bankrupt in the past three years, then decline." Policy rules such as these are based on judgmental lending experience and will impact those that have had such episodes in the past. The concept above, using a bankruptcy score, is more forward-looking in that it converts the policy rule into a statement such as "if the applicant's probability of being bankrupt in the *next* three years is more than *x* percent, then decline." This will impact not just those who have been bankrupt, but may also catch those who have a high likelihood of doing so in the future. Since the action is severe, the decline is usually limited to the bottom few percentage of scores.

The sequential strategy can be fairly blunt, which is why it is used only for isolating the highest risk customers. Where gray areas exist or multiple competing interests need to be balanced, a matrix strategy is much better.

Matrix

In the matrix scoring method, multiple scorecards are used concurrently with decision making based on a combination of the probabilities for the various scorecards. The example in Exhibit 12.8 shows a matrix of expected risk and churn (or attrition), where gray areas have been established.

This approach is most frequently used where a balanced choice needs to be made from different types of, preferably independent,

Exhibit 12.8 Matrix Scoring

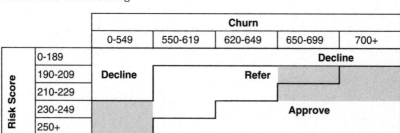

Risk Score		Churn				
		0-549	550-619	620-649	650-699	700+
	0-189				Decline	
	190-209	Decline		Refer		
	210-229					
	230-249			Approve		
	250+					

information. A high score from one scorecard may balance a lower score from another; for example, do you want to approve a low delinquency risk applicant who also has a high probability of attrition, or would you approve someone who is likely to be delinquent but has a low probability of rolling forward to write-off?

The example in Exhibit 12.8 shows:

- Applicants with a high risk score (denoting low risk) and a high churn score (denoting low probability of churn) being approved.
- Applicants with low scores for both delinquency and churn being declined.
- Applicants who are in the gray zone being referred for further scrutiny. For example, those in the top right hand corner represent applicants who have a medium to high probability of delinquency (perhaps 60 days past due), but who are also loyal—most likely because they don't have much choice. From a strategy perspective, these applicants may be approved for low exposure products such as credit cards, but the risk mitigated through actions such as lower starting credit limits, not allowing them to go over their limits or to make purchases if they miss a single payment. These may also be offered cheaper subsidized mobile phones, or lower postpaid monthly plans if applying for cell phone accounts. On the bottom left corner are customers who have a low probability of default, but are also likely to leave—most likely because they do have choices. In this case, the lender may choose to offer them special rates, bonus points, waived annual fees, or other incentives to increase loyalty.
- Applicants with a low delinquency score and a high churn score (i.e., they are high risk and have a low probability of churning) being declined outright.

The mix and number of models used, and what to balance depends on in-house priorities and objectives. Common examples are:

- *Custom in-house behavior versus bureau scores.* Here, payment performance with the existing lender is balanced by performance with other creditors, mostly to foresee future trouble. A customer who has delinquency on an unsecured product elsewhere but is still paying your bank for a mortgage will probably be delinquent with you soon. For application scoring, one can use a matrix of demographic/internal information based scorecards with those built using bureau information only.

- *Mild delinquency versus bankruptcy/charge-off.* This trade-off can help isolate accounts that have a tendency to become mildly delinquent regularly but who eventually self-cure and pay up. These can be a high revenue segment for revolving products.
- *Delinquency vs. cross-sell propensity.* In this case, a bank or telco with multiple products may choose to weigh risk against the probability of cross selling other noncredit products.

The key aspect to note is that measures must be independent of each other and preferably be providing competing information.

In Exhibit 12.8, two measures have been used together in a matrix. Similarly, where appropriate, multidimensional matrices can be designed for more sophisticated decision making. Normally, this is done by first taking a slice-by-slice view and then fine-tuning via a series of two dimensional matrices.

Matrix-Sequential Hybrid

In some multiple-scorecard scenarios, a hybrid of the previously mentioned methods is used, whereby applicants are prequalified using a sequential approach, and then put through a matrix strategy. For example, applicants can be put through a bankruptcy model first, and upon passing the cutoff, be moved to a matrix strategy consisting of delinquency/profit/churn scores. This approach is simpler than a multidimensional matrix and more versatile than sequential scoring. It is best used where more than three independent scorecards are being used, and can balance several competing interests. The hybrid strategy can also be used in conjunction with policy rules to prequalify applicants.

Setting Cutoffs

Most organizations that use scorecards set minimum score levels at which they are willing to accept applicants (or qualify them for any

Exhibit 12.9 Cutoff Strategy Decisions

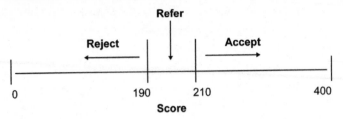

subsequent account treatment with behavior scorecards). This minimum score is referred to as a "cutoff" and can represent a threshold risk, profit, or some other level, depending on the organization's objectives in using the scorecard. A simple example of a cutoff strategy for new account acquisition is shown in Exhibit 12.9.

In this case, anyone who scores above 210 points using the scorecard is accepted automatically, anyone scoring below 190 is declined, and those scoring in between are referred to manual adjudication for further scrutiny. Note that this strategy would be used in conjunction with policy rules, which usually override any scorecard decision. Depending on the existing risk culture, available data, cost of processing, type of product, and maturity with credit scoring, organizations can choose several variations on this. In North America, for example, credit card approval decisions are largely automated—the vast majority are automatically approved or declined without human intervention. This is due to a high level of comfort with credit scoring, availability of good credit bureau data, high cost of staffing, and a relatively low exposure product. For other higher value products such as car loans, there may be a small "refer" zone where manual decisions are made. In the case of small and medium-sized enterprises (SMEs) or mortgage loans in some countries, there are virtually no automated approvals. In such cases, while all applications are scored, the final decision is always manual. In some other cases, the worst x percent may be automatically declined, but the rest are manually adjudicated. Similarly, the refer zone can be of various sizes, depending on the factors cited above.

In account management cases, several cutoff points may exist for actions such as varying collections actions (from soft actions to more stringent ones) or for assigning increasingly higher credit limits. More sophisticated strategies can be developed for more complex applications in account acquisition, for example:

- Assigning different levels of pending "accept," based on the level of due diligence or additional information needed to give final approval to an application—for example, pending real estate appraisals for mortgage loans, or pending confirmation of income. In some cases, cutoffs are set above which income confirmation is not required (this is dependent on the product as well as regulatory requirements—in some countries it is quite common to approve credit card applications without confirmed income). This reduces the workload for low-risk customers or for low-value loans. In addition, more stringent income confirmation methods, such as providing copies of pay stubs to a branch, may be required of higher-risk applicants, whereas low-risk ones may be asked to simply fax theirs in.

- Assigning a "hard lowside cutoff" at a score below which overriding (overturning the scorecard decision) is not allowed. For example, a bank may have a final cutoff of 200 points for approval and may set a hard low-side cutoff of 180. This means that some senior branch staff or adjudicators/credit analysts may override automatically declined applications that score between 180 and 200, if they have good reason to do so (overrides will be covered later in the chapter). There is usually no "hard high-side cutoff." Companies will always override applicants based on policy rules, and so forth, no matter how high they score.

The use of scores alone is only one of the ways to set cutoffs and decisions. Policy rules and human judgment is also widely used by lenders—and for good reason. Models are built on limited information, and need to be used with caution. We will cover overrides and policy rules later in this chapter. There are also other decision making systems in place that combine scorecards with judgment. One such system is the Comprehensive Credit Assessment Framework (CCAF), which is detailed in a wonderful book written by my friends and former colleagues, Clark Abrahams and Sunny Zhang.[3]

Cutoff Analysis

The following example is an overly simplified one, designed to provide a very high level understanding of how adjudication cutoffs are set. In reality, setting cutoffs can be a very complex exercise, usually involving both analytics as well as lots of (political) negotiations between the various stakeholders such as those responsible for risk, marketing, channels, finance, managing branch profitability, and so on. On the customer management side, decisions regarding transaction fraud, collections, and ongoing and initial credit limit or transaction approval strategies using scores will similarly involve multiple stakeholders.

A typical starting point for selecting a suitable cutoff for application scorecards is to analyze the relationship (trade-off) between expected approval and bad rates for different scores. These are only the two most basic considerations. Similar analysis can be done to gauge the impact of selecting a cutoff on other trade-off parameters such as profitability and approval rates, bad rate and revenue, capital and other relevant metrics.

A typical approach in balancing the tradeoff between bad rate and approval rate is to identify two points of reference in the score range:

1. The score cutoff that corresponds to maintaining the current approval rate (and yields the new expected bad rate); that is, answer the question, "What will be my new bad rate if I keep my approval rate the same?"

2. Conversely, the score cutoff that corresponds to maintaining the current bad rate (and yields the new expected approval rate); that is, answer the question, "What will be my new approval rate if I keep my bad rate the same?"

In general, each new generation of scorecards developed should be better than the last, and the preceding analysis should yield results where the organization gets a lower bad rate for the same approval rate, or a higher approval rate while holding the bad rate constant. However, each subsequent generation of scorecards developed on the same segment will have diminishing incremental returns, such as smaller swap sets. This is fairly common in model development, and can be ameliorated thought resegmenting.

Exhibit 12.10 Trade-off Chart

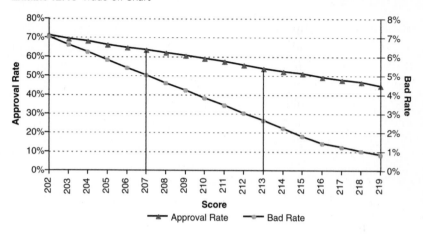

Exhibit 12.10, a trade-off chart, plots the expected total bad rate and expected approval rate across a selected range of scores. This analysis should be done using the most current applicant distribution (from the most recent month or most recent quarter) for plotting expected approval rates, with expected bad rates from the development sample (via the gains chart) or, if available, a more recent sample with a performance period equal to the performance window for the scorecard. In the case of behavior scorecards, one can use the distributions of existing accounts as of the latest month or quarter. The exhibit shows an example for a company whose current portfolio bad rate is about 5 percent and approval rate about 55 percent.

If the objective for developing scorecards is to increase/maximize market share, or if losses are not of concern, the company may choose to maintain its current bad rate levels by choosing a cutoff of 207 (where expected bad rate is 5 percent), and achieve a new, higher expected approval rate of about 62 percent. This means that the organization can be more aggressive in approving more people, yet keep its risk exposure constant by doing a better job of selecting applicants for approval. Consider for a moment the phenomenon that is occurring here—we are going to approve more applicants, yet keep the bad rate the same. Conventional wisdom would hold that for any given portfolio, if you increase the approval rate, the bad rate must also increase. That would be true in a closed system where you use the same data for the same segments. The reason we are able to increase approval rates, and keep bad rates constant, is that we are bringing in new data. The increased approvals from 55 percent to 62 percent represents the "swap set," as discussed in the Reject Inference section of Chapter 10. It is the net impact of bringing in the inferred goods from the previously declined population into the zone above the new cutoff, and now declining the previously approved known bads.

Conversely, if the objective for scorecard development is to reduce or minimize losses, the company may choose a cutoff of 213, maintaining its approval rate at current levels but gaining a lower expected bad rate of about 2.5 percent. This would mean that the company would reduce its risk exposure but take in the same number of new customers. The lowering of bad rates while maintaining approvals is again, due to the swap set, gained via reject inference.

Where a specific objective based on either a desired approval rate or bad rate exists, one of the above two options can be exercised. Typically, where there is no specific objective (for example when redeveloping scorecards as a routine exercise), companies choose cutoffs in between the two key cutoff points (207 and 213 in Exhibit 12.10), where there is both a gain in approval rate and a decrease in expected bad rate.

The choice of cutoff is not limited to between these two points (207 to 213 in Exhibit 12.10). It completely depends on the business strategy, and reasons for developing the scorecard. Some lenders choose to set a cutoff below 207 to get a bad rate higher than current, but with the expectation of higher profitability via a much higher future approval rate. For example, conservative mortgage portfolio managers with current losses in the single digit basis points may decide to lower the cutoff and increase their losses by a few more basis points, in the expectation of a higher future market share and greater overall profitability.

Trade-off charts like the one shown in Exhibit 12.10 can be plotted for other competing interests, depending on the objectives for developing scorecards, for example, risk/profit and risk/churn.

Gauging Impact

Once a preliminary cutoff is selected, its impact on key subpopulations and segments needs to be analyzed. Again, this is to ensure that all possible outcomes are anticipated before a final strategy is developed i.e., no surprises. Reports such as those in Exhibits 11.1, 11.3, 11.4, and 11.5 can be used to analyze expected approval rates and bad rates by scorecard criteria, as well as important segments. A sensible way to identify such segments is to refer to marketing departments and portfolio risk managers to identify future and current target markets, and to the segmentation analyses done earlier that will identify segments that were deemed different enough from a risk perspective but do not yield sufficient data for scorecard development.

For behavior scoring, segments will comprise the groups of people who are likely to be targeted for actions such as collections, cross-selling and up-selling, renewal, and credit line management. This will produce some expected numbers on the volumes of customers who will be subject to specific actions such as being sent collection letters, offered other products, having their credit cards canceled, or having their limits increased. Based on the expected numbers, one can then adjust the proposed strategies, or at least plan accordingly.

As with the trade-off analysis, these reports should also be performed on recent samples of applicants to get a more accurate reflection of expected approval behavior.

It is strongly recommended that these reports be run especially where characteristics containing negative behavior (e.g., ever bankrupt, worst rating, number of times 90 days past due) are used. This is to align organizational expectations and prevent questions such as "How did this person with a bankruptcy get approved?" It is imperative that users understand that based on a chosen overall cutoff, there is a statistical chance that a certain proportion of people with bankruptcy (or other negative behavior) will get approved—if you include this variable in the model. The proportion may be very small, depending on the cutoff and the scorecard's ability to isolate people with bankruptcies into the lower score ranges. This can become an issue, usually when you build scorecards with negative performance indicators. In particular, for lenders new to credit scoring, the most intuitive

Exhibit 12.11 Approval Rate by Score—Worst Delinquency at Bureau

Score	Nvr Delq	30 Days	60 Days	90 Days	120 Days	Bankrupt
210	97%	70%	56%	50%	41%	22%
211	95%	62%	48%	41%	36%	18%
212	92%	58%	41%	38%	31%	12%
213	87%	50%	37%	31%	25%	8%

thing when building scorecards is to include negative information such as those for previous delinquencies. These can cause difficulties, and almost always clash with policy rules.

It must also be understood that, based on statistical analysis, if a cutoff decision has been made with an overall risk profile in mind, these applicants with previous bankruptcies must have scored high enough on other characteristics to reach the cut-off score. An example of such an analysis is shown in Exhibit 12.11.

The exhibit shows that in the range of cutoffs being considered, between 8 percent and 22 percent of previous bankrupts may be approved. If the organization has a level of approvals for people with previous bankruptcies that it is comfortable with, it can then adjust the cutoff based on that comfort level. However, the only way to prevent all previous bankrupts from being approved is to apply a hard policy rule. This is also the case with all negative information, such as "number of times 90 days past due." If the organization chooses to create policy rules to decline people with bankruptcies or other such serious delinquencies, then characteristics such as those based on bankruptcy or delinquency information should not be used in scorecards. This is to make sure that the application of policy rules will not create skewed or biased results, and undermine the performance of the scorecard. This must be understood at the outset when characteristics are being selected for analysis, and also inclusion into the scorecard (initial characteristic analysis). The clash between policy rules and scorecards can also reduce buy-in for scorecards, which is why it is strongly advised to keep the two separate. This point has been covered in previous chapters as well.

In the case where undesirable performance is detected for particular segments, the decision maker has some choices, including:

- Using the same scorecard but with different cutoffs for different segments. For example, assume there are five regions in the country, with differing bad rates corresponding to the proposed overall cutoff. If the overall targeted bad rate is, for example, 2.5 percent, one can select the appropriate cutoff for each segment that would result in a predicted bad rate of 2.5 percent for each one (make sure that such regional cut-off strategies are compliant with regulations in each jurisdiction). This way, the better segments would be rewarded with higher approval rates, while the riskier ones would be penalized, but with the overall portfolio loss goals intact. The analysis can be similarly done with approval rate targets in mind. The same mind-set can be applied to behavior scores and strategies for credit line assignment or repricing. A detailed example of such a strategy has been provided in the previous chapter on scorecard management reports.

- Redeveloping the scorecard with different characteristics. This may mean removal of variables that clash with policy rules.

- Adding policy rules to prevent certain segments from being approved or to impose higher standards for some segments. This can be done if the preceding analysis shows a significantly higher than normal bad rate for a particular segment. Such isolated behavior should not be changed by increasing the overall cutoff, but by more precise actions for the isolated segments. However, this action will cause biased performance in the future, and is not ideal, as you have scorecard variables and policy rules negating each other.

- Exploring further segmentations for segments being over-penalized or over-rewarded. A significant deviation from "average" performance indicates the need for segmentation, especially if the segments in question are particularly important ones. This would be the case where the segment on question is large enough to warrant a separate scorecard. If the segment is too small, then policy rules or separate cutoffs may be the most realistic options.

- In the United States and other countries where fair lending laws exist, negative impacts on protected classes will require changes in cutoffs and strategies.

Strategy Development Communication

The importance of understanding the impact of strategies, and preventing surprises, has been discussed in the previous section. A good practice is to get the various interested parties (mentioned in the Scorecard Development Roles section in Chapter 2) involved in the discussions on strategy design and cutoff setting. These stakeholders can help in anticipating changes, and therefore preparing for it. Examples include:

- *Marketing.* This is a valuable source of information to identify key segments and better predict any impact on marketing initiatives. Marketing can also inform risk management of any ongoing marketing and other acquisition/account management campaigns that may be negatively impacted by introducing new scorecards and cutoffs, or that may explain shifts in applicant or account profiles (during pre-implementation validation). Marketing may also be able to identify any negative impacts on revenue goals, and suggest segment cutoff strategies to mitigate.

- *Information technology (IT).* Expected changes may require involvement from IT, and increase lead times to implementation, especially if scorecards are changed, new scorecards developed, or multiple cutoff strategies adopted (with the corresponding increase in reports and strategies required). In addition, if scorecard scaling is changed, IT may be required to reprogram any hardcoded policy rules, strategies based on scores, and other interfaces used for decision making. This is where flexible infrastructure, discussed earlier in the book, can reduce the implementation time, and avoid the need for the business to compromise strategy just to accommodate technology shortcomings.

- *Adjudication/Authorizations.* Cutoff choices or policy rules that increase the number of "refer" cases may result in higher volumes going into regional or centralized adjudication centers (recognizing that while most banks today have adopted centralized decisioning, some still allow regional lending centers to adjudicate, in particular, for small business loans). Similarly, more credit card transactions being pushed into manual authorizations will require additional staffing in authorization centers to maintain reasonable customer service. In some cases where increasing capacity is not an option, cutoff choices will have to be made with this constraint in mind; that is, the strategies will need to be designed based on the volumes that existing staff/technology can handle, rather than purely based on risk considerations.

- *Collections.* In some cases, a creditor may take additional risks that will increase the volume of cases going into collections. These can be reasonably forecasted, so that collections staff are better prepared in the future to handle the increased volumes. For example, a calculated risk may be taken where the approval rate is significantly increased (along with the expected bad rate), but with expectations of higher profitability. In this case, collections departments may experience a significant volume increase that may require additional staff being hired. In addition, taking more losses (but with higher overall profit due to higher revenues) might be a good idea for the strategy department, but not for someone else whose compensation is based on the amount of losses.

- *Finance.* Information required to calculate the profitability of new strategies typically comes from finance departments. In more recent times, the introduction of the International Financial Reporting Standard (IFRS) 9[4] for predicting losses will require far closer collaboration between risk and finance than before. Lenders may choose to create strategies based on some expected loss rates in the future (as they have done in the past based on capital requirements), rather than simply approval or bad rates.

- *Corporate risk.* Higher credit lines and lower cutoffs will require more capital allocation; risk-based pricing may require changes to hedging. In some cases, overly aggressive strategies may not comply with corporate risk standards. For example, an AAA-rated bank may choose not to market to subprime customers.

- *Customer service.* Calculated negative impacts on various segments will need to be handled. For example, an ongoing campaign targeting a certain segment, who are asked to call in to apply for products, may be negatively impacted if that segment is discovered to be high risk during scorecard development. In this case, the company may choose to provide written scripts to the customer service agents, or offer alternate products to customers who are declined, to minimize this impact. Similarly, if policy rules or cutoff changes are made that increase the volume of accounts or applications going into authorizations or adjudication centers, there may be an unacceptably long wait time for customers who want to make a purchase or who would like a decision on their application. Increasing cutoffs, which result in increased denials for credit, can also have a negative impact on branches and other sales channels. For cell phone companies for example, this would mean less customers buying cell phones and for banks, more irritated customers who may decide to close other existing products. Such actions, based on word of mouth, can lower the overall business to an institution, and result in adverse selection. In jurisdictions such as the United States, negative actions have to be analyzed for adverse and disparate impact in protected classes.

- *Education.* Staff may need to be retrained to understand new scorecard scaling, cutoffs, and strategies. Such education costs can be lowered by standardizing the scaling of scorecards across products and segments, such that new scores will mean the same as previous ones, and a score of, for example, 200 will mean the same across all scorecards. Another strategy to decrease education costs (and better preserve the confidentiality of scores) is to map scores to grades such as A, B, C, D, and so on. This is in the case where scores are being showed to frontline staff such as adjudicators, authorization agents, and collectors. Each new scorecard development will only require the mapping changed at the source, instead of mass reeducation. Appropriate staff members will see the grade, not the score, and policy rules associated with each grade will not need to be changed. Note that it is not recommended to show the score to sales staff such as those in branches. This has in many cases led to manipulation of known unconfirmed application data such as time at address.

- *Legal.* Analyzing the impact of cutoffs on certain geographical areas or other measures such as gender, religion, nationality, and so on may allay fears of "redlining," and reduce the chances of the lender being accused of discriminatory practices.

Risk-Adjusted Actions

At this point, we have a cutoff (or several score breaks for behavior scoring) and therefore know the risk level of marginal applicants, customers in each score band, and those above the chosen cutoff (the approves). We also now know the impacts of various proposed strategies and cutoffs on the various segments, as well as on internal and external stakeholders. Armed with all this knowledge, strategy development should now create risk-adjusted strategies or actions to maximize business objectives. These actions will, of course, differ based on products offered. Strategies can be developed for applicants or existing accounts—the main objective, which is to create risk-adjusted decisions, remains the same. The suggested actions below are high level, and only meant to give the user a general idea of some of the decisions made using scorecards. For example, depending on score and other criteria, various strategies can be developed, such as:

- Risk-adjusted pricing for term loans and other credit products, insurance premiums for new accounts and also for repricing loans coming up for renewals. While risk-based pricing is an enticing concept based on matching price to the specific risk level, it must be done with great caution. Competition and misjudging risk can create complications. For example, if a bank offers high-risk customers a high price, those customers have several choices. They can go somewhere else and try to get a better price. If they have already done so and have been declined elsewhere, they will take that higher price. However, if those customers were actually lower risk, and have been correctly identified as good elsewhere, they will be offered a lower price there and will reject this bank's higher price. The bank practicing risk-based pricing will end up with the bad customers in each score range, but not the good ones. One area where risk-based pricing has worked well is on the customer side for credit cards. In this case, all customers start at the same price. However, if they miss payments, their interest rates go up for a specified period (e.g., six months). Some have further tiers based on the level of delinquencies—for example, if you are up to 30 days past due, the interest rate goes up by 2 percent above the base, and if you go 60 days past due, it goes 4 percent above the base level. Regular payment for, say, six months or a year after curing will bring the interest rate back to normal levels.

- Offering complimentary product upgrades (e.g., premium credit cards) to better customers, even if they have applied for the non-premium ones or inviting them to apply for a lower-interest-rate card based on their risk; offering postpaid accounts to low-risk cell phone customers who may be applying for a prepaid account.

- Setting the level of down payment/deposit for financed products such as auto loans and mortgages, or setting renewal terms. This means setting minimum loan to value or debt service ratios based on risk bands. In some cases, banks use scorecard variables to advise declined customers of the levels of such variables that will result in an approval. For example telling a customer "if you change your LTV from 81 percent to 68 percent, we will approve you." This sort of feedback loop, based on the gap between the existing below-cutoff score and a level above cutoff, can help in retaining loyalty and future business.

- Cross selling of other products to better customers through pre-approvals. Note that risk and propensity scores should always be used in conjunction with ability to service debt in cross selling.

This ensures that cross-sell offers are made to customers who not only will accept the offer and are at a lower risk of default, but also can cope with the additional credit.

- Giving higher line of credit or credit card limit to better customers, both at application and as an existing customer (see example in Exhibit 12.12).

- Setting overall corporate exposure or facility per customer based on the risk profile, to manage concentration risks.

- Using milder collection methods for low-risk customers (e.g., sending letters, sending reminder SMS, using auto-dialers), and harsher actions for high-risk ones (e.g., sending to collection agency). Collections strategy is quite complicated, and involves the correct action and the right timing and channel.

- Varying payments terms for commercial customers (i.e., better customers get more lenient terms, while high-risk ones are asked for payment before goods delivered).

- Allowing low-risk customers to make purchases on their credit cards above their limits, or when they are in early stages of delinquency. In Telco, low risk customers may be allowed to use their cell phones in early delinquency while the high risk one would get their accounts suspended.

- Investigation for fraudulent application (i.e., using fraud scores), or requiring full real estate appraisals for high-risk mortgages.

An example of a credit limit–granting strategy for a credit card is shown in Exhibit 12.12. This is an overly simplified example and is not meant to denote anything optimal. The calculation of exactly how

Exhibit 12.12 Credit Line Strategy

Score	Debt Service Ratio				
	0-10%	11-15%	16-24%	25-35%	36%+
230-234	$ 8,000	$ 6,000	$ 4,000	$ 3,500	$ 3,000
235-239	$ 11,000	$ 9,000	$ 7,000	$ 5,000	$ 3,500
240-244	$ 15,000	$ 13,000	$ 10,000	$ 6,000	$ 4,500
245-249	$ 17,500	$ 14,500	$ 12,500	$ 8,000	$ 5,000
250+	$ 20,000	$ 17,500	$ 14,000	$ 12,000	$ 7,000

much money to give someone is a very complex one. It is dependent not only on risk factors, but also on the amount being asked for, existing relationships, and competition.

The first thing to note in Exhibit 12.12 is that this strategy is based on two independent and relevant measures. The risk score (on the left) measures probability of default on debt (i.e., "Are you going to pay me back?"), and debt service ratio measures the proportion of a person's income being used to service debts (i.e., "Do you earn enough to pay me every month?"). A lower debt service ratio is better, as it indicates that the person has more than sufficient income to make payments on the debt. The strategy shows customers with higher scores and lower debt service ratios getting higher credit limits. Note that a very complex calculated credit line based only on the credit score will not be very useful as it neglects a key part of debt repayment, that is, the calculated capacity. Once the measures to be used for determining credit line assignment are established, the user has various options to assign the actual credit line. Some examples include:

- Determine current line assignment practice based on the two measures, and then use consensus-based judgment to assign higher lines to the better customers and lower to the high-risk ones. For example, the top customers may get a 20 percent increase, and the worse ones a 20 percent decrease. Once the bottom left-hand (best) and the top right-hand (worst) boxes are filled, the rest can be filled in.

- Determine the maximum and minimum credit lines the creditor is willing to give, and assign these to the best and worst customers in the table. Fill in the rest judgmentally based on incremental increases or decreases, as well as knowledge of competition and prevailing credit limits in the business.

- Calculate a more complex optimal credit line, based on approaches such as a predetermined net present value or economic value, optimization of capital and others. One example is based on the total expected loss for a cohort, expected probability of default (PD), the loss given default (LGD), and the exposure at default (EAD) numbers. Using these, one can work backwards to assign optimal maximum exposures (credit limit) for each cell in the matrix above. Some assumptions will need to be made for the distribution of expected loss for each cell. For simplicity, assume that the loss per account for a cell is $500. If the probability of default is 6 percent and the loss given default is 97 percent of the limit, then the maximum credit limit for this cell can be calculated based on:

$$\text{Expected loss} = EAD * PD * LGD$$
$$500 = EAD * 0.05 * 0.97$$
$$EAD = \$10,309$$

The objective of presenting these three choices is not to recommend definitive ways to assign credit lines. The first point here is that the choice of metrics to be used in decision making is key. Many organizations use risk score only to assign credit lines or loan amount. This only presents half the story. As Exhibit 12.12 shows, a balance between probability of repayment and ability to repay makes more sense. The second point is that for every decision, one needs to evaluate options from the simplest to the most complex. Sometimes the simplest options, such as the first two given above, are the best. The first two options are simple, justifiable, and based on two measures that make sense. Risk-adjusted decision making does not necessarily have to be based on complex analytics—it needs to based on a broad-based approach such as the issues discussed in this chapter.

Policy Rules

Policy rules consist of a set of corporate guidelines designed to support the decision-making process. These include legal and risk-related rules such as minimum requirements and risk policies. Examples include:

- Legal age requirements (e.g., age less than 18, then decline).
- Employment (e.g., if not employed, self-employed, or employed less than one year, then decline or refer).

- Bankruptcy (e.g., recent bankruptcy, or bankruptcy less than two years ago, then refer or decline).
- Delinquency limits (e.g., more than two delinquencies at the bureau in the past year, or currently 60 days past due with an existing product at the lender, then decline).
- Application type (e.g., VIP, high net worth or staff application, then refer).
- Previous in-house record (e.g., previous at-fault claim or write-off, then refer).
- Minimum credit line for overrides or certain types of account (e.g., student or previous bankrupt).
- No credit line increase if one has been granted in the last six months.
- No upgrades to premium channels if 90 days past due in the past 12 months.
- If write-off or serious delinquency last two years, then decline for postpaid phone account.

Policy rules are a necessary and prudent part of risk management. The important thing is that they should be based on independent and validated measures. They should also preferably not be based on scorecard characteristics, so as not to undermine the scoring process, and create biased data. For example, if bankruptcy or previous delinquency is taken account of in the scorecard, then preferably these criteria should not be used in policy rules. In situations where the usage of such rules is critical, then it is better to build scorecards using other criteria.

Policy rules are also often judgmental, and are seldom tested empirically. Some policy rules exist merely because someone put them in years ago, and no one bothered to review them after that. Where possible, they should be reviewed, tested, and proven to be effective from time to time (e.g., annually). Credit scorecard development projects can sometimes confirm the effectiveness of some policy rules in the initial characteristic analysis phase. For example, if the WOE analysis for debt service ratio shows a change in gradient (i.e., delinquency increasing at a higher rate) at about 48 percent, the policy rule for it should probably not be at 38 percent. If the policy rule at a lender is such that a person is declined if they have more than three 60 days past due trades in the past two years, this can be assessed via triangulation. Calculate the bad rates for accounts with two and one 60 days past due trades, as well as that for accounts with between one and four 30 days past due trades in the same time frames. The numbers will help in determining whether the current policy rule is at the right level or needs to be changed. Note, however, that post-inferred data should be used, so as to minimize the effects of cherry-picking, since some policy rules are used as blanket refusal policies.

Policy rules are most often used in the overriding process (i.e., reversing decisions made with the cutoff). As with strategies, they should be developed with input from operational, legal, and risk departments so as to ensure that all potential effects are addressed.

Overrides

Overrides refer to manual or automated decisions that reverse the one taken on the basis of score cutoffs (i.e., one that contradicts the decision recommended by the scorecard). This happens in new applicant scoring. There are two kinds of overrides:

1. *Lowside overrides.* Applicants scoring below cutoff who are approved.
2. *Highside Overrides.* Applicants scoring above cutoff who are declined.

Overrides, like policy rules, are a necessary and prudent part of risk management that need to be used judiciously. A general rule for overriding is that it should be done based on *significant information available outside of the scorecard.* Since scorecards are usually developed using empirically tested methods, and represent the analysis of thousands or millions of cases over years of performance, it would be wise to override them only when you know something the scorecard does not. This is based on realistically recognizing the strengths and weaknesses of models. All models are built based on limited data, and many assumptions. The model will always make more consistent decisions and be accurate as long as the assumptions underlying its source data remains the same, and the data set remains limited. Once the assumption changes (e.g., change in population), or information external to the scorecard is introduced, the model will not perform well. These situations, where overriding the scorecard may be justified, include:

- Company policy rules, as discussed earlier.
- Local knowledge. For example, the branch staff in banks may know the applicant and the local environment, and be able to use information such as family income, recent job history, existence of significant deposits in other accounts, local economy, and so forth to make a better decision. This can be both positive information and negative.
- Justifiable derogatory performance. For example, a person was unemployed and missed payments but now has a well-paying job, or a student missed payments on a small debt during vacations.
- Due diligence and paperwork. For example, not being able to furnish satisfactory mortgage/car loan papers, evidence of residency, employment or income confirmation.
- Existing relationships. A model based on demographic or credit data only may ignore customers who have no credit products, but have substantial wealth in savings and checking accounts.
- Presence of strong guarantor or co-applicant.
- Other exceptional circumstances where the predicted risk level using a scorecard alone is not representative.

Overriding levels vary depending on the product, level of confidence in the scorecard, and amount of human intervention allowed in credit processing. Typically, low-value/high-volume products where automated decision making (i.e., a sole-arbiter situation) is used, such as credit cards, have very low override rates. However, high-value products such as business loans and mortgages, which are processed manually and require more due diligence to be performed, have higher override rates. Override rates are also higher in environments where the scorecard is used as a decision support tool, that is, as one of many items looked at, rather than the sole basis for decision making. In addition, in cases where scorecards are developed with too few characteristics (instead of a broad-based "risk profile" scorecard), overriding tends to be high. This is generally because the scorecard only captures a few items, and therefore much more information is left outside of the scorecard for overriding, and because such narrow-based scorecards generate less confidence among adjudicators, leading to higher second-guessing of the scorecard. Scorecards built on large, clean data sets tend to be trusted more, and produce less overrides. For example, credit card data tends to be relatively unbiased, deep and of large volume. It is usually implemented using automated tools, thus producing less biases going forward. However, in the case of low default portfolios or where the model has been developed with partial or biased data, more overriding is expected. For example, SME and wholesale lending is usually not based on a single score cutoff, or automated, and tends to produce higher override numbers.

In either case, lowside overriding should be kept to a minimum, preferably with a "hard lowside cutoff"—and where lowside overriding is allowed, performance must be monitored by "override reason code" where available. Furthermore, every attempt should be made not to allow a "miscellaneous" attribute in the override reason code, because this can become a proxy for judgmental overrides, as opposed to overrides due to more legitimate factors on both the high side and the low side. This is to ensure that overriding done on the basis of experience (or lack thereof) and "gut feel" is validated through performance, and curbed where necessary, in order to be in compliance with fair lending laws.[5] While regulators prefer to minimize overriding, in order to see consistent application of the scoring system, the reasons for overriding are far more important. That is why it is critical to monitor specific reasons for overrides and monitor trends. In mortgage lending, higher override rates for applicants falling into protected classes are a definite red flag, which may invite further regulatory scrutiny. In addition, generally there are more than one override reason for declined applicants. In such cases, monitoring all the reasons make sense and can help in analyzing behavior, such as bad rates by number of override reason.

NOTES

1. http://www.inc.com/magazine/201509/maria-aspan/2015-inc5000-fintech-finally-lifts-off.html
2. http://www.federalreserve.gov/boarddocs/supmanual/cch/fair_lend_over.pdf
3. Clark Abrahams, *Credit Risk Assessment: The New Lending System for Borrowers, Lenders and Investors* (Hoboken, NJ: Wiley, 2009).
4. http://www.ifrs.org/current-projects/iasb-projects/financial-instruments-a-replacement-of-ias-39-financial-instruments-recognitio/Pages/Financial-Instruments-Replacement-of-IAS-39.aspx
5. https://www.fdic.gov/regulations/examinations/supervisory/insights/sisum05/article03_fair_lending.html

CHAPTER **13**

Validating Generic Vendor Scorecards

By Clark Abrahams, Bradley Bender, and Charles Maner

"Trust, But Verify"

—A Russian Proverb given as Advice to
President Ronald Reagan by Suzanne Massie

INTRODUCTION

Economists generally consider the global financial crisis of 2007–2008 to be the worst financial crisis since the Great Depression. While there were many contributors to the crisis, one of the convicted, by the courts of public and regulatory opinion, is the set of underlying statistical or mathematical tools, also known as models. While they are arguably a critical component of making good portfolio, credit and pricing decisions, unmonitored they can be problematic and lead to poor decisions and imprudent risk taking.

A particular class of those models includes mechanisms to ascertain the credit riskiness of individual borrowers, such as credit risk scorecards. Credit risk scorecards are generally developed via three primary channels: (1) fully developed by a firm's internal staff; (2) developed in partnership between internal staff and an outside vendor; or (3) a generic, one-size-fits-most model fully developed by a vendor. The focus of this chapter is primarily on the most challenging case, namely channel 3, but is certainly applicable to channel 2, where there exists less than full disclosure of the system development details. Following the financial crisis in 2011, two U.S. regulatory agencies, the Federal Reserve and the Office of the Comptroller of the Currency, issued very specific guidance for managing model risk: Guidance on Model Risk Management, Supervisory and Regulation Letter 11-7.[1] While the guidance is very specific, its application is arguably more straightforward for the first two classes of models, those fully developed internally or jointly with an external vendor. Complying with the guidance for the third class of models, generic vendor-developed, can be somewhat onerous. The primary reason is due to the strict proprietary treatment vendors place on their models. Their proprietary treatment may span many aspects of model development including:

Exhibit 13.1 Typical Model Development Steps

- The actual data employed for development,
- Filters applied to that data,
- Transformations, applied to the data preceding model development,
- The objective function employed to derive model estimates,
- The method(s) employed to optimize the objective function,
- The model parameter estimates themselves, and, finally,
- Model fit or evaluation metrics.

Exhibit 13.1 depicts the typical model steps for a standard credit risk model, such as a generalized linear model, that is, linear logistic regression. While there are numerous other classes of modeling techniques such as discriminant analysis, neural networks, tree-based methods, etc. (refer to Thomas, Edelman, & Crook, 2002[2] for a more thorough treatment of modeling methods), linear logistic regression is the most common method used globally, and will be the basis of comparison for the remainder of this chapter.

Each of the steps described in Exhibit 13.1 should be fully available for internally developed models, and have been detailed in earlier parts of this book. For models developed by a vendor, but guided or managed internally ("custom developed"), most of the steps are also fully available. The two potential steps that may not be transparent would be the model objective function and methodology for estimating or solving the model.[3] Given the transparency for both internally developed and custom developed model, validation is not only attainable, but also usually straightforward.

However, validation of a proprietary scorecard, or generic score,[4] may pose significant practical challenges. Proprietary scorecard validation is a problem that can be rendered surmountable, provided there is a sufficient level of cooperation from the model developer relative to certain aspects of their scorecard and/or its associated development process. Some have described the exercise as "attempting to *characterize* the conceptual soundness of, and, further, to *prove* the validity of an unknown model produced by an unobservable process." In the case of a vendor credit score, this assessment may be accurate. That is, a vendor may publish the characteristics, but likely not the associated weights, or point values. However, the mechanism to choose the characteristics, especially the weights, is not made available. In either case, the general topic of vendor model transparency is of increasing importance, particularly in the wake of the financial crisis, and especially due to heightened regulatory expectations that press for application of the same standards for vendor scorecard validation as those applied to internally developed scorecards.

This chapter is intended to provide suggestions for augmenting oversight relative to vendor models. While current regulatory model risk guidance is extensive regarding vendor risk, fully achieving its goals are onerous, often due to a lack of vendor transparency. Nonetheless, much can be achieved by collaborating with the vendor and simply asking for pertinent information. To that end, we (the authors) wish to share some specific lessons learned, point to approaches that have generally proved useful, and explore some ideas for enhancing vendor-developed scorecard validation efforts.[5]

Additionally, relative to holistic model risk, the industry (motivated by bank regulators) typically identifies four distinct participants relative to model risk. They are:

1. *Model owner.* The role of model owner involves ultimate accountability and ensures appropriate model use and performance within the framework set by (bank) policies and procedures. Owners are responsible for ensuring models are properly developed, implemented, and employed. Owners further ensure models in use have undergone appropriate validation and approval processes. Owners are accountable for model performance and results. The model owner has responsibility for model documentation and its functioning.

2. *Model developer.* Model developers are technical experts who primarily drive initial development (design and implementation), including choice of theories, inputs, assumptions, methodologies, tests, processing, and design of output, or

subsequent redesign or reconstruction work. Developers typically complete initial model documentation. The model owner retains ultimate responsibility for model use and governance.

3. *Model user.* Model users are the primary consumer(s) of model output. The model user applies or interprets model results and, therefore, utilizes model output or results to guide tactical or strategic decisions or to report estimates for regulatory or financial statement purposes.

4. *Model risk management.* Model risk management is an assurance provider serving as a source of effective challenge over model design, implementation, and use (including ongoing monitoring, outcomes analysis, and change management). Review includes components of the risk management process such as model classification, model validations and reviews as well as the model owners' views on model weaknesses and limitations. Model risk management also (typically) maintains a comprehensive corporate inventory of all models.

Sometimes the individuals or groups of individuals may hold the same role among model owner, model developer, and model user. However, model risk management would be a distinct role. Some of these roles have been covered in Chapter 2 of this book, in the context of internal scorecard development and usage.

VENDOR MANAGEMENT CONSIDERATIONS

Effective vendor management begins with sound policy and governance routines. Vendor reliance requires management to evolve its associates and policies to address the following when considering the use of a vendor scorecard:

1. A risk assessment of the vendor.
2. Due diligence for vendor selection such as a business unit questionnaire.
3. Standardized risk assessments tailored to vendor scorecard evaluation.

4. Knowledgeable contract structuring and sourcing agents within the firm.

5. Monitoring and oversight procedures.

A good practice is for the business unit leadership, sourcing, integration, and internal oversight teams to have continuous and candid dialogue on the business purpose and performance of the vendor scorecard regularly throughout the evaluation, selection, and governance meetings.

Vendor management regiments should be established and considered an ongoing endeavor between each of the aforementioned groups with the following as guiding principles:

1. Foster a true partnership beyond the typical vendor relationship: This relationship may affect the financial performance of the (client) firm.

2. Vendor capacity and maturity: Can the vendor keep up with the rapidly evolving financial technology (FinTech) landscape, handle significant client growth, and integrate products into multiple systems or business lines?

3. Performance: Can vendor performance be monitored with metrics through established contractual language?

4. Partnership/IP transfer: To what extent is the vendor willing to transfer knowledge to internal bank staff, and the level to which they will allow bank staff to participate in the model development project?

5. Transparency: Ensure that the vendor is integrated into your corporate vendor management program. Are vendor performance assessments performed consistently across various (and sometimes siloed) owners? Have they provided sufficiently flexible criteria to preclude being locked into rigid agreements?

Validation of a vendor scorecard ideally involves reviewing each step of the model development process as well as providing effective challenge. There are both quantitative and qualitative aspects to model validation.

Exhibit 13.2 Typical Model Assessment and Performance Monitoring Steps

The typical quantitative validation efforts involved in each step of model development and ongoing validation are shown in Exhibit 13.2.

Selection of a scorecard vendor should be approached from a validation perspective, in addition to other business and technical considerations.[6] A proper validation perspective includes a focus on maximizing transparency as relates to a number of topics, including:

1. *Purpose.* Defining the business need and selection of a scorecard that best fits the stated objective.

2. *Target population.* Determination and specification of the internal population(s) of interest that will ultimately be scored.

3. *Target (and nontarget) definition.* Good, bad, indeterminate, performance group definitions based upon performance and exclusion criteria.

4. *Data.* Vendor data sourcing, inspection, cleansing, and classification of the data prior to any model techniques being applied followed by the selection of a historical sample of the population of interests.

5. *Methodology.* Scorecard development process itself, and incumbent technical assumptions.

    a. Disclosure of derived characteristic construction, including source data elements, formulas or rules for combining them, and any exclusion criteria applied prior to calculation of the characteristic value.

    b. Influence on the candidate set of predictor characteristics and influence on the order in which they are selected.

6. *Validation assessment.* Vendor-performed assessment of the scorecard to ensure the model is robust, and has not been overfit on the development sample, such that it will perform as expected during production. It may include benchmarking, a comparison (e.g., correlation) with other industry, that is, vendor, scores.

7. *Implementation.* Detailed requirements for producing a score in a production environment including limitations or use, storage, and reporting.

8. *Ongoing monitoring.* Recommended methods for monitoring changes in the scorecard's performance, changes in performance group score distributions, changes in the scored population at both aggregate and characteristic levels.

9. *Quality assurance.* Vendor must communicate modifications to the model or drift they observer in the model's performance.

Much of the above will be conceptually familiar to the reader, as they have already been covered in the context of internal scorecard development in this book. It should not come as a surprise to experienced model users that the high-level principles involved in the development and usage of generic vendor scorecards are no different. These topics are addressed along with some tips associated with them through the remainder of the chapter.

VENDOR MODEL PURPOSE

General agreement surrounding the scorecard's intended purpose must be understood and agreed upon by the firm and vendor alike. It is imperative that the firm define the business purpose(s) and ensure the vendor scorecard can address those objectives. Common use cases for scoring include expediting the credit evaluation process, achieving greater consistency of client selection, reducing cost to deliver the credit decision, reducing bias, refining client targeting, reducing credit losses, identifying additional target qualified prospects for product offerings, locating additional lending opportunities for expansion, point-of-sale credit authorization, credit line management, credit account reissuance, and credit collections management. In evaluating the use of a vendor score, the vendor should provide a statement on the general purpose of their proprietary score and indicate the general business purpose(s) for which they have employed it. The vendor should also furnish peer group references along with, ideally, a return on investment calculation depicting how the use cases can be applied to the client firm.

Target Population

On the second point, there should be a clear picture of the population of interest (these have been referred to as "segments" in this book) to be scored. For example, the population could be credit applicants who come to a branch and take a credit application for a specific loan product such as an auto loan. In this case, the population of interest is restricted to branch originated auto loans, as opposed to loan applicants visiting the lender's web site to fill out an online application, or people shopping cars at a car dealership who apply through the dealer network for an auto loan from the bank. The reason specifying the exact development population is important is that the scorecard needs to be derived empirically from a development sample reflecting that specific population of interest. This specification is to ensure its applicability and validity to those who will ultimately be scored. An important caveat, due to business events, is that there may be a legitimate reason for wanting to score a population with a scorecard developed on a different population. By different population, we are referring to a different geographical region, channel, or variant of the use itself, or product associated with it. In those instances, a scorecard adaptability study can be undertaken prior to usage to gauge how well it will perform, compared with the system it will replace, including an examination of swap sets. While we recognize that this may not be theoretically optimal, we also appreciate business reality of situations such as expanding into regions or channels where the banks have not done business before. In such cases, it is sometimes operationally more convenient to use existing (although nonspecific to the segment) scorecards, rather than build new ones.

The authors have seen in practice, although uncommon, that a scorecard may perform better on a population different from the original development sample. One such case occurred when a bankcard scorecard developed for geographic region A was applied to region B, where judgmental credit approval was in use. The scorecard was demonstrably superior to the judgmental system, based on a retrospective analysis of approved accounts having known performance. Moreover, the overall good/bad separation in region B improved by fifteen percent relative to region A in the adaptability test and over a subsequent two-year period nearly 20 percent fewer bads were taken at a comparable acceptance rate! The authors again note that this situation is not usually the norm.

Target Definition

On the third point, to quote John Dewey, educational pioneer, "A problem well-defined is half solved." Considerable care should be taken to understand and properly specify (and have agreement on) population performance definitions. That is, *the details of a problem are its most challenging aspect*! A worst-case example would be if a "bad" is generically defined as a credit applicant you would not have given him/her the loan had you known how they would have performed. In other words, the definition of a bad should be pragmatic and well defined, for example, current/prior bankruptcy, public record (tax liens, court judgments), loan default, charge-off or repossession of collateral, severe delinquency (90 days past due or more), moderate delinquency (minimum number of occurrences of 60 days past due, or isolated 30 day late occurrences.[7] The point to remember is that whether a vendor develops a scorecard tailored specifically for a client with the client's and (perhaps) external data,[8] or if the client employs a generic vendor score, detailed performance definitions should be known and understood.

It is also important to thoroughly understand and align external vendor performance definitions with internal models and policy rules. The authors have observed past experience where vendor scorecards were purchased and later shelved after minimal use, because the vendor's definition of a bad loan *overlapped* with the subprime scorecard owner's definition of a good loan. As a result, the lender determined the vendor scorecard was declining their repeat and refinance customers 60 percent of the time!

As we have discussed for internal development, we need to make sure that the exclusion criteria used by the external vendor is well understood and aligned with internal policies. These exclusion criteria would include for example, not scoring cases where credit would not be approved in any case, where there is insufficient basis to score a candidate reliably, or when the individual falls outside the target population to be scored. Some examples include being under legal age, fraud flag, failure to authenticate, company employee, or VIP customer to name a few. Similarly, other exclusions should be made to the development database to make it relevant for the project at hand. For example, in the case of a vendor-developed personal credit bureau score, one would exclude consumer trade lines that have lost/stolen credit cards, deceased borrowers, business loans, loans less than 12 months old and inactive revolving credit accounts, for example, high balance less than a small amount such as US$50. The owner should bear in mind that if a certain set of rules was used to develop the vendor score, the same criteria should be applied when calculating the characteristics in the scorecard. For example, if delinquencies related to medical trades were not included in the development of the scorecard characteristics, then scorecard implementation logic should apply the same filter. There is more discussion on this topic during vendor scorecard implementation.

Sample Selection

On the fourth point, sample selection should be conducted to draw as representative a group of loans relative to the population of interest as possible. Consider the example in Exhibit 13.3.

First, in the interest of greater transparency and auditability, it is good practice to ask the vendor to share their sampling plan and final sample counts. There should also be assurance that there are no gaps in the sampling plan, and hence no loans missing in the sample, that are in the population of interest. This assurance is to enable an accurate estimate of the population bad rate in cases where oversampling is performed. Note that loans having indeterminate performance comprise nearly a quarter of this sample.

Indeterminates, where relevant, should be sampled even though they may not be utilized in the development process, so that they can be evaluated and their approval rate determined.

In the event segmentation is used, a sampling plan should be chosen, and counts tallied for each segment having its own scorecard. Some common, generic vendor scores have, on average, 10 different segments, based on depth of credit history of the borrower and degree

Exhibit 13.3 Sample Counts for Vendor Scorecard Development

Performance Category	Rule	Period 1	Period n	Total	Percent of Sample
Exclusions	Dispute-Pending	12	8	207	n/a
	Deceased	3	1	28	n/a
	Fraud	7	2	54	n/a
	Insufficient Experience	62	73	1,013	n/a
	Subtotal	84	84	1,302	n/a
Bads	Bankrupt	38	19	760	0.8%
	Charge-Off	109	90	2,461	2.5%
	Ever 3+ 90DPD	59	40	1,261	1.3%
	Ever 2×90DPD	101	82	2,280	2.3%
	90DPD and Rejected for Reissue	37	18	751	0.8%
	Subtotal	319	300	7,513	7.5%
Indeterminate	1×90DPD	319	300	7,513	7.5%
	Ever 3+ 60DPD	467	448	11,054	11.1%
	Rejected for Reissue	92	73	2,055	2.1%
	On Payment Plan	71	52	1,554	1.6%
	Over Credit Limit	100	81	2,263	2.3%
	Subtotal	1,024	1,005	24,439	24.4%
Inactives	Less than 1 year on books	120	101	2,733	2.7%
	High Bal < $50 or fewer than 5 payments	29	10	548	0.5%
	Subtotal	143	124	3,282	3.3%
Goods	Ever 2×60DPD	87	68	1,943	1.9%
	Ever 1×60DPD	181	162	4,188	4.2%
	Ever 30DPD	2,298	2,279	55,009	55.0%
	Never 30DPD	157	138	3,627	3.6%
	Subtotal	2,705	2,686	64,767	64.8%
Total Sample Count		4,191	4,115	100,000	100%

of adverse repayment performance. Such a score may be based upon a very large geographic area that includes regions outside a lender's market area. Vendor score owners should ask vendors about the makeup and weighting of different geographic areas underlying their credit score development sample. In addition to geographic concerns, there may be different options offered by vendors relative to particular products, for example, credit card, installment loans, auto loans, sales finance for consumer durables, mortgage, small business, and so on. There may be further segmented scorecard options for to customers who have performed well versus those who have had derogatory issues in their credit reports. For example, owners of a generic bureau score (i.e., FICO) would score a credit applicant with one of several base scorecards. Then, they would apply an appropriate industry specific scorecard as an overlay to add or remove weight points to the base scorecard resulting in a final score. The final score would relate to the same odds tables, that is, likelihood of a bad, leveraged for the unadjusted base scores. This example is one approach of what has been used in the industry.

MODEL ESTIMATION METHODOLOGY

Relative to model estimation methodology, the scorecard owner should ideally possess a general knowledge of the vendor's scorecard development process. Having this knowledge is important because it should provide a general understanding of what is under the vendor or scorecard developer's control versus what is a by-product of the input data and follows from the application of the mathematical and/or statistical methods employed. For example, knowing that the vendor uses a discrete additive score formula that is quadratic versus linear can help the technical staff with reconstructing an interval odds table for system monitoring or, in the case of origination scorecards, help them better understand how the through-the-door population was reconstructed using data on rejected credit applicants. Knowing the objective function and solution algorithm can also be important for technical owners' staff. Different methods have associated assumptions, such as normality of score distributions of good and bad applicants, or equal variance between the good and bad performance groups. Knowing these assumptions, and the degree to which they influence the model, can help owner technical staff better anticipate areas where the vendor model may have problems, recognize early warning signs and how to investigate results deviating from expectations.

In practice, it is somewhat common for one or more statistical assumptions to be violated. The vendor should be queried as to what key assumptions have been associated with their development methodology. Further, the vendor should be asked if they tested those assumptions, and how those tests were performed, including results found and interpretation of those results. The extent to which one or more scorecard assumptions is *out of range* at development time versus post implementation enables tolerance setting on technical metrics, and then determine linkages to key business performance measures. More elaboration is forthcoming on the topic of vendor scorecard monitoring later in the chapter. A common question posed by bank regulators is the extent to which effective challenge was performed relative to scorecard development, alternatives considered and support for choosing the method ultimately employed. Our experience has been that vendor research teams examine competing technologies, but results are not covered in their scorecard technical review. As such, the client should ask the vendor what alternative methods were considered. Often, the client will be afforded some consideration for attempting to capture that information.

Finally, a best practice is to ensure that the terms and conditions in the contract clearly detail scorecard validation requirements and expectations.

Transparency of Vendor Model Estimation

The case can be made for greater transparency of the scorecard development process relative to its *core elements*. Scorecard development is a highly protected area by most model vendors as they view it as intellectual property and therefore a competitive advantage. At the same time, scorecard owners have a legitimate business need to know more that the simple fact that a "tried-and-true" proprietary development process was used. From a practical standpoint, terms and conditions relating to scorecard development transparency should be included in negotiations with the vendor prior to signing a contract.

There has been some research on competing techniques performed over the years. Some of the challenges associated with comparing different methods for solving real world problems have been recognized,[9] such as assumption about the problem domain that can afford an unfair advantage, degree of model parameterization and fine-tuning, degree and nature of data preprocessing,[10] and modeler domain and technology expertise. To illustrate the point about an unfair advantage due to assumptions about the problem domain, consider a tree algorithm competing with a regression model that has conditional dummy variables representing compensating factors that can strengthen a credit application when there is a weakness in a primary or main effect, variable. The tree algorithm can access all of the variables, both primary and compensating, but it will not know which compensating variables apply to main effect variables. Hence, it will possibly generate unnecessary branches and potentially fail to split on the proper primary variables, relative to one or more compensating variables, so as to accurately reflect the business reality. In addition, the tree will drop observations having missing values for compensating variables whereas the regression model will recognize they are not needed for those observations having strong values for those indicated primary variables that allow for weaknesses to be offset. In this case, the regression model has an unfair advantage over the tree algorithm, and its higher explanatory power is not attributed to the method, but rather to the incorporation of domain knowledge in the regression model formulation and preprocessing. Up until the middle of the last decade, the upshot of numerous reviewed articles is that no model development technology is best in all cases, and that the right technology choice entails domain expertise and good business judgment, coupled with an understanding of the science. Most methods appear to yield similar predictive power, with some edging others out, but not by a large margin.

In 2006, there were a series of thought-provoking exchanges, triggered by an article written by David Hand on classifier technology (see Hand, Classifier Technology and the Illusion of Progress.[11] He made a general reference to the *illusion of progress* in classifier/scoring technology that had been reported, perhaps with some excitement, in the literature over the past decade. It is perhaps important to point out that when comparing methods, such as regression, one should note additional facts, such as the mathematical formulation of the model. For example, a pure main-effects regression, with or without interaction terms, the inclusion of conditional dummy variables may trigger inclusion of yet more variables based upon one or more weaknesses in a main effects variable. These variations are part of *scorecard model formulation*, as opposed to the solution algorithm, which, in this particular example, is logistic regression. The paper noted other differences in classifier model performance might be attributable to data properties, or modeler/scorecard developer expertise, among other factors. The interested reader is encouraged to review authoritative comments on Hand's article, and also his rejoinder.[12]

More recently, some interesting articles have appeared in the literature in the area of classifiers and scoring systems offering additional promise. One such article considers ensemble models made up of a mixture of classifier models. In this case, single model development methodological comparisons have given way to combined approaches (see Ramli, Ismail, & Wooi, 2015).[13] Two other articles in the medical risk-scoring field reflect developments in applied large-scale mathematical programming and another method found to be useful in illness tracking that has potential credit behavior scoring application. By remaining abreast on applications in other disciplines, scorecard development methods may by repurposed to avoid duplication of efforts (see Ustun & Rudin, 2016) and (Dyagilev & Saria, 2016).[14]

The purpose in nontechnical treatment of vendor model validation is to alert scorecard owners/developers and their management that there is some risk with a more complex and sophisticated modeling methodology. While a vendor may claim complex methodologies are demonstrably superior to less complex technologies (by means of results that outperform simpler challenger models during in-sample validation), they may not fare well over time. Reasons may include overfitting the sampled data. Overfitting the sampled data underscores why it is important for the scorecard owner/developer to review relevant and complete vendor documentation ideally covering all aspects of model validation, including *out-of-time* testing results.

Some vendors have their own proprietary data and algorithms for deriving scorecard characteristics.[15] A detailed example of a hypothetical algorithm for deriving a scorecard characteristic called *revolving credit utilization* is provided in Exhibit 13.8 and its subsequent scorecard point value assignments appear in Exhibit 13.3. In general, differences in scorecard predictive power, or lift, can be traced to parts of scorecard build such as variable selection methods, problem formulation, richness and quality of input data, the score weights selection algorithm, and modeler technical expertise combined with business domain knowledge.

It is always a good idea to engage more than one vendor, and make them aware that part of the vendor selection criteria is their degree of willingness to share scorecard development methodology. In some cases, a nondisclosure agreement (NDA) may be necessary to do so. Some vendors may also be open to bank staff participating in some scorecard development activities, or attending post-event briefings. Vendor scorecards must have some form of effective challenge from their owners. Bear in mind that, as far as regulatory agencies are concerned, vendor models should be treated the same as internally developed models, and must be validated to the same standards as internally developed models. Vendors should not be precluded from validation; they should not because they are external and (sometimes) opaque.

Factor Selection

Model owners (certainly developers) may have influence on the candidate set of predictor characteristics including the order in which they are selected. Depending upon the order in which characteristics are allowed to enter the variable selection/weighting algorithm, results can vary. The cases below, using real examples, illustrate the point.

The case in Exhibit 13.4 is one in which the characteristics "total inquiries in the last six months" and the ratio of the total number of trade lines opened during the last twelve months to the total number of trade lines for the credit applicant were selected initially, before any other characteristics.

The case in Exhibit 13.5 is one in which the characteristic "number of major derogatory ratings" and total number of 30- and 60-day ratings for the credit applicant were selected next after "revolving credit utilization," and before the remaining characteristics were selected. The point is that scorecard developers, and the scoring algorithms

Exhibit 13.4 Scorecard Characteristics Ordering Case 1

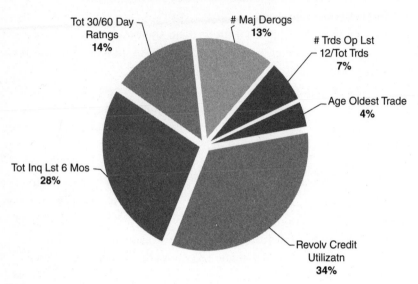

Scorecard Characteristic Information Values–Use
and Search for Credit Emphasized

Tot 30/60 Day Ratngs 14%

\# Maj Derogs 13%

\# Trds Op Lst 12/Tot Trds 7%

Age Oldest Trade 4%

Tot Inq Lst 6 Mos 28%

Revolv Credit Utilizatn 34%

Exhibit 13.5 Scorecard Characteristics Ordering Case 2

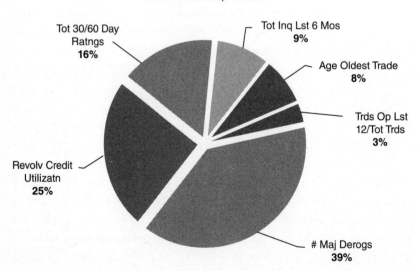

Scorecard Characteristic Information Values–Payment
Performance Emphasized

Tot 30/60 Day Ratngs 16%

Tot Inq Lst 6 Mos 9%

Age Oldest Trade 8%

Trds Op Lst 12/Tot Trds 3%

Revolv Credit Utilizatn 25%

\# Maj Derogs 39%

they use, can result in a variety of different scorecards, which may have comparable predictive value, yet may place emphasis on different credit factors. One such way to influence the order in which characteristics enter a scorecard, using model ordering, has been covered in this book in the chapter on scorecard development. Model owners should know if there is a preference on which factors should have greater emphasis, or should be present in the scorecard. The converse also applies where there is a business rationale for either eliminating or minimizing the impact of a scorecard candidate characteristic.[16]

VALIDATION ASSESSMENT

Concerning vendor responsibilities, it is strongly advised that:

1. Vendors have internal validation groups or engage a third party to validate their models and make that information available to model owners.

2. Vendors claiming the right to protect their intellectual property should be required to provide significant insight into the strengths, weaknesses, and limitations of their models.

3. Vendors provide outcomes analysis and back-testing of their models in various economic cycles, provided sufficient historical data allow.

4. Vendor models should be "tuned" to a firm's specific products or markets and be sure the vendor model works for those products and markets.

Vendor scorecards typically have the same operational form; that is, they consist of a number of characteristics, with each characteristic composed of attribute sets having assigned point values. Conceptually, they are created from a development process consisting of several steps performed in sequence, comprised of both quantitative and judgmental processes, as depicted in Exhibit 13.6.

Exhibit 13.6 High-Level Elements of Vendor Scorecard Development Process

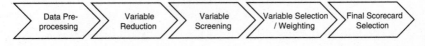

| Data Pre-processing | Variable Reduction | Variable Screening | Variable Selection / Weighting | Final Scorecard Selection |

First, some preprocessing of input data and data cleansing occurs,[17] followed by variable reduction,[18] variable screening,[19] variable selection/weighting,[20] and finally, final scorecard selection among a set of alternative scorecards. It is important to recognize that the end product of the exercise, the final scorecard, is based upon both science and business/technical judgments made along the way. Key model assumptions should be captured by the vendor, documented, and available post-development to the scorecard owner. Model assumption capture is important because the failure of a model assumption during production can evidence itself during on-going monitoring.

For example, suppose "years of employment" is a scorecard characteristic, and bivariate analysis reflects several reversals in the weight of evidence (WOE) trend. One such reversal might indicate that people on the job three years or more are riskier than those on the job less than two years. The model owner may force the WOE trend to be linear/monotone, such that it increases with the length of employment (i.e., with decreased risk). As has been discussed extensively in previous chapters, the (perhaps erroneous or biased) data is effectively being overridden and good business intuition is being employed.[21] Another example might be that a kink is evidenced in the WOE (aka logit) plot for debt ratio, where people at a higher debt ratio are performing better than those with a lower debt ratio. Perhaps in those cases, the individuals have compensating factors such as earnings growth outpacing their obligations, high liquid capital and net worth, among other strengths. In such a case, the modeler may opt to smooth the kink out of the plot, so as not to reward every scored applicant for having a debt ratio in some higher range along the continuum.

An important consideration, relative to vendor model development, is that the scorecard owner will be developing and applying scorecard override rules and criteria, which may be impacted by assumptions made during development of the scorecard. Failure to recognize these assumptions can lead to *overcorrection* by first penalizing the applicant with a lower point assignment for a particular factor, and then again with a policy rule dealing with the same issue for a certain range of scores. If the credit applicant's score fell into the affected range due to a lower point assignment and then penalized again, the combined effect of the credit score plus the business rule(s) will most likely *overstate* the risk for that particular credit factor. In addition, this may also cause sample bias issues in future model development.

Some vendors may use optimization algorithms allowing for specification of floors and caps on attribute point assignments for each scorecard characteristic. Further, policy variables can be "forced into the scorecard" so as to integrate judgmental values with data-based values. This practice has implications for avoiding not only the problem of *overcorrection* caused by a judgmental overlay, but also for reducing the number of scorecard overrides. The model owner will fully need to understand how this overlay is accomplished to determine the best options, and to enable them to explain how the scorecard deals with use cases posing the greatest credit risk to the lender.

In the event the development process is largely unknown, the vendor can be enlisted for help to determine what sort of *sensitivity testing* would be most appropriate to demonstrate the system is valid for use for the intended purpose. At a minimum, all key scorecard assumptions, strengths, weaknesses, and limitations should be identified and well documented so they can be routinely monitored and tested when indicated. The date of the request should be documented for information as well as the vendor reply for any unsuccessful attempts to gather needed information. The regulator or internal auditor will likely ask for this information.

Finally, a final development data sample should be requested from the vendor. If available, a typical logistic regression and WOE approach described earlier can be leveraged to create a "benchmark" scorecard. In some cases, model validation teams at different financial institutions have also built models using several different algorithms, and then compared the results with the final selected scorecard for benchmarking purposes. It will likely not (nor should) achieve the same degree of separation as the final vendor scorecard but should provide some confirmatory analysis. This analysis could be performed using only the known performance population to create a known good/bad scorecard and distributions. A comparison of the rank-ordering based on the two scores to discover any reversals could also be conducted. A comparison plot of the known goods and bads for the two models could also be constructed for comparison. Again, if the models have the same variables, results should align reasonably well, given the starting values are identical for the individual characteristic attribute

WOEs along with their respective bins. Differences should largely be due to characteristic weightings caused by possibly different objective functions and weighting algorithms. In producing the benchmark scorecard, it will be important to understand any adjustments made to the data-based WOEs and any other assumptions/changes associated with vendor scorecard development.

Next, challenges associated with implementing, using, and adapting vendor scorecards and or proprietary vendor scores are examined.

VENDOR MODEL IMPLEMENTATION AND DEPLOYMENT

Successful deployment and incorporation of vendor scorecards should involve an independent deployment assurance function. As previously outlined, vendor engagement is highly encouraged throughout the process and is most critical during implementation. Engagement by the two firms to construct a detailed implementation plan is recommended addressing the following critical areas: scorecard integration technical requirements, implementation testing protocols, ongoing monitoring including business use reporting, and governance standards. Regular meetings between the firm and the vendor should be held to share status updates and results during model predeployment. Representatives from the vendor firm should participate in meetings with the model owner, corporate data management, the information technology deployment and testing team, and line of business leadership. The model owner is responsible for ensuring construction of a plan that is congruent with the contractual terms of the vendor agreement and the firm's internal policies and procedures. Thoughtful consideration should be given to storage and permitted use case conditions, including sufficient documentation evidencing adequate controls are in place to prevent unintended scorecard use.

The authors have typically leveraged the following framework as a generic model implementation plan:

- Executive Summary
  - Overview
  - Background
  - Scorecard Version

- Scorecard Validation
  - Validation Data
  - Methodology Employed
  - Considerations and Effective Challenge
  - Cutoff Score Methodology
- Scorecard Integration
  - Decision Process Flow
  - Operational Deployment
- Implementation
  - Deployment Environment
  - Testing Strategies
    - Parallel Testing Plan
    - Parallel Testing Results Review
    - End-Owner Training Outline
- Ongoing Monitoring and Reporting
  - Validation and Business Use Reporting
  - Population Stability Indices
- Governance
  - Governing Body
  - Model Change Control

Following the successful deployment of the scorecard the vendor should be reengaged on at least a semi-annual basis to discuss performance of the scorecard within the firm. The model owner should request the vendor provide detailed documentation on the models performance and their monitoring results. These ongoing monitoring efforts are critical as they connect the firm and vendor back to the core tenants of the original projects intent and guiding principles outlined previously in the chapter.

CONSIDERATIONS FOR ONGOING MONITORING

Good business practice and regulatory guidance require scorecard owners to have a comprehensive validation process in place that provides for ongoing monitoring including outcomes analysis and implementation/use process verification. This monitoring process represents the key mechanism for ensuring the scorecard and related decision environment can be adjusted if necessary, to avoid serious adverse consequences when there is change.[22] Vendors should recommend methods for monitoring changes in the scorecard's performance, changes in performance group score distributions, and changes in the scored population at both aggregate and characteristic levels. Note some of the common industry reports used for such monitoring have been discussed in the post-implementation reporting chapter in this book. These are needed to assess when/how to adjust policy, strategy, and the depth of monitoring and research. The ability of the scorecard to rank-order credit applicants by their risk of *going bad,* and its ability to separate the good and bad score distributions similar to that witnessed in the development sample is critical. Delinquency (and loss) by score quantiles (typically deciles) can suggest issues with rank-ordering risk. Plots of vintage bad rate curves that are below the modeled benchmark curve may also suggest model drift or deterioration. Multiple tests[23] may be applied to assess the degree and significance of separation between the two score distributions. Temporal analysis can help determine the nature of the shifts, for example, when known changes have occurred, or the degree to which shifts are transitory.

More permanent or different types of distributional shifts may occur more gradually. For the mean[24] there is a simple shift of the score distribution to the right or left and for a logistic regression-based scoring algorithm, this shift would affect only the intercept term,[25] leaving the attribute WOEs unchanged. In these instances, scorecard owners may opt to alter the score cut-off depending on risk appetite and the distributional shift. When comparing two score distributions, homogeneity tests are recommended in the higher moments, which would evidence possible differences in the *shape*[26] of the score distribution(s). Examples include *variance* (spread or dispersion of the distribution), *asymmetry* (a value of zero indicates symmetry, a negative value indicates a left skew, while a positive value indicates a right skew), *kurtosis* (degree of peak or flatness, depending upon the sign, of a density function near its center).[27] In these instances, both the score formula intercept and the coefficients of the characteristics, as well as the WOEs associated with their attributes, are involved. As a result, rank ordering could be compromised, and should be checked. Recalibration of the scorecard is an option, but may prove ineffective obviating the need to redevelop the scorecard.[28]

The vendor should provide baseline values from the scorecard development effort in order to examine the stability of the scored population over time within score bands.[29] The vendor should also recommend thresholds for population stability measures indicating more in-depth analysis is required, as well as ways to spot trends systematically and diagnose suspect causes.[30] If scorecard segmentation is used, analyses should be performed at the segment level.

The authors have experienced a situation when overall population stability index (PSI) appeared insignificant, but some characteristics were very significant. The challenge with only looking at PSI, or spot-checking a few characteristics, is that it can be misleading and convey only part of the story.

The lesson learned from this example is that scorecard owners should pursue a full explanation of changes at a characteristic level, even when the picture looks stable overall, as compensating and offsetting factors may lead to system instability. (The same approach applies to segments, such as geographic groupings, channel, product/subproduct, etc.) It is important to gauge how much, and how rapidly, the through-the-door population is changing over time as it can impact the scorecard's effectiveness.

Characteristic analysis of the applicant population reveals differences in the number of points, on average, that have been assigned over time relative to the development sample for each scorecard characteristic. The vendor should provide instructions on how the information can be sourced for the development sample and how to calculate the baseline characteristic differences by summing over differences at the attribute level.

The vendor should advise what level of score difference in points suggests further analysis, such as five points in a score that is scaled at 20 points doubles the odds of loan default. However, at the attribute level where there may be positive or negative values summed, these may offset to produce a small overall difference in points. It is therefore advisable to examine significant differences at the *attribute level*.

Concerning loan performance monitoring, the vendor should provide template reports and definitions for tracking stages of delinquency, *bad* performance, and charge-off by score interval, over time. The same should be true for portfolio quality trending, including cohort vintage and roll rate analyses, which should be captured on both a dollar and count basis. These reports will help determine how well the scorecard is rank-ordering risk. The vendor should also conduct an out-of-time scorecard validation using a sample of good and bad credit applicants from an identical, most recently available[31] time period and also a sample of recent credit applicants.[32]

It is important to consider the impact of scorecard overrides, whereby score approvals may be declined, and score-declined credit applicants may be approved. Consider Exhibit 13.7, which depicts good and bad population score distributions, along with their overlap on either side of the vertical score cut-off line.

The plotted distributions are both symmetric. The good accounts are depicted by the dotted line and bad accounts depicted by the solid black line, which skew to the right, with an average score falling below the median score. Low-side overrides are aimed at approving the known goods falling below the cutoff score and high-side overrides are directed to declining the known bads scoring above the cutoff. Overrides are usually attempted with policy rules designed to limit risk, factors that

Exhibit 13.7 Plot of Good and Bad Score Distributions[33]

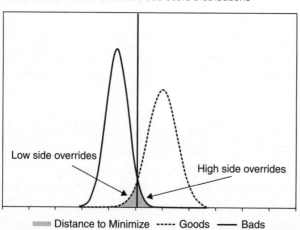

can compensate for weaknesses in one or more of the scorecard characteristics, or additional scores in a dual, or multiple, score matrix.

Scorecard overrides are a focus for scorecard validators. There should be thresholds on the percentages of overrides, both low and high, and solid empirical support and/or business intuition for override rules. As has been covered in this book, acceptable thresholds for overrides can depend on several factors, including risk culture, confidence in the scorecard, and type of product and level of human intervention in the decision. Model vendors should be able to suggest general level of overrides based on similar institution in their customer base.

Examples of Vendor Disclosure Challenges

Scorecard owners should press for full disclosure of derived characteristic construction, including source data elements, formulas or rules for combining them, and any exclusion criteria applied prior to calculation of the characteristic value. For example, suppose *revolving credit utilization* was a characteristic in the vendor scorecard. The process used should be examined to generate its value at the credit bureau, and determine how it was transformed (e.g., binned) and the corresponding point values. A somewhat simplified specification might look as follows in Exhibit 13.8.

The main point here is that whatever algorithm is deployed in system development, the validity of the logic needs to be assessed, attribute definitions ensured to make sense, and codes and values generated mapped appropriately to the scorecard. Any changes made to the calculation of *revolving credit utilization* or the credit bureau fields from which it was derived need to be known in advance. A hypothetical scorecard point assignment for *revolving credit utilization* is provided in Exhibit 13.9.

In practice, the authors experienced an event where the credit bureau changed the derivation of a credit bureau characteristic that happened to be in a scorecard. It was detected a number of months after the fact due to the PSI being out of its normal range, and subsequent characteristic analysis revealed the exact cause. The simple fact is that vendor models using external data, which is often out of the control of the scorecard owner, pose additional risk that is much more difficult to detect than scorecards based on internal credit applicant data—another reason ongoing monitoring is such an important topic.

Exhibit 13.8 *Revolving Credit Utilization* Vendor Calculation Logic

1.	Read in Credit Applicant Credit Bureau file
2.	If Credit Applicant meets exclusion criteria, set Exclusion Flag = Yes, and exit Process Loop
3.	Set all counters to and aggregate amount fields = 0
4.	Read in trade line record from file
5.	If end of trade line records, go to Step (12)
6.	If Trade Line Type = Revolving, Then Revolving Counter = Revolving Counter +1, Else go to Step (4)
7.	If trade line is on a "bypass list,"[34] go to Step (4)
8.	Allowable Counter = Allowable Counter +1
9.	If Status of trade line is "open" and the Outstanding Balance field and High Credit fields have a numerical value, then Valid Counter = Valid Counter +1, Else go to Step (4)
10.	If amount of High Credit > 0 then Aggregate Balance = Aggregate Balance + Outstanding Balance and Aggregate High Credit = Aggregate High Credit + High Credit
11.	Go to Step (4)
12.	If Revolving Counter = 0 then Revolving Credit Utilization = A
13.	Else If Allowable Counter = 0 then Revolving Credit Utilization = B
14.	Else If Valid Counter = 0 then Revolving Credit Utilization = C
15.	Else If Aggregate High Credit = 0 then Revolving Credit Utilization = D
16.	Else Revolving Credit Utilization = (Aggregate Balance * 100) / Aggregate High Credit[35]

Exhibit 13.9 Scorecard Point Value Assignments for *Revolving Credit Utilization*

Attribute Description	Code Value	Scorecard Points
No Revolving Trades	A	15
No Qualifying Trades	B	15
No Valid Qualified Trades	C	15
Aggregate High Credit = 0	D	15
Unused	0%	25
Tier 1 Utilization	$0\% < x < 20\%$	45
Tier 2 Utilization	$20\% \leq x < 35\%$	55
Tier 3 Utilization	$35\% \leq x < 50\%$	60
Tier 4 Utilization	$50\% \leq x < 75\%$	40
Tier 5 Utilization	$75\% \leq x < 90\%$	25
Tier 6 Utilization	90%+	0
Missing/No Information	Blank	15

In another instance, the derivation of a variable programmed at the credit bureau was different from that which was used for scorecard development. It is important to put in place proper controls and quality assurance procedures in order to avoid these situations.

Monitoring in Conjunction with Another Score

Scorecard performance monitoring is typically in the presence of one score. However, it can sometimes be more involved, especially when dual-score matrices are employed either with a custom score developed in-house, or with another vendor score. In these instances, there may be a need for two vendors and additional business rules with judgmental criteria. The motivation for joining two scores explicitly, rather than implicitly, is to maintain factor separability. Conversely, if a separate score, say a vendor score, is incorporated into a model, as in the case of regression, it is then an inseparable part of the model. However, if it is instead maintained separately, such as in a matrix, a vendor or internal model will not affect the original model. In addition, using separate scores in a matrix allows for greater flexibility in creating decision strategies.

In the example displayed in Exhibit 13.10, a risk grade is assigned based on a matrix consisting of two scores for each loan. For example, a loan having an application score of 211 and a credit bureau score of 658 would be assigned a risk grade of 4. There are several reasons why a dual score approach may be appealing, including:

- Improve rank-ordering of risk.
- Increase approval rate/reduce losses.

Exhibit 13.10 Example of a Dual Score Matrix Having a Single Vendor Score[36]

		Application Credit Score							
		< 175	175–184	184–194	195–204	205–214	215–224	225–234	235+
Credit Bureau Score	< 620	7	7	6	6	6	6	6	6
	620–639	7	6	6	5	5	5	4	4
	640–659	6	6	5	4	4	4	3	3
	660–679	6	6	5	4	3	3	3	3
	680–699	6	6	5	4	3	2	2	2
	700–719	6	5	5	4	3	2	1	1
	720+	6	5	5	4	3	2	1	1

■ Reduce overrides and exceptions.

■ Systematic approach/less individual discretion.

■ Preclude or substantially reduce risk of compromising the main scorecard/model should the second score become obsolete or compromised (e.g., no longer available).

Additionally, effective challenge of a custom application scorecard, vendor scorecard, vendor score, or dual-score loan decision model can be based purely on business knowledge. For example, subject-matter experts (SMEs) may specify a "judgmental" scorecard[37] of the type depicted in Exhibit 13.11 for automobile lending.[38]

For example, a loan application with:

1. A debt-to-income ratio of 20 percent (a good rating) would have 8 points assigned.

2. No trade lines having delinquent payments of 60 days past due and fewer than two 30 days past due delinquencies during the past two years (a good rating) would have 18 points assigned.

3. A credit file 18 months (fair rating) would have 3 points assigned; payment to income ratio (PTI) of 17 percent would have 3 points assigned, and so on.

Exhibit 13.11 Effective Challenge via Pure Judgment

Factor	Good Rating	Points	Fair Rating	Points	Poor Rating	Points
Credit payment history	< 2 trades 30 DPD last 24 mos; 0 trades 60 DPD last 24 mos	18	2+ trades 30 DPD last 24 mos; 1+ trade 60 DPD last 24 mos	9	Public record last 24 mos, bankruptcy within last 5 years	3
Debt-to-income Ratio	< 25%	8	26–34%	5	> 35%	2
Credit file depth	2+ years	6	1–2 years	3	< 1 year	1
Dealer advance	< 100%	6	100–114%	4	115%+	0
Down payment Percent	20%+	5	10–19%	3	< 10%	2
Employment Stability	2+ years	6	1–2 years	3	< 1 year	1
PTI Ratio	< 10%	7	10–16%	5	17%	3

With this judgmental system, the highest possible score is 56 points, and the minimum is 12 points, which partitions the loans into at most 44 individual score bins.[39] This type of scorecard can be used to rank-order credit applicants, and it is intuitive in that the stronger credit applications obtain better ratings and conversely for the weaker credit applications.

A typical vendor score will have a range of five hundred or more points (the FICO score ranges from a low of 300 to a high of 850). You can capture the frequencies of individual scores, as well as the typical score band deciles. You should be familiar with the frequencies of your vendor scores, as well as the mean, median, and mode of the score distribution. You may find that for the most part, only a third of the total potential individual scores actually occur in practice. Also, many dual score matrices we have seen use row and column deciles for the score ranges, so that there are 10 times 10 score band combinations, for a total of one hundred entries that require assignment of a risk grade.

At the close of the exercise one would have the vendor score, application score, dual score grade, and judgmental score. Loans could be ranked in the sample based on all four scores individually and results inspected for reversal patterns, as shown in Exhibit 13.12.

In order to construct the ranking by judgmental score, all loans in Exhibit 13.12 should be scored first using the judgmental scorecard and would score in a value range from 12 to 54, and also 56, points. In this example, rank ordering is preserved in general blocks of loans, which were sorted from highest FICO score band to lowest FICO score band. That said, there are opportunities to improve upon the dual-score ranking in this example.

Based on analysis, it may be determined to augment the dual-score matrix with business rules for specific subsets of applicants in various loans grades, where subsets are determined by quantitative methods, such as tree-based algorithms, or by inspection of the ranking table, coupled with results from ongoing monitoring (OGM) of scorecard system performance. In the latter case, 44 bins could be mapped to risk grades 1-7, which correspond identically to risk grades in the dual-score matrix in Exhibit 13.10 based on SME experience and the results of OGM. An example of adjustments appears in Exhibit 13.13. The reader will observe that the dual score assigned grade can be improved through use of appropriate business rules. The "Final Loan Grade"

Exhibit 13.12 Alternative Rankings of a Sample of 300 Loans Based on Four Different Scores

	Rankings (by Type of Score)				
Application ID	Vendor Score	Application Score	Dual Score Risk Grade	Judgmental Score	Final Grade
99-347-001	300	287	290	298	1
99-347-002	299	293	297	287	1
99-347-003	298	289	296	240	1
99-347-004	297	299	297	300	1
...					
99-347-087	223	230	228	235	2
99-347-088	222	218	220	160	2
99-347-089	221	225	224	227	2
99-347-090	220	221	223	231	2
...					
99-347-159	151	168	157	150	3
99-347-160	150	172	160	142	3
99-347-161	149	157	154	163	3
99-347-162	148	139	142	241	3
...					
99-347-233	77	87	82	68	4
99-347-234	76	79	77	18	4
99-347-235	75	84	80	81	4
99-347-236	74	69	72	35	4
...					
99-347-297	4	8	6	20	5
99-347-298	3	12	7	11	5
99-347-299	2	1	1	1	5
99-347-300	1	3	3	3	5

column refers to the adjusted rating, based on criteria specified in preceding columns.

Developing and applying a judgmental evaluation of the vendor model, and/or combining multiple scores, say a vendor and application score, can result in insights that can be used to improve the loan decision process. This translates to tangible added value that can result from a thorough model validation.

Exhibit 13.13 Adjusting Score-Based Grades with Rules[40]

Dual-Score Grade	PTI %	Down Payment %	Advance %	New/Used	Note Amount	Final Loan Grade
1	< 10	20+	5+	Either	< $10K	2
1	< 10	< 20	125+	Used	$10K+	2
1	10–14	5+	< 125	Used	$10K+	3
2	< 10	< 10	< 100	New	Any	1
2	< 10	< 10	125+	Either	Any	4
2	15+	< 20	125+	Either	Any	5
3	10–14	20+	100–124	New	Any	2
3	10–14	20+	100–124	Used	Any	4
3	15+	20+	125+	Either	Any	5
4	< 10	5+	< 100	New	< $10K	2
4	< 10	0–100	125+	Either	Any	5
4	15+	20+	< 100	Either	Any	3
5	< 10	20+	100+	New	Any	4
5	< 10	25+	N/A	Either	Any	2
5	10–14	20+	< 100	Either	Any	3

In the next section, the need for transparency is emphasized with regard to system construction, with special emphasis on characteristic construction and order of selection.

ONGOING QUALITY ASSURANCE OF THE VENDOR

It is generally expected that vendors will validate their scorecards during development using a holdout (or validation) sample. The model owner should request results of that validation, an interpretation of the results and verify all critical assumptions have been tested. The owner should be provided with sufficient information to enable them to conduct their own sensitivity tests on scorecard parameters and assumptions. That said, vendors might not be able to perform scorecard development-time validation on a holdout sample, due to lack of available data (most typically, the number of bads). This limitation is less common in behavioral scorecards than with application scorecards where vendors may use bootstrapping methodology. As a result, there is no 80/20 split with a holdout sample during model development. In these cases, vendors will typically perform out-of-time sample validations, using the most recent year. More than one sample may be drawn, spanning different sets of customers, and the scorecard can be tested for strength of separation between goods and bads. There is also the case of behavioral scorecards, where typically an annual realignment of the score/odds relationship that only affects the intercept term takes place, while the actual scoring model (attribute point values within each scorecard characteristic) remains unchanged.

In the appendix, a checklist of key considerations for vendor scorecard validations is provided for consideration coinciding with points raised in this chapter. Depending upon the way your institution has delineated duties, the following *stakeholders* need to consider their role (e.g., taking the lead, providing input, assurance, and so on) in addressing each item:

1. Vendor
2. Scorecard owner
3. Internal scorecard developer
4. Internal scorecard validator

The idea of using a checklist[41] is to avoid mistakes and to ensure each consideration is addressed by the relevant parties. A possible use would be to assign primary stakeholder responsibility on an item-by-item basis with a number ranging from (1) to (4), instead of a simple check mark (☑). A checklist should be useful, no matter the role; the authors hope the reader finds it of value.

GET INVOLVED

It is highly recommended to take advantage of opportunities to attend vendor conferences, in addition to conferences sponsored by professional risk management associations.[42] The authors have found that such events provide opportunities for meaningful, often insightful, exchanges with technical sales associates, and even the developers themselves in a less formal, more relaxed setting. Membership in owner groups, forums, and Web-based interest groups relative to scorecard development, implementation, use and management is helpful and, therefore encouraged. There, thoughts can be shared, questions asked, opinions voiced and comments as well as recommendations offered, possibly provoking original thought on an important topic. Let your voice be heard!

APPENDIX: KEY CONSIDERATIONS FOR VENDOR SCORECARD VALIDATIONS

	Key Consideration	
1.	For what use(s) was the scorecard designed?	
a.	What question is it attempting to answer?	☐
b.	What is it trying to solve or address?	☐
2.	Is the scorecard based upon sound principles and reasoning? This question should be considered from up to 3 distinct angles: (1) vendor perspective, (2) industry perspective, and (3) owner institution perspective.	
a.	Theories	☐
b.	Facts	☐
c.	Opinions	☐
d.	Business definitions and parameters	☐
i.	What are the population performance definitions (PPDs)? (vendor-supplied, industry-based, or owner specified?)	☐
ii.	Are the PPDs appropriate for the scorecard use and the population of interest to which it will be applied? (Special care must be taken when PPDs are vendor-supplied or industry-oriented.)	☐
iii.	What are the indeterminate performance definitions?	☐
iv.	What are the exclusion criteria for the scorecard development sample and use?	☐
v.	Where is the observation window for the sample positioned relative to the full prevailing economic cycle (boom, recession, recovery)?	☐
vi.	Is the performance window for the sample sufficient based upon sufficient historical experience?	☐
3.	What can the scorecard enable the owner to infer with a high degree of certainty?	☐
4.	What are the scorecard's limitations?	
a.	Per each distinct intended use	☐
b.	Given the supporting theories upon which it is based	☐

	Key Consideration	
c.	Given the data it uses	☐
d.	Over what time horizon	☐
e.	Given uncertainties associated with key scorecard assumptions	☐
f.	Applicable to only certain loan products	☐
g.	Applicable to only certain geographic areas	☐
h.	Applicable to only certain channels	☐
i.	Applicable to only certain combinations of product, geographic area, channel	☐
5.	Scorecard choice effective challenge: What alternatives exist and is there a superior approach?	☐
6.	How does the vendor propose scorecard performance be measured?	
a.	What are the results of the development-time validation relative to that of the hold-out sample?	☐
b.	What out-of-time holdout sample validation was performed and what were the results?	☐
c.	How are periodic "down-the-road" validation(s) and system and population performance on-going monitoring carried out and what thresholds are applied to determine if the scorecard needs to be further studied, recalibrated, or possibly replaced?	☐
d.	Stability of the scorecard inputs?	☐
e.	Stability of the scorecard assumptions?	☐
i.	Vintage Cumulative bad rate for score approved loans	☐
ii.	Vintage Cumulative charge-off rate for score approved loans	☐
iii.	Vintage Cumulative delinquency rate for score approved loans	☐
f.	Stability of the scorecard population (total scored population distributional comparison)	
i.	System level?	☐
ii.	Scorecard characteristic level?	☐
g.	Predictive power (separation of good and bad populations)	
i.	System level?	☐

NOTES

1. David Palmer, Dwight Smith, and Anna Lee Hewko, Board of Governors of the Federal Reserve System, Division of Banking Supervision and Regulation, Guidance on Model Risk Management, Supervisory and Regulation Letter 11-7, Washington, DC, April 4, 2011. https://www.federalreserve.gov/bankinforeg/srletters/sr1107.htm

2. Lyn C. Thomas, David B. Edleman, and Jonathan N. Crook, *Credit Scoring and Its Applications* Philadelphia: Society for Industrial and Applied Mathematics, 2002.

3. An example of a proprietary objective function might be a class of mathematical programming models involving a linear or convex objective function, linear constraints, and bounds or restrictions on decision (e.g., beta) variables.

4. A generic score is more broad based and, in the case of a credit bureau score, is usually designed to capture several credit aspects of the credit risk profile of the borrowing public. Examples include prior credit payment performance, indebtedness, attempts to acquire credit (inquiries), length of time of credit usage and experience for different types of trade lines, for example, credit card, installment loans, mortgage loans, overdraft protection, and so on.

5. The opinions expressed are those of the authors alone, and the experiences are drawn from over three quarters of a century of collective experience in banking and credit spanning financial institutions ranging from $2 billion to $2 trillion in assets, and also direct experience working with, or for, major scorecard vendors.

6. General considerations may include such things as cost, reputation, experience, access to proprietary data, data-specific knowledge and preprocessing capabilities, domain expertise, technical expertise, training, implementation services, and so on.

7. In the case of revolving credit, minimum balance rules are often combined with delinquency experience, for example, instead of 90 days past due as a bad condition. One might define 90 days past due with a loan balance greater than a set amount, say US$200, whereas a situation where there was a loan 90 days past due with a balance less than US$50 would not be considered a bad loan.

8. Such as credit bureaus, rating agencies, business trade data providers, or alternative data providers (e.g., cash payments on obligations like utilities, rent, mobile phones, and so on).

9. See R. D. King, R. Henery, C. Feng, and A. Sutherland, "A Comparative Study of Classification Algorithms: Statistical, Machine Learning and Neural Network," *StatLog, Machine Intelligence* (1995): 13, 311–359, for a discussion of difficulties of comparing classification algorithms.

10. Examples of preprocessing include variable binning and treatment of missing data or outliers.

11. David J. Hand, "Classifier Technology and the Illusion of Progress," *Statistical Science*, 21, no.1 (2006): 1–14.

12. Jerome Friedman, "Comment: Classifier Technology and the Illusion of Progress," Statistical Science, "21, no. 1 (2006): 15–18; Ross W. Galer," Comment: Classifier Technology and the Illusion of Progress, Statistical Science, "21, no.1 (2006): 19–23; Robert C. Holte," Comment: Classifier Technology and the Illusion of Progress, Statistical Science, "21, no.1 (2006): 24–26; Robert A. Stine," Comment: Classifier Technology and the Illusion of Progress, Statistical Science, "21 no.1 (2006): 27–29; David J. Hand," Rejoinder: Classifier Technology and the Illusion of Progress, Statistical Science," 21, no.1 (2006): 30–34.

13. Nor Azuana Ramli, Tahir Mohd Ismail, and Hooy Chee Wooi, "Measuring the Accuracy of Currency Crisis Prediction with Combined Classifiers in Designing Early Warning System," *Machine Learning*, 101 (2015): 85–103.

14. Berk Ustun and Cynthia Rudin, "Supersparse Linear Integer Models for Optimized Medical Scoring Systems," *Machine Learning*, 102 (2016): 349–391; and Dyagilev, Kirill Dyagilev and Suchi Saria, "Learning (predictive) Risk Scores in the Presence of Censoring Due to Interventions," *Machine Learning*, 102 (2016): 323–348.

15. This situation is especially true for FICO and the three major credit bureaus that service the United States' major lending institutions.

16. In either case, the model owner should be prepared to support decisions for inclusion or exclusion of a characteristic, or for emphasizing/deemphasizing the impact of the characteristic. Variable selection is a key area of focus for second line model validators and regulators, who will seek effectively challenge the decision made in this area.

17. Examples include flagging suspect, missing, or erroneous values; imputation, influential data management, derived characteristics, observation exclusion, and so on.

18. This would encompass clustering, calculation of WOE for every characteristic's attributes and information values for each characteristic, consideration of the percent of missing data, use of principal components and possible model segmentation. At this stage, observations should be serialized and flagged randomly for inclusion into either the training or validation sample.

19. Such as transformation of variables (e.g., to combine or linearize relationships), binning, multicollinearity assessment, rank order correlation statistical tests (e.g., Spearman, Hoeffding), univariate histograms, business rationale surrounding seemingly unintuitive characteristic logit plots, model owner preferences, inclusion of characteristics representing a complete risk profile, and so on.

20. This step entails fit statistics, separation of good/bad populations, rank-ordering of risk, and business intuition around the individual variables and their combined effects on the credit decision.

21. There may be a plausible explanation for such a counterintuitive circumstance. An example is a situation where someone changes jobs for a better opportunity involving a significant pay increase and a promotion. Such a population having a relatively short time period in their present job may be better credit risks that those who are more tenured employees, but perhaps earning less because they have not "marked themselves to market" in many years!

22. Examples of areas where change may occur include macro-economic conditions, business/marketing strategy, loan underwriting and pricing policy, portfolio sales/securitization, the credit profile of the incoming loan applicant population, or the degree of risk associated with attributes and the weight of their corresponding characteristics relative to the *through-the-door* (TTD) population as opposed to the scorecard development population.

23. Measures of separation of the score distribution include Kullback's divergence statistic, the Kolmogorov-Smirnoff (KS) statistic, Pearson's chi-square, c-statistic, and the Gini coefficient.

24. Other location parameters include the median and mode.

25. Intercept adjustment would not affect rank ordering, only a linear increase or decrease in odds for all borrowers.

26. One can test for equivalency of shape based upon the moment(s) of a distribution, as is the case with other statistical hypotheses. However, just because a particular moment has a specific value, it does not follow necessarily that the shapes of their distributions are the same. That is, if the third moment of a distribution is zero, it does not imply that the distribution is symmetric! If it is symmetric, the third moment will be zero, not necessarily vice versa. Compound hypotheses have to be tested simultaneously in order to assert equivalency of shape.

27. There exist alternative measures as well, for example, an alternative to variance, in terms of quartiles, which would be the interquartile range. An alternative measure of asymmetry would be to compute the mean minus the median, and divide the quantity the standard deviation. There is also an alternative to kurtosis. However, the authors have not seen much of this alternative measure testing in practice.

28. For example, certain characteristics not included in the scorecard may have increased predictive power that surpassed one or more current scorecard characteristics.

29. Often quantiles (typically deciles) are the basis of tallies and percentage calculations to compare with current production over time by means of a population stability index (PSI). See chapter on post-implementation reporting.

30. Vendors should recommend specific time intervals at which cumulative results should be less influenced by seasonal effects, low volume, and monthly fluctuations. Vendors should also indicate analysis at a characteristic level should be required, based on population instability. However, as noted earlier, that is not the only criterion for performing a characteristic analysis. Sometimes effects can cancel out, so that the overall picture looks fine, yet there are deeper shifts occurring.

31. This time period should be sufficient to provide a minimum number of bad accounts, where the minimum should be specified by the vendor to ensure reliable results.

32. Consisting of both approved and rejected applicants, so that the projected approval rate for the scorecard can be tested for accuracy.

33. The good score distribution is the right-most solid curve and bad score distribution appears as the left-most curve.

34. For example, if medical debts are not to be included, then trade lines related to medical and health would be bypassed. There may be more granularity such that specific trade line types could be excluded within medical, for example, hospitals, pharmacies, dentists, medical clinics or doctors in private practice, labs, optical outlets, veterinarians, chiropractors, funeral homes, and so on. A common trade line excluded from consideration in the United States is *child support obligation*.

35. Rounded to nearest whole percent.

36. Clark R. Abrahams, Mingyuan Zhang, "Credit Risk Assessment: The New Lending System for Borrowers, Lenders, and Investors," (Hoboken, NJ: Wiley, 2009), 147, Exhibit 3.11.

37. See, Clark R. Abrahams and Mingyuan Zhang, "Fair Lending Compliance Intelligence and Implications for Credit Risk Management," (Hoboken, NJ: Wiley, 2008), 185–188, for a discussion of judgmental systems and their strengths and weaknesses; 197–200 for a compilation of scorecard decision variables and their importance across seven credit products for 49 traditional, and 40 credit bureau, characteristics.

38. Ibid., 222–234; 255–264 for seven examples of judgmental credit scorecards.

39. A loan application actually cannot score in 12 of the bins, namely in the ranges of 1–11 and 55, since the first 11 scores fall below the mathematical minimum possible sum of factor points for all "poor" ratings and 55 is not possible because there is no single point differential between the "good" individual factor point value and the "fair" point assignment for any of the factors. While theoretically there are a total of 56 value bins (1-56), in practice only 44 value bins are possible (calculated as 56 − 12 = 44).

40. Abrahams & Zhang, (2008), 255–260, Appendix 6C.

41. The case for using checklists to reduce errors has been popularized by Atul Gawande, The Checklist Manifesto: How to Get Things Right, (New York: Henry Holt & Company, 2009).

42. Examples include Risk Management Association in the United States, Credit Scoring & Risk Strategy Association in Canada, Credit Research Centre University of Edinburgh in the United Kingdom, and PRMIA and GARP (international with local chapters).

## CHAPTER 14

Scorecard Development Process, Stage 7: Post-implementation

"It is better to be roughly right than precisely wrong."

—John Maynard Keynes

Once the scorecard is in production, there are two main areas of post-implementation works:

1. Reporting
2. Review

SCORECARD AND PORTFOLIO MONITORING REPORTS

This section deals with some of the standard reports used by risk practitioners to monitor scorecard and portfolio performance. Scorecard and portfolio monitoring is a fairly wide topic—this chapter is designed to give the user a general idea of the most common reports produced in the industry. In particular, portfolio reporting is almost always customized to the specific needs of senior management as well as portfolio risk managers, while scorecard monitoring is largely driven by the requirements of risk managers, regulators as well as model validation teams. Most scorecard and portfolio management reports that are produced are associated with portfolio and scorecard performance statistics, such as approval rates, bad rates, override rates, and various indices to measure divergence of actual performance from expected values. There are, however, some important business reasons and goals for which these reports should be run. These goals, and the reports used to meet them, are detailed below.

Scorecard and application management reports:

- Confirm "the future is like the past." As has been covered in previous chapters, scorecards are always developed for specific applicant or customer/segment profiles (represented by the expected score or characteristic distribution from the development sample).

The assumption is that as long as the composition of the population remains the same as the one used to develop the scorecard, then that scorecard will be valid. This assumption needs to be validated on an ongoing basis. The reports normally used to monitor the stability of the subject population are:

- System stability (also called population stability and scorecard stability) report.
- Scorecard characteristic analysis.
- Non-scorecard characteristic analysis.

- Monitor and pinpoint sources of change in the profiles of applicants and approves (or customers for behavior scoring). Just knowing that a change has taken place is insufficient, as it does not lead to any actionable items. The source of (and reasons for) the change must also be identified.

- Scorecard and non-scorecard characteristic analysis.
- Analysis of competition and marketing campaigns.
- Drill down analysis by region, channel and other segments.

- Track risk profile of incoming customers and applicants.

- System stability report.
- Scorecard and non-scorecard characteristic analysis.
- Score distribution of approves/customers report. These are also used for forecasting purposes.

- Generate statistics for acceptance and override levels.

- Final score report.
- Override report, including reasons for override.

For portfolio management reports:

- Monitor risk performance of accounts that have been booked.

- Delinquency report.
- Vintage analysis.
- Delinquency migration report.
- Roll rate across time report.

- Monitor and pinpoint the sources of delinquency and profit. As discussed previously, knowing where your losses are coming from allows you to take risk-adjusted decisions.

- Delinquency report, by region, channels, and other segments, in particular when deeply segmented scorecards are not being used.
- Marketing campaign and competitive analysis.
- Estimate future loss rates.
  - Vintage analysis and roll rate report. Note that while these have been the most commonly used methods for forecasting future loss rates, the introduction of the International Financial Reporting Standard (IFRS) 9 rules will likely change the way long-term losses are forecasted at banks. Nevertheless, these reports remain useful for shorter term forecasting of losses. This exercise is not simply one of predicting numbers—it also involves testing various disrupting scenarios that could impact future losses.
- Evaluate bad rate predictions and manage expectations. Tracking actual performance against expected allows for adjustments for future loss forecasts.
  - Vintage analysis.
  - Delinquency report.
  - Delinquency migration report.
  - Measuring the divergence between actual and expected values using various different methods. These are the most common reports used by model validation to evaluate the performance of models at banks.

The preceding applies to both application and behavior scorecard reports.

Needless to say, proper reporting and tracking structures must be in place prior to implementation, so that early results of new scorecard or strategy implementation can be tracked. At the initial stages of scorecard implementation in production environments, it is recommended that weekly reports be produced so that any deviations from expected performance can be identified quickly and remedied. When it is determined that the scorecards or strategies are performing as expected, regular monthly or quarterly reporting is sufficient. In general, performance reports are generated either monthly or quarterly for most retail portfolios, while small and medium-sized enterprise (SME) and wholesale portfolios tend to generate these at quarterly or annual basis. The generation of reports is dependent on lending volumes, the preferences of the model risk and validation functions, regulator reporting needs as well as the frequency at which data is updated. For example, SME and corporate data is usually updated quarterly or annually, and therefore the exposures are normally rated once a quarter or once a year and then reports produced.

While the credit business is dynamic, its pace is fairly slow. Unlike market risk, where fluctuations in risk factors can occur by the minute, retail credit risk indicators and factors tend to change over a longer time frame. It is therefore important to identify significant trends, not quirks, especially when a decision needs to be changed. In the Pre-implementation Validation section in Chapter 12, it was recommended that system stability reports be run on applicants from the past three and six months or longer; the reasoning was to catch long-term trends before deciding whether the scorecard was still valid or not. The reasoning here is no different—whether trying to decide if the scorecard is still valid, or to determine if a cutoff for a particular segment needs to be changed, or to institute harsher delinquency or credit authorization treatment for a particular cohort or segment, you need to be sure that the results are indicative of a long-term continuing trend rather than a one-off event.

Finally, as was emphasized in the previous chapters on scorecard development, the business reasons for changes in profiles and performances must be explained. It is not enough merely to look at approval statistics, bad rates, or stability indices—to be able to make informed/risk-adjusted decisions, you must be able to explain why things are happening. The concept here is the same as that for developing intelligent scorecards, where a combination of qualitative and quantitative measures are best suited for better results.

Model Risk Management

When running model performance reports for regulatory needs, it is best to refer to internal model validation teams, or get some ideas from local regulators. One of the most commonly used documents for guiding model validation reporting is the Basel II Working Paper 14.[1] It is a fairly comprehensive document that provides sound guidance on both qualitative and quantitative aspects of model validation, including suggested fit statistics. While developed for Basel II compliance, it has been adapted by many banks worldwide as a set of best practices. Similar documents that outline good practices for model risk management are the OCC 2011-12 one from the U.S. regulators,[2] and GL-44, issued by the European Banking Authority.

Financial institutions who have been involved in credit scoring have always been aware of model risk, and have been managing it for a long time. However, since the credit crisis of 2008, the topic has taken on greater importance. While it is a common misconception that models or scorecards were responsible for the crisis, the truth is that the event was a complex one with multiple failure points.[3] These include distorted compensation schemes for the frontline brokers, failure of risk management to practice due diligence such as confirming incomes, and the failure to understand both the strengths and weaknesses of models themselves. As has been discussed previously in this book, the development and usage of models is a holistic exercise that involves competence in statistics, teamwork, judgmental oversight and contextual decision making, rather than an academic exercise. For it to be successful, several factors must be present:

- *Continuous checkpoints.* These have been detailed in Chapter 2. The point is to have checkpoints along the way rather than after the exercise is done. Model validation and risk management staff should be involved in interim steps of scorecard development to catch any issues early and resolve them.

- *Management direction.* Senior management need to ensure that model risk is taken seriously, and that model validation teams have the authority and resources to effectively challenge internal development. The position of this function within the corporate hierarchy and direct reporting to C-level staff ensures that it is taken seriously. Management also needs to set and/or approve high-level policies, and ensure compliance and timely remediation of all issues that model risk management has with scorecard development and implementation. Further, there should be an ongoing monitoring plan in place for every score-card, with predetermined thresholds on key performance metrics that are monitored and reported on a regular basis.

- *Integrated infrastructure.* Disparate infrastructures for development, validation and deployment adds to model risk. Some of the issues have been discussed in Chapter 3. Inability to replicate results, recoding of models and "lost in translation" issues have been flagged by regulators as risks with some of my customers.

- *Independent validation with clear accountabilities.* Clear lines of accountabilities must be drawn between the model developers, end users and validation. Without these, the process can very quickly come to a stalemate. While mutually agreed to results (via teamwork) are ideal for each stage of scorecard development, when it comes to it, one person needs to take accountability and make a decision. In general, the model validation team has the final decision on most regulatory model development issues, as they need to be answerable to the regulators. In some institutions, where models are developed for operational (nonregulatory) uses, the risk management function often has the final say as they are the end users. The levels of model validation differs from bank to bank. Some have only one independent model validation function, while others may have internal audit as an additional final layer.

- *Robust methodologies.* This book presents only one methodology to develop scorecards. But we know that there are numerous other ways to develop models and scorecards. Institutions need to have formalized and documented methodologies for their model development, bearing in mind issues such as appropriateness of the methodology for the volume and type of data available, transparency/explainability, regulatory needs, type of product, decision required and skill sets of both validation and development staff.

- *Appropriate controls.* Some checkpoints have been suggested in Chapter 2 of this book. Institutions should have their own controls in place to make sure that the models are being developed, validated and used properly. This point is related to both management oversight and independent staff being able to mount challenges effectively. In addition, documentation and approval standards, as well as escalation protocols should be established to make ensure adherence to policies, and a standardized framework for managing model risk.

- *Feedback loops.* While there are some global best practices around model risk management, each organization needs to develop a set of conditions that work for it, given its risk culture, organization, decisioning process and level of maturity around credit scoring. In order to continuously improve, there should be an honest feedback loop that can be used to close any gaps, and create better processes.

The preceding list is not mean to be exhaustive. The science of model risk management continues to evolve—each organization should develop a set of protocols that are the most pertinent for its own culture, environment, and size. While global practices present a set of good ideas, ultimately what is "best practice" is what works best for a particular bank.

Credit Application Analysis Reports

These reports are sometimes called "front-end" reports because they are used to track the distributions of incoming applications, as well as the quality of the booked population (based on application scores).

System/Population/Scorecard Stability Report

This report has been covered in detail previously (in Chapter 12) the context of pre-implementation validation. During pre-implementation validation, the score distributions of the latest batch of applicants were compared with those of the development sample to make sure that the scorecard was stable before usage started. The objective and method here are similar, except in this case we measure the stability on an ongoing basis to make sure the scorecard is still stable. The stability report is the forward looking health check for scorecards. The ongoing report also compares the distributions by score of the latest applicant population ("actual") with those of the development sample ("expected"). As before, this is done to detect shifts in the applicant profile, represented by the distribution of applications by score. The report can easily be modified for behavioral scoring by comparing distributions of existing customers with the distributions by score of the development sample. "Actual" in some cases may be the applicants from the last month, or last quarter, depending on the frequency of reporting, and the volume of applicants. This comparison provides two pieces of information:

1. It validates the "the future is reflected by the past" assumption (i.e., bad rate predictions are based on a future applicant profile that is similar to the one used for predictive modeling). While not conclusive, evidence of similarity provides a comfort level. At the same time, it provides a forward looking assessment of the models performance (note all indicators dependent on actual vs. expected performance are backward looking).

2. It provides an indication of the quality of applicants/accounts (e.g., if the shifts in scores are downward, that may point to a deteriorating quality of applicant pool, or existing customers).

While historically, system stability reports were produced monthly, in recent time many banks have started to produce them quarterly—especially in the mortgage sector, where the applicant population tends to be more stable. A point to note is that for a pure system stability report, the applicant population must be generated using the same exclusion criteria as the development sample. Needless to say, for segmented scorecards, the report should be produced separately for each. Companies that choose to score exclusions, however, perform a second set of analyses for the scorecard cutoff, in which all applicants are included. This is to provide a more realistic analysis of the expected approval rate, and of the effects of the cutoff on key segments.

An example of a system stability report is shown in Exhibit 14.1. Note that the system stability report is also sometimes referred to as the population stability or scorecard stability report.

The "Actual %" and "Expected %" columns denote the distribution of cases for recent and development samples, respectively, for each of the score ranges specified. Note that in the exhibit, the scores have been engineered such that each score bucket contains 10 percent of the "expected" population. This has been done for efficiency, so that

Exhibit 14.1 System Stability Report

Score Range	Actual %	Expected %	A – E	In(A/E)	Index
0–169	7%	10%	–3%	–0.3567	0.0107
170–190	6%	10%	–4%	–0.5108	0.0204
191–197	6%	10%	–4%	–0.5108	0.0204
198–202	7%	10%	–3%	–0.3567	0.0107
203–207	9%	10%	–1%	–0.1054	0.0011
208–218	13%	10%	3%	0.2624	0.0079
219–225	13%	10%	3%	0.2624	0.0079
226–259	11%	10%	1%	0.0953	0.0010
260–292	13%	10%	3%	0.2624	0.0079
293+	15%	10%	5%	0.4055	0.0203
Index					**0.1082**

any shifts upward or downward can easily be identified (by setting the base for each group to 10 percent). In the preceding example, we can easily detect a shift to the higher scores.

There are two types of analyses that can be done with Exhibit 14.1. First, the nature of the population shift can be confirmed by looking at the chart above, or viewing a graph of the actual versus expected applicant/account distributions by score. This can provide additional information (e.g., whether the shift in scores is downward, upward, or kurtosis). In addition, displaying the distributions for historical periods in addition to the most recent month or quarter—for example, for the past three months, past six months, and so forth—on the same graph will help in tracking long-term trends. This will indicate whether, for example, there is slowly deteriorating quality or whether the distribution tends to follow cyclical variations. A change that is a long-term trend can be taken as a stable event and therefore reacted to with policy changes and other decisions. This is a better way to guide decision making, as opposed to reacting to monthly variations that are not stable. Detailed examples of how to spot one-time, seasonal, and long-term trends were provided in Chapter 12.

Exhibit 14.2 compares the distributions of expected, most current actual, actual from last three months, and actual from last six months on the same graph. The numbers for current actual and expected have been taken from Exhibit 14.1. Exhibit 14.2 clearly shows that the

Exhibit 14.2 System Stability Trend

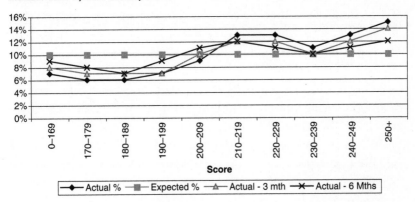

applicants have been consistently scoring higher and higher for the past six months. Similar to what was done in Chapter 12, we would do further analysis to find out for example, if specific marketing activities were done six months ago, or look further into the past to figure out why the distribution has changed.

In addition to looking at the shift visually via charts and graphs, we can also measure the magnitude of the shift mathematically. This is nothing more than measuring the difference between two distributions, and there are many ways of doing this. One method is by using an industry standard measure, as calculated in Exhibit 14.1. The index, known as the System Stability Index (SSI) or Population Stability Index (PSI), as shown at the bottom right hand corner of Exhibit 14.1, measures the magnitude of the population shift between recent applicants and expected (from development sample). This index is calculated as:

$$\Sigma \,(\% \text{ Actual} - \% \text{ Expected}) \times \mathit{ln} \,(\% \text{ Actual} / \% \text{ Expected})$$

for all score ranges.

This calculation is exactly like that for Information Value, seen earlier in Chapter 10; which also measures the deviation between two distributions.

In general, the index can be interpreted as follows:

- Less than 0.10 shows no significant change.
- 0.10–0.25 shows a small change that needs to be investigated.
- Greater than 0.25 points to a significant shift in the applicant population.

As mentioned previously, the above are industry rules of thumb and are not conclusive. Other methods, such as chi-square for binned data, with some level of significance, may also be used to measure the magnitude of the shift. The method shown here is one used widely by credit risk managers. As with most analytics, the results of the system stability analysis is only reliable when there is enough data. If you have a low volume product, producing monthly reports for a few dozen applicants will not be very useful. The index is also sensitive to the size of the bins. Most analysts use equal score bands for the report, which produces nonuniform distribution of cases across. Too large concentrations or sparse groups will both cause problems. Producing the report with scores engineered to represent for example, a uniform 10 percent or 5 percent distribution of expected cases in each bucket may alleviate some of those concerns.

This index is not an end-all measure; it only provides a general indication. In fact, it only tells us whether a shift has occurred or not, and provides an indication of the magnitude of the shift. Factors such as trends (Is the change a temporary occurrence or something more long term?), magnitude of the shift, and reasons for change should be taken into account before deciding if a population shift is significant. From the perspective of being able to use this report to generate decisions, the more important task here is to find out the reasons for the shifts in scores.

Shifts in scores can be due to several reasons (these have been detailed in Chapter 12, and as such, only a summary will be provided here):

- Independent change in applicant profile (e.g., demographic change) due to a change in the general population thru immigration or intense economic growth.

- Market dynamics that include things such as marketing campaigns, niche competition, and product design. For example, if the recent month's applicants were noticeably younger or were concentrated in a particular area, this may be due to focused marketing activity. Changes in product design such as the addition of loyalty programs, changes in fee structure, "no interest for six months"–type sweeteners, or shift to nontraditional channels can also attract a different type of applicant. External competition attracting a particular demographic may also affect the makeup of your applicants. Examples include institutions that target customers through product design (e.g., Telcos using advertising and handsets to attract young customers), loyalty programs, and higher interest rates. One bank that did not have a loyalty program associated with its credit card found that its applicant quality became consistently worse over time—analysis showed that most of its applicants were those who were rejected by banks that offered loyalty programs with their credit card (i.e., those who could, got credit cards that offered fringe benefits, while those who could not went to this particular bank). In behavior scoring, more aggressive authorizations or credit line management strategies, introduction of loyalty programs, repricing, cross selling, and other such activities can change the score profile of existing customers.

- Error in coding. This is typically a systematic error.
- Mistakes in data capture, whereby the data represents a non-random or incorrectly segmented sample, or where exclusions from the development sample are included.

There are several ways to perform further investigation to pinpoint the cause of the shift. These include:

- Performing a scorecard characteristic analysis to analyze shifts in characteristics in the scorecard. (This may sound obvious, but this is done because the scores are based on the scorecard. Again, this underscores the importance of building a widely based "risk profile" scorecard so that shifts indicated in these analyses reflect reality and are not just caused by fluctuations in one or two characteristics of a narrowly based scorecard.)
- Analyzing shifts in non-scorecard characteristics. These fall into three main categories:
  - Strong characteristics that did not enter the scorecard. (Since these are risk rankers, their distributions should confirm qualitatively if the population is getting better or worse.)
  - Characteristics related to those that are in the scorecard. (These should move in the same direction as those in the scorecard, thus providing confirmation for shifts in the scorecard characteristics.)
  - Numerators and denominators for ratios in scorecard.

■ Gathering information on changes in regulations, recent marketing campaigns internally and by the competition, and product changes for both.

Scorecard Characteristic Analysis Report

The scorecard characteristic analysis report compares current versus development distributions for each scorecard characteristic, and the impact on the score of any distribution shifts. This report can further pinpoint the reasons for any shifts in scores, and is generally produced quarterly, or whenever the system stability report indicates a significant shift. As with the system stability report, it is again advisable to compare expected distributions with those from the most recent period as well as historical periods, to detect trends.

An example of a scorecard characteristic analysis for "age" is shown in Exhibit 14.3.

"Expected percent" and "Actual percent" again refer to the distributions of the development and recent samples, respectively. There are two analyses that can be performed with this data. First, the expected and current, as well as historical, distributions for each characteristic can be plotted on a chart, like the one shown in Exhibit 14.2. That will provide a visual indication of the nature of the shift.

Second, we can calculate the magnitude of that shift mathematically. In this case, we will calculate the impact of that shift in terms of scores. This impact, or the scorecard characteristic index, is calculated simply by:

$$\Sigma\,(\%\text{ Actual} - \%\text{ Expected}) \times (\text{Points})$$

for all score ranges.

Exhibit 14.3 Scorecard Characteristic Analysis

Age	Expected %	Actual %	Points	Index
18–24	12%	21%	10	0.9
25–29	19%	25%	15	0.9
30–37	32%	28%	25	–1
38–45	12%	6%	28	–1.68
46+	25%	20%	35	–1.75
Index				**–2.63**

Note that including a "% Accept by criteria" column in this analysis can provide indication of whether the scorecard is systematically discriminating against a particular segment, or presenting an approval rate trend that is illogical. In addition, some risk managers also include a "bad rate" by attribute column as an additional check for risk ranking. The bad rates by attribute should follow a logical trend, similar to WOE curves. I have also seen analysts calculate "average current score" and "average development score" by attribute to check whether the total score is also logical by attribute.

Exhibit 14.3 shows a shift toward a younger applicant, resulting in applicants scoring about 2.63 points less than expected for age.

Similar reports are produced for all the other characteristics in the scorecard, and usually placed on one page to be analyzed. An example of this (from a partial application scorecard) is shown in Exhibit 14.4.

Analyzing the characteristics shown above, one can conclude:

- Applicants are getting younger (therefore riskier).
- They are living at their residences less (riskier). Other time-related characteristics outside of the scorecard, such as time at employment and oldest trade at bureau, should also point in the same direction. If they don't this may point to potential fraud, or some other problem.
- They have not moved geographically. The bands shown in this example above have been aggregated—in reality they would be broken into much finer zones. Logically, this would mean that the lower time at address is not because of migration—which means it is likely due to some action on the part of the lender.
- They have a significantly higher number of inquiries at the credit bureau in the last 6 months (riskier). Analysis of inquiries in the last 3 months, 12 and 18 months will confirm whether this is a short-term or seasonal phenomenon or something more permanent. See Chapter 12 for a detailed example of how to check for seasonality.
- The number of delinquencies from bureau and internal performance is higher (riskier). Other bureau delinquency related characteristics should confirm this.
- Utilization of revolving credit from bureau data is lower (less risky).

Exhibit 14.4 Full Scorecard Characteristic Analysis

Age	Expected	Actual	Points	Index	# Delq	Expected	Actual	Points	Index
18–24	12%	21%	10	0.9	0	80%	65%	45	-6.75
25–29	19%	25%	15	0.9	1–2	12%	21%	20	1.8
30–37	32%	28%	25	-1	3–5	5%	8%	12	0.36
38–45	12%	6%	28	-1.68	6+	3%	6%	5	0.15
46+	25%	20%	35	-1.75					**-4.44**
				-2.63	**Utilization at Bureau**				
Time at Res					0	12%	8%	15	-0.6
0–6	18%	29%	12	1.32	1–9	10%	19%	40	3.6
7–18	32%	32%	25	0	10–25	14%	20%	30	1.8
19–36	26%	22%	28	-1.12	26–50	22%	25%	25	0.75
37+	24%	17%	40	-2.8	50–69	11%	6%	20	-1
				-2.6	70–85	13%	9%	15	-0.6
Region					86–99	14%	8%	10	-0.6
Major Urban	55%	58%	20	0.6	100+	4%	5%	5	0.05
Minor Urban	26%	24%	25	-0.5					**3.4**
Rural	19%	18%	15	-0.15					
				-0.05					
Inq 6 mth									
0	63%	34%	40	-11.6					
1–3	19%	31%	30	3.6					
4–5	10%	16%	15	0.9					
6+	8%	19%	10	1.1					
				-6					

While all other indicators point to a higher-risk pool of applicants, the lower utilization levels indicate otherwise. Counterintuitive trends like these should be investigated. As advised earlier, we must track the numerators and denominators of every ratio in the scorecard to explain sources of changes. In this case, the balances and credit lines (i.e., the numerator and denominator for calculating utilization) were tracked separately. While average balances showed slight increases from historical levels, the credit lines had increased by a higher amount. This had happened in a highly competitive environment where banks had started cross selling their products to a higher risk segment, and concurrently increased the credit lines of customers to be more competitive. Therefore applicants were scoring higher for utilization, but this did not represent lower risk. The issue here is that the scores being given to customers for utilization does not represent the true risk level/bad rate associated with that score. This has the potential to affect the expected bad rates, and risk ranking of the model.

The deeper business reasoning analysis will help in making the right decision for the right problem. It helps to understand activities such as marketing campaigns, competition, economic environment and product changes as these help explain shifts in your customer base.

In cases such as these, where the risk manager is aware that applicants are scoring higher than they should, some options that can be considered are:

- Reduce points assigned for utilization, for higher-risk applicants. This is not ideal as you will be penalizing the low risk customers with low utilization as well.

- If the scorecard is fairly new, replace utilization with a variable that assigns the applicants the appropriate points based on their actual risk level. This will reduce the average score of the population and shift the score distributions slightly downwards, but that would be indicative of reality.

- Increase the cutoff. Even if the strategy to target higher risk people was deliberate, the overallocation of points can skew expected performance. Increasing the cutoff will bring the expected bad rates back nearer to calculated levels.

- Adjust expected loss/bad rates to reflect a higher actual risk than what is indicated by scores. Various analyses can be used for this, including extension of vintages as shown in Exhibit 12.6 in Chapter 12. It does not change the risk level of those who apply and are approved, but it makes the expectations more realistic.

The preceding analysis is therefore enhanced from a simple calculation of score shifts to something resembling a key risk indicator (KRI)-type analysis for applicants (or customers, for behavior scorecards).

A natural extension of this analysis is to compare development and current distributions for other characteristics outside of the scorecard. These can include:

- Characteristics that are not in the scorecard, but are believed to have an impact on applicant quality. These include strong characteristics that did not make it into the scorecard. For example, if shifts in the scorecard characteristics point to a deteriorating quality of applicants, reviewing these strong non-scorecard characteristics will help to confirm that movement. This ensures that judgments on applicant quality are made with a wider variety of information and therefore more robust.

- Characteristics that are similar to the ones in the scorecard. For example, if "age" is in the scorecard, tracking other time-related characteristics—such as time at employment or address, and age of oldest trade—may explain further reasons for the shift in applicant profile. If "inquiries in the past 6 months" is in the scorecard, tracking inquiries in the past 3 and 12 months will help to further explain the shift in inquiries. In the example in Exhibit 14.4, the distribution for "inquiries in the past 12 months" did not show any significant change. This meant that the increase in inquiries may be due to increasing competition in the last six months, or it may mean that factors such as product change or marketing in the last six months may be attracting a more credit-hungry applicant. Inquiries also tend to increase before major holidays. Related characteristics should all move in the same direction (e.g., older applicants should have higher tenures at work or older files at the bureau). Examples of other information types for which this can be done include trades, demographics, inquiries, and financial ratios.

- Where ratios are used in the scorecard, distributions of the denominator and numerator should also be tracked to explain changes in the ratio itself. For example, if utilization (balance divided by credit limit) has decreased, it may be due to either balances moving lower or credit limits being increased (as shown in Exhibit 14.4).
- Characteristics that are used in policy rules as well as for over-riding. These will help in determining the effectiveness of policy rules, biases in the data and for compliance purposes.

Again, these analyses should be performed to compare development data with recent historical data over the last one to six months to detect any trends and to validate that the shifts in distributions are not a temporary phenomenon.

The shifts in scored and nonscored characteristics should be consistent and explainable using logic and business considerations. If, for example, analysis shows that applicants are getting younger, yet have higher "time at employment," coding errors may be occurring. Such illogical shifts must be investigated and explained.

REACTING TO CHANGES

The preceding reports will indicate whether shifts have taken place, some indication of the level, and through investigation, reasons for the change. At regular intervals, the risk/validation manager will be called upon to decide what to do with the scorecard when changes happen. The key criterion is to decide whether the changes are significant. In general, the following considerations will apply:

- *Trend across time or one-time event.* This, in my opinion, is the most important reason. Changes due to one-time events such as specific marketing campaigns, balance transfer promotions and major festivals are not significant enough to warrant changing the scorecard. Those are one time blips (although with some credit card portfolio, blips that occur very often). On the other hand, shifts due to population, product, policy, regulation or loyalty program changes tend to be permanent. If for example, the loyalty program for a credit card shifts from earning travel points to hardware store points, that will very likely change the demographics of those apply for it. In this case, the scorecard will need to be redeveloped.

- *Level of shift.* If the change results in a very small change, say less than 5 percent shift in the distribution, is that worth redeveloping the scorecard? The cost and effort involved will likely be more significant. In such cases, most risk managers adjust strategy and continue to use the same scorecard. Ideally, one should measure the impact on the expected bad rates due to the shifts in populations, and then use that number to decide. This would be similar to the exercise we did to determine whether segmentation was worth the effort.

- *Systematic errors (input/calculation).* In some cases, very large deviations can be caused by input errors, missing inputs, or calculation errors. Calculation errors should be checked before the model is put into production. In the case of inputs, it is usually an education issue to make sure the frontline staff are inputting correct values instead of choosing the default option in drop-down lists, for example. Inputting done from paper applications in offices or customer service centers have a different profile compared to applications inputted directly in stores or booths. For some demographic variables, frontline staff will also sometimes leave them blank to save time. For credit scoring, this has two main impacts: the proportion of "missing" becomes higher than expected, and we lose data for future analysis.

- *Age of the scorecard.* If the scorecard is fairly new, options can include redeveloping it with different variables, that is, replacing the unstable ones, or adjusting expectations using recent vintages (discussed in Chapter 12). If the scorecard has been used longer than the performance window, redeveloping it is a better option.

- *Time since change.* Stability reports are forward-looking, which means they will catch some changes immediately. For example, if regulations change to reduce the maximum loan to value (LTV) for mortgages, that change will be effective immediately. Whereas changes in the applicant population due to demographic shifts or economic cycles will be slower. Redeveloping scorecards only becomes a viable option if the changes happened long enough in the past to yield actual analyzable performance. Otherwise, our options are limited to actions such as guesstimating the effects of the change and changing cutoffs or policies for example. If the maximum LTV is reduced, we can analyze the performance of the truncated sample (meaning remove the applications and accounts between current and future maximum LTVs), and then adjust strategies accordingly. In some cases, scorecards can be fully redeveloped based on the truncated sample as well. If the changes happened long enough to generate some vintages, we can also use vintage extrapolation to estimate future loss rates, and adjust cutoffs/strategies accordingly.

- *Technology issues.* As much as modelers and risk managers would wish immediate implementations of newly developed models, in many cases technology infrastructure limitations means waiting for many months. This is separate from validation and legal overviews, which in countries such as the United States can take a long time as well. In some cases, banks have a 15- to 18-month cycle just to build and implement a model, whereas the leading ones manage to do this in around 2 months. If technology does not allow for introducing new variables, then reweighting the model is a good option. This means running the full scorecard development exercise using the same variables, and same attribute bins as before, but on a more recent data set. The new regression run will generate new weights and scores. Realigning the scorecard is also possible where expected bad rates for each score band is recalculated for the same scorecard. Again, this is an alternate option to full redevelopment of models.

- *Isolated effects.* If the changes are due to instability in one or two variables only, replacing them is an option. Otherwise, reweighting, realigning, and adjusting expectations can all be done. The cause of shifts in those isolated variables will determine the best course of action, which can include changing cutoffs and recalculating expected bad rates. Another case of isolated insta-bility is when the change occurs in one identifiable segment. In this case, remedial strategies can include resegmenting the scorecard, assigning different cutoffs for the affected segments or changing expected performance.

Based on the considerations identified above, the risk manager, in consultation with the model development and model validation staff, can then make a decision on the best course of action for unstable scorecards. Once again, making this, and other business decisions is the goal of the exercise (in addition to generating regulatory reports). This should be the main issue driving the types of reports, subsegments and circulation of those reports in any scorecard using company.

Final Score Report

The final score report is used for application scorecards and is produced to obtain operational numbers such as approval rate and override rate. It can also be used to monitor excessive overriding and gauge the qual-ity of applicants and approved accounts. Exhibit 14.5 shows a typical final score report, using a scorecard with a cutoff of 200 points.

Exhibit 14.5 Final Score Report

Score Range	Applicants	Approved	% Appr	Not Taken Up	Lowside	Highside
0-169	700	-	0%	0	0	
170-179	800	16	2%	0	16	
180-189	700	35	5%	0	35	
190-199	900	99	11%	0	99	
200-209	1,100	924	84%	3%		176
210-219	1,100	968	88%	3%		132
220-229	1,000	900	90%	5%		100
230-239	1,200	1,092	91%	8%		108
240-249	1,100	1,045	95%	11%		55
250+	1,400	1,344	96%	15%		56
	10,000	6,423	64.2%	8%	150	627
Above Cutoff	6,900	6,273			4.84%	9.09%
Below Cutoff	3,100	150				

This exhibit shows an approval rate of 64.2 percent, and low-side and high-side override rates of 4.84 percent and 9.09 percent, respectively. Note that some lenders calculate override rates based on the total applicants as the denominator, while others use the number of applicants below or above cutoff as the denominator (for low-side and high-side override). If regulators or internal validation teams have specified a particular way to calculate this number, then clearly that's the one that should be used. Otherwise, pick one method and adhere to it consistently. In some cases, companies also calculate a "total override" based on the sum of all over-rides divided by total applications. While this is an interesting ratio, I don't find it very useful for decision making as the nature of low-side and high-side overriding is fundamentally different, and as such must be tracked and counted separately.

For products such as SME loans, and retail mortgages and term loans, an additional "Not Taken Up" column is also created to denote those who were approved by the lender but chose not to accept the offer. In other words, loans that were approved but not booked. In scorecard development, these are considered indeterminate (treatment options for these have been covered in detail in Chapter 10). In particular, the "not taken up" rate should be monitored in the top score ranges. There will always be some people who will walk away from a bank due to a better offer elsewhere—this is due to the differences in how banks rate their credit applicants. If the number of people walking away remains stable over time, it's somewhat normal behavior. However, if this number starts rising across time, it may mean that the bank is not price or credit limit competitive. Given that we are monitoring this in the top score ranges, logically, we would have offered the approved applicant our best price/offer. If that best offer is still not good enough, it is likely a pricing issue. Note that this can be part of a deliberate strategy. Some banks don't like to decline applicants, so they approve with a deliberately higher–than-competitive price. This would technically counts as a score-approved applicant, but the (hopeful) net result is that the customer voluntarily walks away. This should be done with caution as it may result in adverse selection—the customer who would take up the offer may do so because they have no other option and may not be able to carry the loan at the price point accepted.

From both scorecard development and monitoring perspectives, users needs to understand that product pricing practices can have an impact on portfolio quality and behavior of data.

The report in Exhibit 14.5 is typically produced for each scorecard, but many users will also generate it for various subpopulations and segments. This is done to ensure that a valuable segment is not being penalized, or that approval rate by score is consistent across various segments. Evidence indicating that this is not happening may mean that the scorecard is either not predicting as designed, or that excessive overriding is going on. In the first case, alternate segmentation may be required, whereas in the second, further investigation and controls would be called for.

A variation of Exhibit 14.5 is one that tracks the quality of booked business across time. An example is shown in Exhibit 14.6.

This exhibit shows the distribution of booked accounts by application score, over three time periods. These are compared to the expected distribution to determine if the quality of accounts is worse or better than what was expected. Exhibit 14.6 shows a constant decline in quality, where the proportion of approves in the 200–209 score band (just above cutoff) is increasing, while those in the top score band are decreasing.

Exhibit 14.6 Account Quality

Score	Expected	Q1 16	Q2 16	Q3 16	Q4 16
0–169	0%	0%	1%	1%	
170–179	0%	1%	3%	4%	
180–189	0%	2%	3%	5%	
190–199	0%	2%	4%	5%	
200–209	20%	26%	28%	26%	
210–219	15%	19%	20%	20%	
220–229	20%	22%	22%	20%	
230–239	16%	15%	12%	11%	
240–249	18%	4%	3%	5%	
250+	11%	9%	4%	3%	
Total	100%	100%	100%	100%	

In addition, not only is the percentage of low-side overrides gradually increasing, but they are being done at increasingly lower scores.

While the System Stability and Final Score reports show quality of applicants, this report indicates the quality of approved accounts. This report helps to generate a better expected bad rate of each new intake of accounts, instead of relying on a simple approval rate/bad rate relationship derived from the gains tables. That relationship—which tells you that if your approval rate is, for example, 70 percent, then you can expect a total bad rate of 3 percent—is based on the assumption that the distribution of accounts above cutoff remains stable. As shown in Exhibit 14.6, once that assumption is no longer valid, one must reevaluate the bad rate predictions. In some cases, the approval rate can stay the same for a given portfolio, but if the mix changes, then the predictions from the gains tables are no longer valid.

Override Report

This report tracks the number of low-side and high-side overrides by override reason. In situations where decisions are made by a combination of manual (humans) and automatic (software) methods, the overrides need to be tracked by both those decision types as well.

As discussed in the "Overrides" section of Chapter 12, excessive and uncontrolled overriding results in increased losses, yet some overriding is justified and should be done. This report therefore acts as a control tool to alert management when override levels increase, or when overriding is done for unspecified reasons. It can also be used to determine the quality of overrides being done within the organization. Where possible, all overriding should be done based on justifiable and trackable reasons, so that analysis can be done to determine which override reasons are appropriate and which ones should be abandoned. One way of determining this is to generate a report of performance (bad rate) by override reason.

A sample override report is shown in Exhibit 14.7.

This exhibit shows overrides by reason and decision type. Note that the definitions of system and manual decisions will vary across companies, depending on their approval process. Some organizations require an adjudicator to review and confirm system decisions

Exhibit 14.7 Override Report

Override Reason	Number	System "D"	System "A"	Manual "D"	Manual "A"
Lowside					
Local Knowledge	34	34	0		34
Justifiable Delq	96	96	0		96
VIP	12	12	0		12
VP Override	8	8	0		8
	150	**150**	**0**		**150**
Highside					
Bankruptcy	125	120	0		5
Local Knowledge	102	0	102	102	
Derogatory	200	0	200	185	15
Policy 1	55	55	0		
Policy 2	73	73	0		
Policy 3	92	92	0		
	647	**340**	**302**	**287**	**20**

for all applications, while others automatically approve or decline the majority of applications with few manual reviews. The report shown in Exhibit 14.7 can therefore be customized to include "Preliminary Decision" and "Final Decision" instead of system and manual decisions. The point is to monitor overrides by both reason and method.

Note also that this report does not include "Other" or "None Specified" as reason codes. These should, of course, be minimized, or better, eliminated. A good practice before designing application processing systems and reports is to survey credit risk policy teams and adjudicators and compile a comprehensive list of all reasons that can be used to override applications. These reasons can then be subdivided into groups, and used in drop-down lists or codes for adjudicators to use. This practice minimizes the chances of overrides based on reasons that cannot be entered into a system.

For lowside overrides, all decisions are shown as "System D" and "Manual A," meaning that the system declined all of them (for scoring below cutoff), but they were all finally approved by someone, based on a specified reason. The delinquency performance of these overrides should be monitored by reason to determine the better reasons.

The high-side override portion has a few variations:

- "Bankruptcy" shows that all 125 overrides were declined by the system, indicating that presence of bankruptcy is probably an automated policy decline, and uses online information from the credit bureau. However, five people were ultimately approved by an adjudicator, despite having previous bankruptcy. The performance of these approves should be monitored separately, as they are in principle like low side overrides.

- Policy rules 1, 2, and 3 are also examples of automated policy declines, again, likely based on either online bureau or internal information (for existing products).

- "Local Knowledge" shows all 102 applicants being approved by the system, and then being subsequently declined manually by someone, possibly at the regional adjudication centers or branches. This may have been due to negative information available outside the scorecard.

- "Derogatory" (i.e., delinquent performance at the bureau or in-house) shows an interesting situation. All 200 applicants were initially approved by the system—meaning that the particular derogatory performance is not an automated policy rule, but most likely something the adjudicator noticed through manually checking the full credit bureau reports, internal records or other documents. Subsequently, while 185 of them were manually declined due to the derogatory information, the adjudicator decided to approve 15. These 15 should be treated like low-side overrides and monitored separately.

The setup shown in Exhibit 14.7 can therefore be used to monitor overrides better than a simple distribution by override reason, which can sometime mask certain sorts of decisions, such as the highside override manual approves for bankruptcy shown. If a report is generated based on the logic of "if score > cutoff and decision = approve" to define approved accounts, it will fail to recognize the five bankrupts as overrides and include them as normal approves. One can also argue that the 15 applicants with some derogatory information that were manually discovered and approved are also overrides. In such cases, these should be tracked separately to gauge the effectiveness of the decision to approve accounts with that derogatory information.

In environments where the override rate is high, an additional report should be done, outlining the risk profile of the overrides. This can be done in various ways, for example:

- Compare scorecard and non-scorecard characteristics for overrides and nonoverrides, especially for negative performance characteristics such as "Worst Delinquency."
- Score distribution of overrides across time.

This is to enable a qualitative assessment of the risk profile of those being overridden.

Portfolio Performance Reports

Portfolio performance reports are often called "back-end" reports. They involve analyzing the delinquency performance of accounts thought various measures.

Delinquency (or Performance) Report

Delinquency (or performance) reports are used to determine the performance of the portfolio. These typically consist of charts displaying bad rates by score for different definitions of bad. In addition, this report is also generated for various segments (e.g., region, channel, demographics) to identify particular areas of high or low delinquencies. This report is also produced for accounts by "month opened" to identify any specific cohorts that present a higher risk (vintage analysis will be covered later).

An example of a delinquency report by account for a credit card portfolio is shown in Exhibit 14.8.

This report is normally generated for both counts (as shown in Exhibit 14.8) as well as dollars receivable, and is applicable to both behavior and application scoring. Exhibit 14.8 shows:

- Performance for an application scorecard with a cutoff at 200.
- A separate column for active accounts (i.e., those who have utilized their available credit). The definition of "active" differs between lenders but is typically based on transactions of some minimum amount, recency of usage or the existence of

Exhibit 14.8 Delinquency Performance Report

Score	Accounts	Active	%	Current	%	1–29 Days	%	30–59	%	60–89	%	90+	%	Write-off	%	Bankrupt	%
0–169	2,865	2,702	94.30%	783	29.00%	594	22.0%	459	17.00%	297	11.00%	216	8.00%	135	5.00%	216	8.00%
170–179	1,750	1,622	92.70%	691	42.60%	324	20.0%	243	15.00%	101	6.20%	89	5.50%	68	4.20%	105	6.50%
180–189	986	886	89.90%	444	50.10%	142	16.0%	115	13.00%	51	5.80%	37	4.20%	31	3.50%	66	7.40%
190–199	1,478	1,391	94.10%	814	58.54%	209	15.0%	153	11.00%	64	4.60%	46	3.30%	36	2.56%	70	5.00%
200–209	12,589	10,399	82.60%	6,977	67.10%	1,248	12.0%	832	8.00%	458	4.40%	354	3.40%	218	2.10%	312	3.00%
210–219	21,996	17,949	81.60%	13,162	73.33%	1,705	9.5%	1,095	6.10%	628	3.50%	449	2.50%	336	1.87%	574	3.20%
220–229	35,786	27,197	76.00%	22,579	83.02%	1,496	5.5%	1,224	4.50%	598	2.20%	435	1.60%	321	1.18%	544	2.00%
230–239	26,143	18,222	69.70%	15,871	87.10%	893	4.9%	583	3.20%	346	1.90%	237	1.30%	109	0.60%	182	1.00%
240–249	15,997	10,926	68.30%	10,041	91.90%	350	3.2%	229	2.10%	153	1.40%	76	0.70%	22	0.20%	55	0.50%
250+	16,442	11,509	70.00%	10,899	94.70%	230	2.0%	184	1.60%	115	1.00%	46	0.40%	23	0.20%	12	0.10%
Total	136,032	102,803	76%	82,263	80%	7,191	6.99%	5,118	4.98%	2,812	2.73%	1,985	1.93%	1,299	1.26%	2,135	2.08%

a balance. This column will not be relevant for reports on term loan portfolio such as mortgages or car loans.

- For term loans, an additional column is also sometimes added for "paid out." This would track the number of customers who have paid off their balances in full before the term of their loans. This column is however, more relevant for vintage reports.

- "Bad rate" for each delinquency level, using the total number of active accounts as the denominator. Some lenders elect to use the total number of opened accounts as the base for revolving portfolios. Regulatory requirements, model validation guidance as well as historical practices all determine the way the delinquency numbers are calculated. For term loan products such as mortgages and loans, the total accounts opened or currently having balances should be used as the denominator. If the scorecard was developed based on a complex bad definition such as "1 × 90 days or 2 × 60 days or 3 × 30 days," then a column needs to be added with that definition so that the actual performance of the scorecard can be evaluated. Note that if behavior scorecards were being developed, this report would provide an indication of the approximate number of bads that may be available for development.

- A trend of increasing bad rate as the score decreases, as should be the case. This shows that the scorecard is risk ranking.

- An approximate doubling of bad rates for each "points to double the odds" interval (20 points in this case). This, as well as the actual bad rates, are of course dependent on the level of high and low-side overrides, conditions, mix of the booked customers and other factors. As such, we look for approximate behavior rather than exact.

The definition of "bad" here can be based on either "ever" bad or "currently" bad. Most lenders produce reports based on both these definitions, as they serve different purposes.

In some cases, the performance of accounts just below cutoff, for example the low-side overrides up to 10 or 20 points below, can be close to or better than those just above cutoff. This is mainly due to better "cherry-picking"—those just below cutoff were manually selected after careful review as "best of the bunch," while those above cutoff were automatically approved. This also shows that cherry picking can be usually be done with some success close to the cutoff, but not too far below it. Of course, this depends on building good rank ordering models using full un-biased data sets to start with.

This report is based on delinquency performance—similar reports can be generated for churn, profit, revenue, recovery, or any other objective for which the scorecard was developed.

Another object of performance monitoring is to evaluate the predictive accuracy of the scorecard. This is generally done by comparing the actual bad rate by score or pool to the expected. In addition, many statistics measuring the difference between those two numbers can be generated. A good resource for such statistics is the Basel II Working Paper 14.[4] For a proper comparison, the actual account performance should be based on the same criteria as the scorecard development sample (i.e., with the same "bad" definition, segmentation, performance window, and exclusions). An example of such a comparison is shown in Exhibit 14.9.

This exhibit shows the actual bad rate of a portfolio (Act Bad percent) compared to that expected at development (Exp Bad percent). There are several factors to note here:

- Since this report cannot be generated until the performance window has been reached, it has limited operational value (for immediate/ongoing decision making). However, it is one of the key

Exhibit 14.9 Scorecard Accuracy

Score	Accts	Active	%	Act Bad	%	Exp Bad %
0-169	200	198	99%	89	44.9%	23.0%
170-179	348	300	86%	79	26.3%	18.0%
180-189	435	367	84%	56	15.3%	14.0%
190-199	466	387	83%	24	6.2%	10.0%
200-209	2,456	1,876	76%	122	6.5%	8.0%
210-219	4,563	3,600	79%	151	4.2%	5.0%
220-229	5,678	4,325	76%	166	3.8%	4.0%
230-239	7,658	4,598	60%	88	1.9%	2.0%
240-249	5,786	3,546	61%	38	1.1%	0.8%
250+	4,987	2,176	44%	20	0.9%	0.5%
Total	32,577	21,373	66%	833	4%	

reports that is required by both internal validation as well as regulators. Generally for immature cohorts, vintage analysis and charts like the one shown in Exhibit 6.4 are used to track the performance of individual cohorts against the expected at each time period. For example, if a cohort has better performance at six months compared to the development at six months, it is likely that that its actual bad rate at maturity would be less than expected, and vice versa. This information is useful for managing accounts and for forecasting. More discussion on vintages will be in the next section.

- Actual performance is almost always different from expected, due to high-side and low-side overrides, account management strategies, economic cycles, increased risk due to debtors obtaining more credit elsewhere and other events that happen between the granting of credit for one product and the end of the performance window. What is important to the risk manager is to be able to accurately predict the expected performance at any given time.

- The ongoing monitoring of bad rates by time opened, and comparisons to expected performance are used to evaluate whether or not the scorecard is indeed working. In most cases, good scorecards do rank risk, but the predicted bad rates are not exactly as expected. Where the scorecard does not rank risk, it may need to be replaced. In cases where there is disparity between expected and predicted performance, actions such as changing cutoffs (for some segments if applicable), changing policy rules, or reweighting the scores may be necessary.

Vintage (or Cohort) Analysis

Vintage, or cohort, analysis involves generating the bad rates for different cohorts (accounts opened within a particular time frame) by time on books. While model monitoring staff would prefer to look at this report by accounts, risk managers may also want to generate the same for balances so as to get a more accurate picture of the amount of losses.

As with the delinquency report, this report is also produced for different definitions of bad, and for various segments and subpopulations. The report is used to:

- Identify high-risk cohorts (i.e., if accounts opened in a particular month or quarter are a higher-risk than others).

- Tracks bad rate development over time—note that Exhibit 6.4, which shows the development of bad rate over time, was developed using information from a cohort analysis table shown in Exhibit 6.2. This information is used to compare the performance of new cohorts to long-term performance, in order to manage expectations and produce more accurate forecasts.

- Identify time based subpopulations that contribute disproportionately to losses. Further analysis is done to identify the causes, and if possible, remedies.

An example of a vintage analysis is shown in Exhibit 14.10. It shows the performance of accounts opened from January 2015 to March 2016, measured after equivalent time as accounts. In other words, we are comparing the bad rate of accounts opened in different months, but after equal performance periods, in this case, based on quarters. Note that similar reports can be generated for other metrics such as churn, profit, bankruptcy, recovery, and so forth, based on business objectives as well as the target specified for scorecard development. This report can be run for different definitions of bad (e.g., ever 90 days, ever

Exhibit 14.10 Vintage Analysis

Open Date	1 Qtr	2 Qtr	3 Qtr	4 Qtr	5 Qtr
Jan-15	0.00%	0.44%	0.87%	1.40%	2.40%
Feb-15	0.00%	0.37%	0.88%	1.70%	2.30%
Mar-15	0.00%	0.42%	0.92%	**1.86%**	**2.80%**
Apr-15	0.00%	**0.65%**	**1.20%**	**1.90%**	
May-15	0.00%	0.10%	0.80%	1.20%	
Jun-15	0.00%	0.14%	0.79%	1.50%	
Jul-15	0.00%	0.23%	0.88%		
Aug-15	0.00%	0.16%	0.73%		
Sep-15	0.00%	0.13%	0.64%		
Oct-15	0.20%	**0.54%**			
Nov-15	0.00%	**0.46%**			
Dec-15	0.00%	0.38%			
Jan-16	0.00%				
Feb-16	0.00%				
Mar-16	0.00%				

60 days, and so forth). Exhibit 14.10 shows that accounts opened in March and April 2015 are of a higher risk than those opened in other months. We can see that their bad rates are higher after two or three quarters as customers. At this point, one can refer to system stability and other reports from March and April 2015 to find out reasons for this disparity in performance. It may be due to factors such as adverse selection, changes in cutoff, seasonal effects, marketing efforts targeted to high-risk groups, system errors whereby high-risk customers were inadvertently approved, or excessive overriding. In short, one needs to be able to use nearly all the reports covered in this chapter as well as information on historical business practices to get these reasons.

Once those reasons are known, it can be determined if they represent a one-off event, or if the conditions are in place to cause a repeat. In the case of the latter, steps can be taken to avoid approving such high-risk accounts. From the numbers in the exhibit above, it looks like whatever happened in March and April was probably a one-time event. The reason is that accounts from May onwards exhibit normal delinquency behavior. If the event in March/April was deliberate and permanent, all cohorts below it would have had higher than average bad rates. The other comparison that must always be done is with accounts opened during similar months in the past two or three years. This is to establish whether the effects are seasonal, and happen each year.

The only reason all cohorts after a certain month should have higher than average bad rates is deliberate action. This means that the lender has lowered their cutoff, loosened policy rules or otherwise made a conscious decision to accept a higher-risk customer. In all other cases, after perhaps two or three quarters of higher-than-average performance, the risk and validation managers should be able to quickly ascertain that something is wrong, find out what caused it and remedy it. If it is a change in applicant distribution due to product design or other issues discussed earlier in the book, they can then decide to increase the cutoff or tighten up other lending policies and make sure future cohorts come back to normal expected bad rates. If it is due to a change in policy, marketing, product, or other factors that impact applicant quality, then changes to those can be considered as well.

In addition, once it is discovered that particular cohorts are of a higher risk compared to others in their peer groups, risk-adjusted decisions can be made to control them. These include:

- Increasing pricing for loan renewals, if the loans are renewable, or not renewing them.
- Not renewing credit cards for higher risk customers (note that due to the quick vintage maturity of credit card products, in practice by the time the renewal dates come around, most of the high risk customers have already become bad).
- Curbing automated credit line increases by flagging high-risk cohorts so that their credit limits are only increased only on request and after careful review.
- Curbing credit card customers from using their cards during early delinquency or from going over their assigned credit limit.
- Introducing more stringent collections actions for these cohorts.
- Decreasing credit limits. Note this has become more common in the Basel II era as banks are required to set aside capital for unused limits. For controlling losses, credit limit for the high risk cohorts can be decreased to just above their balance, or to below existing limits on other credit cards. Of course, decreasing limits should be done after careful strategy planning, and only on the highest risk accounts that have no other business at the bank, or on accounts that are clearly delinquent on all other products and not like to generate profits for the institutions in the future. This is because decreasing credit limits is a hostile action which will cause the customer to go elsewhere—and that is what you are counting on. Again, in this context we have recognized that particular cohorts are high risk, and we want to reduce our future losses.

The Vintage Analysis report is also very widely used for forecasting. The idea is to extrapolate vintages for newer cohorts based on the long term vintage development of older cohorts. This way, bad rates for newer cohorts can be forecasted for any number of months/ quarters into the future. When used for portfolio forecasting for say 12 month into the future, we would extrapolate all cohorts that exists at the bank for 12 months into the future using one particular long term cohort as the base case. It has also been suggested that vintage analysis can be used for Basel II backtesting.[5]

Using information from reports to drive this kind of decision making is key. It makes the report a decision-making tool, and not just an exercise in generating paperwork and statistics.

The sort of research into the past mentioned previously (to understand the reasons for disparity in cohort performance) is made easier if certain items are documented. These include:

- Changes in scorecards, cutoffs, policy rules, products, marketing strategy, rewards programs (existence of, type of rewards, redemption changes) and regulatory environment.

- Information on major marketing initiatives such as cross sell campaigns, on-site campaigns at events, balance transfers, and so on.

- Any other information that could help find out reasons for score shifts and account performance.

These should be captured for each portfolio, and documented such that future diagnosis and troubleshooting is made easier. Such documentation is common in credit scoring, and is often referred to as the Portfolio Chronology Log. Note that this is separate from the Data Change Log, which captures all changes to databases within the organization.

Delinquency Migration Report

On a month-to-month basis, most lenders track the movement of accounts from one delinquency bucket to another. An example of such a delinquency migration report is provided in Exhibit 14.11.

The report shown in Exhibit 14.11 measures the migration of number of accounts from one delinquency class to another, from "previous month" to "this month." Note that the "%" measure in the "Previous Month" column is a column-wise distribution. The "%" fields under "This Month" are a row-wise distribution. For example, of all accounts that were 30 to 59 days past due last month, 40 percent are now current, 10 percent are 1 to 29 days past due, 14.5 percent are 30 to 59 days past due, and so forth. The same report is also produced

Exhibit 14.11   Delinquency Migration

This Month → / Previous Month ↓	Previous Month #	Previous Month %	Current #	Current %	1–29 Days #	1–29 Days %	30–59 Days #	30–59 Days %	60–89 Days #	60–89 Days %	90–119 Days #	90–119 Days %	120–179 Days #	120–179 Days %	180+ #	180+ %	Bankrupt #	Bankrupt %
Current	54,782	72%	52,591	96.0%	2,082	3.8%											210	0.2%
1–29 days	12,640	17%	10,112	80.0%	632	5.0%	1,871	14.8%									85	0.2%
30–59 days	3,254	4%	1,302	40.0%	325	10.0%	472	14.5%	1,139	35.0%							59	0.5%
60–89 days	2,271	3%	182	8.0%	204	9.0%	227	10.0%	227	10.0%	1,413	62.2%					39	0.8%
90–119 days	1,449	2%	55	3.8%	65	4.5%	80	5.5%	87	6.0%	72	5.0%	1,065	73.1%			42	2.1%
120–179	887	1.2%	16	1.8%	12	1.4%	19	2.1%	20	2.2%	27	3.0%	64	4.0%	550	78.0%	150	7.5%
180+	632	0.8%	1	0.2%	8	1.2%	11	1.8%	16	2.5%	13	2.0%	3	3.0%	371	60.3%	210	29.0%
Total	75,915		64,258	85%	3,329	4%	2,679	3.5%	1,488	2.0%	1,524	2.0%	1,132	1.5%	921	1.2%	585	0.8%

for dollars in each delinquency bucket, as well as different time periods. Some banks produce this by quarters, and for Basel II purposes, many banks produce this report by pools. That report is known as Pool Migration Report.

Reports such as these can help in forecasting as well. This one can be modified to provide long-term roll rates over many years. In some cases, where the development of 90-day or charge-off models is not possible due to low default numbers, models to predict lesser delinquency, for example, 60 days, can be developed as an interim step. The forecast from the 60-day model can then be combined with roll rate information (percent roll from 60 to 90, for example) to then predict 90-day delinquency or charge-off. The report is similar to the roll rate analysis discussed in Chapter 6, and provides similar evidence of "point of no return" for delinquency. The report above shows that 80 percent of those who were 1 to 29 days past due last month paid up to become current, while only 2 percent of those who were 90 to 119 days past due paid up fully.

In some cases, institutions also develop transition state models to predict the likelihood of accounts migrating from one bucket to all possible buckets within a specified period of time. For example, one can predict the likelihood of a current account migrating to paid off or 30 days past due in the next 1 month, or the likelihood of a 30 days past due account migrating to paid off, current or 60 days past due in the same time frame. These models are also used for forecasting.

Roll Rate across Time

A modification of Exhibit 14.11 tracks the number of accounts and dollars outstanding in each delinquency bucket across time. An example of such a report is shown in Exhibit 14.12, which only shows two delinquency buckets, for illustration purposes. In reality, it would be produced for all delinquency buckets.

This report helps you to understand the development of delinquency across time, in terms of both accounts that are delinquent and dollars. The relative growth of dollars delinquent to account also gives an indication of rising balances and whether the loss given default is rising or not.

Exhibit 14.12 Roll Rate

Month	Total Receivable		Current					1–29 Days		
	Accounts	Dollars	Accounts	%	Dollars	%	Accounts	%	Dollars	%
May-16	80,895	$ 256,987	71,188	88.0%	$ 230,260	89.6%	6,472	8.0%	$ 35,978	14.0%
Jun-16	81,229	$ 277,125	71,075	87.5%	$ 245,533	88.6%	6,986	8.6%	$ 36,026	13.0%
Jul-16	86,985	$ 289,541	75,851	87.2%	$ 251,901	87.0%	6,872	7.9%	$ 41,115	14.2%
Aug-16	89,524	$ 298,654	77,796	86.9%	$ 261,322	87.5%	7,162	8.0%	$ 41,513	13.9%
Sep-16	92,458	$ 311,897	80,069	86.6%	$ 270,103	86.6%	7,027	7.6%	$ 39,923	12.8%
Oct-16	97,114	$ 318,694	84,004	86.5%	$ 276,626	86.8%	7,478	7.7%	$ 40,155	12.6%
Nov-16	99,365	$ 322,145	85,851	86.4%	$ 283,488	88.0%	7,651	7.7%	$ 39,302	12.2%
Total	627,570	$2,075,043	545,834	87.0%	$1,819,233	87.7%	49,647	8%	$ 274,012	13.2%

The above reports are again, not meant to be an exhaustive list. They are a small selected examples of some of the common ones run by those who use scorecards. In reality, there are hundreds of reports run by banks to both manage scorecards as well as monitor their portfolios. The reports are custom designed to cater to the requirements of the different stakeholders, and the decisions each needs to make.

Some common business reports run include the ones below. Note they are all also produced by subsegments:

- Active versus inactive customers.
- Revolvers versus transactors by percent.
- Credit limit utilization.
- Default rates by utilization.
- Average purchases and payments by time.
- Average interest and interchange revenue.
- Exposure at default reports.
- Loss given default reports.
- Credit conversion factor reports.
- Prepayment reports for term loans.
- Account closure reports.
- Collection reports on dollars collected, average days in collections, days to payment, percent paid, average $ paid, cure rates, self-cure rates, time to cure.
- Renewal rates for term loans.
- Measures for model performance[6]:
  - (1-PH) Statistic
  - Accuracy
  - Accuracy Ratio (Gini)
  - G^2 Likelihood Ratio Statistic[7]
  - Area Under the Curve (AUC)
  - Bayesian Error Rate
  - Conditional Information Entropy Ratio
  - D Statistic

- Error Rate
- Information Statistic
- Kendall's Tau-b (p-value)
- Kolmogorov-Smirnov Statistic
- Kullback-Leibler Statistic
- Pietra Index
- Precision
- Sensitivity
- Somers' D (p-value)
- Specificity
- Validation Score
- Measures for model calibration[5]:
  - Chi-Square Test (p-value)
  - Correlation Analysis
  - Hosmer-Lemeshow Test (p-value)
  - Observed versus Estimated Index
  - Mean Absolute Deviation (MAD)
  - Mean Absolute Percent Error (MAPE)
  - Mean Squared Error (MSE)
  - Brier Skill Score
  - Spiegelhalter Test

REVIEW

"Twice and thrice over, as they say, good is it to repeat and review what is good."

—Plato

Once scorecards are built and implemented, a post-implementation review is a good way to identify gaps or shortcomings in the overall scorecard development and implementation process, and conversely, to recognize areas of effectiveness. This serves to make subsequent scorecard development projects more efficient and effective. The review should be done with all parties involved, as detailed in Chapter 2.

Some key questions that should be covered are:

- Was data cleansing required? If it was, logic for the cleansing should be stored and operationalized so that it can be reused by others in the future. Ideally this should be incorporated into automated extract-transform-load (ETL) algorithms.

- Were any new derived variables created? if so, they should be shared in a way where they can be reused by other members of a team, preferably through a graphical user interface (GUI) where there is an audit trail. As with data cleansing, these should also be added to automated ETL processes so that they can be created in the future and added to risk data marts. Automation reduces model risk and avoids repeated auditing of the same thing. It also ensures consistent calculations.

- Was the interviewing process with, for example, adjudicators and collectors, successful in identifying predictive variables and changes in characteristics across time? This process should then be repeated for future projects. In cases where the scorecard development analyses proved that the information given by the interviewees may not have been correct, such information should be passed back to the adjudicators, for example, so that they can adjust their expectations. For example, adjudicators may have thought that young people living in urban centers were high-risk because they had high rents and moved jobs as well as homes frequently, but analysis showed that they were good risks because those are considered "normal" behavior in urban centers. In most cases, the results of interactive grouping can be presented to those responsible for adjudication or portfolio management, since the information is fairly intuitive, visual, and easily understood. It can also lead to improved risk management through a better understanding of the risk factors affecting your portfolio.

- Were there any specific elements that made your portfolio unique, such as seasonality or periods of abnormal activity? If so, such information should be documented for future development as well as portfolio reviews.

- Were there any occasions when the project stood still due to indecision or technology? Could something be done in the future to avoid such occurrences? These include waiting for data, inability to interpret results or data, decision making stalemate due to unclear responsibilities/jurisdictions, failure of other departments to do their part due to bad planning, not being able to implement the scorecard, technology issues, inability to agree on a cutoff or other strategy, and so forth. Some of these can be rectified through better planning, creating clear accountabilities and better teamwork.

- Was there any "data tricks" or transformation of data that made the job of scorecard development easier?
- Were there any data elements that caused problems?
- Were there any surprises or unintended consequences once strategy was developed and implemented? Was this a communications issue (i.e., those affected did not know) or was it a failure to forecast? If so, more "what if" type analysis should be done.
- Was the reporting implemented before the scorecard?
- How can the intelligence and intellectual property generated through this project be better shared with other members of the team, and preserved in the institution?

Most of these questions—and their answers—have been covered in the book. Nevertheless, mistakes often get made. The important thing, however, is to learn from them and to ensure that each successive scorecard development project gets more efficient, better organized, and—above all—more intelligent.

NOTES

1. Article I, "Studies on the Validation of Internal Rating Systems (revised)." BCBS Working Papers No. 14, Bank for International Settlements, May 2005.
2. OCC 2011-12, "Supervisory Guidance on Model Risk Management." Board of Governors of the Federal Reserve System/Office of the Comptroller of the Currency, April 2011.
3. J. R. Bohn, "Credit Portfolio Risk and Performance Metrics: Lessons from the Sub-Prime Crisis." Shinsei Bank, 2008.
4. P. Siarka, "Vintage Analysis as a Basic Tool for Monitoring Credit Risk," *Mathematical Economics* 14, no. 7 (2011): 213–228.
5. Ibid.
6. *SAS® Credit Scoring 6.1 for Banking: User's Guide* (Cary, NC: SAS Institute, 2016).
7. Y. Bishop, S. Fienberg, and P. Holland, *Discrete Multivariate Analysis* (Cambridge, MA: MIT Press, 1975), 125, equation (4.2-2).

A:

Common Variables Used in Credit Scoring

The thought process behind selection of variables for developing scorecards has been covered in detail in a previous chapter. The variables used are, of course, dependent on the product, segment, country, regulations, and the availability of data from sources such as credit bureau. The following list is not meant to be exhaustive; it contains data elements that are most commonly used worldwide for the development of retail credit risk scorecards. Scorecard developers should make sure that a particular data element can be used in their jurisdictions before using them.

Demographics

- Age
- Time at residence
- Time at recent employment
- Number of unique addresses last five years
- Time in industry or total time in employment
- Number of unique jobs last five years
- Postal code; usually grouped using some business logic
- Residential status
- Employment status/type
- Occupation type
- Industry type
- Highest education level attained
- Number of dependents
- Number of children
- Marital status
- Guarantors count
- Number of income earners at home
- Number of borrowers
- Owns car? Motorcycle?

Collateral Data

- Type of home being purchased: apartment, detached, semi-detached, bungalow, split
- Some use square footage, number of rooms, age of home, etc.

- New home or existing
- First mortgage for customer or renewal
- First, second, or third lien
- Used or new car
- Brand of car
- Mileage on used car
- Owner occupied/investment
- Age of used car

Internal/Financial Data

- Number of products internally
- Length of tenures for different types of products at bank
- Safety deposit box at bank?
- Investment account at bank?
- Salary deposited at bank?
- Income—normally used in ratios with other variables
- Total assets
- Total liabilities—used in ratio with assets
- Net worth; also liquid net worth
- Total overall debt/income
- Total monthly debt service amount
- Total debt service ratio
- Gross debt service ratio
- Revolving debt/total debt (amount and number of products)
- Price of car or house divided by income
- Loan to value
- Worst delinquency at bank: for revolving and term loans, and for last 12/24/36 months
- Time since last 30/60/90 days past due at bank
- Number of times 30/60/90 DPD at bank; for last 12/24/36 months
- Number of other bank cards
- Total deposits at bank
- Total deposits/total outstanding balances

- Average difference between deposits and withdrawals for different accounts, done for last 12/24/36 months
- Average ATM withdrawals; also ratios between current and last 12 months
- Average withdrawals thru all channels and historical ratios
- Average deposits last month/last 12 months
- Behavior score current
- Behavior score trends; for example, average last 6 or 9 months
- Payment last month/average payment last 12 months for revolving loans
- Months since continuous payment
- Best credit product at bank; mortgage to credit cards hierarchy
- Days to payment in collections
- Average balance at delinquency, by product
- Number of products prepaid before term
- Utilization of revolving facilities at bank and historical ratios

Bureau Data
- Bureau score
- Time at bureau, or age of the oldest trade at the bureau
- Total inquiries
- Inquiries last 3/6/12 months—used in multiple ratios
- Total trades and total open trades
- Trades opened last 3/6/12 months—used in ratios with total trades open
- Total open trades as a ratio of total inquiries within a given time frame
- Total active trades—also used in ratios
- Total term trades and total revolving trades—used in ratios with total trades
- Number of trades current, 30/60/90, etc. days past due—also used in ratios
- Total credit lines—revolving
- Total balance—revolving

- Total utilization—also can be used in ratio across time
- Worst rating of all current trades; also by time, for example, last 12/24 months
- Time since last 30/60/90 DPD at bureau
- Number of public records
- Type of record: bankruptcy, arrest, foreclosure, suits, liens, judgments, or other such records
- Months or years since bankruptcy
- Number of collection items
- Existence of loan from subprime lender

Macroeconomic Variables

- GDP: all below used as ratios to determine direction of growth/contraction
- Unemployment
- Employment
- Housing starts
- Consumer price index
- House price index
- Inflation

Credit Card Only

- Time as customer
- Amount of purchases—used in ratio over time such as average last month divided by average for 3 months, 6 months, 12 months, life
- Number of transactions and ratios over time
- Interest income—averaged and used in ratios as in purchases
- Service fee income
- Amount of payments—used in ratios as in purchases
- Cash withdrawals: averages, number, and historical trends
- Percentage payment last month—and used in ratios
- Spending habits—on staples/total spend and on other categories like fast food, restaurant, entertainment, luxury stores, etc.
- Number of Internet transactions and long-term ratios

Internal bank scorecard characteristic candidates (*Note:* P = primary—most predictive; S = secondary—found in scorecards). (*Source:* Abrahams & Zhang, *Fair Lending Compliance Intelligence and Implications for Credit Risk Management* [Hoboken, NJ: Wiley, 2008], 197–199.)

Exhibit A.1 Internal Bank Scorecard Characteristic Candidates

Factors	Direct Auto	Indirect Auto	Credit Card	Home Equity	Mortgage	Other Secured	Small Business
Credit history	P	P	P	P	P	P	P
Credit bureau score	P	P	P	P	P	S	S
Debt-to-income ratio	P	P	P	P	P	P	S
Payment-to-income	S	P	S	n/a	n/a	n/a	n/a
Loan-to-value	P	S	n/a	P	P	P	n/a
Payment shock	n/a	n/a	n/a	n/a	S	n/a	n/a
Credit limit/Mo. Inc.	n/a	n/a	S	n/a	n/a	n/a	n/a
Net worth	n/a	n/a	n/a	n/a	S	n/a	S
Liquidity	S	S	S	S	S	P	P
Months of reserves	n/a	n/a	n/a	n/a	S	n/a	n/a
Employment stability	S	S	S	S	S	S	S
Housing ratio	n/a	n/a	n/a	S	S	n/a	n/a
(Trade in + cash)/price	P	P	n/a	n/a	n/a	n/a	n/a
Co-app bureau score	S	S	S	n/a	n/a	S	n/a
Loan term	P	S	n/a	S	S	S	S
Custom credit score	P	P	P	P, n/a	P	P	P
Years in profession	S	S	S	S	S	S	S
Residence stability	S	S	S	n/a	n/a	S	n/a
Deposit relationship	S	S	S	S	S	S	S
Prior loan experience	S	S	S	S	S	S	S
Age of vehicle	S	P	n/a	n/a	n/a	n/a	n/a
Loan amount	S	S	S	S	S	S	S
Owner-occupancy	n/a	n/a	n/a	S	S	n/a	n/a
Add-ons-to-unpaid bal.	n/a	S	n/a	n/a	n/a	n/a	n/a
Income tier	n/a	n/a	S	n/a	n/a	S	n/a
Financial performance tier/trend	n/a	n/a	n/a	n/a	n/a	n/a	P
Quick ratio	n/a	n/a	n/a	n/a	n/a	n/a	S
Current ratio	n/a	n/a	n/a	n/a	n/a	n/a	S
Working capital	n/a	n/a	n/a	n/a	n/a	n/a	S
Debt/net worth ratio	n/a	n/a	n/a	n/a	n/a	n/a	S
Return on assets	n/a	n/a	n/a	n/a	n/a	n/a	S
A/R inv AP turn	n/a	n/a	n/a	n/a	n/a	n/a	S
Receivables aging	n/a	n/a	n/a	n/a	n/a	n/a	S
Management quality	n/a	n/a	n/a	n/a	n/a	n/a	P
Industry	n/a	n/a	n/a	n/a	n/a	n/a	P
Life ins./credit life ins.	S	S	S	S	S	S	S
Geographic concentration	n/a	n/a	n/a	n/a	n/a	n/a	P
Market diversity	n/a	n/a	n/a	n/a	n/a	n/a	P
Type of ownership	n/a	n/a	n/a	n/a	n/a	n/a	S
Disability ins.	S	S	S	S	S	S	S
Prof. ins./bonding	n/a	n/a	n/a	n/a	n/a	n/a	S
LTV below threshold	S	S	n/a	S	S	S	n/a
Strong co-applicant	S	S	S	S	S	S	S
Savings pattern	n/a	n/a	n/a	S	S	S	n/a
Cash flow analysis	n/a	n/a	n/a	n/a	S	n/a	S
Relationship	S	S	S	S	S	S	P
Diversification of customer base	n/a	n/a	n/a	n/a	n/a	n/a	S
Education	n/a	n/a	S	S	n/a	n/a	S
Own/rent	S	S	S	n/a	n/a	S	S

Commonly encountered credit bureau scorecard characteristic candidates (*Note:* P = primary—most predictive; S = secondary—found in scorecards).

Exhibit A.2 Credit Bureau Scorecard Characteristic Candidates

Factors	Direct Auto	Indirect Auto	Credit Card	Home Equity	Mortgage	Other Secured IL	Small Business
# Tradelines	S	S	S	S	S	S	S
# New recent tradelines	S	S	S	S	S	S	S
# Satisfactory ratings	S	S	S	S	S	S	S
% Satisfactory trades	S	S	S	S	S	S	S
# 30-day late revolving	S	S	P	S	S	S	S
# 30-day late installment	P	P	P	S	S	S	S
# 30-day late mortgage	P	P	P	P	P	P	P
Total # 30-day late	S	S	S	S	S	S	S
# 60-day late revolving	S	S	P	S	S	S	S
# 60-day late installment	P	P	P	S	S	S	S
# 60-day late mortgage	P	P	P	P	P	P	P
Total # 60-day late	S	S	P	S	S	S	S
# 90-day late revolving	S	S	P	S	S	S	S
# 90-day late installment	P	P	P	P	P	P	P
# 90-day late mortgage	P	P	P	P	P	P	P
Total # 90-day late	P	P	P	P	P	P	P
# Open trades by type	S	S	P	S	S	S	S
# Liens or judgments	P	P	P	P	P	P	P
# Foreclosures or repos	P	P	P	P	P	P	P
Bankruptcy last 5 years	P	P	P	P	P	P	P
# Derog items	P	P	P	P	P	P	P
# Current past dues	P	P	P	P	P	P	P
Ratio sat/tot trades	P	P	S	S	S	S	S
# Inquiries < 6 mos	S	S	P	S	S	S	S
# Inquiries < 12 mos	S	S	P	S	S	S	S
Ratio of bal/cred lmt	S	S	P	S	S	P	S
Age of oldest trade	S	S	S	S	S	S	S
# Collections > $X	S	S	S	S	S	S	S
# Derog > $X	S	S	S	S	S	S	S
Condition on last 12 mos	S	S	S	S	S	S	S
Condition on last 24 mos	S	S	S	S	S	S	S
Ratio of type/tot trades	S	S	S	S	S	S	S
Prev ratios by type trd	S	S	S	S	S	S	S
Depth of credit file	P	P	P	P	P	P	P
Ratio of install/tot trds	P	P	S	S	S	P	S
Ratio of rev/tot trds	S	S	P	S	S	S	S
Revolving tot utilization	S	S	P	S	S	S	S
Total major derogs	P	P	P	P	P	P	P
Ratio nondeling/tot trd	P	P	P	P	P	P	P
Mos since last past due	P	P	P	P	P	P	P

APPENDIX **B:**

End-to-End Example of Scorecard Creation

The following is an end-to-end example to show how a scorecard is created. This is a highly simplified one, designed to show how the final scores are calculated from the inputs and formulae discussed in earlier chapters of the book. In reality, a scorecard development project would be far more complex, with many other tasks.

The example is based on SAS Enterprise Miner, including the Credit Scoring nodes add-on.

The sample data set we will use in our example is a fairly standard North American one, consisting of some demographic, bureau, and financial information.

Note that the variable "Ever60dpd" is our target variable (Exhibit B.1).

Exhibit B.1 Some Selected Variables in the Sample Data Set

Variables - Ids			

(none) ▼ ☐ not Equal to ▼

Columns: ☐ Label

Name	Role	Level	Report
Bal_cc	Input	Interval	No
Bureau_score	Input	Interval	No
Car_price	Input	Interval	No
Ever60dpd	Target	Interval	No
Judgments	Input	Interval	No
LTV	Input	Interval	No
Loan_requested	Input	Interval	No
Mth_oldest_trade	Input	Interval	No
Open_trades	Input	Interval	No
Price_2	Input	Interval	No
Reason	Input	Nominal	No
Term_mths	Input	Interval	No
Total_lim_cc	Input	Interval	No
Utilisation	Input	Interval	No
_num_rev_trades	Input	Interval	No
app_id	ID	Nominal	No
applicants	Input	Interval	No

Exhibit B.2 WOE Curve and Table for Utilization

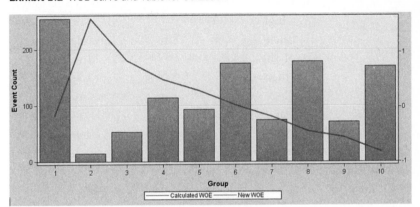

Label	Group	Calculated WOE
Utilisation< 2, _MISSING_	1	-0.15669
2<= Utilisation< 5	2	1.61812
5<= Utilisation< 12	3	0.84963
12<= Utilisation< 27	4	0.50146
27<= Utilisation< 39	5	0.2956
39<= Utilisation< 62	6	0.02892
62<= Utilisation< 71	7	-0.17937
71<= Utilisation< 92	8	-0.44191
92<= Utilisation< 100	9	-0.55603
100<= Utilisation	10	-0.82186

The Interactive Grouping Node was used to bin some of these variables.

The first variable binned is "utilization," which produced the curve and table seen in Exhibit B.2.

Similarly, the variable Months Oldest Trade was binned into seven buckets (Exhibit B.3).

Other variables in the data set were then also binned, and their attribute weights of evidence (WOEs) obtained.

Next, the Scorecard node was used to build a logistic regression model on the variables and create a scorecard. This was done in two steps.

The first step was to build a logistic regression model, and get parameter estimates as well as other regression statistics. The results are shown in Exhibit B.4.

Note again that the scorecard is oversimplified and for illustration purposes only. We can see five variables in the model.

Exhibit B.3 WOE Curve and Table for Months Oldest Trade

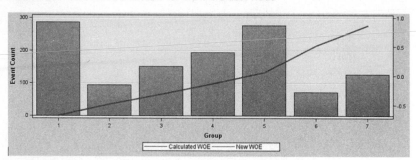

Label	Group	Calculated WOE
Mth_oldest_trade< 42, _MISSING_	1	-0.67511
42<= Mth_oldest_trade< 58	2	-0.48587
58<= Mth_oldest_trade< 86	3	-0.30944
86<= Mth_oldest_trade< 125	4	-0.13248
125<= Mth_oldest_trade< 178	5	0.06331
178<= Mth_oldest_trade< 216	6	0.51694
216<= Mth_oldest_trade	7	0.86825

Exhibit B.4 Output of Logistic Regression Run

Analysis of Maximum Likelihood Estimates

Parameter	DF	Estimate	Standard Error	Wald Chi-Square	Pr > ChiSq	Standardized Estimate	Exp(Est)
Intercept	1	-2.9323	0.0343	7307.07	<.0001		0.053
WOE_Bureau_score	1	-0.8024	0.0459	305.69	<.0001	-0.4183	0.448
WOE_LTV	1	-0.9783	0.0803	148.58	<.0001	-0.2406	0.376
WOE_Mth_oldest_trade	1	-0.2713	0.0733	13.72	0.0002	-0.0789	0.762
WOE_Total_lim_cc	1	-0.3791	0.0638	35.35	<.0001	-0.1411	0.684
WOE_Utilisation	1	-0.2662	0.0704	14.29	0.0002	-0.0846	0.766

Based on the output, we can then start assigning scores to each binned attribute. Let's start with specifying the scaling parameters, which are *Odds of 50:1 at 200 points, and 20 points to double the odds.*

Based on the formula shown in Chapter 10, we can calculate the "offset" and "factor."

Factor = PDO/ln(2) = 20/0.6932 = **28.85**

Offset = Score − {Factor * ln (Odds)} = 200 − (28.8517 * 3.9120)

= **87.13**

Finally, using the WOEs in Exhibit B.3 for Months Oldest Trades, as well as the estimates, intercept, and number of variables (five) from the regression output, we now apply the formula below to start calculating points for each bin.

$$-\left(woe_i * \beta_i + \frac{a}{n} \right) * factor + \frac{offset}{n}$$

For the first bin, Months Oldest Trade less than 42 or missing, we would calculate points as such:

$$-((-0.67 * (-0.27)) + (-2.93/5)) * 28.85 + (87.13/5)$$
$$= (-(-0.40) * 28.85) + 17.42 = \mathbf{29.06}$$

And the next bin, for Months Oldest Trade between 42 and 58:

$$-(-0.49 * (-0.27)) + (-0.59) * 28.85 + 17.42$$
$$= (0.4577) * 28.85 + 17.42 = \mathbf{30.62}$$

The points distribution for the variable Months Oldest Trade would look as shown in the second column in Exhibit B.5. The scores have been rounded to whole numbers for ease of use. Also shown in the column on the far right are the WOEs for each bin.

The points distributions for the other variable shown in this example, Utilization, is shown in Exhibit B.6.

Exhibit B.5 Points Distribution for Months Oldest Trade

Mth_oldest_trade< 42, _MISSING_	1.00	29	-0.68
42<= Mth_oldest_trade< 58	2.00	31	-0.49
58<= Mth_oldest_trade< 86	3.00	32	-0.31
86<= Mth_oldest_trade< 125	4.00	33	-0.13
125<= Mth_oldest_trade< 178	5.00	35	0.06
178<= Mth_oldest_trade< 216	6.00	38	0.52
216<= Mth_oldest_trade	7.00	41	0.87

Exhibit B.6 Points Distribution for Utilization

Utilisation< 2, _MISSING_	1.00	33
2<= Utilisation< 5	2.00	47
5<= Utilisation< 12	3.00	41
12<= Utilisation< 27	4.00	38
27<= Utilisation< 39	5.00	37
39<= Utilisation< 62	6.00	35
62<= Utilisation< 71	7.00	33
71<= Utilisation< 92	8.00	31
92<= Utilisation< 100	9.00	30
100<= Utilisation	10.00	28

Similarly, we would calculate the scores for all other attributes for all the other variables in the scorecard.

Bibliography

Abdou, H., El-Masry, A., and Pointon, J., On the Applicability of Credit Scoring Models in Egyptian Banks, *Banks and Bank Systems* 2, no. 1 (2007): 4–20.

Abrahams, C. R., and Zhang, M., *Credit Risk Assessment: The New Lending System for Borrowers, Lenders, and Investors*. Wiley, 2009.

Abrahams, C. R., and Zhang, M., *Fair Lending Compliance: Intelligence and Implications for Credit Risk Management*. Wiley, 2008.

Abrahams, C., Burnett, F., and Jung, J. W., Using Data Mining Technology to Identify and Prioritize Emerging Opportunities for Mortgage Lending to Homeownership-Deficient Communities, October 2000 Southeast SAS Users Group Paper #-501, 2000.

Anderson, R., *The Credit Scoring Toolkit: Theory and Practice for Retail Credit Risk Management and Decision Automation*. Oxford University Press, 2007.

Ash, D., and Mester S., Best Practice in Reject Inferencing. Presentation at Credit Risk Modeling and Decisioning Conference. Wharton FIC, University of Pennsylvania, 2002.

Avery, R., Brevoort, K., and Canner, G., Credit Scoring and Its Effects on the Availability and Affordability of Credit, *Journal of Consumer Affairs* 43, no. 3 (2009): 516–537.

Back, B., Laitinen, T., Sere, K., and Van Wezel, M., Choosing Bankruptcy Predictors Using Discriminant Analysis, Logit Analysis, and Genetic Algorithms. Turku Centre for Computer Science Technical Report, no. 40, September 1996.

Baesens, B., Developing Intelligent Systems for Credit Scoring Using Machine Learning Techniques. PhD thesis, Katholieke Universiteit Leuven, 2003.

Baesens, B., Van Gestel, T., Viaene, S., Stepanova, M., Suykens, J., and Vanthienen, J., Benchmarking State-of-the-Art Classification

Algorithms for Credit Scoring. *Journal of the Operational Research Society* 54 (2003): 627–635.

Bailey, M., *Practical Credit Scoring: Issues and Techniques*. White Box Publishing, 2006.

Banasik, J., Crook, J., and Thomas, L., Sample Selection Bias in Credit Scoring Models, *Journal of the Operational Research Society* 54 (2003): 822–832.

Basel Committee for Banking Supervision,: Sound Practices for Backtesting Counterparty Credit Risk Models, Bank for International Settlements, December 2010.

Basel Committee on Banking Supervision,. Use of Vendor Products in the Basel II IRB Framework. Bank for International Settlements, 2006.

Basel Committee for Banking Supervision, Guidance on Credit Risk and Accounting for Expected Credit Losses, Bank for International Settlements, December 2015.

Basel Committee for Banking Supervision, Working paper 14, Studies on the Validation of Internal Rating Systems (revised). Bank for International Settlements, May 2005.

Basel Committee on Banking Supervision,. Working paper 17, Vendor Models for Credit Risk Measurement and Management. Bank for International Settlements, 2010.

Bhardwaj, G., and Sengupta, R., Credit Scoring and Loan Default, RWP 15-02. The Federal Reserve Bank of Kansas City, 2015.

Board of Governors of the Federal Reserve System and Office of the Comptroller of the Currency, SR Letter 11-7, Supervisory Guidance on Model Risk Management. Washington, DC: Federal Reserve.

Boyle, M., Crook, J. N., Thomas, L. C., and Hamilton, R., Methods for Credit Scoring Applied to Slow Payers in Credit Scoring and Credit Control. Oxford University Press, 1992.

Carey, M. S., and Treacy, W. F., Credit Risk Rating at Large U.S. Banks, Federal Reserve Bulletin, November 1998: 897–921.

Choy, M., and Laik, M., A Markov Chain approach to determine the optimal performance period and bad definition for credit scorecard, *International Journal's Research Journal of Social Science and Management* 1, no. 6 (October 2011): 227–234.

Comptroller of the Currency, OCC Bulletin 2006-16, Model Validation. Comptroller of the Currency, 2006.

Constangioara, A., Consumer Credit Scoring, *Romanian Journal of Economic Forecasting* 3 (2011): 162–177.

Crone, S. F., and Finlay, S., Instance Sampling in Credit Scoring: An Empirical Study of Sample Size and Balancing, *International Journal of Forecasting* 28 (2012): 224–238.

Crook, J. N., Edelman, D. B., and Thomas, L. C., Recent Developments in Consumer Credit Risk Assessment. *European Journal of Operational Research* 183, no. 3 (2007): 1447–1465.

Crook, J. N., and Banasik, J., Does Reject Inference Really Improve the Performance of Application Scoring Models? *Journal of Banking and Finance* 28 (2004): 857–874.

Davison, A., and Hinkley, D., *Bootstrap Methods and Their Application.* Cambridge University Press, 1997.

Delamaire, L., Abdou, H., and Pointon, J., Credit Card Fraud and Detection Techniques: A Review, *Banks and Bank Systems* 4, no. 2 (2009): 57–68.

Demyanyk, Y., Did Credit Scores Predict the Subprime Crisis? *The Regional Economist,* Federal Reserve Bank of St. Louis, October 2008: 12–13.

Dil, S., Complying with the New Supervisory Guidance on Model Risk. *The RMA Journal,* 2012: 46–50.

Dimitru, M., Avramescu, E. A., and Caracota, C. R., Credit Scoring for Individuals, *Economia* 13, no. 2 (2010): 361–377.

Dyagilev, K., and Saria, S., Learning (Predictive) Risk Scores in the Presence of Censoring due to Interventions, *Machine Learning* 102 (2016): 323–348.

Dzidzeviciute, L., Application and Behavioural Statistical Scoring Models, *Economics and Management* 15 (2010): 1046–1056.

Efron, B., and Tibshirani, R., *An Introduction to the Bootstrap.* Boca Raton, FL: Chapman and Hall/CRC, 1994.

El Tabba, M., Introducing Credit Scoring in Microlending in ABA/SME. *Proceedings of 2007 IFC Conference: Next Generation Access to Finance,* 2007.

Einav, L., Jenkins, M., and Levin, J., The Impact of Credit Scoring on Consumer Lending, *RAND Journal of Economics* 44, no. 2 (Summer 2013): 249–274.

Finlay, S., *Predictive Analytics, Data Mining and Big Data*. Palgrave Macmillan, 2014.

Fishelson-Holstein, H., Credit Scoring Role in Increasing Home-ownership for Underserved Populations, in *Building Assets, Building Credit: Creating Wealth in Low-Income Communities*, edited by Nicolas P. Retsinas and Eric S. Belsky. Brookings Institution Press, 2005.

Frame, W. S., Srinivasan, A., and Woosley, L., The Effect of Credit Scoring on Small-Business Lending. *Journal of Money, Credit and Banking* 33 (2001): 813–825.

Friedman, J., Comment: Classifier Technolody and the Illusion of Progress. *Statistical Science*, 21, no. 1 (2006): 15–18.

Frunza, M.-C., Computing a Standard Error for the Gini Coefficient: An Application to Credit Risk Model Validation. *Journal of Risk Model Validation*, 2013, 61–82.

Fryzel, S. R., Technology Is Great, but Remember to Validate. *Illinois Banker*, November–December 2013: 18–19.

Gawande, A., *The Checklist Manifesto How to Get Things Right*. Henry Holt and Company, 2009.

Gayler, R. W., Comment: Classifier Technology and the Illusion of Progress—Credit Scoring. *Statistical Science* 21, no. 1 (2006): 19–23.

Goldstein, M., and Dillon, W. R., *Discrete Discriminant Analysis*. Wiley, 1978.

Hababou, M., Cheng, A. Y., and Falk, R., *Variable Selection in the Credit Card Industry*. North East SAS User Group, SAS Institute, 2006.

Hand, D. J., and Henley, W. E., Can Reject Inference Ever Work? IMA *Journal of Mathematics Applied in Business and Industry*. 5 (1993): 45–55.

Hand, D., Sohn, S. Y., and Kim, Y., Optimal Bipartite Scorecards, *Expert Systems with Applications* 29 (2005): 684–690.

Hand, D. J., and Henley, W. E., Statistical Classification Methods in Consumer Credit Scoring: A Review, *Journal of the Royal Statistical Society: Series A (Statistics in Society)* 160 (1997): 523–541.

Hand, D. J., The Improbability Principle, *Scientific American/Farrar*, Straus and Giroux, February, 2014.

Hand, D. J., Classifier Technology and the Illusion of Progress. *Statistical Science* 21, no. 1: 1–14.

Hand, D. J., Rejoinder: Classifier Technology and the Illusion of Progress. *Statistical Science* 21, no. 1 (2006): 30–34.

Hasan, M. N., Session 5. Monitoring and Benchmarking. *OCC Validation of Credit Rating and Scoring Models*. Office of the Comptroller of the Currency.

Hoadley, B., A Survey of Modern Scoring Technology. Interact96, A Fair Isaac Forum. Session 31, San Francisco: Fair Isaac & Co, (1996): 649–731.

Holte, R. C., Elaboration on Two Points Raised in Classifier Technology and the Illusion of Progress, *Statistical Science* 21, no. 1 (2006): 24–26.

Hsia, D., Credit Scoring and the Equal Credit Opportunity Act, *Hastings Law Journal* 30, no. 2 (November 1978): 371–448.

Islam, S., Zhou, L., and Li, F., Application of Artificial Intelligence (Artificial Neural Network) to Assess Credit Risk: A Predictive Model For Credit Card Scoring, MScBA Thesis, School of Management, Blekinge Institute of Technology, Spring 2009.

Janeska, M., Sotiroski, K., and Taleska, S., Application of the Scoring Model for Assessing the Credit Rating of Principals, *TEM Journal* 3, no. 1 (2014): 50–54.

Joanes, D. N., Reject Inference Applied to Logistic Regression for Credit Scoring. *IMA Journal of Mathematics Applied in Business and Industry* (1993): 35–43.

Joseph, M., A PD Validation Framework for Basel II Internal Ratings-Based Systems, *Credit Scoring and Credit Control IX*, September 2005.

Kaplan, M., and Kaplan, E., Chances Are . . .: Adventures in Probability, Penguin Book, February 2007.

Kennedy, K., Low-Default Portfolio/One-Class Classification: A Literature Review, DITAIG School of Computing, April 2009.

King, R. D., Henery, R., and Sutherland, A., A Comparative Study of Classification Algorithms: Statistical, Machine Learning and Neural Network. In Machine Intelligence 13, Machine Intelligence and Inductive Learning, edited by K. Furukawa, D. Michie, & S. Muggleton, pp. 311–359. Oxford University Press, Inc.

Klepac, G., Integrating Seasonal Oscillations into Basel II Behavioural Scoring Models, *Financial Theory and Practice* 31, no. 3 (2007): 281–291.

Kolesar, P., and Showers, J. L., A Robust Credit Screening Model Using Categorical Data. *Management Science* 31, no. 2 (1985): 123–133.

Kosoff, J., Best Practices in Model Risk Audit, Improving Model Control Processes Around the Three Lines of Defense, *The RMA Journal*, 2016, 36–41.

Koo, J.-Y., Park, C., and Jhun, M., A Classification Spline Machine for Building a Credit Scorecard, *Journal of Statistical Computation and Simulation* 79, no. 5 (2009): 681–689.

Kullback, S., *Information Theory and Statistics*. Dover Publications, 1968.

Lynas, N., and Mays, E., Structuring an Efficient Program for Model Governance, *RMA Journal*, March 2010: 44–49.

Mays, E., *Handbook of Credit Scoring*. Glenlake Publishing Company, 2001.

Mays, E., *Credit Scoring For Risk Managers: The Handbook For Lenders*. South-Western Educational Publishers, 2003.

Mays, E., Systematic Risk Effects on Consumer Lending Products. Credit Scoring Conference CRC, Edinburgh, 2009.

Mester, L., What's the Point of Credit Scoring? Federal Reserve Bank of Philadelphia Business Review, 1997: 3–16.

Montrichard, D., *Reject Inference Methodologies in Credit Risk Modeling*. South East SAS Users Group, SAS Institute, 2007.

Mood, A. M., Graybill, F. A., and Boes, D. C., *Introduction to the Theory of Statistics*, 3rd edition. McGraw Hill, 1974.

Moorthy, P., *Vendor Model Validation: Challenges and Proposed Solutions*. Global Association of Risk Professionals, 2015.

North American CRO Council, Model Validation Principles Applied to Risk and Capital Models in the Insurance Industry. Deleware: North Americal CRO Council Incorporated, 2012.

OCC, Supervisory Guidance on Model Risk Management, OCC Bulletin 2011-12. OCC, Office of the Comptroller of the Currency, 2011.

Osipenko, D., and Crook, J., The Comparative Analysis of Predictive Models for Credit Limit Utilization Rate with SAS/STAT®, Paper 3328-2015, SAS Global Forum, 2015.

Onderej, J., Mathematical Applications in Credit Risk Modelling, Aplimat Journal of Applied Mathematics 1, no. 1 (2008): 431–438.

Pezzuto, I., Miraculous Financial Engineering or Toxic Finance? The Genesis of the U.S. Subprime Mortgage Loans Crisis and Its Consequences on the Global Financial Markets and Real Economy, SMC Working paper, Swiss Management Centre, Issue 12, 2008.

Potts, W. J. E., and Patetta, M. J., Predictive Modeling Using Logistic Regression: Course Notes. SAS Institute, 2000.

Przanowski, K., and Mamczarz, J., Consumer Finance Data Generator—A New Approach to Credit Scoring Technique Comparison, University of Warsaw, September 2012.

Ramli, I., and Wooi, H. C., Measuring the Accuracy of Currency Crisis Prediction with Combined Classifiers in Designing Early Warning Systems. *Machine Learning* 101 (2015): 85–103.

Rezac, M., and Rezac, F., How to Measure the Quality of Credit Scoring Models, *Czech Journal of Economics and Finance*, 61, no. 5 (2011): 486–507.

Rud, O. P., *Data Mining Cookbook*. Wiley, 2001.

Scallan, G., Selecting Characteristics and Attributes in Logistic Regression. Credit Scoring Conference CRC, Edinburgh, 2011.

Schreiner, M., Credit Scoring for Microfinance: Can It Work? Paper presented at the III Foro Interamericana de la Microempresa, Barcelona, Spain, 2000.

Securities Industry and Financial Markets Association, Recommendations of the Securities Industry and Financial Markets Association. Credit Rating Agency Task Force, SIFMA, July 2008.

Siddiqi, N., *Credit Risk Scorecards: Developing and Implementing Intelligent Credit Scoring*. Wiley, 2006.

Silver, N., *The Signal and the noise: The Art and Science of Prediction*, Penguin Press, 2013

Sleath, M., A Case Study in Comparing Scoring Technologies. Interact 96, A Fair Isaac Forum. San Francisco: Fair Isaac & Co., 1996: 811–839.

Stahl, G., Nill, E., Siehl, B., and Wilsberg, J., Risk Modeling and Model Risk—The IRBA Case, Bundesanstalt fur Finanzdienstleistungsaufsicht (BaFin), Bonn, August 2007.

Stein, R. A., Comment: Classifier Technology and the Illusion of Progress. *Statistical Science* 21, no. 1 (2006): 27–29.

Stein, R. M., *Benchmarking Default Prediction Models: Pitfalls and Remedies in Model Validation.* Moody's KMV, 2002.

Strijov, V., Model Generation and Model Selection in Credit Scoring, *Proceedings of Euro 2010,* 2010.

Taylor-Schoff, S., and Panichelli, P., Validating and Comparing Predictive Models—Statistical Measures and Beyond. Interact98, A Fair Isaac Forum. San Francisco: Fair Isaac & Co., 1998: 1–18.

Thomas, L., A Survey of Credit and Behavioural Scoring: Forecasting Financial Risk of Lending to Consumers, *International Journal of Forecasting,* 16 (2000): 149–172.

Thomas, L. C., Edelman, D. B., and Crook, J. N., *Credit Scoring and Its Applications,* Volume 6 of Monographs on Mathematical Modeling and Computation, Society for Industrial and Applied Mathematics, 2002.

Trinkle, B., and Baldwin, A., *Interpretable Credit Model Development via Artificial Neural Networks.* University of Alabama, 2005.

Ustun, B., and Rudin, C., Supersparse Linear Integer Models for Optimized Medical Scoring Systems. *Machine Learning,* 102 (2016): 349–391.

Van Sang, H., Ha Nam, N., and Duc Nhan, N., A Novel Credit Scoring Prediction Model Based on Feature Selection Approach and Parallel Random Forest, *Indian Journal of Science and Technology* 9, no. 20 (May 2016). doi: 10.17485/ijst/2016/v9i20/92299

Wagner, H., The Use of Credit Scoring in the Mortgage Industry. *Journal of Financial Services Marketing* 9, no. 2 (2004): 179–183.

Yobas, M. B., Crook, J. N., and Ross, P., Credit Scoring Using Neural and Evolutionary Techniques, *MA Journal of Mathematics Applied in Business and Industry,* 11 (2000): 111–125.

Zeliade Systems, *Model Validation: Theory, Practice and Perspectives.* Zeliade Systems SAS, 2011.

About the Author

Naeem Siddiqi is the author of *Credit Risk Scorecards: Developing and Implementing Intelligent Credit Scoring (Wiley & Sons, 2005)*, and has advised and trained bankers in over 30 countries on the art and science of credit scoring. Naeem has worked in retail credit risk management since 1992, both as a consultant and as a risk manager at financial institutions.

At SAS, Naeem played a key role in the development of several products relating to credit scoring. He is currently responsible for managing SAS's end-to-end credit scoring solution. He continues to meet and advise between 30–40 financial institutions worldwide annually.

Naeem has an Honours Bachelor of Engineering from Imperial College of Science, Technology and Medicine at the University of London, and an MBA from The Schulich School of Business at York University in Toronto.

About the Contributing Authors

Clark Abrahams is SVP, Credit Model Validation Group Manager at BB&T. A former bank CRO, Clark possesses over 25 years of banking experience. At FICO, he built and validated scorecards and evaluated competing scoring technologies. At SAS, he co-invented a new credit system, including a patented method for credit model validation. Clark was a contributor to the first edition of this book, and has co-authored two other books on lending. A San Francisco native, UC Berkeley graduate, and Stanford engineer, Clark has been a strong voice for transparency and ensuring that lending systems are valid and fair.

Dr. Billie Anderson is an Associate Professor of Data Analytics at Ferris State University in Big Rapids, Michigan. She received her PhD in Applied Statistics from the University of Alabama in 2008. Dr. Anderson is also a contract SAS Analytical Trainer. In this role, she teaches courses in data mining and credit scoring applications. Dr. Anderson travels to customer sites, where she teaches and assists customers in implementing data mining and credit scoring solutions. She has developed training courses for SAS in credit scoring. Dr. Anderson has published SAS Global Forum papers, journal articles, and book chapters in the credit scoring field.

Brad Bender is SVP, Community Bank Senior Model Risk Manager at BB&T. As model owner, he leads the execution of an effective model risk management framework for consumer, small business, and commercial lines of business. Previously, he has held a number of credit and portfolio risk management roles supporting commercial, government guaranteed, and small business lending segments. A Winston-Salem, North Carolina, native and University of North Carolina at Greensboro

427

graduate, Brad has developed and advocated best practices for model integration, process alignment, monitoring, and governance standards within business operations and financial services industry groups.

Charles Maner is EVP, Quantitative Credit Risk Executive within Risk Management at BB&T, where he focuses on quantitative analytics for traditional credit risk across commercial, small business, and consumer lines of business. Previously, at Bank of America, he led development and evaluation efforts focused on internal commercial risk rating methodologies compliant with Basel AIRB. A Winston-Salem, North Carolina, native and UNC Chapel Hill and Georgia Institute of Technology graduate, Charles has championed the integration of quantitative techniques from the traditional field of statistics and operations research.

Dr. Hendrik Wagner is an independent consultant with Risk Parameters. In the early part of his career, he worked on scorecard development tools at SAS EMEA and managed their data mining solutions. Since 2007 he has been developing and validating rating models in Basel II projects for banks globally. Clients include leading banks in Thailand, Malaysia, South Africa, Finland, Hungary, Great Britain, and Germany. Other work interests include fraud modeling and mobile telecommunications. His PhD in science informatics, from the University of Bielefeld, dealt with the modularization of neural networks. For more detail, visit his page on LinkedIn: https://de.linkedin.com/in/drhendrikwagner

Index